Bipartisanship and US Foreign Policy

T0355193

"Polarization has certainly undermined partisan comity but Jordan Tama's careful and illuminating research demonstrates that Democrats and Republicans in Congress still vote together on foreign policy issues surprisingly often. Tama's explanation for the persistence of bipartisanship is a major contribution to research on the politics of foreign policy."

—**Benjamin O. Fordham**, Professor of Political Science, Binghamton University

"Despite unprecedented levels of partisan polarization, Jordan Tama argues bipartisanship remains surprisingly common in foreign affairs. However, not all bipartisanship involves legislators from both sides of the aisle backing presidential policies. Rather, Tama critically shows how cross-partisan and bipartisan coalitions frequently push back against the president with considerable effect."

—**Douglas L. Kriner**, Clinton Rossiter Professor in American Institutions, Cornell University

Bipartisanship and US Foreign Policy

Cooperation in a Polarized Age

JORDAN TAMA

OXFORD
UNIVERSITY PRESS

Oxford University Press is a department of the University of Oxford. It furthers
the University's objective of excellence in research, scholarship, and education
by publishing worldwide. Oxford is a registered trade mark of Oxford University
Press in the UK and certain other countries.

Published in the United States of America by Oxford University Press
198 Madison Avenue, New York, NY 10016, United States of America.

Library of Congress Cataloging-in-Publication Data
Names: Tama, Jordan, 1976– author.
Title: Bipartisanship and US foreign policy : cooperation in a polarized age / Jordan Tama.
Other titles: Bipartisanship and United States foreign policy
Description: New York : Oxford University Press, [2024] |
Includes bibliographical references and index.
Identifiers: LCCN 2023013843 (print) | LCCN 2023013844 (ebook) |
ISBN 9780197745670 (pb) | ISBN 9780197745663 (hb) | ISBN 9780197745694 (epub)
Subjects: LCSH: United States. Congress. | Coalitions—United States. | United States—
Politics and government—Decision making. | United States—Foreign relations.
Classification: LCC JK1021 .T26 2024 (print) | LCC JK1021 (ebook) |
DDC 324.273/011—dc23/eng/20230601
LC record available at https://lccn.loc.gov/2023013843
LC ebook record available at https://lccn.loc.gov/2023013844

DOI: 10.1093/oso/9780197745663.001.0001

Paperback printed by Marquis Book Printing, Canada
Hardback printed by Bridgeport National Bindery, Inc., United States of America

For my father

Contents

Acknowledgments

The seeds for this book were planted more than two decades ago during my work as a speechwriter for former US Representative Lee Hamilton. Lee was one of the most influential foreign policy voices in Congress during the latter part of the 20th century and had become the head of the Woodrow Wilson Center, a research institution in Washington, DC, after retiring from Congress. One of my assignments for him was to draw on his insights and experience to draft a series of speeches that he delivered on the foreign policy role of Congress, which we later published as a book. This project was the beginning of my education in the domestic politics of US foreign policy. In Lee, I observed a leader who always placed the national interest above partisan considerations. He was highly respected across the aisle, which made him not only a very effective lawmaker but also an ideal leader of nonpartisan institutions, including the Wilson Center and the 9/11 Commission, which investigated the September 11, 2001, terrorist attacks on the United States.

Some years later, I served as an American Political Science Association Congressional Fellow on the Tom Lantos Human Rights Commission in the House of Representatives. In that role, I worked for another highly effective foreign policy leader: US Representative Jim McGovern, the co-chairman of the commission. Jim is a progressive Democrat who is deeply committed to fundamental values of human rights and skillfully forges politically diverse coalitions to promote and defend those ideals. He has partnered with Democrats and Republicans across the ideological spectrum to advance an array of important foreign policy legislation. My work for him on a bill he introduced known as the Magnitsky Act, which imposed sanctions on Russian officials who committed major human rights violations and was enacted into law with strong bipartisan support in Congress, led me to decide to write a book on the nature of foreign policy bipartisanship today.

I'm grateful to a number of institutions for generous support that facilitated my work on the book. A residential fellowship from the Wilson Center enabled me to return to the institution in a scholarly capacity, begin intensive research for the project, and get early feedback on it. A grant from the Social Science Research Council allowed me to further advance the research and receive more helpful suggestions. Support from the School of International Service at American University made it possible for me to present drafts of parts of the project at conferences of the American Political Science Association and International Studies Association, as well as to receive feedback from other scholars on a draft of the entire manuscript at a book workshop. I also thank the institutions and workshops that invited me to present papers or ideas from the project, including the DC IR Workshop, the Finnish Institute of International Affairs, the National Capital Area Political Science Association American Politics Workshop, Kaiserslautern University, Partnership for a Secure America, Southern Methodist University, the University of Heidelberg, the University of Maryland at College Park, and the University of Quebec at Montreal.

Many people gave me valuable guidance, feedback, and suggestions as I worked on the book. Jim Goldgeier, Miles Kahler, David Karol, Doug Kriner, Frances Lee, and Sarah Snyder read a full draft of the book and provided extensive and insightful comments on it at my book workshop. Numerous other scholars also generously gave their time to discuss the project with me or provide helpful feedback on draft papers or chapters from it. I thank, in particular, David Auerswald, Florian Böller, Philip Brenner, Sarah Burns, Shannon Carcelli, Ralph Carter, Audrey Kurth Cronin, Charles-Philippe David, Chris Deering, Colin Dueck, Ben Fordham, Gordon Friedrichs, Glenn Hastedt, Bob Hathaway, Ryan Hendrickson, Will Howell, Bruce Jentleson, Maya Kandel, Josh Kertzer, Ron Krebs, Anna Kronlund, Jim Lebovic, Dov Levin, Robert Litwak, Yonatan Lupu, Sarah Maxey, Kelly McHugh, Dumitru Minzarari, Shoon Murray, Randy Newnham, Autumn Perkey, Stefano Recchia, Josh Rovner, Elizabeth Saunders, Jim Scott, George Shambaugh, Jim Thurber, Matt Timmerman, Wolfgang Wagner, and Don Wolfensberger. The book is a much better product as a result of the willingness of all of these scholars to offer their input.

I was fortunate to have some terrific research assistants during the project. I'm grateful to Harrison Brooks, James Bryan, Margaret Carlough, Gabriel Exposito, Thomas Flaherty, and Balazs Martonffy for their excellent work. At Oxford University Press, I thank David McBride for his interest in the project and for shepherding it through the review process. I also thank the anonymous peer reviewers who provided thoughtful and constructive comments on the manuscript.

When researching the political dynamics of contemporary policy debates, it is invaluable to learn from the experiences and insights of people who were directly involved in those debates. I'm indebted to the more than 100 members of Congress, congressional staff, executive branch officials, and advocates and experts outside government who agreed to be interviewed by me as part of my research for the book. Several dozen of these interview subjects are named in the book in connection with my use of quotes or information from the interviews. Many other interview subjects requested anonymity so that they could speak with me candidly, and I therefore cannot acknowledge them by name. But all of them enhanced my understanding of important dimensions of the foreign policy debates discussed in the book.

My completion of this book would not have been possible without the constant support and warm encouragement of my wonderful wife Julia. My delightful children Amos and Jesse made the years during which I worked on it tremendously joyful and meaningful. Looking back further, I'm deeply grateful to my parents, grandparents, and aunts for giving me a strong foundation for intellectual endeavors and a fulfilling life. I dedicate this book to my father, who has always been a rock of support for me and from whom I have learned so much.

PART 1
CONCEPTS AND PATTERNS

1

The persistence and forms
of bipartisanship

During the fall and winter of 2019–2020, Washington, DC, appeared entirely consumed by partisan division as the US Congress considered whether to hold President Donald Trump to account for pressuring the government of Ukraine to conduct investigations that could benefit him politically. The impeachment proceedings in the House of Representatives and trial in the Senate were marked by intensely partisan rhetoric. Republicans accused Democrats of engaging in a witch hunt, while Democrats charged that Republicans were placing loyalty to Trump above loyalty to the country.[1] In a series of House and Senate votes on whether to impeach and convict Trump for abuse of power and obstruction of justice, a total of just four out of 535 members of Congress crossed party lines.[2] A *Washington Post* article noted that the main takeaway from the impeachment process was that "partisanship reigns" in Washington.[3]

Yet even as Democratic and Republican lawmakers battled one another over Trump's impeachment, they cooperated on a variety of substantive foreign policy issues. While the impeachment proceedings and trial were taking place, large bipartisan majorities in the House and Senate approved legislation adopting a major trade agreement negotiated by Trump with Mexico and Canada,[4] mandating sanctions on officials responsible for human rights violations in Hong Kong,[5] creating a space force as the sixth branch of the US military,[6] prohibiting the US executive branch from withdrawing from NATO,[7] and rejecting a Trump proposal to slash US spending on diplomatic and foreign aid programs.[8] On some of these issues, such as the trade agreement and space force, the bipartisan congressional majorities backed Trump's positions. On other issues, such as NATO and international affairs spending, legislators in both parties joined together to constrain or challenge the president.

These examples show that the full reality of contemporary American politics is more nuanced than what many headlines and high-profile partisan

Bipartisanship and US Foreign Policy. Jordan Tama, Oxford University Press. © Oxford University Press 2024.
DOI: 10.1093/oso/9780197745663.003.0001

battles suggest. Yes, partisan polarization has increased dramatically in recent decades, and Democrats and Republicans routinely fight tooth-and-nail for political advantage. But this polarization coexists with bipartisanship that remains surprisingly common. Such bipartisanship continues to exist in both domestic and international issues, but it remains most prevalent in foreign affairs.

However, bipartisanship is not necessarily what you think it is. Whereas the classic conception of bipartisanship involves Democrats and Republicans joining together in unity, bipartisanship is not always synonymous with consensus in Washington. Instead, bipartisan cooperation in Congress can take several forms, from bipartisan support of the president, which I call *pro-presidential bipartisanship*; to bipartisan opposition to the president, which I call *anti-presidential bipartisanship*; to bipartisan coalitions generated by intra-party divisions, or *cross-partisanship*.[9] Each of these alignments characterizes important contemporary foreign policy debates, even as American politics has grown increasingly polarized on the whole. Put another way, Democrats and Republicans lack overarching consensus about foreign policy, but they nevertheless work together on international issues in a variety of ways.

In this book, I document the extent to which bipartisanship persists in foreign policy and show that it remains more common in international rather than domestic issues. I also explain why bipartisan coalitions still develop in many international issues and why foreign policy bipartisanship often coincides with intra-party or inter-branch divisions.

Understanding these political dynamics is important because they can shape the conduct and effectiveness of US foreign policy. While the president is the leading actor in foreign policy, Congress also possesses critical international responsibilities, from the appropriation of funds for defense and foreign aid to the approval of international treaties. When Democrats and Republicans are polarized on an issue, Congress will tend to be incapable of taking the steps needed to address it. Polarization also can make it more difficult for presidents to send clear signals to other countries and can lead US policy to shift sharply when a president from one party is succeeded by a president from the other party. These pathologies, in turn, can reduce the credibility of US commitments and damage America's global standing.[10]

By contrast, bipartisanship tends to strengthen US foreign policy, but different varieties of bipartisanship generate different effects. Pro-presidential bipartisanship can facilitate robust action to address global challenges, make US policies more durable, and bolster the credibility of US commitments.

Anti-presidential bipartisanship can be harmful in stymieing worthy presidential initiatives or beneficial in blocking unwise unilateral presidential moves. Cross-partisanship, for its part, can generate either gridlock or legislative action, depending on how the intra-party divisions stack up. Importantly, none of these forms of bipartisanship always results in "better" policy than polarization—even pro-presidential bipartisanship can involve support for a bad policy—but the ways that Democrats and Republicans line up have a large impact on the US role in the world.

Polarization in American politics

Partisan polarization in American politics has risen steadily over the past several decades to reach record levels. As recently as the 1960s and 1970s, more than a quarter of US representatives and senators were best described as conservative Democrats or liberal Republicans.[11] In a pattern of behavior that may seem hard to imagine today, many of these lawmakers voted more often with colleagues in the other party than with colleagues in their own party. Furthermore, many major policy issues that now sharply split Democrats and Republicans lacked such fixed divisions. Consider that President Richard Nixon, a Republican, backed the creation of the Environmental Protection Agency and proposed establishing a sweeping program of national health insurance.[12]

Since then, largely due to a massive realignment of the parties in the wake of the civil rights era, polarization has steadily increased, and the positions of Democratic and Republican elected officials have become far more distinct.[13] When representatives and senators are placed based on their voting records on a number line in which −1 represents the most liberal position and 1 represents the most conservative position, the average gap between the median Democratic lawmaker and median Republican lawmaker rose from .60 during the Congress that operated during 1979–1980 to .88 during the 2019–2020 Congress.[14] At the same time, the share of congressional roll call votes in which a majority of Democrats voted against a majority of Republicans increased from 38% to 70% in the House and from 46% to 64% in the Senate from 1980 to 2020.[15] Today, the voting record of every Democratic senator and representative falls to the left of the voting record of every Republican senator and representative, and the two party caucuses are more polarized than at any other time since the creation of the Republican Party in the 1850s.[16]

Foreign policy debates have not been immune to this polarization.[17] Following an early Cold War period characterized by relatively strong bipartisan support for an internationalist and anti-communist foreign policy, partisan divisions became more common on international issues after the failed US military intervention in Vietnam.[18] Some studies also find that polarization on international issues increased after the end of the Cold War,[19] or they identify a more gradual, long-term trend of growing polarization on overseas matters.[20] Moreover, throughout the modern period, partisan motivations have regularly shaped the foreign policy behavior of elected officials, even on questions of war and peace.[21]

At the same time, polarization extends well beyond Washington to the American electorate. The average gap separating the share of the Democratic public and share of the Republican public who approve the president's performance increased from 27% under Jimmy Carter to 81% under Donald Trump.[22] In the 2020 election, 95% of Democrats voted for Biden, while 94% of Republicans voted for Trump.[23]

Even more troubling, many Republican and Democratic voters now have deeply ingrained hostile feelings toward members of the other party, a phenomenon known as "affective polarization," or negative partisanship.[24] When asked in a 2019 public opinion survey to rate their feelings about members of the other party on a zero to 100 thermometer scale, in which zero represents the coldest reading and 100 the warmest reading, 79% of Democrats and 83% of Republicans gave members of the other party a rating of 49 or below.[25] A 2022 public opinion poll further found that political disagreements had damaged the friendships or family relationships of one in five Americans.[26] Democrats and Republicans even discriminate against each other more than they discriminate against members of another race.[27] Such patterns point to powerful social polarization based on partisan identities, fueled by biases and emotion rather than rational thought.[28] Political scientist Liliana Mason observes: "Partisanship can now be thought of as a mega identity."[29]

Given these troubling trends, the dominant perspective on contemporary American politics centers on its polarization. The leaders of an American Political Science Association task force on negotiating agreement in politics write: "Today politics is dominated by intense party polarization and limited agreement among elected representatives on even basic facts about policy problems and solutions."[30] Political analyst Ezra Klein comments that the "master story" of American politics today is "the logic of polarization."[31] Newspaper headlines regularly proclaim that bipartisanship is "dead."[32]

In a similar vein, scholars of US foreign policy observe that polarization now characterizes the political landscape on international issues. Charles Kupchan and Peter Trubowitz note: "The domestic consensus that long supported US engagement abroad has come apart in the face of mounting partisan discord and a deepening rift between urban and rural Americans."[33] Daniel Drezner writes: "Foreign policy discourse was the last preserve of bipartisanship, but political polarization has irradiated that marketplace of ideas."[34] In a 2018 survey, foreign policy practitioners and experts rated polarization as the most critical threat to the United States.[35]

Yet some recent research offers grounds for hope about the prospects for bipartisan cooperation during this highly polarized era. Political scientists James Curry and Frances Lee find that when Congress enacts landmark laws today, the majority party still does so by negotiating with the minority party rather than by ramming partisan bills through the legislature.[36] Other work shows that it remains common for Democrats and Republicans to join together in cosponsoring legislation.[37] In foreign policy specifically, some scholars find that bipartisan support for liberal internationalism remains relatively robust,[38] the Democratic and Republican party platforms continue to embrace deep international engagement,[39] and distinctions between the two parties on international issues are rather muted overall.[40]

In this book, I build on this and other research by developing a new conceptualization of political alignments that goes beyond the binary distinction between bipartisanship and polarization. I also investigate the frequency of these alignments in important policy debates and examine factors that enable or hinder different alignments. My findings show that bipartisanship occurs more often today than conventional wisdom indicates and suggest that some analysts underestimate the prevalence of bipartisanship because they adopt an overly narrow definition of it. I offer, too, novel understandings of factors that contribute to polarization or different forms of bipartisanship, highlighting the key roles of ideological commitments, advocacy groups, and institutional incentives in shaping how elected officials line up.

Types of political alignments

My conceptualization of political alignments takes into account the extent of inter-party, intra-party, and inter-branch agreement or disagreement on issues. Binary definitions of polarization and bipartisanship typically define polarization as instances where most members of the two parties oppose each other and define bipartisanship as instances where most members of the two parties line up together. While these definitions offer useful simplicity, they fail to capture some important nuances. One such nuance concerns the degree to which parties are internally divided on issues. For instance, a situation where 95% of Democrats vote against 95% of Republicans has a markedly different character than a situation where 60% of Democrats vote against 60% of Republicans. By the same token, the nature of a bipartisan coalition is quite different when nearly all Democrats and Republicans agree with each other than when just a bare majority of the members of each party do so. To capture such differences, I distinguish between cases of strong bipartisanship or strong polarization, in which intra-party division is minimal, and cross-partisanship, in which a substantial share of elected officials in one or both parties opposes their own party's dominant position.

A second nuance concerns whether Democrats and Republicans in Congress are supporting or opposing the president. To capture this nuance, I distinguish between pro-presidential bipartisanship and anti-presidential bipartisanship, with the former term referring to instances in which majorities of both parties in Congress support the president and the latter term describing instances in which majorities of both parties in Congress are at odds with the president. In foreign policy, it is particularly important to take into account this inter-branch dimension of bipartisanship given the president's preeminent role in shaping the United States' role in the world.

Each of these political alignments has been common in US foreign policy debates. In the remainder of this section, I illustrate the historical prevalence of four of them: pro-presidential bipartisanship, anti-presidential bipartisanship, strong polarization, and cross-partisanship.

Pro-presidential bipartisanship

I begin with pro-presidential bipartisanship because it represents the standard image of bipartisanship, associated with the notion, which dates back to a comment by Daniel Webster during the War of 1812, that partisan divisions should "cease at the water's edge."[41] A century later, President William Howard Taft made the same point, arguing, "In its foreign affairs, the United States should present to the world a united front."[42] During the

Cold War, US leaders expressed this perspective so often that the idea that politics should stop at the water's edge became a cliché. While presidents have advanced this view in an effort to persuade opposition party lawmakers to support them on foreign policy, opposition party lawmakers have sometimes used the same language in an effort to persuade presidents to give them a say in national security decision-making.[43]

Pro-presidential bipartisanship characterized some of the most important US foreign policy decisions of the early Cold War years, including congressional approval of Harry Truman's proposals to provide aid to Europe under the Marshall Plan and join newly established NATO.[44] However, even the early Cold War featured some fiercely partisan debates over foreign policy. For instance, congressional Republicans attacked Harry Truman for "losing China" after the communist revolution in that country, and congressional Democrats charged that Dwight Eisenhower allowed the Soviet Union to acquire more military power than the United States.[45] Overall, the era between World War II and the Vietnam War featured broad US consensus in support of an internationalist and anti-communist foreign policy, coupled with intense disputes on international issues where presidents were politically vulnerable.[46]

In other words, the United States has never experienced a period of consistent bipartisan congressional support for the president. Nevertheless, pro-presidential bipartisanship has marked a variety of important foreign policy debates. Since the 1990s, the Senate has approved six waves of NATO enlargement—bringing a total of 16 countries into the alliance—by voice vote or with at least three-quarters of Democrats and Republicans voting for the expansion.[47] After the September 11, 2001, terrorist attacks, Congress authorized the use of military force against the perpetrators of the attacks with just a single member of Congress voting in opposition.[48] In 2003, large majorities of Democrats and Republicans voted to establish the President's Emergency Plan for AIDS Relief, a major program designed to combat HIV/AIDS and other infectious diseases in Africa.[49] The approval by Congress of the United States-Mexico-Canada Agreement (USMCA), the major trade deal negotiated by Trump to replace the North American Free Trade Agreement (NAFTA), also involved strong pro-presidential bipartisanship.[50] Most recently, the vast majority of Democrats and Republicans joined together in support of the provision of large amounts of military aid to Ukraine and the imposition of major sanctions on Russia by the Biden administration following Russia's 2022 invasion of Ukraine.[51]

Anti-presidential bipartisanship

Anti-presidential bipartisanship has received less attention from observers of American politics, but it has also been prevalent in US foreign policy.[52] In 1950, the House and Senate voted overwhelmingly to override Harry Truman's veto of the Internal Security Act, which gave the Justice Department new authority to deport aliens on security grounds, and established the Subversive Activities Control Board to investigate claims of communist subversion.[53] Two decades later, as bipartisan congressional dissatisfaction with the Vietnam War intensified, majorities of Democrats and Republicans voted to restrict US military activities in Southeast Asia. In 1973, a majority of Senate Republicans and nearly half of House Republicans joined most Democrats in voting to override Richard Nixon's veto of the War Powers Resolution, which set limits on the president's authority to take the country into war.[54]

Anti-presidential bipartisanship has been especially common in the area of economic sanctions. In 1986, majorities of Democrats and Republicans in the House and Senate voted to override Ronald Reagan's veto of legislation imposing sanctions on the apartheid-era government of South Africa.[55] Congress has also approved many other bipartisan sanctions bills—targeting countries ranging from Cuba to China—that were resisted by presidents who worried that the sanctions would antagonize foreign governments or make it more difficult for the United States to advance international priorities.[56]

Under Obama, anti-presidential bipartisanship characterized some important terrorism debates. In 2016, large majorities in both parties voted to override a veto by Obama of legislation allowing US courts to hear cases against foreign officials charged with culpability for acts of terrorism committed on US soil, which Obama worried would lead Saudi Arabia and other countries to retaliate against the United States.[57] Congress also blocked Obama from transferring detainees in Guantánamo Bay to facilities on the US mainland, thereby preventing him from fulfilling his pledge to close the Guantánamo detention facility.[58]

Under Trump, anti-presidential bipartisanship characterized an array of foreign policy issues, including relations with Russia, NATO policy, spending on diplomacy and foreign aid, and the US military presence on the Korean Peninsula.[59] In most of these cases, Democratic and Republican lawmakers joined together to counter or prevent steps by Trump that would turn the

United States away from liberal internationalist values or commitments. In a reflection of the intensity of some of these inter-branch clashes under Trump, eight of the 10 bills that he vetoed concerned foreign policy.[60]

Strong polarization

Still other foreign policy debates have been marked by strong polarization. One of the most important cases of foreign policy polarization involved the Senate's consideration of the Treaty of Versailles, which established the League of Nations, in 1919. Only one Republican senator joined 37 Democrats in voting for the treaty in the form submitted to Congress by President Woodrow Wilson, while just a handful of Democrats joined the vast majority of Republicans in a key pair of votes on reservations to the treaty.[61] During the Clinton administration, just four Senate Republicans joined 44 Senate Democrats in voting to approve the Comprehensive Test Ban Treaty, resulting in the treaty falling well short of the two-thirds support needed for approval.[62] Congress also became strongly polarized during George W. Bush's presidency over the Iraq war. At the nadir of the war, all but 14 House Democrats voted for legislation setting a deadline for withdrawing US troops from Iraq, while all but two House Republicans voted against the legislation.[63]

Congress has been quite polarized on climate change and nuclear diplomacy with Iran too. In a key congressional vote on climate change in 2009, 95% of House Republicans voted against a Democratic proposal to mandate reductions in emissions of greenhouse gases in various sectors of the economy.[64] Thirteen years later, not a single Democrat or Republican crossed party lines when voting on landmark legislation backed by Joe Biden designed to support a US transition to clean energy.[65] On the nuclear issue, as I discuss in Chapter 7, every Republican senator voted in 2015 against the Joint Comprehensive Plan of Action (JCPOA) negotiated by Obama with Iran, which lifted sanctions on Iran in return for Iran's acceptance of constraints on its nuclear activities, while 40 out of 44 Senate Democrats voted for it.[66] Recent Congresses have also been sharply divided along partisan lines on foreign policy investigations that had the potential to tarnish the president or other party leaders—on issues ranging from the 2012 killing of four Americans in Benghazi, Libya, to the impeachment of Trump over his handling of Ukraine policy.[67]

Cross-partisanship

Cross-partisanship merits its own consideration. On issues marked by strong bipartisanship in Congress, intra-party division is minimal. Similarly, intra-party division is low when nearly all Democrats line up against nearly all Republicans. But on issues marked neither by strong bipartisanship nor by strong polarization, cross-party coalitions become central to congressional activity. For the empirical sections of the book, I define cross-partisanship as instances where more than 10% of the members of a party oppose their party's dominant position. Cross-partisanship is not mutually exclusive with pro-presidential or anti-presidential bipartisanship, but it is worth highlighting this alignment as a distinct category because the existence of substantial intra-party division often affects the ability of Congress to approve legislation or exercise influence in other ways.

Cross-partisanship has been especially common in recent decades in votes on trade agreements, with a substantial minority of Democrats often joining a majority of Republicans in support of trade liberalization.[68] In 1993, 40% of House Democrats and 49% of Senate Democrats joined 75% of House Republicans and 77% of Senate Republicans to approve NAFTA.[69] In 2015, as I discuss in Chapter 8, 15% of House Democrats and 30% of Senate Democrats joined 79% of House Republicans and 90% of Senate Republicans in voting to give the president trade promotion authority and thereby facilitate negotiation by Obama of the Trans-Pacific Partnership.[70] The overwhelming bipartisan approval of the USMCA in late 2019 and early 2020 represents an exception to the pattern of limited Democratic support for recent trade agreements.

Cross-partisan votes have also marked other important international agreements. In a 1978 Senate vote on the Panama Canal Treaties, which turned control of the canal over to the government of Panama, 52 Democrats and 16 Republicans provided the two-thirds majority needed for approval of the treaty negotiated by Jimmy Carter, while 10 Democrats and 22 Republicans voted against it.[71] Three decades later, 13 of 39 Senate Republicans joined all Senate Democrats in voting for the New START nuclear arms control agreement negotiated by Obama with Russia.[72]

Many debates over military intervention—in places ranging from Bosnia and Kosovo during the 1990s to Libya and Syria following the Arab Spring— have also generated intra-party divisions. For instance, in a key 2011 House vote during the US intervention in Libya, 19% of Democrats joined 38% of Republicans in voting to restrict funding for the military operation.[73] Two years later, as I detail in Chapter 4, both parties were internally divided over whether to use the military to enforce a red line set by Obama regarding the use of chemical weapons by the government of Syria.

Why foreign policy bipartisanship persists

So, why does bipartisanship persist in foreign policy during a highly polarized era, and why does bipartisan cooperation on international issues regularly take multiple forms? These questions are especially worthy of investigation given that there often exist major obstacles to bipartisanship. In particular, the incentives for elected officials to engage in partisan behavior can be quite powerful. In recent decades, small margins have tended to separate the two parties in presidential election vote totals and congressional seats, placing control of the levers of power in Washington up for grabs nearly every time voters go to the polls. Faced with the prospect of gaining or losing so much power in each election, elected officials are strongly incentivized to do everything they can to make their own party look good and make the opposing party look bad. The results are often strong feelings of teamsmanship within each party and approaches of no-holds-barred warfare between the parties.[74]

Yet there are countervailing forces that sometimes lead elected officials to act in bipartisan ways. Some of the motivations for elected officials to engage in bipartisanship are not specific to foreign policy. Legislating in the US system of government is no easy task. A bill must be approved by the House, approved by the Senate (where a supermajority of 60 votes is often needed for passage), and signed by the president in order to become law. If the president vetoes a bill, it will only become law if two-thirds of the members of the House and Senate agree to override the veto. Given these realities, some support from both parties is usually needed to enact legislation. This means that individual members of Congress and the leadership of the parties have a strong incentive to seek bipartisan backing if they wish to advance their legislative priorities.[75] This incentive is often bolstered by an electoral motivation, in that it can be beneficial politically to members of Congress and the parties as a whole to show voters that they are solving public problems.[76]

In foreign policy specifically, national security crises and international threats can also be sources of bipartisanship. Here, too, an electoral motivation can be important. During perilous times, the public may rally around the flag and expect elected representatives in both parties to put partisan concerns aside.[77] Consider that in the immediate aftermath of the September

11, 2001, attacks, 90% of the American public approved of President George W. Bush's job performance.[78] In such a context, challenging the president on a national security issue can be politically risky for members of Congress, while supporting the president can be politically advantageous for them. The result is likely to be pro-presidential bipartisanship, as occurred when Democrats and Republicans banded together to authorize Bush to use military force against the perpetrators of the 9/11 attacks. In addition, even during less tumultuous periods, bipartisanship may sometimes occur because the president and many legislators recognize that international engagement is necessary to protect US security in the face of various global challenges.[79]

While these factors explain many cases of bipartisanship, they do not account well for the multiple forms of bipartisanship. For instance, the incentive of members of Congress to reach across the aisle in order to be successful legislatively or show constituents that they are solving public problems does not explain well the prevalence of cross-partisanship, which often makes legislating more difficult. Similarly, if foreign policy bipartisanship is motivated by a shared desire to rally around the flag or protect US security, one would not expect to see both parties in Congress at odds with the president. National security crises, for their part, represent the exception more than the rule in contemporary American politics. Even after 9/11, the president's popularity quickly returned to more normal levels.

Other factors fill in these important gaps, helping explain why some degree of bipartisanship marks many foreign policy debates even in the absence of a crisis, as well as why bipartisan cooperation is often not synonymous with unity. In an argument that I develop in greater detail in Chapter 3, I highlight three key contributors to political alignments among elected officials in policy debates: (1) the ideological landscape associated with the debate, (2) the advocacy landscape associated with the debate, and (3) the differing incentives and prerogatives of lawmakers and the president.[80]

The limits of ideology

The limits of liberal and conservative ideology provide one part of the story. Bipartisan behavior by elected officials is common in foreign policy in part because the ideological landscape—among both policy elites and voters—is still not consistently polarized on international issues. The views of lawmakers are shaped by a foreign policy ecosystem that includes experts and other elite professionals in think tanks and the media. At the same time, on salient issues, members of Congress need to be responsive to the attitudes of their constituents. When liberal or conservative ideology leads the views of policy elites or voters on an issue to divide along left-right lines, members of Congress will be likely to follow their lead, particularly since legislators may open themselves up to a primary challenge if they do not hew to their party's ideological orthodoxy. By contrast, if an issue does not break down along left-right lines among policy elites or the mass public, the views of elected officials will tend not to be polarized and lawmakers will have more political leeway to cooperate across party lines.

Whereas large gaps separate the views of liberal and conservative elites and voters on many domestic issues, their opinions are less consistently distinct on major foreign policy issues.[81] Although conservatives typically place more value than liberals on military power and attribute less importance than liberals to cooperation with other countries, positions in many foreign policy debates do not map onto a one-dimensional, left-right ideological spectrum.[82] On such issues, Republican and Democratic elected officials have greater freedom to cooperate with one another. At the same time, since many international issues are not salient to voters, lawmakers have the flexibility to follow their own compass in many foreign policy debates, facilitating cross-partisanship. In these ways, ideas influence the behavior of members of Congress through both electoral pressures and the principled beliefs of lawmakers.

This ideological fluidity in many areas of foreign policy helps explain how Donald Trump could become the Republican standard-bearer in 2016, even though his stances on international issues ranging from Russia and NATO to trade and US military involvement in the Middle East departed from the views of most Republican leaders.[83] It is much harder to imagine someone becoming the Republican nominee for president today while espousing views on core domestic issues, such as taxes, abortion, or government regulation of the economy, that deviate sharply from the Republican Party's standard positions.

The role of advocacy groups

My account of bipartisanship also differs from most other analyses of polarization and bipartisanship by attributing greater importance to advocacy groups. Although it is well-known that interest groups have considerable influence on policymaking, much of the literature on polarization and bipartisanship gives little attention to the role of outside groups in pushing elected officials together or apart. Yet whether advocacy groups are themselves split along partisan lines, working together in a politically diverse coalition, or inactive on an issue can greatly influence how elected officials line up.[84]

In domestic affairs, most major advocacy groups, from Planned Parenthood to the National Rifle Association, have a strong pro-Democratic or pro-Republican orientation, making them forces for polarization. By contrast, advocacy groups that lobby the government on foreign policy—which include ethnic constituencies, defense contractors, and values-based nongovernmental organizations—are less one-sided on the whole in their campaign contributions and lobbying.[85] As a result, whether they represent mass constituencies or elite interests, foreign policy advocacy groups often foster bipartisan action by lawmakers.

In addition, there are some areas of foreign policy in which powerful advocacy groups typically do not play a major role.[86] For example, outside advocacy has been relatively unimportant in many recent debates regarding whether the United States should intervene militarily in countries experiencing civil war or brutal repression. In such cases, elected officials often have considerable freedom to reach across the aisle. The upshot is that it is less common on international than on domestic issues for groups to pressure elected officials to resist compromising with their colleagues in the other party.

The ideological and advocacy landscapes further help explain why political alignments on foreign policy take a variety of forms. Pro-presidential bipartisanship is more likely if the president's position on an issue is compatible with liberal and conservative perspectives or if important advocacy groups linked to both parties share the president's position. Anti-presidential bipartisanship is more likely if the president's position is out of sync with liberal and conservative outlooks or if influential groups tied to both parties oppose it. Strong polarization is more likely if an issue features a clear left-right ideological divide or if groups with partisan orientations are advocating on opposite sides of it. Cross-partisanship typically occurs if competing policy positions cannot be mapped on a left-right ideological spectrum or if party-affiliated groups are split or uncommitted on the issue.

The influence of institutional incentives

I also bring inter-branch dynamics more directly into the understanding of polarization and bipartisanship by considering how differences in the incentives and prerogatives of lawmakers and the president generate anti-presidential bipartisanship. To the extent the literature on congressional polarization has considered the relationship between Congress and the president, this has usually been to explain how party identity and positions of the president influence the positions of legislators. For instance, studies have shown that legislators in the president's party are more likely than ones in the opposition party to support presidential positions, and presidents fuel stronger polarization in Congress when they make an issue a top priority.[87] But scholars have given less attention to instances where Democrats and Republicans in Congress join together to challenge the president.[88] Understanding this phenomenon requires consideration of the differing electoral incentives and institutional prerogatives of lawmakers and the president, which my account brings to the fore.

Since presidents are elected by the entire American population and are held accountable by voters for national welfare, they have a strong electoral motivation to pursue policies that advance overall national interests.[89] By contrast, legislators are not generally held accountable for the outcomes of policy decisions, giving them more political leeway to adopt positions that reflect their personal values or resonate with domestic constituencies.[90] This difference makes lawmakers in both parties more likely than the president to place principle before pragmatism when adopting foreign policy positions.

In addition, since presidents are responsible for diplomacy and the execution of foreign policy, they tend to oppose legislative mandates that might limit their diplomatic flexibility or antagonize governments with which they seek to cooperate. Lawmakers, for their part, sometimes seek to protect congressional foreign policy prerogatives by constraining presidential discretion or unilateralism. These differing institutional perspectives can foster inter-branch conflict in areas including sanctions, treaties, and military action. To be sure, many members of Congress tend to acquiesce in, rather than oppose, the unilateral exercise of presidential power. But, as I show in the remainder of the book, bipartisan congressional efforts to challenge the president occur regularly.

The importance of individual agency

While the factors I highlight involve broad forces and powerful incentives acting upon elected officials, it is important to recognize that the individual agency of lawmakers is also essential when it comes to particular instances of bipartisanship. Ultimately, it is individual members of Congress who make decisions about whether to pursue or reject compromises with colleagues in the other party or whether to vote for or against pieces of legislation. On some issues—particularly very salient ones—the key decisions in the legislative process are made by congressional leaders, who wield tremendous power in the contemporary Congress.[91] But on other issues, committee leaders or rank-and-file legislators shape bipartisan bills and drive legislative negotiations.

Some members of Congress have played a particularly outsized role on foreign policy issues.[92] After the fall of communism, Democratic Senator Sam Nunn and Republican Senator Richard Lugar designed the Cooperative Threat Reduction Program, a major, multidecade investment in securing various nuclear facilities and materials in countries of the former Soviet Union.[93] In 2016, Democratic Senator Ben Cardin, Republican Senator John McCain, Democratic Representative Jim McGovern, and Republican Representative Christopher Smith spearheaded the enactment of the Global Magnitsky Act, a landmark law that authorized sanctions on individuals in any country who have committed gross violations of human rights.[94]

Some of the key congressional foreign policy figures of recent decades are no longer serving in Congress, due to retirement, reelection defeat, or death. The departure from the institution of foreign policy giants such as Nunn, Lugar, McCain, and former Democratic Representative Lee Hamilton has raised the question of whether Congress can still play an important role in foreign policy.[95] But many legislators remain active in foreign policy, including in the development of bipartisan legislation and coalitions. In recent years, for instance, Democratic Representative Barbara Lee, Democratic Senators Tim Kaine and Chris Murphy, and Republican Senators Mike Lee and Todd Young have led bipartisan efforts to restrict presidential war powers authorities; Republican Senator Lindsey Graham and Democratic Senator Patrick Leahy have worked together to build and maintain a robust budget for diplomacy and foreign assistance; and Republican Senator Marco Rubio and Democratic Senator Bob Menendez have cooperated to advance human rights sanctions on China.

Most of these lawmakers have been motivated at least in part by their personal views—from a belief in the importance of human rights to a desire to protect national security—when engaging in foreign policy debates. As a major 2018 Center for Strategic and International Studies study concluded: "Rather than operating as an insular, parochial institution defined solely by constituent interests, members of Congress hold a nuanced set of views on the US role in the world and have a wide variety of motivations for becoming engaged in foreign policy decisionmaking."[96]

Yet the ability of lawmakers to reach across the aisle on a given issue is often conditioned by partisan and electoral pressures, such as demands for party loyalty or lobbying by influential constituencies. Put another way, policy views and political constraints both matter when it comes to the prospects for bipartisan cooperation.[97] In the book's case studies (Chapters 4–9), I show how political pressures and the ideological, advocacy, and institutional landscapes make it easier or harder for individual legislators to act in bipartisan ways on different issues.

In short, there is much more to the story of contemporary US foreign policy than rising polarization. Admittedly, on highly salient issues with major stakes for the fortunes of the two parties, partisan incentives tend to crowd out any interest elected officials might have in reaching across the aisle. But the vast majority of foreign policy issues do not have large electoral stakes, opening the door for different forms of bipartisanship. Notably, these varieties of bipartisanship are shaped by bottom-up, top-down, and outside-in forces, including the attitudes of voters, the views of leaders, lobbying by activists, and the differing incentives and responsibilities of the president and Congress.

Why foreign policy bipartisanship matters

The political alignments of Democrats and Republicans, in turn, shape the ability of the United States to carry out an effective foreign policy. High levels of polarization foster legislative gridlock, thereby weakening the capacity of Congress to address important challenges.[98] As Congress scholar Sarah Binder notes: "When elections yield more polarized parties and chambers, bargaining is more difficult and compromises more out of reach."[99] Polarization has also contributed to a long-term decline in expertise on Capitol Hill as the two parties in Congress have prioritized investments in communications and leadership office staff over investments in committee staff,[100] and it has frayed the social fabric of Congress as lawmakers have interacted less with colleagues in the other party.[101] These trends have led scholars to catalog the institution's dysfunction in books with bleak titles such as *The Broken Branch*, *It's Even Worse Than It Looks*, *Congress Overwhelmed*, and *Kill Switch*.[102]

Foreign policy polarization is particularly worrisome because it diminishes the capacity of the United States to attend to important global challenges and support a rules-based international order.[103] The United States cannot fund multilateral institutions, provide foreign aid to other countries, or develop new military capabilities without congressional approval of funds for these activities. By reducing the likelihood of Congress approving an international agreement or of a president's successor remaining party to an agreement, polarization also gives other countries less incentive to negotiate or partner with the United States.[104]

At the same time, by making it more difficult for Congress to act, polarization gives the president greater incentive to pursue unilateral foreign policy initiatives that can be executed without congressional involvement in areas ranging from military intervention to diplomacy.[105] Polarization also makes it harder for Congress to muster the majorities needed to check such unilateral actions, since lawmakers in the president's party often prioritize loyalty to the president over the preservation of checks and balances.[106] Moreover, pushback against the president from just one party in Congress is usually less effective than bipartisan pushback because the president can denigrate it as partisan sniping and the media may depict it in the same way. Yet unilateral presidential initiatives tend to be less effective or durable than policies instituted through legislation or bipartisan cooperation.[107] Political scientist Kenneth Schultz observes: "As the parties become more ideologically distinct, there is a danger of greater swings from one administration to the next if the party in power changes. And as Congress loses its bipartisan center, it becomes less of a stabilizing force to keep swings in check."[108]

Indeed, Congress often allows the president to sit in the driver's seat on foreign policy.[109] In recent decades, Congress has frequently acquiesced in unauthorized wars and other presidential assertions of national security power,[110] allowed the president to put international agreements into effect without submitting them to the Senate for ratification,[111] permitted the military instrument of US foreign policy to be strengthened at the expense of civilian foreign policy tools,[112] and neglected to conduct adequate oversight of executive branch actions.[113] US foreign policy scholars Jim Goldgeier and Elizabeth Saunders argue that these patterns reflect the "unconstrained exercise of executive power."[114]

Yet, even as Congress has deferred to the president on many international issues, it has played an important role on many others.[115] Generally, Congress has tended to act more independently and assertively on foreign policy issues that involve spending or are connected to the domestic economy than ones that involve the use of military force.[116] Studies have documented the impact of Congress on policymaking in areas including trade,[117] multilateral institutions,[118] international agreements,[119] human rights,[120] foreign aid,[121] and economic sanctions.[122] Even on questions of military intervention and civil-military relations, Congress is frequently more influential than many observers realize.[123]

This book's case studies show that Congress continued to shape important areas of foreign policy during the presidencies of Barack Obama and Donald Trump, when polarization generally reached its highest levels in more than a century. Most strikingly, this congressional influence sometimes involved anti-presidential bipartisanship, in which Democrats and Republicans in Congress momentarily set aside their partisan identities to band together to challenge presidential policies. Such acts of bipartisanship suggest that Congress remains capable of fulfilling its constitutional responsibilities as a coequal branch of government, though it certainly has not exercised these responsibilities consistently in recent years.

Preview of remaining chapters

In the remainder of the book, I analyze data on the prevalence of different political alignments in congressional foreign and domestic policy votes (Chapter 2); explain more fully how ideology, advocacy groups, and congressional and presidential incentives influence alignments among elected officials (Chapter 3); examine the political dynamics associated with six major foreign policy debates of the Obama and Trump presidencies (Chapters 4–9); and discuss some key implications of my findings (Chapter 10).

I use the congressional voting data, based on 2,737 important votes from 1991 to 2020, to explore overall patterns of polarization and bipartisanship. The data reveal that polarization has been increasing in both international and domestic issues but has been doing so more slowly in international issues. The data also show that bipartisanship is more common in foreign than in domestic policy. Turning to different types of bipartisanship, the data further reveal that pro-presidential bipartisanship, anti-presidential bipartisanship, and cross-partisanship each occur regularly when lawmakers turn their attention overseas.

I use the case studies to evaluate the factors that shape the positions of elected officials. These case studies, which span the Obama and Trump administrations, examine important recent debates over military intervention in the Syrian civil war, the repeal or replacement of post-9/11 laws authorizing the use of military force, the imposition and removal of sanctions on Russia, the placement and lifting of sanctions on Iran, the Trans-Pacific Partnership trade agreement, and the US budget for diplomacy and foreign assistance.

I selected these debates for in-depth study for several reasons. First, they represent a cross-section of major areas of foreign policy, including the security, economic, diplomatic, and humanitarian dimensions of international affairs. To the extent that my argument holds up across these different debates, we can have more confidence that it is broadly applicable. Second, as I explain in Chapter 3, these policy areas involve differing ideological and advocacy group landscapes, enabling me to evaluate how the ideological and advocacy contexts of an issue influence political alignments on it. Third, each debate spanned the Obama and Trump presidencies, as well as periods in which one party controlled both branches of government and periods when it did not. This variation in the political context ensures that the findings in each case are not specific to a particular president or political configuration. Fourth, given that overall polarization in American politics reached new heights under Obama and Trump, these presidencies offer hard tests for my argument that foreign policy bipartisanship is common—making evidence of multiple types of bipartisanship in the cases all the more striking. I discuss my case selection process and rationale in more detail in the last section of Chapter 3.

Collectively, the case studies illustrate how ideology, advocacy groups, and institutional incentives contribute to polarization and different forms of bipartisanship. My analysis in the cases draws on legislative and executive branch documents; surveys of public and elite opinion; records of advocacy group activity; contemporaneous reporting by journalists; memoirs by government officials; the work of other scholars and analysts; and more than 100 interviews that I conducted with members of Congress, congressional staff, senior and mid-level executive branch officials, think tank experts, and advocates who were heavily involved in the debates.[124]

In the book's final chapter, I synthesize my findings, highlight the persistence of multiple types of bipartisanship during the first two years of Joe Biden's presidency, and discuss implications of my findings for efforts to foster bipartisanship in foreign policy.

2

Bipartisanship in congressional voting

In this chapter I outline overall patterns in political alignments on policy issues based on analysis of an original data set of important congressional votes from 1991 to 2020. The biggest takeaways from the chapter are that bipartisanship remains more prevalent in international than in domestic issues and that multiple forms of bipartisanship consistently characterize foreign policy debates. This analysis sets the stage for Chapter 3, in which I shift from identifying patterns of political alignments to explaining why foreign policy bipartisanship persists and why elected officials line up in different ways on different issues.

This is not the first study to examine patterns of polarization and bipartisanship in US foreign policy. As discussed in Chapter 1, scholars have previously found that polarization increased in domestic and international issues after the 1970s. Studies have also found that US lawmakers have been less polarized on foreign policy than on domestic policy,[1] and that bipartisanship has been more common on issues involving military intervention or national security than on issues involving international spending or economics.[2]

I provide a fresh look at patterns of polarization and bipartisanship using more recent data and taking into account different types of bipartisanship. I begin the analysis by using the standard binary conceptions of bipartisanship and polarization. I then go beyond those categories to examine patterns involving more nuanced alignments, including pro-presidential bipartisanship, anti-presidential bipartisanship, and cross-partisanship. I also consider the strength of bipartisanship and polarization, distinguishing between stronger and weaker versions of these alignments. This approach enables a more fine-grained understanding of the ways Democrats and Republicans align with and against one another.

I find that multiple types of bipartisanship have remained common in foreign policy in recent years and that alignment patterns differ across policy areas. Strong polarization is rare in foreign policy, whereas pro-presidential bipartisanship, anti-presidential bipartisanship, and cross-partisanship each occurs regularly in international issues. Bipartisanship is also more frequent

Bipartisanship and US Foreign Policy. Jordan Tama, Oxford University Press. © Oxford University Press 2024.
DOI: 10.1093/oso/9780197745663.003.0002

in important foreign policy issues than in important domestic policy issues. The gaps between foreign and domestic policy in rates of anti-presidential bipartisanship and strong polarization are especially striking, with the former alignment occurring much more often in international issues and the latter far more prevalent in domestic matters.

Moreover, while bipartisanship declined in both international and domestic issues during the past three decades, the drop in bipartisanship in foreign policy was less pronounced, suggesting that international policy debates have been less heavily affected than domestic policy ones by the overall rise in polarization in American politics. Finally, important congressional votes on international security issues are marked more often by strong bipartisanship and less often by cross-partisanship than important votes on international economic matters, but bipartisanship occurs more frequently in both of these major foreign policy areas than it does on domestic matters.

Collectively, the chapter's findings point to a glass half-full/glass half-empty situation. If one's reference point is the early decades of the Cold War, when overall foreign policy bipartisanship reached a peak, recent Congresses look depressingly polarized on international issues. But if one's reference point is instead the contemporary politics of the most salient domestic issues, bipartisanship seems remarkably prevalent and persistent in foreign affairs. The patterns described in this chapter also imply that factors other than partisan incentives influence the decisions of elected officials on many foreign policy issues, and that the pressures facing legislators vary across different policy areas. After reviewing alignment patterns in this chapter, I turn to discussing the factors that influence this variation in alignments in Chapter 3.

Congressional voting data

My analysis in this chapter is based on a data set I created of important congressional votes with the help of research assistants.[3] To be sure, congressional votes do not represent the only type of governmental activity that involves polarization or bipartisanship. One could also evaluate patterns of polarization or bipartisanship by examining public statements by elected officials, the conduct of congressional hearings or investigations, the cosponsorship of legislation, control of the congressional agenda, or the appointment of executive branch officials, to name a few other important activities.[4] But votes provide a particularly rich source of data for examining patterns concerning different forms of bipartisanship. Since the president takes a position on some legislation prior to votes on it, voting data are particularly useful for investigating rates of pro-presidential and anti-presidential bipartisanship. Votes also reveal the extent of intra-party divisions, facilitating analysis of patterns of cross-partisanship.

I created a new data set, rather than basing the analysis on existing data sets of congressional votes, because many congressional votes deal with trivial matters.[5] While the alignment of lawmakers on trivial votes is of little consequence, the alignment of elected officials on important issues can influence the welfare and security of people within the United States and overseas. My data set homes in on important votes and sets aside trivial ones.

The votes span the years 1991 to 2020, from the 102nd through the 116th Congress. This was a period during which polarization in American politics was generally high and rising. The end of the Cold War just before the start of this period had also diminished the perception of international danger that had sometimes brought Democrats and Republicans together during previous decades. Given these domestic and international trends, the prevalence of foreign policy bipartisanship during this period is particularly notable.

The data set includes votes from 1991 to 2020 that were highlighted as important by Congressional Quarterly (or CQ), a highly regarded news outlet that focuses on congressional activity. More specifically, the data set includes all congressional votes included in annual CQ lists of "key votes," which represent the votes CQ considered to be most important each year, as well as all votes highlighted in articles in every third edition of CQ Almanac, an annual summary of important congressional action.[6]

I classified a vote as a foreign policy vote if the Congressional Research Service (CRS) categorized the legislation in one of the following policy areas: armed forces and national security, international affairs, foreign trade and international finance, or immigration. This method identified a total of 594 important foreign policy votes and 2,141 important domestic policy votes in the House and Senate. Among these votes, 71% of the foreign policy votes and 74% of the domestic policy votes were roll call votes. The remaining votes were voice votes or unanimous consent votes, in which the votes of individual legislators were not recorded.[7] Twenty-three percent of the foreign policy votes and 21% of the domestic policy votes were procedural or amendment votes, which involved the legislative process or changes to bills, rather than votes on the final passage of legislation. Fifty-six percent of the votes took place in the House, and 44% of them occurred in the Senate.

Bipartisanship in foreign and domestic policy votes

The data reveal that a large share of important congressional votes over the past three decades involved some degree of bipartisanship and that bipartisanship occurred more often on international than on domestic issues. For Congress as a whole, a majority of Democrats and a majority of Republicans voted together in 64% of the foreign policy votes and 54% of the domestic policy votes.[8] In the House, this degree of bipartisanship marked 61% of foreign policy votes and 51% of domestic policy votes. In the Senate, the corresponding rates were 69% and 60%. (See Figure 2.1.) The rates of bipartisanship in the House and Senate were also higher on international than on domestic issues when the tabulations are restricted to roll call votes; when procedural and amendment votes are dropped from the tabulations; when immigration votes are excluded;[9] when votes on spending measures are excluded; when the data are restricted to votes identified by CQ as key votes; and regardless of whether the House and Senate or the presidency and the voting chamber were controlled by the same party when a given vote occurred. (See Figures 2.2 and 2.3.) Collectively, these tabulations show that

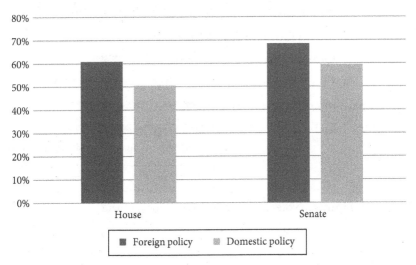

Figure 2.1 Bipartisan votes

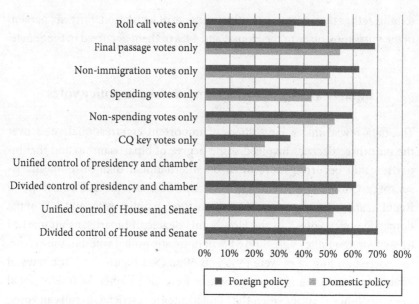

Figure 2.2 Bipartisan votes under various conditions, House

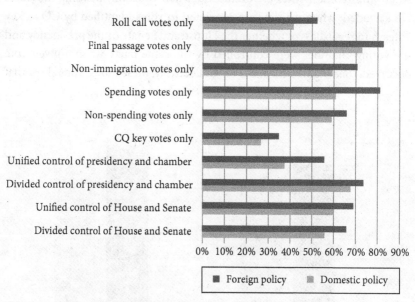

Figure 2.3 Bipartisan votes under various conditions, Senate

bipartisan voting has remained common in Congress during an era known for its polarization and this has been particularly the case for international issues.[10]

It is worth noting that these data are not perfect indicators of the level of polarization or bipartisanship in Congress. On the one hand, they might overstate the overall level of agreement between Republican and Democratic legislators on important issues, since legislation that advances far in the legislative process is more likely than other legislation to involve bipartisanship and be considered important by journalists. Relatedly, most of the votes in the data set represent votes on the final passage of legislation, and disagreements in earlier stages of the legislative process have often already been resolved through compromises by the time legislation reaches the final passage stage. On the other hand, highly salient issues tend to be more polarized than less salient ones, and legislation may attract more media attention when it is controversial, suggesting that legislation considered important by journalists might be more likely than other legislation to involve polarization.[11] Indeed, the CQ key votes, which represent the most salient votes, feature higher levels of polarization than the other important votes included in the data set.

Regardless of any such patterns, it is clear from the data that bipartisanship has continued to occur regularly in Congress and that it is more prevalent in international than on domestic issues. Moreover, other data on congressional voting in recent decades also indicate higher levels of bipartisanship on foreign than on domestic policy. For instance, a study of all roll call votes taken within House committees between 1995 and 2016 found that the foreign affairs, armed services, and intelligence committees—the three committees focused on international issues—each ranked in the top six among all 20 House committees in rates of bipartisan voting.[12]

The data set further reveals that strong polarization is much less common in foreign policy than in domestic policy. In the House, at least 90% of Democrats and at least 90% of Democrats voted on opposite sides of each other on 25% of roll call votes on domestic issues and just 15% of roll call votes on foreign policy issues. (See Figure 2.4.) In the Senate, this gap was even greater, with polarization of this severity characterizing 25% of domestic policy roll call votes and only 8% of foreign policy roll call votes. (See Figure 2.5.) Given that severe polarization creates especially large obstacles to effective governance, it is striking that it occurs much less often on international matters.

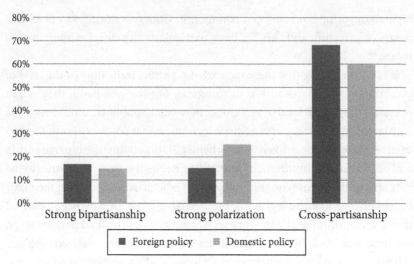

Figure 2.4 Variations of bipartisanship and polarization, House

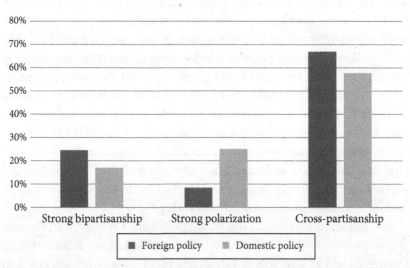

Figure 2.5 Variations of bipartisanship and polarization, Senate

Cross-partisanship is also more common on foreign than on domestic policy, though it characterizes large shares of both sets of votes. For the purpose of this analysis, I define cross-partisanship as instances where more than 10% of the members of a party oppose their party's dominant position. The defection of that share of lawmakers from their party's prevailing position typically has large consequences given the relatively small margins of party majorities in the contemporary Congress and the supermajoritarian requirements for enacting legislation in the US system of government. Indeed, since several decades of Democratic dominance of Congress ended in the 1994 election, the majority party has only governed with a margin exceeding 10% of their seats in the chamber during a total of six years in the House and four years in the Senate. The result is that a majority party is rarely able to enact legislation on an issue if 10% of its members defect, unless it is able to attract countervailing support from the other party. By the same token, a defection of this scale sometimes enables the opposition party to advance legislation successfully.

Across the House votes included in the data set, more than 10% of the members of a party voted against their party's dominant position in 68% of roll call votes on international issues and 60% of roll call votes on domestic issues. (See Figure 2.4.) A similar pattern marked Senate voting, with 67% of foreign policy roll call votes and 58% of domestic policy roll call votes meeting the threshold for cross-partisanship. (See Figure 2.5.) These data suggest that substantial intra-party division is the norm in policy debates and that such intra-party divides are especially prevalent in foreign affairs.

A different subset of the data further shows that it is more common for Congress to challenge the president in a bipartisan manner on foreign than on domestic policy. The president took a clear public position on 990 of the votes in the data set.[13] Caution is warranted when analyzing such "presidential position" votes because the president's public position on a bill does not always reflect the president's actual view of the bill.[14] Sometimes, the president might endorse legislation for strategic or political reasons—for instance, because the bill is popular with voters—despite having serious reservations about it. In other cases, the president might publicly oppose legislation for strategic or political reasons—for instance, because the president wants to negotiate a better deal with lawmakers—despite considering the bill to be in the best interest of the country. As a result, one should interpret individual presidential position votes with some caution. But these votes are still highly informative for identifying broad patterns of anti-presidential and pro-presidential bipartisanship.

Of the House presidential position votes in the data set, a majority of Republican legislators and a majority of Democratic legislators voted against the president's position in 13% of the foreign policy votes and 5% of the domestic policy votes. Among the Senate presidential position votes, 16% of foreign policy votes and 7% of domestic policy votes involved anti-presidential bipartisanship. Although 13% and 16%, respectively, might not seem like high figures, it is remarkable that most Democratic and Republican lawmakers would vote against the president on foreign policy during an era of high polarization that frequently. At the same time, rates of pro-presidential bipartisanship were similar on foreign and domestic policy. A majority of House members in both parties voted with the president in 20% of presidential position votes on international issues and 17% of presidential position votes on domestic issues, while the corresponding percentages in the Senate were 22% and 23%, respectively—differences that were not statistically significant. (See Figures 2.6 and 2.7.)

Taken together, these rates of anti-presidential and pro-presidential bipartisanship point to a need to update understandings of the "two presidencies"—the idea that the president receives more support from Congress on foreign than on domestic matters.[15] The data presented here suggest that, to the extent that two presidencies exist, they may actually involve a greater congressional proclivity to challenge, rather than back, the president on international than on domestic issues.

The data further reveal, unsurprisingly, that the House and Senate are less likely to challenge the president when they are controlled by the president's party. In the House, anti-presidential bipartisanship characterized 17% of presidential position votes on foreign policy when the presidency and the

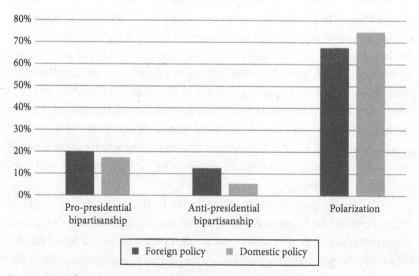

Figure 2.6 Alignments on presidential position votes, House

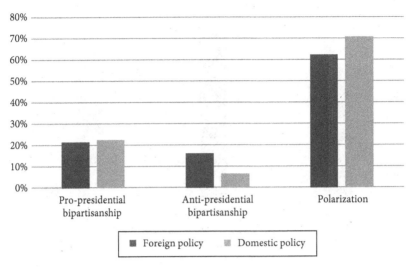

Figure 2.7 Alignments on presidential position votes, Senate

House were controlled by different parties but did not characterize any presidential position foreign policy votes when the presidency and that chamber were controlled by the same party. In the Senate, anti-presidential bipartisanship marked 20% of presidential position foreign policy votes in the former circumstance and 7% of presidential position foreign policy votes in the latter condition. These differences most likely reflect the influence of partisan concerns on decisions by congressional leaders regarding which bills to bring to the House or Senate floor. Congressional leaders in the opposition party will often be enthusiastic about bringing to the floor bipartisan legislation that the president opposes, since approval of such legislation can embarrass the president. Conversely, congressional leaders in the president's party will frequently have an incentive to keep such legislation off the floor, since their party's overall standing can be tarnished if the president suffers a resounding legislative defeat. In this way, partisanship paradoxically even infuses congressional action on bipartisan legislation.[16]

Bipartisanship over time

The data also show a trend of declining bipartisanship in both foreign and domestic policy over the course of the three decades represented in the data

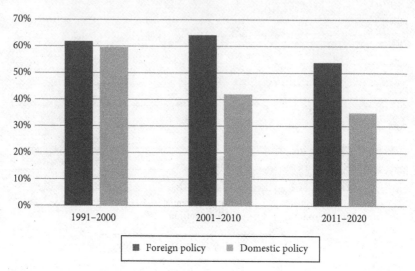

Figure 2.8 Bipartisan votes over time, House

set, with a sharper drop on domestic than on international issues. The share of important House foreign policy votes on which a majority of Democrats and a majority of Republicans voted together dropped from 62% between 1991 and 2000 to 54% between 2011 and 2020. On domestic policy, this drop was even larger, from 60% to 35%. (See Figure 2.8.) In the Senate, rates of bipartisanship also dropped more on international issues than on domestic matters between the earlier and later periods, with the share of bipartisan votes declining from 73% to 54% in foreign policy and from 67% to 38% in domestic policy. (See Figure 2.9.) These differences suggest that the gap in levels of bipartisanship between foreign and domestic policy actually grew over the course of this period.

These patterns are the same—with bipartisanship declining in both domains but doing so to a greater extent on international issues—when procedural and amendment votes are excluded from the tabulations, indicating that the increase over time in polarization was not simply an artifact of the increased use of more divisive legislative processes.[17] On House votes on the final passage of legislation, the share of bipartisan foreign policy votes declined from 74% between 1991 and 2000 to 57% between 2011 and 2020, while the share of bipartisan domestic policy votes dropped from 66% to 35% between those decades. In the Senate, these respective drops were from 85% to 69% on foreign policy and from 80% to 50% on domestic policy. Overall,

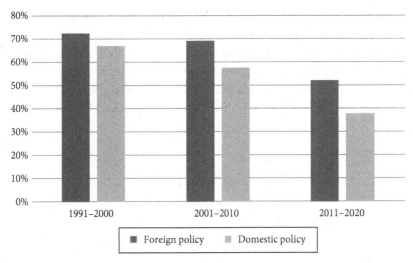

Figure 2.9 Bipartisan votes over time, Senate

these data on temporal trends suggest that foreign policy debates have not been immune to the heightened partisan divisions that have characterized American politics over the past few decades but that rising polarization has been infecting foreign policy debates at a slower rate.

Breaking down the data by presidential term further illustrates these trends, while pointing to the role of events in influencing bipartisanship. The highest levels of bipartisanship in the data set are associated with the presidency of George H. W. Bush (Bush Sr.), who is the first president represented in the data set, and the first term of George W. Bush (Bush Jr.), whose first term coincided with the initial US response to the 9/11 terrorist attacks. Those attacks led many Democrats and Republicans to join in rallying around the flag, which likely drove the high rate of bipartisanship during Bush Jr.'s first term. But the frequency and strength of bipartisan voting plummeted in Bush Jr.'s second term, as the fight against Al Qaeda moved off the front burner of American politics and Democrats increasingly clashed with Republicans over the Iraq war. After that, through the presidencies of Barack Obama and Donald Trump, levels of foreign policy bipartisanship remained well below the high watermarks of Bush Sr.'s presidency and the immediate aftermath of the 9/11 attacks.

But the frequency and strength of bipartisanship plunged still further on domestic issues under Obama and Trump, widening the bipartisanship gap between foreign and domestic policy. Remarkably, under Trump, a majority of Democratic and Republican members of Congress voted together on important international issues nearly twice as often as they did on domestic matters. In the House, this degree of bipartisanship marked 52% of foreign policy votes and 29% of domestic policy votes, while in the Senate, these rates were 58% and 29%, respectively. (See Figures 2.10 and 2.11.) The upshot is

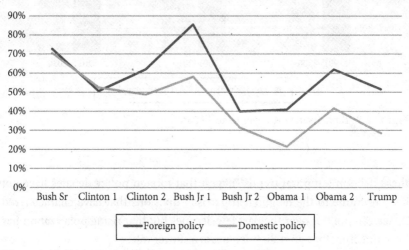

Figure 2.10 Bipartisan votes by presidential term, House

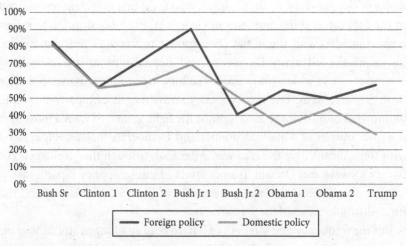

Figure 2.11 Bipartisan votes by presidential term, Senate

that polarization soared to new heights under recent presidents, but it did not rise as dramatically in foreign affairs.

Bipartisanship across areas of foreign policy

The data further reveal similarities and differences in patterns of bipartisan-. ship across different areas of foreign policy. Of the 594 foreign policy votes in the data set, 52% concerned legislation identified by the Congressional Research Service as involving armed forces and national security, 28% concerned legislation identified by CRS as involving international affairs, 12% concerned legislation identified by CRS as involving foreign trade and international finance, and 7% concerned legislation identified by CRS as involving immigration.[18]

The armed forces and national security votes concern annual legislation authorizing and funding defense and intelligence programs; legislation making organizational changes to government agencies involved in national security policy; and legislation on a variety of specific national security issues, such as overseas troop deployments, weapons programs, electronic surveillance, and counterterrorism policy. Examples of important votes in this area include a 1993 Senate vote on legislation prohibiting funding for US military operations in Somalia after a period of six months, a 2004 House vote on legislation establishing a new director of national intelligence to coordinate US intelligence activities, a 2006 Senate vote on legislation authorizing military tribunals to try detainees as part of the war on terrorism while denying these detainees the right of habeas corpus, and a 2014 House vote on legislation barring the deployment of US troops in a sustained combat role in Iraq unless Congress specifically authorized such a deployment.[19] To simplify language, I label the armed forces and national security votes simply as "national security" votes for the remainder of this chapter.

The international affairs votes are more of a hodgepodge, covering annual bills authorizing State Department programs, annual foreign aid appropriations bills, and legislation in areas such as economic sanctions, export financing, arms control, democracy promotion, human rights, policy toward multilateral institutions, and policy toward individual countries. They include a 1992 Senate vote on legislation linking aid to Russia to the withdrawal of Russian forces from Baltic countries, a 1997 House vote on legislation allowing aid to nongovernmental organizations that use their own

funds to perform abortions in other countries, a 2006 House vote on legislation allowing the United States to conduct civilian nuclear cooperation
with India if that country provides the United States with a plan to separate
civilian and military nuclear programs, and a 2013 House vote on legislation
imposing a variety of sanctions on Iran.[20]

The foreign trade and international finance votes involve international
trade agreements, the Export-Import Bank, economic sanctions, and foreign
investment.[21] Examples include a 1991 Senate vote on legislation prohibiting
the granting of most favored nation trading status to China until the president certifies that China has made progress on human rights, a 1993 House
vote on legislation approving the North American Free Trade Agreement, a
1997 Senate vote on legislation creating an expedited process for the approval
of trade agreements negotiated by the president, and a 2012 House vote
establishing permanent normal trade relations with Russia while mandating
sanctions on Russian officials who had committed human rights violations.[22]
To simplify language, I call these "international economics" votes hereafter.

The immigration votes span legislation involving the entry of non-citizens
into the United States, the status and treatment of undocumented immigrants
residing in the country, the granting of citizenship to immigrants, the admission of refugees, border security, and decisions by some US cities to stop
enforcing federal immigration laws. They include a 2007 Senate vote on legislation granting permanent resident status to immigrants who entered the
United States before turning 16 years old, a 2013 Senate vote on legislation
providing all undocumented immigrants with a pathway to citizenship and
strengthening border security, and a 2019 House vote on a national emergency declared by Trump to build a wall on the border with Mexico.[23]

When comparing levels of bipartisanship across these areas of foreign
policy, I combine House and Senate votes because the number of important votes in a particular policy area in one chamber is relatively low. I find
that levels of bipartisanship were high across the national security, international affairs, and international economics categories but lower in immigration debates. A majority of Democrats and Republicans in Congress
voted on the same side in 66% of national security votes, 67% of international affairs votes, and 65% of international economics votes. (See Figure
2.12.) Each of these rates exceeds the 54% rate of bipartisanship on domestic policy issues. These data show that high levels of bipartisanship are
not limited to just one area of foreign policy but rather span a wide range of
foreign policy debates.

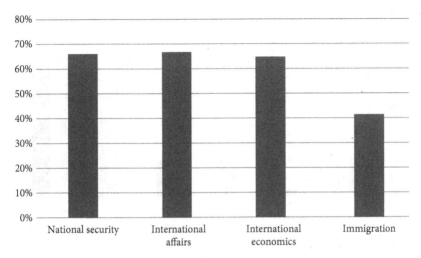

Figure 2.12 Bipartisan votes across foreign policy areas, House and Senate

The immigration votes are a clear exception to this pattern. They featured a 41% rate of bipartisan voting. This figure is not only much lower than the rate of bipartisanship in the other foreign policy areas but it is also lower than the rate of bipartisanship on the domestic policy votes. A closer look at the immigration votes suggests that the lower level of polarization on these votes than on the domestic policy votes is a function of a much higher share of the immigration votes occurring during the later years in the data set when congressional polarization was higher overall.[24] When controlling for the year when a vote occurred, there does not exist a statistically significant difference between the rate or strength of polarization on the immigration votes and the rate or strength of polarization on domestic policy votes. The upshot is that congressional voting on immigration matters resembles congressional voting on domestic issues more than it resembles congressional voting on other foreign policy issues. This probably reflects in part the fact that most immigration debates include domestic as well as international dimensions. It also likely reflects the ideological and advocacy landscape, as liberals are generally much more supportive than conservatives of open immigration policies and immigration debates typically feature intensive lobbying on opposite sides of the issue by Democratic-affiliated and Republican-affiliated groups.[25]

Focusing on different types of bipartisanship reveals some additional patterns across areas of foreign policy. Although levels of bipartisan voting

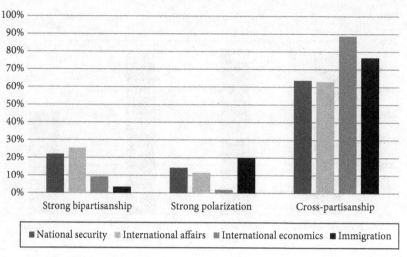

Figure 2.13 Variations of bipartisanship and polarization across foreign policy areas, House and Senate

were generally similar across national security, international affairs, and international economics issues, intra-party division was much more common on international economic matters than in the other two areas. Whereas at least 10% of the members of a party voted against their party's dominant position in a little over 60% of the national security and international affairs roll call votes, this level of cross-partisanship characterized nearly 90% of international economics roll call votes. (See Figure 2.13.) This pattern most likely reflects the cross-cutting nature of many trade debates. As I discuss in Chapter 3, attitudes regarding trade do not break down along left-right ideological lines, and lawmakers often face strong pressures in trade debates from economic constituencies that imperfectly align with their party affiliations.[26]

By contrast, strong bipartisanship, in which at least 90% of the members of each party vote in support of legislation, is more common on national security and international affairs issues than on international economic ones. (See Figure 2.13.) This difference reinforces previous research finding stronger bipartisan agreement during earlier periods of US history on international security than on international economic issues.[27]

Limiting the analysis to presidential position votes further reveals that pro-presidential bipartisanship is particularly common on international economic issues, with majorities of Democratic and Republican lawmakers voting in support of the president 37% of the time. Conversely, majorities of

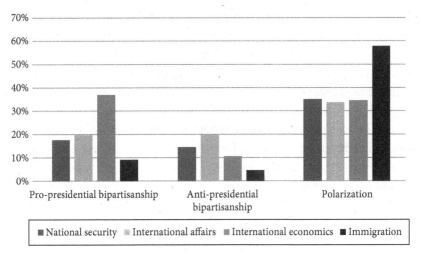

Figure 2.14 Alignments on presidential position votes across foreign policy areas, House and Senate

lawmakers in both parties voted in opposition to the president in 14% of national security votes, 20% of international affairs votes, 11% of international economics votes, and 5% of immigration votes. (See Figure 2.14.) With the exception of the immigration votes, each of these rates of anti-presidential bipartisanship exceeds the 6% rate of anti-presidential bipartisan voting on domestic issues.

The data also reveal that bipartisan voting has occurred more often on foreign policy spending legislation than on other foreign policy legislation.[28] Whereas majorities of Democrats and Republicans voted together in 74% of congressional votes on foreign policy spending measures, they did so only on 63% of votes on non-spending foreign policy legislation. Since interest groups tend to be particularly active on spending bills, which can influence their bottom lines or funnel resources to valued priorities, the high levels of bipartisanship on spending votes suggest that groups engaging in intensive advocacy on defense and foreign aid have built and maintained strong bipartisan ties.

Overall, these data indicate that bipartisanship occurs regularly across most areas of foreign policy and that the bipartisanship gap between domestic and foreign affairs spans national security, international economic, and other foreign policy issues. The big exception to this pattern is immigration policy, which features levels of polarization that are closer to polarization levels on domestic issues than to those associated with other foreign policy areas. At the same time, international economic debates tend to involve particularly high levels of cross-partisanship, underscoring the importance of taking into account intra-party divisions when analyzing the politics of foreign policy.

In the next chapter, I move from identifying overall patterns of polarization and multiple forms of bipartisanship to explaining why elected officials align in varying ways on different issues. The subsequent chapters then draw on a wide array of sources to illustrate the importance of these drivers of polarization and bipartisanship in several major foreign policy debates of the Obama and Trump eras.

3

Enablers of bipartisanship

In this chapter, I move from describing patterns of political alignments to explaining why bipartisan behavior continues to characterize many areas of foreign policy and why foreign policy bipartisanship takes multiple forms. In a nutshell, I argue that it remains common for elected officials to act in a bipartisan manner on foreign policy because the ideological and advocacy landscapes are not consistently polarized across international issues. Whereas some foreign policy debates break down on left-right ideological lines or feature advocacy by interest groups with strong partisan affiliations, other debates feature little disagreement between liberals and conservatives, ideological cross-pressures, advocacy by groups with strong ties to both parties, or minimal interest group activity. These circumstances facilitate bipartisan agreement or intra-party splits rather than polarization.

At the same time, the differing electoral incentives and institutional prerogatives of lawmakers and the president sometimes fuel inter-branch clashes. Lawmakers have less electoral accountability than presidents for the overall effectiveness of foreign policy, making it easier for them to support policies that reflect deeply held values or the views of domestic constituencies, even if those policies might make it more difficult to advance other US interests or priorities. Lawmakers and the president also often see the value of checks and balances differently, with members of Congress sometimes seeking to limit presidential unilateralism and presidents usually seeking to maintain policymaking flexibility and control.

Admittedly, these are not the only factors that influence political alignments. Democratic and Republican elected officials regularly distance themselves from one another not only because they have different policy views or are pressured by activists to take extreme positions but also because of incentives to engage in partisan teamsmanship or partisan warfare, in which they approach politics primarily as a partisan struggle for power.[1] This competition between the parties has been intensified by the small size of congressional majorities in recent decades, which have placed party control of the House and Senate up for grabs in nearly every election.[2] Issues also tend

Bipartisanship and US Foreign Policy. Jordan Tama, Oxford University Press. © Oxford University Press 2024.
DOI: 10.1093/oso/9780197745663.003.0003

to become more polarized when they are highly salient.[3] On such matters, legislators have a stronger incentive to engage in partisan combat because the debates may influence the national standing of the parties and thereby shape the future electoral prospects of lawmakers.

Conversely, legislators have greater political freedom to cooperate across party lines on issues that lack intense public scrutiny or large political stakes.[4] Members of Congress also retain pragmatic and electoral incentives for pursuing bipartisanship in that some support from both parties is almost always needed to enact legislation and legislative accomplishments can boost the reelection prospects of lawmakers.[5] The existence of an international threat and a strong economy tend to foster bipartisanship too.[6]

In this book, though, I focus on the roles of ideology, advocacy groups, and the differing incentives of lawmakers and the president because these factors have received relatively little attention in prior studies of polarization and bipartisanship, as well as because they go a long way toward understanding not only why some issues are more or less polarized but also why bipartisanship regularly takes several forms.

More generally, I aim in what follows to illustrate the variety of pressures that shape the behavior of elected officials and how different incentives sometimes come into conflict with each other. While achieving reelection is often the principal goal of members of Congress,[7] lawmakers are frequently also motivated by the goals of advancing their vision of good public policy or boosting their stature.[8] On issues that involve strong ideological orthodoxies or feature intensive advocacy by party-affiliated groups, electoral pressures will tend to be very pronounced, and lawmakers will have powerful incentives to toe the party line. But on other issues, elected officials often have more political leeway, making it possible for them to prioritize the advancement of their own policy preferences or institutional prerogatives rather than party loyalty—opening the door to cross-partisanship, pro-presidential bipartisanship, or anti-presidential bipartisanship.

The argument I develop in this chapter departs from perspectives that emphasize a single overriding motivation for congressional behavior, such as partisan goals or ideological commitments. Yes, partisan goals are often very important, but they do not always drive the behavior of lawmakers. At the same time, many foreign policy debates do not revolve around liberal or conservative orthodoxies. And while elite or public views heavily constrain elected officials on some issues, advocacy groups or institutional considerations are more consequential on others. In short, a full understanding of the behavior of elected officials requires consideration of a variety of forces that sometimes come into conflict with each other and that remain important even as American politics becomes increasingly polarized overall.

Ideology and policy preferences

Political scientist Hans Noel defines ideology as "a nearly complete set of political issue preferences that is shared by others," or a system that "ties together political ideas, especially someone's positions on political issues, such as abortion, taxes, or gun control."[9] Other scholars offer similar definitions. International relations scholars Patrick Cronin and Benjamin Fordham note: "Virtually all accounts of ideology treat it as a set of shared ideas with implications across a wide range of political issues."[10]

While an ideology is broad and somewhat abstract, it becomes more concrete in the form of public or elite opinion on specific policy issues. Put another way, ideology represents the fundamental ideas that underlie policy preferences.[11] In the following discussion, I use the term "ideology" to refer to an overarching framework of ideas, such as liberalism or conservativism, and use the terms "public opinion" and "elite opinion" to refer to the attitudes of the mass public or public policy elites about particular issues, such as military intervention or trade.[12] As I will show, public and elite opinion are heavily shaped by ideology on many, but not all, issues.

There exist two main mechanisms through which ideology can generate polarization or some form of bipartisanship in the behavior of elected officials. The first involves ideological agreement or division among policy elites themselves. Democratic and Republican elected officials will be more likely to adopt the same position on an international issue if they share common ideas about it and will be more likely to take opposing positions if they do not.[13] Importantly, though, even elected officials who are ideologically out of step with their party on an issue may face pressure to conform to the party's prevailing position on it if the party's elites possess a strong orthodoxy about it. For instance, if a Republican politician backs gun control measures or a Democratic politician calls for reducing government spending on healthcare programs, they will be likely to receive sharp criticism and potentially a primary challenge from elites within their own party. In this way, left-right ideological divisions tend to entrench partisan discord.

By contrast, cross-partisanship is facilitated when there do not exist clear liberal or conservative positions on an issue, either because a policy debate lacks much ideological content or because liberal and conservative values can each point toward opposing positions on an issue. For example, in many debates over military intervention to prevent mass atrocities overseas, liberalism's commitment to the promotion of social welfare points toward intervention while its skepticism of military power suggests refraining from the use of force, and conservativism's high regard for military power points toward intervention while its wariness of government activism suggests a more hands-off approach. On issues featuring such ideological cross-currents, elected officials in the same party will tend to have more discretion to adopt a variety of stances without running afoul of party gatekeepers.

The second mechanism through which policy preferences can influence political alignments runs through voters. Given the overriding desire of almost all lawmakers to get reelected,[14] lawmakers in the two parties will have greater incentive to adopt the same position on issues on which Democratic and Republican voters see eye to eye than on issues that separate the two electorates. But on issues where voters in each party are internally split or on which most voters lack a strong view, lawmakers will have greater freedom to act based on their own principled views, which can enable the formation of cross-partisan coalitions. In an interview, former Senate Foreign Relations Committee Chairman Bob Corker noted: "Generally members of Congress have more leeway on foreign policy because the American people pay less attention to it."[15]

Domestic and foreign policy attitudes

The relationship between ideology and political parties has evolved over time. During the 19th century, the political views of American elites could not be mapped meaningfully on a one-dimensional ideological spectrum— in other words, elites did not espouse sets of views that could be labeled as left wing or right wing—and a person's party identity was often driven by regional and other considerations more than by ideology. By 1950, however, pundits and opinion writers had clearly defined competing liberal and conservative worldviews, and most political commentators could be easily identified with one of these two schools of thought.[16] Since then, liberalism and conservativism have retained certain core beliefs about the economy and society. Scholars Christopher Ellis and James Stimson write: "Liberals, by and large, support the expansion of government power where necessary to provide equal opportunity and remediate social injustice. Conservatives, by and large, support economic freedom and traditional patterns of social order."[17]

The ideological polarization that took root among elites later contributed to the rise of partisan polarization in Congress, as party coalitions increasingly conformed, starting in the 1970s, to the liberal-conservative divide in elite opinion. Ideological polarization among elites was also followed by the sorting of the American public into more ideologically distinct partisan camps, with liberals becoming the base of the Democratic Party and conservatives becoming the base of the Republican Party.[18] This polarization is particularly evident today on major domestic policy issues. In 2019, the Pew Research Center asked Americans a series of questions about their political values in different issue areas. By margins ranging from 35% to 55%, far more Democrats than Republicans indicated that they favored stricter gun control laws, stricter environmental regulations, greater assistance for needy Americans, the provision of healthcare coverage to all Americans, and greater government regulation of business.[19]

By contrast, the ideological landscape on major foreign policy issues has remained less polarized on the whole. Noel finds that, in 1990, the most recent year covered by his analysis of the history of ideology in the United States, the fit, on a scale of zero to one, between a one-dimensional model of ideology and the actual positions of pundits and opinion writers was .92 on economic issues, .87 on social issues, and .87 on racial issues, but just .53 on foreign policy issues.[20] A separate study, based on American National Election Studies (ANES) surveys, finds that the correlation between the political ideology of respondents and their positions on specific issues was lower from 1972 to 2004 on a set of six foreign policy issues than on any other set of issues, including economic issues, civil rights issues, and moral issues.[21] Moreover, ideological polarization increased over the course of this 32-year period at a slower rate in foreign policy than it did in other areas, making the gap in ideological polarization between foreign policy and other issue areas greater in 2004 than it was in 1972.[22]

Other data reveal that ideological polarization has remained weaker on foreign than on domestic policy in recent years. ANES publishes trend data for questions that it has regularly asked in its quadrennial surveys. Among questions on public policy issue positions asked by ANES in 2008, 2012,

2016, and 2020, an average gap of 19% separated liberals and conservatives on military and foreign policy issues, whereas an average gap of 44% separated liberals and conservatives on domestic policy issues.[23] This pattern reflects the relatively weaker link on foreign than on domestic policy between issue positions and core elements of liberal or conservative ideology.[24]

The smaller degree of ideological polarization on international than on domestic issues is even evident in stereotypes that citizens hold about the policy positions of the two parties. Surveys conducted in 2014 and 2018 revealed that members of the public associated competing policy positions with one of the two parties much more consistently on major domestic issues than on major foreign policy issues.[25]

This is not to say that liberals and conservatives see all international issues in the same way. In fact, there exist key differences between liberal and conservative approaches to foreign policy, which stem from broader differences in the moral values and psychological dispositions of liberals and conservatives. For instance, liberals tend to be concerned altruistically with the well-being of strangers and to value reciprocity, whereas conservatives tend to value respect for authority and the maintenance of order.[26] These different values and dispositions shape attitudes about foreign policy, just as they shape attitudes about domestic affairs.[27]

Most importantly, liberals generally favor a more cooperative and less militarized approach to international affairs than conservatives. This tends to lead liberals to be less supportive than conservatives of high levels of defense spending and military action against perceived adversaries and more supportive than conservatives of multilateral institutions, such as the United Nations.[28] Indeed, in 2018 surveys, the Chicago Council on Global Affairs (Chicago Council) found that 75% of Republican foreign policy experts and decision-makers, along with 70% of the Republican public, considered maintaining superior military power worldwide to be a very important goal for the United States, but only 39% of Democratic foreign policy elites and 41% of the Democratic public shared this view.[29] A 2016 Chicago Council survey also found that support among Republican foreign policy elites and the Republican public for the use of military force to stop Iran from obtaining a nuclear weapon was more than 30% greater than the corresponding rates of support among Democratic foreign policy elites and the Democratic public.[30]

Conversely, among both elites and the public, more Democrats than Republicans favor participating in international treaties on issues ranging from the arms trade, to human rights, to climate change.[31] The stronger backing of liberals than conservatives for social welfare programs also leads Democrats at both the elite and public levels to favor higher levels of economic aid to other countries than Republicans.[32] On an issue that involves both international cooperation and economic aid, liberal lawmakers were 31% more likely than conservative lawmakers from 1944 to 2009 to support the appropriation of funding for the International Monetary Fund.[33]

Ideological polarization is quite limited on many other foreign policy issues, though. In the big picture, roughly equivalent shares of liberal and conservative voters favor international engagement by the United States. In the 2020 ANES survey, 81% of liberals and 73% of conservatives said they disagreed with the notion that the United States should not concern itself with world problems.[34] Along similar lines, Chicago Council surveys in 2018 found that 75% of the Democratic public, 70% of the Republican public, 97% of Democratic foreign policy elites, and 97% of Republican foreign policy elites thought the United States should play an active role in the world.[35]

Some more specific foreign policy debates feature broad consensus too. For instance, there exists strong support across the political spectrum for the use of security alliances. The 2018 Chicago Council surveys found that 98% of Democratic foreign policy elites, 94% of Republican foreign policy elites, 87% of the Democratic public, and 66% of the Republican public favored increasing the US commitment to NATO or keeping it the same, whereas much smaller percentages of each of these populations favored decreasing the commitment or withdrawing from NATO entirely.[36] In the same surveys, about five-sixths of elites in both parties and two-thirds of the publics of both parties said that they thought the United States should have long-term military bases in South Korea and Japan.[37] There also exists broad consensus that international terrorism and cyberattacks on US computer networks represent critical threats to the United States, with at least two-thirds of the publics of each party endorsing these points of view.[38]

Still other foreign policy debates lack broad consensus but involve divisions within one or both parties as much as or more than polarization. For instance, there have existed high levels of intra-party division on trade policy in both parties in recent years, as documented in Chapter 8 of this book.[39] To take another issue, 50% of the Republican public and 48% of the Democratic public said in 2022 that they favored the United States committing to defend Taiwan if China invaded it.[40] More generally, intra-party debates over foreign policy have been especially pronounced in the Republican Party in recent years—in particular, between Trump's brand of populist nationalism and the more internationalist orientation of many establishment Republicans.[41] In this context, some liberal and conservative thought leaders who favor a robust US role in the world have joined together in calling for the United States to take assertive steps to counter authoritarian governments and exercise international leadership on an array of global challenges.[42]

When foreign policy debates do not break down on a simple left-right spectrum, they can generate strange ideological bedfellows. In these cases, liberals and conservatives might agree about what to do on an issue even if they do not share the same perspective about why to do it.[43] For instance, some liberals and conservatives support strong US action to promote human rights or protect besieged populations overseas—though conservatives are more likely to be motivated by a desire to challenge US adversaries or aid threatened religious minorities, while liberals are more likely to be motivated by a desire to help any victims of human rights abuses or disasters.[44] Former Democratic Senator Russell Feingold, a liberal who served as chair of the Africa subcommittee of the Senate Foreign Relations Committee, noted in an interview: "Sometimes the most conservative senators would work with me on Africa issues because they saw religious persecution issues that concerned them."[45] But human rights hawks and supporters of humanitarian intervention are sometimes countered by a strange bedfellows coalition of progressives and libertarians who recoil from government efforts to get deeply involved in the affairs of other countries.[46]

To take a couple of other examples, moderate Republicans and Democrats are more supportive of intrusive intelligence surveillance programs designed to prevent acts of terrorism than conservative Republicans or liberal Democrats,[47] and social and economic libertarians are more supportive of free trade than other Democrats and Republicans.[48] These kinds of opinion constellations are particularly conducive to cross-partisanship among elected officials.[49]

The relationship between public and elite opinion

While the preceding discussion treats elite and public attitudes in much the same way, it is also important to recognize how elite and public opinion interact with each other. In particular, public opinion on foreign policy issues is itself often influenced by cues from elected officials and other national elites in the form of statements communicated through the media.[50] These cues can heavily shape public polarization, as the public tends to develop greater consensus on an issue when elites are united on an issue and to divide more along partisan lines when elites in the two parties express different views on it.[51] Yet there are important limits to the extent of elite influence on public foreign policy attitudes. As a result, public opinion sometimes shapes the foreign policy decisions of elected officials.

The influence of elite rhetoric on public attitudes was evident during the Trump presidency with respect to views of Russia. The share of the Republican public viewing Russia favorably increased from 19% to 30% between February 2015, when Republican leaders almost uniformly espoused negative views of Vladimir Putin and the Russian government, and February 2019, when Trump's more positive rhetoric about Putin had become familiar to the Republican electorate. By contrast, the Democratic public moved in the opposite direction during this period—probably influenced by intelligence assessments that the Russian government had interfered in the 2016 election on behalf of Trump—with the percentage of Democrats viewing Russia favorably dropping from 26% to 17%.[52]

Nevertheless, the attitudes of voters are not entirely malleable, as the views of individuals on international issues are also shaped by their core values, principles, or predispositions.[53] The limits of elite influence on public opinion are underscored by the large gaps that separate elite and public attitudes on some foreign policy issues. For instance, in 2018, the Republican and Democratic publics were 55% and 40% more likely, respectively, than Republican and Democratic foreign policy elites to consider large numbers of immigrants and refugees entering the United States to be a critical threat, and 41% and 34% more likely, respectively, to think the protection of American jobs should be a very important foreign policy goal of the United States.[54] On other issues, a 2012 survey found that Republican and Democratic voters were much more likely than experts to favor retaliation against currency manipulation by China and much less likely than experts to support military intervention in Syria.[55] The public has also long been much less supportive than elites of liberalized trade and the provision of economic aid to other countries.[56] More generally, a review of contemporaneous surveys of public and elite opinion on foreign policy issues over a 30-year period found that public and elite views differed by at least 10 percentage points on 73% of survey questions.[57]

All of this raises the question of whether elected officials take public opinion into account when adopting foreign policy positions. While some studies have found little evidence that public opinion shapes foreign policy,[58] other research has found that public attitudes have influenced congressional and executive actions on issues including the defense budget,[59] arms control,[60] the use of military force,[61] trade,[62] and presidential unilateralism.[63] On the whole, several scholars observe that "the literature on American foreign policy substantiates the influence of public opinion on foreign policy, albeit an inconsistent influence."[64] Importantly, public opinion has greater impact on policymaking on highly salient issues than on issues that receive little public attention—since only the former set of issues is likely to shape how people vote.[65]

When it comes to Congress, it is also important to distinguish between overall public opinion and the attitudes of vocal or politically active constituents, as lawmakers are often influenced less by general public opinion than by constituents who contact their office, attend political events in their state or district, or support their political campaigns.[66] This tendency reflects in part the fact that on most issues opinion polls are never conducted in individual states or districts—meaning that legislators do not have concrete information about the attitudes of their constituents aside from their direct contact with them.[67] In the absence of such information, the perceptions of elected officials about the views of their constituents can be skewed by the relatively small number of constituents with whom they interact directly.[68] This effect can be compounded by the fact that legislators have a strong incentive to be responsive to politically active constituents on particular issues because such constituents may vote based on the positions of legislators on the issues in question. An anecdote told by former House Foreign Affairs Committee Chairman Lee Hamilton in an interview illustrates this tendency: "One time I was discussing US policy toward Greece and Turkey with [then-Representative] Ray Madden on the floor of the House. Ray said to me, 'Everyone in my district is on the side of the Greeks.' I said to him, 'Well, how do you know that?' He said, 'I went to four Greek Orthodox picnics and everyone there was on the Greek side.'"[69]

Nevertheless, on issues where national public opinion surveys can enable legislators to infer that a position in a policy debate has strong or weak support in their state or district, legislators will typically take that survey data into account when formulating their positions. Both general public opinion and particularly vocal or active constituents can therefore influence congressional positions on foreign policy.

Returning to the theme of bipartisanship, the limited degree of ideological polarization on many foreign policy issues facilitates the formation of bipartisan coalitions regardless of whether the positions of elites are influencing public attitudes or influence is being exercised in the opposite direction. On the one hand, elected officials will have more political leeway to engage in bipartisanship if liberal and conservative elites are not polarizing public attitudes by expressing diametrically opposed positions. On the other hand, bipartisanship will be more feasible if liberal and conservative members of the public are not pushing Democratic and Republican lawmakers in opposing directions. Since elites and the public both tend to be less divided along left-right lines on international than on domestic policy issues, lawmakers usually have more capacity to cooperate on foreign policy matters.

Advocacy groups

The advocacy group landscape can also facilitate polarization or one of several types of bipartisanship. When Democratic-affiliated groups and Republican-affiliated groups stake out opposing positions on an issue, they drive elected officials in the two parties apart. But when advocacy on an issue is dominated by groups that have close ties to both parties or when influential groups are inactive on an issue, broad bipartisan agreement or cross-partisanship becomes more likely in Congress.

Advocacy groups include groups representing private sector firms as well as nonprofit organizations committed to certain principled values or goals.[70] In general, advocacy groups are important actors in American politics that exercise influence in a variety of ways, including through campaign contributions to politicians, the provision of information and ideas to policymakers, media advertising, and the rallying of public support or opposition to policy proposals.[71] Although the difficulty of changing the status quo in Washington typically limits the ability of interest groups to instigate major policy changes,[72] business groups generally have substantial influence on federal government activity,[73] and a variety of groups have shaped many landmark US laws.[74] In foreign policy, economic, ethnic, religious, and values-based groups have influenced US policies on an array of issues, including defense spending,[75] arms sales,[76] international trade,[77] international finance,[78] human rights,[79] debt relief for poor nations,[80] policies toward countries with diaspora populations in the United States,[81] and grand strategy.[82]

Links between advocacy groups and policymakers in both parties are particularly important as a contributor to political alignments on Capitol Hill because advocacy groups generally have greater access to Congress than to the executive branch.[83] Legislators are particularly responsive to groups that are rooted strongly in the states or districts that they represent.[84] Advocacy groups tend to have the most influence on issues with relatively low public salience, since elected officials will be more likely to follow the lead of such groups, rather than voters, on issues about which voters lack strong views.[85]

On many issues, advocacy groups contribute to polarization among elected officials. Campaign contribution patterns have grown steadily more polarized since 1980 with campaign donors becoming more likely over time to give money to staunch liberals or conservatives.[86] Today, most highly influential groups have close ties to one of the parties and weaker ties to the other party. For instance, many labor unions, environmental groups, civil rights organizations, pro-choice groups, consumer protection organizations, and groups based on broad progressive values are strongly linked to the Democratic Party, whereas many business associations, pro-life organizations, evangelical Christian groups, anti-tax organizations, pro-gun groups, and groups grounded in broad conservative values are strongly linked to the Republican Party.[87]

In fact, some research suggests that the two parties are best understood as coalitions of interest groups and policy activists.[88] These groups and activists tend to foster polarization among candidates and elected officials by using their campaign contributions, political endorsements, and other sources of influence to apply pressure on politicians in the party with which they are linked to adopt and remain faithful to their preferred policy positions.[89] This pressure makes it more difficult for candidates and elected officials to deviate from party orthodoxies.[90] Foreign policy scholars have also shown that the core constituencies of the parties can influence major policy choices of those parties, on issues ranging from grand strategy to the financing of wars.[91]

In foreign policy, however, a smaller proportion of important advocacy groups has strong partisan associations. Groups that engage in advocacy on international issues include organizations representing ethnic constituencies or diaspora communities, such as Armenian Americans, Cuban Americans,

Jewish Americans, and Vietnamese Americans; defense contractors, such as Lockheed Martin; business associations, such as the US Chamber of Commerce; labor unions, such as the AFL-CIO; human rights groups, such as Amnesty International; and foreign governments, from the United Arab Emirates to Japan. While many business associations are closely linked to the Republican Party and most labor unions are closely tied to the Democratic Party, many of the other major foreign policy advocacy groups have close ties with members of both parties. For instance, many ethnic constituencies and defense contractors have strong allies among Democratic and Republican legislators.[92]

These patterns are illustrated by data on campaign contributions by interest groups. A study of all federal campaign donations by groups from 2007 to 2011 found that organizations lobbying the government on international issues clustered near the middle when placed on a left-right ideological spectrum based on their campaign contribution patterns, whereas organizations lobbying on domestic issues included greater shares of groups near the liberal and conservative ends of the ideological spectrum.[93] In a similar vein, a study based on contributions to congressional candidates by political action committees (PACs) from 1980 to 2010 found that PACs concerned with foreign policy or defense issues were more likely to donate to a candidate at the center of the ideological spectrum than to a liberal or conservative candidate.[94]

More recent campaign contribution data further highlight the variation in patterns of partisanship across different types of advocacy groups. In the 2016 election cycle, 92% of the campaign contributions of business associations to political candidates and party committees went to Republicans, whereas 88% of the contributions of labor unions went to Democrats. In 2020, the share of business association contributions going to Republicans dropped considerably, but remained rather high at 69%, while the share of labor contributions going to Democrats stayed at 88%.[95] The large difference in the political orientation of business and labor largely explains why trade agreements typically receive more support from Republican legislators than from Democratic legislators.[96]

Some other sectors involved in foreign policy tend to split their donations between Democrats and Republicans more evenly. For instance, during the 2016 and 2020 electoral cycles, defense contractors gave 61% and 52% of their campaign contributions, respectively, to Republicans, while pro-Israel groups gave 53% and 63% of their donations, respectively, to Democrats.[97]

Such contribution patterns are more conducive to fostering bipartisanship in Congress.

At the same time, even groups that are closely tied to one of the parties sometimes foster bipartisanship by forming alliances with groups that are closely tied to the other party. For instance, influential evangelical leaders have aligned with left-leaning international development, humanitarian, and feminist NGOs to press lawmakers to support debt relief to poor countries, aid to address the HIV/AIDS pandemic in Africa, and measures to combat global sex trafficking.[98] As detailed in Chapter 9, humanitarian and development NGOs have also forged alliances with the business, military, and religious communities on behalf of foreign assistance spending.

Similarly, progressive and libertarian activists have teamed up in recent years in an effort to scale back US military activity overseas. In one manifestation of this effort, George Soros and Charles Koch joined forces in 2019 to launch a think tank, the Quincy Institute for Responsible Statecraft, that is committed to anti-militarism.[99] They have also been among the leaders of an effort spanning a variety of liberal and conservative advocacy groups that seeks to reassert congressional control over decisions to use military force, which I discuss in Chapter 5.[100]

An additional attribute of the advocacy landscape further facilitates bipartisanship on some foreign policy issues. While few important domestic debates lack advocacy by powerful interest groups, some important foreign policy debates feature relatively little such advocacy, as political scientist Aaron Wildavsky first noted more than five decades ago.[101] In general, interest groups tend to play a more important role on issues that can create large and concentrated gains or losses for particular segments of the US population than on issues that have more diffuse effects on the American people.[102] This pattern tends to result in greater advocacy activity about issues of "low politics," such as international trade and domestic economic and social programs, than on issues of "high politics," such as military deployments and other security policies.[103] As one indication of the more limited role of interest groups on some national security issues, the members of the congressional armed services committees receive a much smaller proportion of their campaign contributions from groups concerned with committee issues than do the members of committees that address domestic matters.[104] More generally, a major study of interest groups found that only three of the 30 public policy issues marked by the most advocacy activity concerned foreign policy to a substantial degree.[105]

These characteristics of the advocacy landscape on foreign policy can foster polarization or different forms of bipartisanship in several ways. First, strong polarization is likely if powerful Democratic-affiliated and Republican-affiliated advocacy groups pressure politicians in the two parties to support opposing positions. Second, if groups with close ties to both parties engage in intensive advocacy on the same side of an issue, Republican and Democratic politicians will tend to experience similar pressure to support the positions of those groups, facilitating strong bipartisanship in Congress. Third, if a debate does not feature advocacy by powerful interest groups, politicians in both parties will typically have more discretion with respect to their policy positions.[106] This context can enable strong bipartisanship, if the policy preferences of Democrats and Republicans largely coincide, or cross-partisanship, if the issue splits Democrats or Republicans in terms of their policy views.

Inter-branch differences

Ideology and advocacy groups also provide a partial explanation of anti-presidential bipartisanship. This alignment tends to result when presidential policies conflict with prevalent attitudes in both parties or with the preferences of groups that possess close ties to both parties. However, the differing electoral incentives and institutional prerogatives of lawmakers and the president further help explain why foreign policy bipartisanship sometimes takes an anti-presidential form.

Since presidents are generally considered by the American people to be responsible for the overall well-being of the United States, they have an electoral incentive to pursue foreign policies that they believe are likely to advance overall national welfare and interests.[107] American politics scholars William Howell and Terry Moe note: "Quite unlike most legislators, presidents are institutionally predisposed to think in national terms about national problems, and their overriding concern for their historical legacies drives them to seek durable policy solutions to pressing national problems."[108] The institutional responsibility of presidents for international diplomacy and the execution of other dimensions of foreign policy also gives them reason to take into account how actions on one foreign policy issue may have repercussions for other US priorities—for instance, influencing the willingness of other countries to cooperate with the United States—and to resist legislative initiatives that would limit their foreign policy flexibility.[109] As a result, presidents often have incentives to prioritize their foreign policy objectives over the views of domestic constituencies when determining their positions on international issues.

To be sure, presidents are not immune to parochialism. Political pressures regularly influence presidential policies on both domestic and international issues.[110] Nevertheless, presidents are frequently concerned with the promotion of economic growth and national interests when formulating their approach to world affairs. Since World War II, these incentives have typically led presidents to pursue internationalist policies.

Donald Trump certainly did not conform to the internationalist mold that shaped the foreign policies of his predecessors in both parties for 70 years.[111] But even he opposed congressional initiatives that might hamstring his ability to cooperate with other countries. For instance, as the coronavirus, which originated in China, threatened to become a pandemic in February 2020, Trump resisted calls from lawmakers and experts to place more pressure on the Chinese government to provide information and access about the disease. The *Washington Post* reported that Trump took this stance based on a concern that Chinese President Xi Jinping "will not work with the United States if it says anything negative about the country."[112] Similarly, Trump opposed congressional efforts to place pressure on the governments of Russia, Saudi Arabia, and Turkey, prioritizing instead the pursuit of cooperation with the leaders of those countries.[113]

Meanwhile, the weaker electoral accountability and fewer responsibilities of legislators in foreign policy give legislators an incentive to support foreign policies that are favored by advocacy groups or constituents, even if those policies might antagonize foreign governments or make it more difficult for the United States to achieve other goals. This tendency is bolstered by the fact that legislators are often held responsible by constituents and groups for the positions that they take but are rarely held responsible for the resulting policy outcomes.[114] Moreover, even though the public is usually prudent about the use of military force,[115] the public is often less supportive than elites of cooperation with governments engaged in behavior that appears to conflict with US values or interests.[116] This can give legislators a particular incentive to favor "tough" stances short of military action toward governments responsible for objectionable actions.

At the same time, many legislators regularly adopt foreign policy positions based on their own deeply seated convictions or prior personal experiences.[117] Indeed, a personal interest in the substance of foreign policy is a common motivation for legislators to join one of the foreign affairs committees.[118] Yet even among lawmakers with strongly held foreign policy views of their own, legislators' low level of electoral accountability for foreign policy outcomes gives them greater ability than presidents to promote their preferred policies without having to weigh carefully whether those policies will be effective or incur undesirable costs. In other words, legislators have more political leeway than presidents to place principle over pragmatism when making foreign policy decisions.

These dynamics are often evident in sanctions policymaking. Legislators in both parties frequently favor the imposition of punitive sanctions on governments responsible for human rights violations, armed conflict, weapons proliferation, drug trafficking, or economic policies that place the United States at a disadvantage.[119] This common congressional position is facilitated by the positions of advocacy groups, public opinion, and the personal views of lawmakers. Advocacy groups—ranging from ethnic diaspora communities and human rights organizations to industries vulnerable to import competition—often encourage Congress to impose sanctions on other countries, and many of these groups have ties to both parties.[120] At the same time, sanctions tend to be popular among voters.[121] A 2015 Chicago Council public opinion survey found that 68% of Democrats and 58% of Republicans considered the placement of sanctions on other countries to have been a very or somewhat effective means of achieving the foreign policy goals of the United States.[122] This outlook is consistent with the public's tendency to favor one-dimensional policies that attack problems directly.[123] Yet foreign policy elites in both parties also believe the United States should regularly employ sanctions. A 2018 Chicago Council survey of foreign policy decision-makers and experts found that 81% of Democrats and 73% of Republicans supported pressuring a non-democratic government with some economic sanctions, such as reduced trade with the United States.[124] Such data suggest that congressional support for sanctions is driven by the policy views of lawmakers as well as the attitudes of constituents and outside groups.

By contrast, presidents often resist congressional sanctions proposals because they worry that the sanctions will do more harm than good by generating substantial costs to the United States, either directly through restrictions on American business activity in the target country or as a result of the diplomatic and economic friction that they generate between the United States and governments upset by the sanctions.[125] David Kramer, who has been heavily involved in many sanctions debates as a senior State Department official and president of Freedom House, a major human rights organization, observed: "There's more freedom and liberty as a member of Congress to take on these causes because one member isn't likely to have to explain the security or economic consequences of their support for sanctions, whereas the executive has to worry about those kind of concerns."[126] At the same time, presidents often worry that sanctions legislation will constrain their flexibility—by taking away their ability to choose when to impose sanctions and when to lift them. Indeed, sanctions laws have made it harder for presidents to reach diplomatic agreements with countries, such as Iran and Cuba, because presidents could not make credible commitments to those countries that they could induce Congress to repeal the laws.[127]

In other cases, lawmakers in both parties band together in attempts to rein in presidential unilateralism and protect authority assigned to Congress under the Constitution.[128] In this way, the exercise of presidential power sometimes leads to anti-presidential bipartisanship. During Obama's presidency, this dynamic contributed to the enactment of a bipartisan law that gave Congress a say over whether to carry out the nuclear deal that Obama negotiated with Iran, which Obama planned to put into effect unilaterally.[129] During Trump's presidency, it contributed to bipartisan congressional initiatives to block the president from withdrawing from the NATO treaty, intervening militarily in the war in Yemen, or using force against Iran without explicit congressional authorization.[130] By contrast, since presidents cannot take as many consequential unilateral actions in domestic affairs, there is usually less reason on domestic matters for lawmakers to protect their institutional prerogatives. Challenging the president on a high-profile foreign policy issue can also be an effective means for members of Congress to gain notoriety and a respected place in history, providing an additional incentive for inter-branch conflict.[131] Remarkably, out of 27 major laws enacted by Congress that involved the reassertion of congressional authority vis-à-vis the executive from 1789 through 2012, 17 of them involved foreign policy.[132]

None of this is to suggest that members of Congress always, or even usually, stand up to presidential unilateralism. To the contrary, many lawmakers are content to leave the president in the driver's seat on foreign policy, particularly when challenging the president carries electoral risks. Moreover, most members of the president's party routinely place party loyalty above the protection of congressional prerogatives. This reality partly explains the decline in congressional oversight on foreign policy over the past several decades.[133]

But party loyalty pressures do not always carry the day, enabling instances of anti-presidential bipartisanship facilitated by countervailing electoral motivations or institutional concerns. As US foreign policy scholars Ralph Carter and Jim Scott have found, "congressional foreign policy behavior is highly context-dependent."[134]

Summary of expectations

Collectively, the preceding analysis of the roles of ideology, advocacy groups, and inter-branch differences generates the following expectations about how these factors contribute to foreign policy alignments.

- Members of Congress will tend to be strongly polarized along partisan lines if a policy debate centers on a left-right ideological fault line or important pro-Democratic and pro-Republican advocacy groups favor opposing positions on the issue.
- Members of Congress will tend to form cross-partisan coalitions if a policy debate does not feature a left-right ideological fault line or involve important pro-Democratic advocacy groups lined up against important pro-Republican advocacy groups.
- Members of Congress in both parties will tend to support the president's position if that position is popular across much of the ideological spectrum or advocacy groups with strong ties to both parties favor that position.
- Members of Congress in both parties will tend to oppose the president's position if that position is unpopular across much of the ideological spectrum or advocacy groups with strong ties to both parties oppose that position.
- The differing institutional incentives and prerogatives of lawmakers and the president will tend to contribute to anti-presidential bipartisanship in foreign policy.

The choice and conduct of case studies

In the remainder of the book, I probe the plausibility of this argument through case studies of important recent US debates involving military intervention, economic sanctions, trade, and spending on diplomacy and foreign aid. I chose these issue areas because they range across the major domains of foreign policy and feature a variety of ideological and advocacy landscapes. The intervention and trade debates represent, respectively, the security and economic dimensions of foreign policy, while the sanctions debates bridge security and economics. Debates over the budget for the State Department and Agency for International Development, meanwhile, concern the diplomatic and development pillars of US foreign policy and involve the key congressional power of the purse. Collectively, these policy domains are broadly representative of the principal foci and tools of US foreign policy. If case studies across these areas provide evidence consistent with my argument, this would suggest that the argument offers a plausible account of political alignments in foreign policy.

These domains also generally involve differing ideological and advocacy contexts. With respect to ideology, there often exist sizable gaps between liberals and conservatives in their views of military intervention and civilian foreign policy spending, with conservatives more likely to favor the former and liberals more likely to support the latter.[135] However, the placement of sanctions on governments engaged in objectionable behavior tends to be broadly popular.[136] Debates over trade agreements, for their part, are typically marked by ideological cross-pressures. Whereas right-wing economic libertarianism and left-wing support for international cooperation point toward pro-trade positions, right-wing nationalism and left-wing concern with solidarity and equity point toward protectionism.[137]

With regard to advocacy groups, debates over international economic matters tend to generate more intensive lobbying than debates over military and security policies since they more directly affect domestic economic constituencies.[138] Advocacy on trade is also often dominated by groups with partisan orientations, with pro-Republican business associations aligned against pro-Democratic labor unions.[139] By contrast, sanctions debates frequently feature advocacy by ethnic diaspora communities, particular industries, or nongovernmental organizations that possess ties to both parties.[140] As I show in Chapter 9, advocacy on the budget for diplomacy and foreign assistance also has a strongly bipartisan character.

Within each of these four issue areas, I used the annual publication *CQ Almanac* to identify major policy debates that spanned the Obama and Trump administrations. More specifically, I identified debates that were the subject of *CQ Almanac* articles during the presidencies of both Obama and

Trump. This approach enabled me to select cases that were not specific to just a single presidency, thereby allowing me to consider whether political dynamics on an issue changed from one president to the next. To the extent that my argument is supported by evidence from both presidencies, this should strengthen confidence in the argument. If a policy debate began before the Obama administration, I also briefly examine important earlier developments on it.

In the area of military intervention, *CQ Almanac* highlighted congressional debates regarding intervention in Syria and against ISIS during both the Obama and Trump administrations. I focus on debates over the provision of arms to Syrian rebels, the establishment of no-fly zones over Syria, and the conduct of airstrikes against Syrian government forces and installations in Chapter 4. I turn to debates over congressional authorization for the use of military force against ISIS and related war powers proposals in Chapter 5. As I detail in the chapters, these debates were marked by cross-partisanship, which was facilitated by weak links between liberal or conservative ideology and competing policy stances in the debates, as well as by the non-partisan identities of the advocacy groups that were active in them.

In the area of sanctions, *CQ Almanac* covered congressional debates about the placement of sanctions on Russia, Iran, and North Korea under both administrations. Given space constraints, I make only Russia and Iran sanctions the subjects of case studies. In Chapter 6, I analyze debates over sanctioning Russia for human rights violations, its 2014 intervention in Ukraine, and its interference in the 2016 US election. In Chapter 7, I evaluate debates over the imposition of sanctions on Iran before Obama entered nuclear talks with the country, the lifting of sanctions on Iran under the 2015 Joint Comprehensive Plan of Action, and the reimposition of sanctions on Iran by Trump. I show that many of these debates were marked by anti-presidential bipartisanship, fueled by strong public and advocacy group support for sanctions as well as by differing congressional and presidential incentives, but that congressional positions on Iran sanctions became much more polarized once the debate began to center on a multilateral agreement that represented a signature achievement of Obama.

In the area of trade, *CQ Almanac* discussed action under Obama and Trump related to the Trans-Pacific Partnership (TPP), including debates over the provision to the president of trade promotion authority to facilitate negotiation of the TPP, the TPP itself, and Trump's withdrawal from the agreement. I examine these debates and provide a briefer overview of two other major trade debates of the Trump era—over tariffs and the United States-Mexico-Canada Agreement (USMCA)—in Chapter 8. I document how the coexistence of pro-trade and protectionist stances on both sides of the left-right ideological spectrum facilitated cross-partisanship in the TPP debate, and I highlight how a rare convergence in the positions of business and labor organizations enabled pro-presidential bipartisanship in the USMCA debate.

In the area of diplomatic and foreign assistance spending, *CQ Almanac* reviewed debates over the budget for the State Department and Agency for International Development under both Obama and Trump. I investigate these debates in Chapter 9. I show that a strange bedfellows coalition of development and humanitarian aid NGOs, major corporations, retired military officers, and faith-based leaders has fostered bipartisan congressional support for civilian international affairs spending. While this bipartisanship had a pro-presidential form under Obama, who sought to maintain this part of the federal budget, it took an anti-presidential form under Trump, who sought to slash it sharply.

In each case study, I use an array of sources and data to determine how elected officials lined up on the issue and to investigate the factors that influenced their positions. These sources include congressional and presidential statements; legislative proposals; transcripts of congressional hearings; congressional voting records; surveys of public opinion and the attitudes of foreign policy professionals; data on interest group positions and lobbying; reporting by journalists; memoirs by government officials; work by other scholars; and interviews of individuals who were deeply involved in these debates. In all, I conducted more than 100 interviews of US representatives and senators from both parties; House and Senate staff in both parties; Obama and Trump administration officials from the White House, State Department, Defense Department, Treasury Department, Commerce Department, US Agency for International Development, and Office of the US Trade Representative; think tank-based experts; and advocates from economic interest groups, ethnic diaspora groups, and values-based organizations.

I identified people to interview after having done extensive research on each case and gained an understanding of who some of the key players were on the issue. I then requested interviews with these individuals and if they agreed to my request, closed my interviews with them by asking for suggestions of other people to contact who would be very knowledgeable about political dynamics on the issue. Since this "snowball sampling" technique could result in an imbalanced interview pool—for instance, including many Democratic officials but few Republican officials—I also sometimes sought to identify and recruit interview subjects with certain affiliations to ensure that the interview pool would include all relevant perspectives.[141] I allowed each subject to choose whether I would treat the conversation as an on-the-record or not-for-attribution interview. I used a semi-structured technique for conducting the interviews, asking some of the same broad questions to many of the respondents but tailoring most of the questions to the particular aspects of the case the subject would likely be very knowledgeable about.[142] I recorded many of the interviews, but I took notes by hand when doing so was more feasible or acceptable to the interview subject.

Generally, the debates covered in the book should be hard cases for generating any type of bipartisanship since they occurred during years when overall polarization in American politics reached record levels. Given the over-time trend of increasing polarization during the past several decades, the existence of different types of bipartisanship during the Obama and Trump presidencies is more notable than their existence under George H.W. Bush or Bill Clinton. Moreover, parts of the military intervention, sanctions, and trade debates were publicly salient—a characteristic that tends to foster polarization, as discussed earlier in this chapter. To the extent that elected officials developed and maintained bipartisan coalitions when these debates were salient, the cases provide particularly powerful evidence of the persistence of foreign policy cooperation across the aisle in the contemporary era. In addition, the years covered by the case studies include periods in which the president's party controlled both chambers of Congress and periods in which it did not. Congressional acts of strong anti-presidential bipartisanship during both types of periods suggest that Congress remains capable, in certain circumstances, of putting aside partisan loyalties to challenge the president in foreign affairs.

PART 2

CASE STUDIES FROM THE OBAMA AND TRUMP YEARS

4

Military intervention in Syria

On September 4, 2013, the Senate Foreign Relations Committee (SFRC) voted on a resolution to authorize the use of military force by the United States in Syria.[1] The committee vote occurred two weeks after Syrian government forces had killed more than 1,400 people in a chemical weapons attack—an atrocity that had clearly crossed a "red line" that President Barack Obama had set regarding the use of chemical weapons in Syria, leading Obama to ask Congress for an authorization for use of military force (AUMF) against the government of Bashar al Assad.

Consistent with expectations of partisan loyalty, the request from a Democratic president attracted more Democratic than Republican support among lawmakers on the SFRC. But in a reflection of intra-party divisions that characterized US policy toward the war that had broken out in Syria in 2011, bipartisan coalitions formed on both sides of the issue. Whereas congressional supporters of air strikes in both parties argued that the United States needed to act forcefully to hold the Syrian government to account and deter the future use of chemical weapons, congressional opponents asserted that intervention could prove counterproductive and lead to ever-deeper US involvement in the war.[2] In the committee's 10-7 vote approving the AUMF, seven Democrats and three Republicans lined up against five Republicans and two Democrats.[3]

The close vote in the SFRC, which tended to be more supportive than the rest of Congress of extensive US engagement in international affairs, boded poorly for the resolution's prospects of passing the full Senate and House of Representatives. With public opinion surveys showing that most voters opposed conducting air strikes in Syria, a growing percentage of lawmakers in both parties came out against the AUMF, and the resolution appeared headed for defeat, particularly in the Republican-controlled House.[4] But before Congress held any further votes on the issue, Obama reached an agreement with Russia for the removal of chemical weapons from Syria that enabled him to call off the AUMF push.[5]

Bipartisanship and US Foreign Policy. Jordan Tama, Oxford University Press. © Oxford University Press 2024.
DOI: 10.1093/oso/9780197745663.003.0004

The intraparty divisions evident in the SFRC's vote on the Syria AUMF were a microcosm of congressional splits over involvement in Middle East conflicts that emerged during the Arab Spring. In 2011, both parties in Congress were similarly split internally over whether the United States should intervene in Libya to prevent the army of Libyan dictator Moammar Qaddafi from carrying out mass atrocities.[6] I focus in this chapter, though, on an interrelated set of debates over military involvement in Syria, including the provision of arms to the Syrian opposition, the creation of no-fly zones to protect vulnerable parts of the Syrian population, and the execution of air strikes against Syrian military targets.

In this case study, I explore how and to what extent the ideological and advocacy landscapes shaped the cross-partisanship that marked US debates over intervention in Syria. To gauge the role of ideology, I investigate whether public and elite opinion on these questions broke down along left-right lines, involved consensus across the ideological spectrum, or revealed differences of views among liberals or among conservatives. To evaluate the role of advocacy groups, I examine the political orientation and strength of groups that were active in these debates. The chapter focuses mainly on the Obama years since debates over intervention in Syria were most intense during his presidency. But I also cover the positions of Democrats and Republicans on Syria under Trump, who conducted air strikes against Syrian targets in response to Syria's use of chemical weapons on two occasions. In Chapter 5, I turn to war powers debates following the rise of ISIS, including Obama- and Trump-era debates over the repeal or replacement of AUMFs that had been enacted into law in 2001 and 2002.

I find that cross-partisanship in debates over military involvement in Syria was enabled by ideological and advocacy landscapes that made it relatively easy to forge bipartisan coalitions but difficult to create consensus in Congress. Neither public nor elite attitudes toward the war were marked by a left-right fault line, enabling Democrats and Republicans to take similar positions without deviating from an ideological orthodoxy. However, most voters in both parties were wary of the United States getting entangled in the conflict through the direct use of force, contributing to weak support among lawmakers in both parties for the most robust types of intervention. Meanwhile, advocacy activity in these debates was largely limited to groups that lacked a strong partisan orientation, particularly Syrian-American organizations, foreign policy experts at think tanks, and human rights NGOs. These groups generally urged US action to address the Syrian crisis, thereby contributing to the development of bipartisan initiatives by internationalist lawmakers. But the groups did not speak with one voice and lacked the political clout needed to have a major effect on congressional activity. Taken together, these conditions facilitated the creation of competing bipartisan camps on Syria policy. On the one hand, hawkish and humanitarian impulses led some Republican and Democratic lawmakers to favor forceful steps to address the crisis in Syria. On the other hand, dovish or libertarian attitudes and concerns about the likely effectiveness or consequences of military steps led other lawmakers in both parties to oppose involvement in the conflict.

Partisan pressures were certainly not entirely absent from debates over intervention in Syria. Since Obama's standing was placed on the line as he sought congressional approval of military action in 2013, lawmakers had an incentive to side with the president if they belonged to his party and side against him if they did not. Conversely, Republican lawmakers had more incentive than Democratic lawmakers to back the air strikes ordered by Trump in 2017 and 2018. During such moments, strong partisan incentives came into direct conflict with personal policy preferences for many members of Congress. Some lawmakers responded to this conflict by choosing partisanship over principle. But even during these moments of heightened partisan pressure, some members of Congress departed from the position of their party leader, enabling cross-partisan coalitions to persist.

While my focus in this chapter is explaining the positions of elected officials in Syria intervention debates, I also consider the impact of Congress on the US approach to the war. The intra-party divisions over Syria policy made it very difficult for lawmakers to pass legislation on the issue, thereby limiting the influence of Congress and leaving key decisions largely in the hands of Obama and Trump. In this way, the case highlights how internal divisions within Congress weaken the ability of lawmakers to shape US foreign policy. Nevertheless, Congress did influence some important elements of US policymaking regarding the Syria conflict. Under Obama, the push by hawks in both parties for more assertive US action contributed to some steps by the administration to place more pressure on the Assad government, while the strength of antiwar sentiment in Congress during the red line debate amplified reservations held by Obama—who was deeply reluctant to involve the United States in another war in the Middle East—about going forward with air strikes. Under Trump, resistance from key lawmakers in both parties to a withdrawal of US troops combating ISIS in Syria influenced decisions by Trump to backtrack from plans for a complete military pullout from the country.

Arms transfers and safe areas

In March 2011, the Arab Spring, which had begun a couple of months earlier in Tunisia, spread to Syria in the form of large protests against the repressive Assad government. In response, the Assad government deployed security forces in an effort to stamp out the protests. The government's crackdown soon escalated to the targeting of demonstrators by tanks, artillery, and attack helicopters, leading to a quickly rising death toll among Syrian civilians. By August, Syrian security forces had killed more than 2,000 people.[7] In response, some Syrian opponents of the Assad government began arming themselves to resist government forces, forming the Free Syrian Army. All of this marked just the beginning of a conflict that would take more than 400,000 lives and force over 11 million people to flee their homes.[8]

As the Syrian government's crackdown intensified, some members of Congress in both parties began pushing for a strong US response. In May 2011, Senator Joseph Lieberman, an Independent Democrat, and Marco Rubio, a Republican, introduced a resolution calling for the placement of certain sanctions on Assad and other Syrian officials.[9] One week after the resolution's introduction, Obama issued an executive order imposing the sanctions suggested by it.[10] Three months later, Democratic Senator Kirsten Gillibrand, Republican Senator Mark Kirk, and Lieberman introduced a new bill authorizing the placement of sanctions on companies engaging in economic transactions involving Syria's petroleum sector or doing other specified forms of business with Syria.[11] Two weeks after this bill's introduction, Obama imposed the sanctions it authorized by executive order.[12] Shortly thereafter, Obama also said publicly that "the time has come for President Assad to step aside."[13] This statement echoed an increasing number of calls by lawmakers for Obama to take this position.[14]

While Congress was not entirely responsible for these early administration steps regarding the conflict, it influenced them. Robert Ford, who served as the US ambassador to Syria from 2011 to 2014, recalled of this period: "There was a lot of pressure on Obama from Republicans and even some Democrats to take a tougher line on Assad. People were denouncing the administration as weak. The White House began taking a tougher stance in part because of politics."[15]

By early 2012, as mass killings by Syrian government forces proliferated, some lawmakers in both parties began proposing that the United States assist the Syrian opposition directly. In February 2012, Democratic Senator Bob Casey and Rubio—both of whom served on the SFRC—introduced a resolution that called on the administration to begin providing anti-government groups with "substantial material and technical support."[16] In a statement accompanying the resolution, Casey highlighted the need to "support the people of Syria during this terrible hour in their history," while Rubio argued that such aid was necessary to "hasten Assad's departure from power."[17] Although the resolution's language did not call explicitly for the provision of lethal assistance to the opposition, it opened the door to that option. Other lawmakers, including Lieberman and Republican Senators John McCain and Lindsay Graham, began calling explicitly for providing arms to anti-government groups or taking more direct military action against Syrian government forces.[18]

But proposals to aid the opposition also faced considerable resistance within each party. Adam Smith, the senior Democrat on the House Armed Services Committee, commented that "it would be very difficult to act . . . in a way that would make a difference [in Syria]."[19] In a similar vein, Richard Lugar, the senior Republican on the SFRC, cautioned that "we should not overestimate our ability to influence events [in Syria]."[20] Some Democrats and Republicans were especially critical of the idea of providing arms to the opposition given the paucity of information about the anti-government groups and the difficulty of ensuring that arms would not end up in the hands of factions with anti-American agendas.[21]

In April, the SFRC approved the Casey-Rubio resolution calling for aid to the opposition by a vote of 13-6. Whereas nine Democrats and four Republicans endorsed the resolution, one Democrat and five Republicans voted against it. However, this cross-partisan vote occurred only after Casey and Rubio had agreed to amend the resolution to add the qualifier "non-lethal" to the language about the aid, which mitigated some of the concerns about the measure.[22]

Around the same time, some Democratic and Republican lawmakers developed interest in the idea of creating humanitarian "safe areas" on the Syrian border for the purpose of shielding parts of the Syrian population threatened by Assad's forces. In most versions of this idea, the safe areas would be protected by the establishment above them of no-fly zones policed by US, Turkish, NATO, and/or other non-Syrian forces. The idea was proposed or endorsed in 2012 by several prominent lawmakers in both parties, including McCain and Carl Levin, the Democratic chairman of the Senate Armed Services Committee.[23]

But many other congressional Democrats and Republicans remained wary of any substantial US involvement in the conflict. One journalist following the debate closely in 2012 highlighted the push by interventionist lawmakers for a "more muscular policy," but reported that most members of Congress fell into one of two bipartisan groups: (1) those who wanted "no part of a greater US military role" in Syria, and (2) those who were open to limited steps but who remained "deeply suspicious of another Middle East quagmire."[24] As a result, supporters of forceful US action could enact into law nothing more during the second year of the Syrian conflict than a requirement that the Pentagon report to Congress on the feasibility of certain military options.[25]

In the meantime, a parallel debate about providing arms to the opposition to Syria was occurring within the Obama administration. In the summer of 2012, Central Intelligence Agency Director David Petraeus developed a plan, backed by Secretary of State Hillary Clinton and Secretary of Defense Leon Panetta, to provide light weaponry to vetted opposition groups.[26] But Obama, in addition to seeking to reduce America's entanglements in the Middle East, was worried that the arms might be insufficient to tip the balance against Assad and that many of the weapons could end up in the wrong hands. He declined to approve the plan.[27]

In March 2013, the policy debate intensified in Washington as reports emerged of chemical weapons attacks killing more than two dozen people in Syria.[28] In the wake of these reports, proponents of more forceful steps led a new push for legislative action. Representative Eliot Engel, the senior Democrat on the House Foreign Affairs Committee, and Representative Mike Rogers, the Republican chairman of the House Intelligence Committee, introduced a bill that urged the provision of military aid to vetted Syrian opposition forces.[29] In a separate bipartisan push, Senators Levin and McCain called on Obama to conduct air strikes on Syrian forces and then work with Turkey to create a safe zone inside Syria's northern border.[30] McCain and Levin argued that the creation of such a zone would both facilitate the provision of humanitarian aid and provide a space where opposition forces could organize and receive military assistance, thereby putting greater pressure on Assad.[31]

But proposals to take stronger action in Syria continued to face bipartisan opposition. Representative Ileana Ros-Lehtinen, a senior Republican on the House Foreign Affairs Committee, commented in March 2013, "I sincerely do not believe that it is time for the US to arm the rebels. Too many questions remain about who the rebels are, and with whom they will swear allegiance."[32] Senator Jack Reed, a senior Democrat on the Senate Armed Services Committee, said in April that establishing a safe zone in Syria "could involve a serious engagement of US forces which is hard . . . to reverse, and second, extraordinarily expensive."[33]

The most important legislative push of the first half of 2013 centered on arming the opposition. In May, the SFRC considered a bill introduced by Bob Menendez and Bob Corker, the senior Democrat and Republican on the committee respectively, that authorized the provision of weapons and training to vetted Syrian opposition groups.[34] In promoting the bill, Menendez argued, "The choice here is not between arming and not arming. The choice is between the United States stepping in and trying to do this in a responsible fashion or leaving it to others who will simply arm the extremists."[35] But a few anti-interventionist committee members, including libertarian Republican Rand Paul and progressive Democrats Chris Murphy and Tom Udall, opposed the proposal. Paul charged that aiding Syrian rebels was tantamount to funding "allies of Al Qaeda."[36] Udall commented, "After a decade of war overseas, now is not the time to arm an unorganized, unfamiliar, and unpredictable group of rebels. Now is not the time to rush headlong into another Middle Eastern civil war."[37]

The SFRC approved the Menendez-Corker bill on May 21 by a vote of 15-3. Eight Democrats and seven Republicans approved the bill, while Paul, Murphy, and Udall rejected it.[38] This vote provided the strongest congressional pressure yet on the administration to provide arms to the opposition.[39] Nevertheless, the bill's prospects of passing the full Senate were not strong. Ilan Goldenberg, who handled the issue as a Democratic SFRC aide from 2012–2013, noted that Senate Majority Leader Harry Reid did not wish to bring the bill to the floor of the Senate "because the president didn't support it and there was division within the [Democratic] caucus on the issue."[40]

Three weeks after the SFRC vote, Obama authorized the provision of some US lethal assistance to the rebels for the first time. This limited aid, to be provided by the Central Intelligence Agency (CIA), was reported to include small arms and ammunition, but not heavy weaponry.[41] The announcement came shortly after the US intelligence community completed an assessment that the Assad government was responsible for multiple uses of chemical weapons over the preceding year.[42]

Some Obama administration officials who were involved in Syria policy said this decision was influenced by pressure from Congress and from US allies and partners in the Middle East who were seeking greater US involvement in the conflict.[43] Amanda Sloat, who served at the time as a senior advisor on the National Security Council with responsibility for Middle East issues, recalled, "The administration's Syria strategy was a little muddled, and so the administration ended up backing into piecemeal efforts because there was pressure to do more, but the administration never went all-in on these efforts."[44] However, then-National Security Advisor Susan Rice commented, "On arming and equipping the rebels, we made the decisions that we thought were the right decisions on the merits, not because of political pressure."[45]

Obama's decision took away some of the impetus for Syria legislation, but it did not satisfy congressional proponents of more forceful US action in either party. On June 18, Senators Levin, McCain, and Menendez wrote a letter to Obama urging "more decisive military actions in Syria."[46] Meanwhile, Democratic and Republican critics of US involvement argued the provision of military aid to rebel groups went too far. Representative Adam Schiff, the senior Democrat on the House Intelligence Committee, said in July that "primary for me is the concern that if we become an arms supplier . . . we'll be sucked into another sectarian civil war."[47] In a similar vein, Rand Paul commented that month, "I'm not in favor of sending arms or weapons or boys or girls to fight some war for stalemate."[48]

The Obama red line debate

The Syria policy debate took a new turn following a chemical weapons attack in the Ghouta region of the country on August 21, 2013, that killed over 1,400 people, including more than 400 children.[49] A year earlier, Obama had said at a press briefing, while talking about the war in Syria, that "a red line for us is we start seeing a whole bunch of chemical weapons moving around or being utilized."[50] Following the Ghouta chemical weapons attack, which the United States determined was ordered by Syrian government officials, congressional advocates of intervention intensified their calls to take stronger action against the Assad government. McCain criticized Obama harshly for not enforcing his red line charging: "The word of the president of the United

States can no longer be taken seriously."[51] Eliot Engel, the senior Democrat on the House Foreign Affairs Committee, also used strong language to urge intervention, though without the direct swipe at Obama: "The US has two options—continue to largely stand on the sidelines as the regime slaughters its own people, or tip the balance of power against a brutal dictator by degrading its ability to attack civilians."[52] Meanwhile, some US allies moved toward military action, as French President François Hollande and British Prime Minister David Cameron said intervention was necessary to hold the Syrian government accountable for the chemical attacks.[53]

In this context, Obama began preparing to order a set of air strikes on Syrian military facilities and units.[54] But after the British Parliament rejected Cameron's proposal to take part in military action in Syria on August 29, Obama chose to request authorization from Congress before conducting the strikes. In a statement on August 31, Obama noted that "we are prepared to strike," but added, "I'm also mindful that I'm the President of the world's oldest constitutional democracy . . . and that's why I've made a second decision: I will seek authorization for the use of force from the American people's representatives in Congress."[55]

Obama's decision to turn to Congress reflected his reluctance about getting involved in the war in the first place, as well as a concern that entering the conflict without the backing of Congress would leave him very vulnerable to future criticism by lawmakers if the intervention did not go well.[56] Then-US ambassador to Syria Robert Ford commented: "Obama didn't want to get into an escalation scenario in Syria where Congress would be free to snipe at him as the conflict went on."[57] Obama's concern with gaining congressional support was surely only heightened by the low levels of public support for intervention in Syria, which I detail later in this chapter. In that context, it was natural for Obama to worry that congressional criticism of intervention could further erode public support for it.[58]

For the next two weeks, the Obama administration lobbied lawmakers in an effort to achieve approval of the AUMF.[59] The president's major stake in the high-profile debate provided members of Congress with a political incentive to polarize along partisan lines, and as the debate proceeded, some polarization did in fact occur. Most strikingly, some Republicans who had previously called for US action, such as Marco Rubio, opposed the use of force authorization. Susan Rice observed with dismay, "Republicans would never want to do anything to give Obama a victory."[60] However, Jamil Jaffer, who served at the time as Republican chief counsel on the SFRC, said that policy concerns, rather than politics, weakened Republican support for the AUMF: "For many Republicans, the president hadn't laid out a path to success in the conflict."[61] Democrats, meanwhile, felt a pull of loyalty toward their party leader. Margaret Taylor, who served at the time as Menendez's deputy chief counsel on SFRC, noted, "Some Democrats felt that since Obama was asking for this, they needed to deliver."[62]

Nevertheless, a substantial degree of cross-partisanship persisted on the issue. While the resolution's supporters included proponents of a muscular foreign policy in both parties, opponents represented what the *Washington Post* called "an unlikely alliance" between "tea party conservatives" and "liberal doves."[63] Democratic Representative Alan Grayson, a progressive opponent of military action, noted the latter coalition stemmed from a viewpoint shared across the political spectrum about Syria that "we just need to mind our own business," adding, "that's not a liberal or conservative concept."[64]

In a further reflection of how positions in the debate did not map onto a left-right spectrum, both opponents and supporters of military action cited a variety of reasons for being for or against the proposed air strikes. For instance, among supporters of intervention, Senate Democrat Tim Kaine emphasized the need to "stand up for the principle that chemical weapons . cannot be used," while Senate Republican Lindsay Graham highlighted the need to counter Iran (which was propping up the Assad government).[65] Opponents, meanwhile, pointed to an array of concerns, from the costs of military action, to the potential effects of strikes on Syrian civilians, to the lack of a clear US strategic interest in Syria, to the possibility of a slippery slope carrying the United States into a larger military operation.[66]

As the debate proceeded, the bipartisan coalition opposing intervention quickly outgrew the bipartisan coalition supporting it—particularly among Republicans—and it became clear that the full Congress would probably not approve the resolution. Among all representatives and senators who took a clear position on the AUMF resolution before Obama reached the agreement with Russia that allowed him to call off the push for military action, 30 Democrats and 15 Republicans said they backed the resolution, whereas 42 Democrats and 158 Republicans said they opposed it.[67]

While the September 2013 debate showed that most lawmakers opposed direct US military intervention in Syria, congressional hawks, such as McCain, Engel, and Levin, continued in subsequent months to push for stronger action to address the crisis.[68] In May 2014, the Senate Armed Services Committee, led by Levin, approved an annual defense bill containing a provision authorizing the Defense Department to provide military equipment and training to vetted members of the Syrian opposition.[69] A proposal to strike this provision from the defense authorization bill was rejected by the committee—which tends to be more hawkish than the rest of Congress—in a 23-3 vote, with just one Democrat and two Republicans voting against it.[70] Congress enacted the provision into law in December 2014.[71]

A few days after the committee's resounding vote in support of arming the opposition, Obama announced a closely related plan.[72] This initiative, which expanded the lethal aid begun in 2013 and housed the new program in the Pentagon rather than the CIA, was formalized in a June administration request for Congress to provide $500 million to train and equip Syrian opposition fighters.[73] Journalists reported that Obama's decision to propose this expansion in military assistance was influenced by the pressure from Congress.[74] But it was also driven by Obama's growing concern about the rise of ISIS and the likelihood that the Syrian opposition would radicalize further without US involvement.[75]

Before Congress completed approval of the defense authorization bill or acted on Obama's proposal, the beheading by ISIS of American journalists James Foley and Steven Sotloff on August 21 and September 4, 2014, respectively, gave new urgency and a new rationale to the idea of training and equipping Syrian opposition fighters. Those killings, along with other ISIS beheadings and the rapid expansion of ISIS-controlled territory in Iraq and Syria during 2014, led to a shift in the principal purpose of the train-and-equip proposal from countering Assad to countering ISIS. With this shift, on September 17 and 18, 2014, the House and Senate approved the administration's proposal as an amendment to a must-pass spending bill by votes of 273-156 and 78-22, respectively.[76] While these votes demonstrated bipartisan backing for arming anti-government groups for the purpose of countering ISIS, they also revealed continued intra-party splits, with most hawks and centrists on one side and many libertarians and progressives on the other.[77] In the House vote, 159 Republicans and 114 Democrats lined up against 85 Republicans and 71 Democrats. In the Senate vote, 44 Democrats and 33 Republicans lined up against nine Democrats and 12 Republicans.

The approval by Congress of the Syrian opposition train-and-equip program represented the most substantial action taken by the institution with respect to US military involvement in the Syrian war since the conflict had begun three years earlier. Yet the program turned out to be less consequential than its supporters expected. While the administration intended for the program to train as many as 5,000 fighters, news reports a year later revealed that only a handful of fighters had gone through the program successfully, leading the administration to cancel the program.[78] In the meantime, the attention of some lawmakers concerned with the ongoing conflict shifted to questions related to the authorization of military action against ISIS, with which the United States entered direct combat in the fall of 2014. I discuss this AUMF debate in-depth in Chapter 5.

Public and elite opinion

As noted in Chapter 3, ideology becomes concrete in the form of public and elite opinion regarding specific policy issues. In this section, I use public and elite opinion data to investigate the extent to which debates over intervention in Syria involved left-right ideological division, consensus across the ideological spectrum, or ideological divisions within each of the parties. On the whole, these data show that there did not exist a left-right divide in public or elite views of military involvement in Syria, though there did exist intra-party splits in opinion. This opinion constellation meant that Democratic and Republican elected officials were not constrained by a liberal or conservative orthodoxy in Syria intervention debates, facilitating cross-partisan behavior in Congress.

Voters in both parties had similar views regarding the importance of addressing the Syria conflict. A December 2012 Pew survey found that 66% of the Republican public and 61% of the Democratic public said they did not think the United States had "a responsibility to do something about fighting in Syria."[79] Six months later, after the first reports of chemical weapons being used in the war, more Americans voiced support for some type of action, but still without much of a partisan gap: a June 2013 Pew survey found that 58% of Democrats and 49% of Republicans thought the United States had "a moral obligation to do what it can to stop violence in Syria."[80]

Public perspectives on particular policy options also did not break down sharply along left-right lines. Across all public opinion polls I could find between 2011 and 2014 that included a breakdown of the data by party affiliation, an average of just 29% of Democrats and 27% of Republicans said they supported providing arms to Syrian anti-government groups.[81] (See Table 4.1.) Conversely, an average of 56% of Democrats and 63% of Republicans said they favored creating a no-fly zone in Syria.[82] (See Table 4.2.) Taken together,

Table 4.1 Public and elite opinion on arming Syrian opposition, 2011–2014

Pollster	Survey period	Group polled	Democrats in support	Democrats opposed	Republicans in support	Republicans opposed
Chicago Council[a]	May–June 2012	Public	28%	72%	34%	66%
Pew[b]	June 2013	Public	25%	66%	20%	71%
Quinnipiac[c]	June–July 2013	Public	32%	51%	26%	63%
Wash Post/ ABC[d]	September 2013	Public	30%	65%	28%	70%
Chicago Council[a]	May 2014	Public	29%	68%	31%	62%
Chicago Council[a]	May– August 2014	Elites	52%	48%	60%	40%

Note: The table includes all US opinion polls I could find that asked whether respondents supported providing arms to Syrian opposition groups between the outbreak of the Syrian conflict in March 2011 and the killing of James Foley by ISIS in August 2014 and which broke down the data by party affiliation.

[a] "Would you support or oppose the United States and its allies sending arms and supplies to anti-government groups in Syria?"

[b] "Would you favor or oppose the US and its allies sending arms to anti-government groups in Syria?"

[c] "Do you support or oppose the US sending arms and military supplies to anti-government groups in Syria?"

[d] "Do you support or oppose the United States and its allies supplying weapons to the Syrian rebels?"

these data highlight the coexistence within both parties of sentiments favoring and opposing greater US action to address the crisis.

The views of foreign policy elites from this period also reveal a lack of polarization. I found only one survey that asked foreign policy elites about Syria policy choices between the start of the Syrian conflict and the beheading of James Foley by ISIS in August 2014. In this Chicago Council on Global Affairs (Chicago Council) survey of foreign policy professionals, 60% of Republicans and 52% of Democrats supported providing arms to Syrian anti-government groups, whereas 56% of Republicans and 47% of Democrats favored creating a no-fly zone in Syria.[83] (See Tables 4.1 and 4.2.) In conjunction with the public opinion data, these data also indicate a sizable elite-public gap in attitudes regarding arming the opposition, with the share of elites favoring this step nearly twice as large as the share of the public favoring this step—consistent with the broader pattern in which foreign policy elites favor more extensive international involvement than the public.

Table 4.2 Public and elite opinion on creating a no-fly zone in Syria, 2011–2014

Pollster	Survey period	Group polled	Democrats in support	Democrats opposed	Republicans in support	Republicans opposed
Chicago Council[a]	May–June 2012	Public	61%	39%	67%	33%
ABC/Wash Post[b]	December 2012	Public	60%	N/A	67%	N/A
Chicago Council[c]	May 2014	Public	47%	49%	56%	39%
Chicago Council[c]	May– August 2014	Elites	61%	39%	65%	35%

Note: The table includes all US opinion polls I could find that asked whether respondents supported US enforcement of a no-fly zone in Syria between the start of the Syrian conflict in March 2011 and the killing of James Foley by ISIS in August 2014 and which broke down the data by party affiliation. Table entries indicating "N/A" represent survey results that the pollster did not report.

[a] "Would you favor or oppose the US and its allies enforcing a no-fly zone over Syria?"

[b] "What if US military aircraft were used to create a no-fly zone, but no ground troops were involved? In that case would you support or oppose US military involvement in Syria?"

[c] "Would you favor or oppose the US and its allies enforcing a no-fly zone over Syria, including bombing Syrian air defenses?"

During the 2013 air strikes debate, direct intervention attracted more opposition than support among both Democratic and Republican members of the public, though opposition was greater among Republicans.[84] Across seven surveys conducted in late August and early September of that year, an average of 40% of Democrats and 31% of Republicans said they favored US military action against Syria, while an average of 51% of Democrats and 60% of Republicans said they opposed it.[85] (See Table 4.3.) The survey data also reveal a growing partisan gap on air strikes as the debate proceeded, as Republican public opinion grew more sharply opposed to military action over the course of these weeks. This trend likely stemmed from Obama's party identity: with a Democratic president making the case for military action, some Republican voters probably turned against intervention in part due to their general opposition to Obama.[86] Nevertheless, the relatively limited polarization in public attitudes regarding direct military intervention provides further evidence that the Syria debate did not generally pit liberals against conservatives.

Anecdotal evidence suggests that vocal constituents were even more heavily tilted against military action than the general public, and the high

Table 4.3 Public opinion on air strikes against Syria, 2013

Pollster	Survey period	Democrats in support	Democrats opposed	Republicans in support	Republicans opposed
Wash Post/ABC[a]	Aug 28–Sept 1	42%	54%	43%	55%
Pew/USA Today[b]	Aug 29–Sept 1	29%	48%	35%	40%
Gallup[c]	Sept 3–Sept 4	45%	43%	34%	53%
Wash Post/ABC[a]	Sept 4–Sept 8	41%	55%	24%	71%
Pew/USA Today[b]	Sept 4–Sept 8	35%	53%	21%	70%
Fox[d]	Sept 6–Sept 8	46%	51%	30%	66%
CBS/NYT[e]	Sept 6–Sept 8	41%	50%	28%	65%

Note: The table includes all public opinion polls I could find that asked whether respondents supported conducting military strikes on Syria after it was reported that Obama was preparing to order strikes and before he reached a deal with Russia for the removal of Syria's chemical weapons and which broke down the data by party affiliation.

[a] "The United States says it has determined that the Syrian government has used chemical weapons in the civil war there. Given this, do you support or oppose the US launching missile strikes against the Syrian government?"

[b] "Would you favor or oppose the US conducting military airstrikes against Syria in response to reports that the Syrian government used chemical weapons?"

[c] "Would you favor or oppose the US taking military action against Syria in order to reduce that country's ability to use chemical weapons?"

[d] "Do you favor or oppose using US military force to punish Syria for using chemical weapons?"

[e] "In response to the Syrian government's use of chemical weapons, do you favor or oppose the United States launching military airstrikes against Syrian military targets?"

degree of salience of the September 2013 debate made lawmakers highly attuned to constituent views during this period. Representative Justin Amash, a Michigan Republican, reported that out of 400 constituents he had heard from on the issue, 95% opposed military action in Syria.[87] Following those interactions, Amash tweeted, "If you're voting yes on military action in #Syria, might as well start cleaning out your office. Unprecedented level of public opposition."[88] Representative Jim McDermott, a Washington Democrat, also described hearing far more opposition than support from his constituents.[89]

Overall, public and elite views regarding US policy options toward the conflict in Syria help explain the high levels of congressional cross-partisanship on the issue and the difficulty lawmakers faced in passing legislation on it. Many Democrats and Republicans wanted the United States to do something to address the conflict in Syria, but most members of both parties wanted to avoid a possible military entanglement and were particularly wary of direct intervention. The option that received the most attention on Capitol Hill—arming the opposition—was viewed favorably by a sizable share of foreign policy elites in both parties but viewed unfavorably by most voters in both parties. In short, there was neither a Democratic nor a Republican Party orthodoxy regarding Syria, which allowed lawmakers to take a range of positions regarding possible steps to address the crisis.

At the same time, the relatively low level of public interest and advocacy activity on the issue—aside from the September 2013 air strikes debate—gave lawmakers some freedom to follow their own compass, but it also meant that legislative action would garner them few political benefits. Former SFRC Democratic aide Ilan Goldenberg noted, "Most of the Syria debate didn't resonate a lot with the public, and so the positions of members mainly came down to their personal views."[90] In this context, most lawmakers had little incentive to prioritize the issue, and those lawmakers that did care about it faced an uphill battle trying to forge consensus around legislative options. This limited the extent of Congress's influence over US Syria policy, though lawmakers on either side of the debate did act at times as a prod or constraint regarding presidential action toward Syria.

At the same time, strong public opposition to intervention during the September 2013 AUMF debate meant that lawmakers faced real political risk if they voted for intervention. This risk was made all the more salient in the minds of many members of Congress by the recent experience of the Iraq war, in that many lawmakers had paid a large political price for backing US intervention in Iraq. Tommy Ross, who handled Syria policy as a national security aide to Senate Majority Leader Harry Reid at the time, commented, "Members didn't want to have to go back to their constituents and explain why they had voted to authorize another war and put themselves in the same position as the people who had voted for [the] Iraq [war]."[91]

Advocacy group activity

The advocacy landscape also facilitated cross-partisanship in US debates about Syria policy options. With the exception of the September 2013 AUMF debate, these debates did not elicit lobbying by America's most influential interest groups, but they did feature advocacy by human rights NGOs, Syrian-American diaspora organizations, and foreign policy experts outside government.[92] This advocacy helped bring attention to the Syrian crisis on Capitol Hill and contributed to the development of activist legislative initiatives. Since many of the groups involved in Syria advocacy lacked partisan orientations, they were particularly well-suited to building some support for these initiatives in both parties. But the groups were not united when it came to policy choices and lacked the clout needed to sway many congressional votes.

One accomplishment of these groups was to raise awareness of the severity of the crisis and the horror of the atrocities perpetrated by the Assad regime. In 2013, a defector from a Syrian military police forensic photography unit with the pseudonym Caesar smuggled more than 50,000 photographs out of Syria that showed evidence of crimes against humanity and war crimes by government forces, including the torture and death of thousands of detainees. Human rights and Syrian diaspora groups worked with Caesar to publicize the images through the US media and on Capitol Hill, where Caesar testified before the House Foreign Affairs Committee and met with lawmakers with his identity concealed.[93] Exposure to such images contributed to the desire of some lawmakers to do more to address the crisis.[94] This advocacy effort influenced the enactment of laws authorizing efforts to promote accountability for atrocities in Syria and mandating additional sanctions on the Syrian government and its foreign backers.[95]

But while human rights groups urged the United States and other Western governments to apply non-military forms of pressure on the Assad government, they generally refrained from taking a position on potential military action.[96] For instance, Maria McFarland, the Washington deputy director of Human Rights Watch, a leading NGO, testified before Congress in March 2012: "Human Rights Watch is limited in its ability to advise on whether any of the options involving the use of military force would make the situation in Syria better or worse."[97] Other prominent human rights organizations, such as Amnesty International and Human Rights First, also limited their advocacy to non-military steps, such as tightening sanctions on the Assad government and prosecuting war crimes and crimes against humanity at the International Criminal Court.[98] Tommy Ross, the former aide to Senate Majority Leader Harry Reid, recalled, "I don't remember a lot of outside groups coming to Congress with particular military solutions. I do remember a lot of discussion with outside groups about the humanitarian consequences of what was going on, but that didn't yield any obvious answers about how to stop the conflict."[99]

Some Syrian-American diaspora groups, including the Syrian American Council, Syrian Emergency Task Force, and Coalition for a Democratic Syria, did advocate intensively for some form of military action.[100] Rather than reaching out only to lawmakers in one of the two parties, these groups targeted Democrats and Republicans who represented Syrian-American constituencies.[101] The bipartisan reach of Syrian-American groups is evident in the membership of the House caucus on Syria, which includes 25 Democratic representatives and 22 Republican representatives as of this writing.[102] These groups were also partly responsible for the support of some lawmakers for proposals to provide arms to the opposition. A House Republican aide who handled the issue noted, "The pro-opposition groups did have an impact. I don't think many members would have cared about the opposition without them."[103]

But the influence of the Syrian-American community was weakened by some internal splits. Broadly, it was split between Sunni Muslims, who tended to favor forceful action against the Assad government, and Alawites and Christians, who tended to be relatively pro-Assad.[104] Although the anti-Assad portion of the community greatly outnumbered the pro-Assad portion, Syrian-American groups who opposed Assad were themselves not always on the same page. Syria policy expert and human rights advocate Radwan Ziadeh observed, "There are too many Syrian American organizations, and there is too much division among them."[105] Another advocate involved in the debate recalled, "Many Syrian ex-pat groups called for a no-fly zone or arming rebels. But they weren't unified and made different policy recommendations."[106]

The influence of Syrian-American groups was further limited by the small size of the Syrian-American population. As of 2014, the number of Americans who were born in Syria or possessed Syrian heritage totaled about 191,000, or less than one out of every 1,000 Americans. Of these Syrian-Americans, 18% lived in California, 10% in Pennsylvania, 8% each in New York and New Jersey, and the rest in various other states.[107] Lawmakers representing some of these more sizable Syrian-American communities—such as Senator Casey of Pennsylvania and Senator Menendez of New Jersey—were among the strongest congressional advocates of more forceful US action in Syria. But few lawmakers stood to gain many votes from activism on this issue.

Some prominent foreign policy experts in both parties also called for greater US involvement in the Syria conflict. In February 2012, Princeton professor and former Obama administration official Anne-Marie Slaughter wrote an op-ed in the *New York Times* calling for the creation of safe areas in Syria that would protect innocent civilians.[108] Three months later, 62 foreign policy experts—many of whom had served in Republican administrations—promoted the safe zone idea in a letter organized by the hawkish Foreign Policy Institute and Foundation for Defense of Democracies.[109] Other think tank experts urged more forceful US action in Syria in congressional testimony and policy papers. Tamara Cofman Wittes, a Middle East expert and former Obama administration official at the Brookings Institution, argued in 2012 that "dithering over diplomatic measures [concerning Syria] while ruling out more coercive options is the quickest path to irrelevance for US policy."[110] Kimberly Kagan, founder of the Institute for the Study of War, called in 2013 for the provision of "funds, weapons, equipment, and training" to the Syrian opposition.[111] In a similar vein, Democratic and Republican experts at the Washington Institute for Near East Policy urged in 2012 and 2013 that the United States provide arms to Syrian opposition groups, establish no-fly zones, and/or plan for direct military intervention against Syrian government forces.[112]

These and other experts outside government played an important role in shaping the perspectives of some congressional officials and suggesting legislative ideas.[113] But, like the Syrian-American diaspora groups, they lacked the political clout that comes from being a major campaign donor or representing a large constituency. A House Democratic foreign policy aide who handled Syria policy noted, "There was no Syrian-American constituency of any magnitude to push home the idea of getting aggressive in Syria."[114]

The limits of advocacy group influence on Syria policy debates are also illustrated by lobbying data. For groups that do not represent a large constituency of voters, attaining great political influence usually requires making substantial campaign contributions to politicians. But while some diaspora groups and think tank experts endorsed bills concerning the provision of aid to Syrian opposition groups or the creation of safe areas in Syria, no interest group that made campaign contributions to US lawmakers took a public position on one of these bills.[115] Moreover, no Syrian-American diaspora group or other Syria-specific advocacy organization made any campaign contributions to US lawmakers or congressional candidates during the 2012 or 2014 election cycles.[116] Some human rights groups that were engaged in the Syria debate, such as Human Rights Watch and Human Rights First, did make such campaign contributions during this period.[117] But, as noted above, these groups did not take policy positions on military options regarding Syria, limiting their influence over these debates.

Some heavyweight groups did engage in advocacy when Congress considered the high-profile request from Obama to authorize air strikes against the Assad government in 2013. In a strange bedfellows advocacy alliance, the major progressive group MoveOn.org and major conservative group FreedomWorks urged lawmakers to vote against authorizing the strikes.[118]. While MoveOn.org argued that strikes against Syria would take the United States into an unnecessary war, FreedomWorks emphasized that the cost of strikes would add to the national debt.[119] On the other side of the debate, the American Israel Public Affairs Committee, which maintained close ties to lawmakers in both parties, argued that the strikes were needed to dissuade Syria from further use of unconventional weapons and to counter Iran.[120] While these groups possessed the clout needed to influence congressional voting, their particular alignments in this debate meant that both Democratic and Republican lawmakers would satisfy one group and disappoint another group regardless of which position they took—a situation conducive to cross-partisanship.

Air strikes and withdrawal steps under Trump

Following the start of the US military campaign against ISIS in 2014—to which I return in Chapter 5—US debates regarding Syria focused mainly on efforts to weaken and defeat ISIS, rather than on efforts to counter the Assad government. But the latter type of action took center stage again in April 2017 after a determination by US intelligence agencies that the Syrian military had killed more than 80 people in a new chemical weapons attack in Idlib province. Two days after the attack, President Trump ordered 59 cruise missiles to be launched at a Syrian airfield that had been used to conduct the chemical warfare.[121] In this case, unlike in 2013, the president did not ask Congress for authorization before taking military action.

Congressional reaction to the missile strikes revealed continued cross-partisanship concerning military action in Syria although, in a mirror image of the pattern in the red line debate that reflected the power of partisan incentives, the Republican president's action generated more support among Republicans than among Democrats on Capitol Hill. Congressional leaders in both parties endorsed the strikes, including Senate Majority Leader Mitch

McConnell and Speaker of the House Paul Ryan (both Republicans), as well as Senate Minority Leader Chuck Schumer and House Minority Leader Nancy Pelosi (both Democrats).[122] But Schumer also called on the administration to develop a clearer Syria strategy, while Pelosi urged the administration not to pursue further military action without first getting approval from Congress.[123] Pelosi stated soon after the strikes: "Tonight's strike in Syria appears to be a proportional response to the regime's use of chemical weapons. If the President intends to escalate the US military's involvement in Syria, he must come to Congress for an Authorization for Use of Military Force which is tailored to meet the threat and prevent another open-ended war in the Middle East."[124]

Many senior foreign policy voices on Capitol Hill in both parties—including McCain, Rubio, Engel, and Senator Ben Cardin, who had become the senior Democrat on the SFRC—also offered support to the missile barrage, with Republicans generally providing the strongest backing.[125] Rubio said, "By acting decisively against the very facility from which Assad launched his murderous chemical weapons attack, President Trump has made it clear to Assad and those who empower him that the days of committing war crimes with impunity are over."[126] Notably, some of the Republicans who backed the strikes, including Rubio, had opposed the Syria AUMF in 2013, underscoring the influence of partisanship on congressional positions even on this relatively unpolarized issue.[127]

However, some lawmakers in both parties were sharply critical of the strikes. Democratic Senator Tim Kaine and Republican Senator Rand Paul called them "unconstitutional."[128] Democratic Senator Chris Murphy said Trump had taken military action "based off of an emotional reaction to the images on TV, and it should worry everyone about the quixotic nature of this administration's foreign policy."[129] Republican Representative Thomas Massie tweeted, "Didn't the missile attack just make the situation better for ISIS?"[130]

A wide array of views was also expressed by lawmakers at a House Foreign Affairs Committee hearing three weeks after the strikes. Ed Royce, the Republican chairman of the committee, said the use of force was "proportional" and "legitimate," but he called for more "forceful diplomacy" to isolate Assad.[131] In a similar vein, Engel said the strikes were "appropriate" but added that a "pinpoint missile strike is not a strategy."[132] Meanwhile, Republican committee member Dana Rohrabacher argued that Assad was no worse than other leaders in the Middle East whom the United States supported, and he sharply criticized the strikes, commenting, "I do believe there is a moral equivalency between dropping a bomb on people and killing those same people with gas."[133] Many Democrats on the committee, meanwhile, insisted that the administration not take any further military actions against Syria unless Congress authorized them.

A year later, congressional reactions in both parties were similarly mixed in response to a new set of missile strikes ordered by Trump on Syrian targets in response to a chemical weapons attack that killed more than 40 Syrians.[134] In describing those reactions, the *Los Angeles Times* highlighted the kind of cross-partisan alignments that had characterized Syria intervention debates since the start of the Syrian conflict: "Hawkish conservatives favored the aggressive response to Assad. So did some liberals, who applauded the airstrikes as a way to stop the horrors of chemical weapons, which have become a grim feature of the Syrian civil war. But it also created another group of strange bedfellows—liberals and conservatives upset that Trump neglected to consult Congress."[135]

Yet it is also notable that congressional sentiment was more supportive overall of Trump's air strikes than it had been toward the proposed AUMF in 2013. This difference likely reflected the prospective versus retrospective nature of these debates. In 2013, Obama was asking lawmakers to put their political necks out in support of an intervention whose length and outcome were highly uncertain. In 2017 and 2018, by contrast, lawmakers were responding to a limited missile barrage that had already been completed successfully, at least in a tactical sense. As one former Senate foreign policy aide noted about the Trump air strikes, "These were one-offs. If Trump had asked for congressional support for further military action, that would have generated a different conversation."[136] In addition, the later debates occurred at a time when the United States was already carrying out military operations in Syria, albeit against ISIS rather than the Assad government. Former SFRC Democratic aide Ilan Goldenberg noted, "In 2013, this would have been opening a new military front. In 2017, we were already fighting a war in Syria, so a few more air strikes didn't seem like such a big deal."[137]

The Syria policy debate took yet another turn in December 2018, when Trump suddenly announced a complete and rapid withdrawal of the roughly 2,000 troops deployed in Syria as part of the campaign against ISIS, tweeting, "After historic victories against ISIS, it's time to bring our great young people home!"[138] In a video posted on Twitter, Trump added, "Our boys, our young women, our men—they're all coming back, and they're coming back now."[139]

In making this withdrawal decision, which reflected his overarching view that the United States should pull its troops out of hotspots like Syria, Iraq, Afghanistan, and the Korean Peninsula, Trump had overruled his most senior foreign policy and military advisers.[140]

Trump's decision prompted sharp bipartisan criticism from Capitol Hill.[141] Lindsey Graham charged that it was "akin to surrender," while fellow Republican Senator Ben Sasse warned that "a lot of American allies will be slaughtered if this retreat is implemented."[142] On the Democratic side of the aisle, Senator Jeanne Shaheen labeled the move "dangerous" and "premature," while Bob Menendez called it a "foolhardy" step that put security in the Middle East in "great peril."[143] In February 2019, the Senate approved by a vote of 70-26, with 46 Republicans and 24 Democrats endorsing it, a resolution introduced by Senate Majority Leader Mitch McConnell that expressed opposition to the decision, warning that a "precipitous withdrawal" of US forces "could allow terrorists to regroup" and "create vacuums that could be filled by Iran or Russia."[144] In response to the pushback from Congress, as well as from advisors and US allies, Trump modified his decision a couple of weeks later, agreeing to leave several hundred US troops in Syria.[145]

History repeated itself on this issue in late 2019, when Trump again suddenly announced a withdrawal of US troops from Syria, whose number totaled about 1,000 at the time. Following Trump's announcement, McConnell said that the withdrawal "would only benefit Russia, Iran, and the Assad regime" and "increase the risk that ISIS and other terrorist groups regroup."[146] A week later, the House approved a resolution that expressed opposition to the administration's decision by a vote of 354-60, with more than two-thirds of Republicans joining all Democrats in support of it.[147] Partly in response to this strong pushback from Congress, Trump modified his decision, agreeing to leave at least several hundred of the approximately 1,000 US troops in Syria, ostensibly to guard the country's oil fields.[148] These developments provide further evidence that Congress influenced US policy toward the war in Syria.

Conclusion

The persistence of cross-partisanship in Syria intervention debates across the Obama and Trump presidencies shows how some major foreign policy issues feature neither bipartisan consensus nor partisan polarization, underscoring the importance of a more nuanced understanding of political alignments. The character of public and elite opinion, as well as of advocacy activity, associated with these debates is also consistent with the argument developed in the book that cross-partisanship is facilitated when a debate does not break down on left-right ideological lines or involve advocacy by powerful groups with strong partisan associations. At the same time, the somewhat greater polarization that marked the red line debate illustrates how increased political stakes lead the pressures of partisan loyalty to carry more sway relative to principled views.

The internal divisions on Capitol Hill over the war in Syria usually allowed Obama and Trump to set the course for the US response to the conflict. When it came to congressional influence, cross-partisanship acted as a double-edged sword. On the one hand, bipartisan coalitions on either side of the debate sometimes constrained the president, either by applying pressure on the president to take steps to address the crisis or by signaling weak support for more robust military intervention. On the other hand, the lack of consensus on the issue on Capitol Hill meant that Congress was unable throughout most of the crisis to act coherently to force US policy to move in a particular direction.

5

War powers authorities

On April 16, 2018, Republican Senator Bob Corker and Democratic Senator Tim Kaine led a bipartisan group of senators in introducing a resolution that would authorize the use of military force against ISIS, Al Qaeda, and the Taliban while repealing use of force authorizations that Congress had enacted into law in 2001 and 2002.[1] Under this authorization for use of military force (AUMF) proposal, the president would be required to tell Congress where the United States was conducting military operations against the designated groups, and Congress would follow an expedited process for modifying or repealing the new AUMF every four years. In announcing the introduction of the legislation, Kaine commented, "For too long, Congress has given Presidents a blank check to wage war. We've let the 9/11 and Iraq War authorizations get stretched to justify wars against multiple terrorist groups in over a dozen countries, from Niger to the Philippines. Our proposal finally repeals those authorizations and makes Congress do its job by weighing in on where, when, and with who we are at war."[2]

The resolution, which was cosponsored by Republican Senators Jeff Flake and Todd Young, as well as Democratic Senators Christopher Coons and Bill Nelson, represented the latest step in a multiyear effort by these and other lawmakers to find middle ground on the scope of presidential war powers in the context of US military operations against ISIS and other armed groups. On one side of this debate, Republican hawks, such as Senator Lindsey Graham and House Armed Services Committee Chairman Mac Thornberry, argued that Congress should give the president an entirely free hand in the conduct of counterterrorism operations overseas. On the other side of the debate, some progressives and libertarians, such as Democratic Representative Barbara Lee and Republican Senator Rand Paul, pressed for major restrictions on US military action with respect to ISIS and other armed groups. Corker, Kaine, and the legislation's other cosponsors sought to thread a needle between these opposing camps by developing a proposal that placed modest limitations on presidential authority to deploy the military for

Bipartisanship and US Foreign Policy. Jordan Tama, Oxford University Press. © Oxford University Press 2024.
DOI: 10.1093/oso/9780197745663.003.0005

counterterrorism operations while institutionalizing a greater congressional oversight role.

A month after introducing the resolution, Corker, as chairman of the Senate Foreign Relations Committee (SFRC), convened an SFRC hearing to discuss it. At the hearing, Corker highlighted how the bipartisan proposal balanced executive branch and congressional prerogatives: "Our legislation gives the administration the flexibility necessary to win this fight while strengthening the rightful and necessary role of Congress."[3] But it quickly became evident that the legislation faced an uphill battle in Congress. Noting that the Constitution gives Congress the power to declare war, Bob Menendez of New Jersey, the committee's senior Democrat, said the extensive leeway granted to the president under the legislation "reverses the roles the Constitution gave to the executive and legislative branches."[4] Other Democrats on the committee, including Ben Cardin of Maryland and Christopher Murphy of Connecticut, joined Rand Paul in arguing along similar lines that the resolution gave too much latitude to the president.[5] The Trump administration, for its part, had indicated that the resolution was unnecessary because the pre-existing 2001 AUMF, which authorized the use of force against any groups responsible for the 9/11 terrorist attacks, provided it with sufficient authorities for military action against ISIS and other terrorist groups.[6] In this context, Corker refrained from pushing for a committee vote on the legislation, and the proposal did not advance in Congress.

In this chapter, I examine the political dynamics associated with efforts to enact AUMF and other war powers legislation after ISIS became widely viewed as a security threat in 2014. Like the debates over intervention in Syria following the Arab Spring, these war powers debates were generally characterized by cross-partisanship in Congress. Democrats and Republicans committed both to intervention against ISIS and to congressional involvement in war powers decisions developed a series of bipartisan proposals to update the 2001 AUMF so that it would directly authorize the use of force against ISIS while giving Congress greater opportunity to object to presidential efforts to expand the scope of US military action against terrorist groups. Yet these proposals faced resistance from other lawmakers in both parties. While many Republicans objected to placing any restrictions on the authority of the commander-in-chief, most Democrats, along with some libertarian Republicans, argued for more substantial limits on the scope of military action.

The argument developed in this book suggests that ideology, advocacy groups, and differing incentives of lawmakers and the president shape political alignments on policy issues. In this chapter, I examine whether and to what extent these factors contributed to cross-partisanship in war powers debates. With respect to ideology, the stronger support of conservatism than of liberalism for military-led approaches to international problems largely explains why most congressional Republicans were more willing than most congressional Democrats to grant the president broad war powers discretion. But libertarianism's skepticism of government authority led some on the right to share the view of progressives that presidential authority to use military force should be sharply restricted, creating the conditions for a strange bedfellows alliance. This alliance was bolstered by a politically diverse set of advocacy groups that favored restrictions on presidential authority. These groups, which included civil liberties and human rights organizations with close ties to Democrats as well as conservative organizations with close links to Republicans, pressed Congress to simply repeal the 2001 AUMF and a separate AUMF that had authorized military action against Iraq in 2002, rather than granting the president any new authority to conduct military operations against terrorist groups.

Institutional prerogatives also contributed to bipartisanship in this case. Whereas presidents sought to preserve their flexibility regarding military action, some lawmakers in both parties argued that Congress had a constitutional responsibility to determine when and in what circumstances the US military is deployed. However, for most lawmakers, this institutional prerogative was outweighed by an electoral calculation that pointed toward congressional passivity—the concern that voting to repeal or replace an AUMF would bring lawmakers more electoral risk than electoral benefit. On the one hand, few voters cared a great deal about this type of legislation, meaning that electoral rewards associated with action on it would be minimal. On the other hand, an AUMF repeal or replacement vote had the potential to attract criticism in the future, depending on how security conditions or military operations subsequently unfolded. As a result of these electoral disincentives to action, both the Obama and Trump presidencies ended with the 2001 and 2002 AUMFs remaining on the books.

Toward the end of the chapter, I briefly examine two other Trump-era war powers debates involving legislative proposals to restrict military intervention in Yemen or against Iran. These debates were also characterized by cross-partisanship, highlighting a broader pattern of contemporary intra-party division over use of force authorizations.

The AUMF debate under Obama

Some US lawmakers had considered repealing or replacing the 2001 AUMF, which authorized the use of force against the perpetrators of the September 11, 2001, attacks and any country that harbored those responsible for those attacks, prior to the rise of ISIS.[7] In 2013, for instance, a bipartisan group of senators, including Corker, Republican Senator John McCain, and Democratic Senators Richard Durbin and Carl Levin, began working on a resolution that would supersede the 2001 AUMF and authorize military action only against Al Qaeda, affiliate groups, or organizations designated by Congress as terrorism supporters.[8] That same year, Democratic Representative Adam Schiff introduced an amendment that would have cut off funding for any activities under the 2001 AUMF at the end of 2014. The House rejected the amendment by a vote of 185-236 in July. In an indication of the cross-partisanship that would continue to mark the AUMF debate in subsequent years, Democrats voted 155-39 in support of the amendment, while Republicans voted 30-197 against it.[9]

Members of Congress renewed debate over AUMF issues following the rise of ISIS. From late 2013 through the summer of 2014, ISIS took over a rapidly growing swath of territory in northern and western Iraq and northeastern Syria. Despite his long-standing reluctance to intervene in the Middle East, President Obama began to respond militarily to these advances in the summer of 2014. On August 7, three years after he had pulled the last of US troops out of Iraq, Obama launched a limited set of airstrikes against ISIS fighters moving on the Kurdish city of Erbil and threatening thousands of members of the Yazidi minority who were stranded on an Iraqi mountaintop.[10]

Obama escalated the scope and intensity of US military action following the videotaped beheading of American journalists James Foley and Steven Sotloff on August 19 and September 2, 2014, respectively. On September 10, Obama announced the beginning of a campaign of airstrikes against ISIS, designed to "degrade, and ultimately destroy," the group.[11] In conjunction with the airstrikes, Obama ordered the deployment of US troops to support efforts by Iraqi and Kurdish allies to fight ISIS on the ground.[12] While the US military effort was initially focused on Iraq, it quickly spread to Syria. The intervention, which President Trump continued, ultimately forced ISIS out of all the territory that it had conquered.

While Obama's intervention against ISIS may have seemed inconsistent with his earlier reluctance to intervene in Syria against Assad, for him there existed a key distinction between intervention against a dictator who threatened his own people but did not threaten Americans and intervention against a group that did endanger Americans. Obama said when making the case for action against ISIS: "If you threaten America, you will find no safe haven."[13] The threat ISIS appeared to pose to the United States also resulted in bipartisan support in Congress and among the American public for intervention against the group.[14] Opinion polls from the fall of 2014 showed that Americans backed US airstrikes against ISIS militants in Iraq and Syria by margins of about two to one.[15] On Capitol Hill, even Democratic Socialist Senator Bernie Sanders, who had opposed nearly all US military interventions during his career, said he supported airstrikes in this case.[16]

Approving an AUMF focused on ISIS would prove to be much more contentious, however. In a reflection of the common presidential desire to preserve freedom of action in foreign policy, the Obama administration argued that it did not need direct authorization from Congress for military action against ISIS. In congressional testimony soon after the launch of US airstrikes against ISIS, Secretary of State John Kerry said the administration would "welcome" updating the 2001 AUMF but argued that the 2001 AUMF provided the administration with sufficient authority for the military campaign because ISIS began as an offshoot of Al Qaeda.[17]

However, some lawmakers in both parties argued that a new AUMF was needed to give the president the authority for a long-term military campaign against ISIS.[18] In a September 2014 letter to House leaders, a bipartisan group of 12 representatives led by Democrat Jim McGovern and Republican Tom Cole wrote: "The time has come to take up and debate an authorization regarding US military operations in Iraq. We believe such a debate and vote is required, will enhance our national security and the ability of Congress and the Executive to carry out US foreign and defense policies abroad."[19]

In the Senate, Tim Kaine introduced a resolution the same month that would authorize air strikes against ISIS and provide military support to forces fighting ISIS for a period of one year while repealing the 2002 AUMF immediately and repealing the 2001 AUMF in two years.[20] In a speech making the case for his proposal, Kaine, who emerged as a leader of efforts to enact a new AUMF in just his second year in the Senate, linked his commitment to the issue to a strong personal concern with preserving a congressional role in use of force decisions: "People come into elected office with passions and interests, and I have many. But I have one obsession, and this is it . . . how the nation makes a decision to go to war and what are the right processes that would engage Congress, the President and the American public—it is an obsession of mine, and I'm going to be focused on it as long as I'm blessed to be here."[21]

Other lawmakers in both parties also argued that Congress should act. Bob Menendez, the Democratic chairman of the SFRC, commented, "The 9/11 AUMF was adopted to counter Al Qaeda in the wake of the September 11 attacks. . . . I do not believe that it provides the authority to pursue a new enemy in different countries under completely different circumstances than existed 13 years ago."[22] Republican Senator Jeff Flake said, "I hope that the administration will . . . ask firmly for an AUMF, and I hope Congress gives it."[23] In a later interview, Flake, who served for several years as Kaine's principal partner on the issue, evoked the same sense of institutional responsibility emphasized by Kaine:

> The 2001 AUMF brought the country together. It let our troops know we were behind them and let our allies and adversaries know that the commander-in-chief and Congress were together. But then these wars started to morph into something different and it became clear to me that we needed a new template that gave Congress a role but didn't unnecessarily tie the hands of the executive. Without skin in the game, Congress is far more likely to just complain about what the president is doing, rather than taking responsibility. That's why a bipartisan AUMF is so important.[24]

However, many other members of Congress in both parties were reluctant to vote on a new AUMF because of the electoral risks associated with such a vote. Whereas voting for a new AUMF would place lawmakers on record in support of military action that might go awry, voting against a new AUMF would open lawmakers to potential criticism that they had failed to protect the country from terrorism.[25] Republican Representative Jack Kingston said of his colleagues, "A lot of people would like to stay on the sideline and say, 'Just bomb the place and tell us about it later. We can denounce it if it goes bad, and praise it if it goes well and ask what took [Obama] so long.'"[26] Recognizing the electoral risks associated with the issue, Democratic and

Republican congressional leaders sought to avoid having an AUMF resolution brought to the floor of the House or Senate.[27]

In addition to the reluctance of many lawmakers to go on record on the AUMF issue, efforts to enact a new AUMF ran up against disagreements among lawmakers regarding an authorization's potential scope and limitations. In December 2014, the SFRC considered a proposal by Menendez for an AUMF that would authorize the use of force against ISIS for three years (such a legislative time limit is known as a "sunset provision") while prohibiting ground combat operations against the group.[28] The proposed resolution also repealed the 2002 AUMF and terminated the 2001 AUMF after three years. In debating it, most Democrats on the committee voiced support for its prohibition on ground troops and three-year sunset provision. For instance, Democrat Chris Coons argued that while ISIS is a "real and present threat to the United States and our allies in the region," Congress should not "write another blank check for war."[29]

However, most Republicans on the committee argued that Menendez's proposal was too restrictive. Republican John Barrasso commented, "Congress should either be authorizing the use of force or not authorizing force. Congress should not try to micromanage a war through an authorization."[30] The Obama administration, meanwhile, joined Republicans in expressing opposition to the prohibition on the use of ground troops, arguing that Congress should not "preemptively bind the hands of the Commander in Chief or our commanders in the field in responding to scenarios and contingencies that are impossible to foresee."[31]

The SFRC approved Menendez's proposal on a 10-8 party line vote in December 2014.[32] This vote would likely have broken less sharply along partisan lines were it not for the impending shift in Senate control from the Democrats to the Republicans in January 2015, which gave Democrats an incentive to back an authorization that was more restrictive than what Republicans would likely advance when they gained control of the chamber and gave Republicans an incentive to delay Senate action until that time.[33] With the House under Republican control, the bill nevertheless had little chance of being enacted into law, and Senate leaders did not bring it to the floor before the end of the 113th Congress.

However, the committee's activity on the issue and the calls by many lawmakers for a new AUMF led the administration to begin engaging more directly with lawmakers and their staffs in an effort to develop an AUMF that could attract bipartisan support and be acceptable to the administration. An

Obama administration legislative affairs official recalled, "There was a constant refrain from the Hill, 'We want to see a request for AUMF legislation.' We were responsive to that."[34]

Accordingly, the White House engaged senior staff in the offices of Democratic and Republican congressional leaders in an extensive set of discussions about a new AUMF in late 2014 and early 2015.[35] A former Obama administration official recounted:

> We had serious discussions with them about what a new AUMF might look like, what sort of authorities should go in there, when it would expire, any geographic limits. Then we started talking about what each caucus could stomach. On the Republican side, they thought that under no circumstance should an AUMF tie the president's hands in any way. Their ulterior motive was that [Obama's] not going to be president forever and the next "tough" Republican president is really going to fight these guys, so we want to be able to let him off the leash. . . . On the Democratic side, it was a rehashing of the lessons learned from the Iraq war and 2001 AUMF. They wanted a clear sunset, geographic limits, or else—and their ulterior motive was that the next Republican president is going to go "ape shit" and get us into an endless war.[36]

A Democratic congressional aide involved in some of these discussions recalled similarly, "Republicans said, 'You can't tie the hands of the commander-in-chief.' They were closer to the White House on this in many ways than Democrats were. Democrats wanted explicit provisions that would limit the deployment of ground forces, but we weren't in agreement among ourselves. There were ten different ways we were talking to the White House."[37]

Following these interbranch consultations, Obama issued his own proposal for a new AUMF in February 2015.[38] The proposed resolution authorized the use of force against ISIS and associated forces, prohibited "enduring offensive ground combat operations," expired after three years, repealed the 2002 AUMF, and did not repeal the 2001 AUMF.[39] The proposal was less constraining than that of Menendez, particularly by allowing ground combat operations that were not enduring and offensive and in leaving the 2001 AUMF on the books indefinitely.

As a result of these looser restrictions on military action, Flake, who had voted against Menendez's resolution, voiced support for Obama's proposal, adding: "I think we need to value . . . language that can get a good bipartisan majority. . . . In this body, we never get everything we want. So I commend the administration for coming forward, for listening to us on this committee as this AUMF was formulated, and for consulting and listening to others as well."[40] However, most Republicans on Capitol Hill said the proposal was still too restrictive.[41] House Armed Services Committee Chairman Mac Thornberry expressed the prevailing Republican view: "We already put too many encumbrances on our troops in carrying out the missions they are assigned, in my opinion, so going into battle with a lawyer nearby to decide whether a particular action is enduring or offensive or a ground combat operation seems problematic."[42]

Yet Obama's proposal attracted little support from Democrats. In one exception, Eliot Engel, a relatively hawkish Democrat, spoke positively about the proposal: "The language sent to us by the President with the AUMF isn't perfect, but I believe it's a good start. So let's work together to craft a bipartisan AUMF."[43] But most other Democrats said the proposal left the president with excessive discretion. Menendez and Cardin expressed concern that the proposal's prohibition of "enduring offensive ground combat operations" was vague and could still allow the deployment of large numbers of US troops to the Middle East.[44]

In June 2015, Kaine and Flake, in an effort to advance a bipartisan approach, introduced an AUMF resolution that was similar in most respects to Obama's proposal, but it replaced the "enduring offensive ground combat operations" language with a provision stating that the use of "significant United States ground troops" was not consistent with the authorization's purpose.[45] But Corker, who had become chairman of the SFRC at the beginning of 2015, did not bring the resolution forward for a vote in the committee, at least in part out of concern that there did not exist sufficient support in the Senate for the legislation to advance further.[46]

Some House members also continued to push for action to no avail. Soon after the Obama administration announced steps in October 2015 that represented an escalation of the US military campaign against ISIS, including an increase in the intensity of airstrikes and the deployment of special operations forces into Syria, a group of 17 Democratic and 18 Republican representatives led by Jim McGovern and Tom Cole sent a letter to Speaker of the House Paul Ryan urging him to schedule a House debate on an AUMF. The lawmakers highlighted institutional prerogatives in making the case for such a debate, writing: "We do not share the same policy prescriptions for US military engagement in the region, but we do share the belief that it is past time for Congress to fulfill its obligations under the Constitution and vote on an AUMF that clearly delineates the authority and limits, if any, on US military engagement in Iraq, Syria, and the surrounding region."[47] In response, Ryan charged House Majority Leader Kevin McCarthy and House Foreign Affairs Committee Chairman Ed Royce with gauging the prospects for advancing a new AUMF, but these discussions did not result in any legislative action.[48] A Democratic congressional aide observed that House Republican leaders had little political incentive to bring AUMF legislation forward with Obama in the White House: "They were in a position where they could shit all over the president, saying he didn't have a strategy [for defeating ISIS] and lacked leadership, but in no way have to own the campaign."[49]

The AUMF debate under Trump

For all the differences between Obama and Trump, the AUMF debate did not change much under the new president, who continued the US military campaign against ISIS. Kaine and Flake renewed their efforts to develop bipartisan agreement on a new AUMF, but Congress remained split on the issue, and most lawmakers still had more electoral incentive to neglect than to prioritize the issue. At the same time, progressive Democrats and libertarian Republicans joined together to seek a simple repeal of the earlier AUMFs. This repeal effort gained some momentum early in Trump's presidency, though it also failed to attract enough support to be enacted into law. In 2019 and 2020, however, a confluence of external events, including growing concern in both parties about actions by Saudi Arabia and the possibility that Trump might bring the United States into a new war in the Middle East, fueled new bipartisan war powers efforts, as the Democratic-led House and Republican-led Senate approved resolutions restricting the president's authority to take military action in Yemen or Iran.

In May 2017, Flake and Kaine introduced a new version of their proposal, which superseded the 2001 and 2002 AUMFs by authorizing the use of force against Al Qaeda, the Taliban, ISIS, and associated forces for five years while establishing a process through which Congress could reject any presidential plans to expand the scope of military action geographically or in terms of the groups being targeted.[50] At an SFRC hearing, Flake argued that the proposal represented an effort to strike a balance between executive and legislative prerogatives.[51] A few other committee members in both parties, including Democrat Christopher Coons and Republican Todd Young, also spoke favorably about the proposal. Young commented that US troops in the field "need to know that the American people through their elected representatives have their backs."[52]

But even if a new AUMF passed the Senate, the prospects for passing it in the House were dim. In June 2017, Engel, the senior Democrat on the House Foreign Affairs Committee, issued a discussion draft of a new AUMF that, like the Kaine-Flake proposal, staked out a middle ground on the issue.[53] The draft authorized for three years military action against ISIS without any geographic restriction, including the use of ground troops in limited operations, but it required presidential reporting to Congress on any more expansive use of ground troops and established an expedited congressional process for rejecting such presidential plans for the broader use of ground troops.[54] However, Engel could not attract much support for his approach from colleagues in either party. On the one hand, congressional Democrats generally favored greater restrictions than Engel envisioned.[55] On the other hand, most congressional Republicans maintained that any new AUMF should not restrict presidential flexibility at all. At a House Foreign Affairs Committee hearing in July 2017, Representative Adam Kinzinger argued that any new AUMF should place "no limitation on what the President can do because that makes us Commander in Chief."[56]

Yet there also continued to be cross-partisanship on AUMF issues in the House. As the House Appropriations Committee considered a defense appropriations bill in June 2017, Representative Barbara Lee, a progressive Democrat, introduced an amendment to repeal the 2001 AUMF within eight months. The amendment replicated a bill Lee had introduced in each Congress since 2010, which stated that the 2001 AUMF "has been used to justify a broad and open-ended authorization for the use of military force and such an interpretation is inconsistent with the authority of Congress to declare war."[57]

During the committee's debate over the amendment, several Republicans on the committee endorsed it based on their view that Congress had an institutional responsibility to debate and authorize military action against ISIS directly. For instance, Representative Scott Taylor, a former Navy SEAL, commented, "I think we've seen a disproportionate sacrifice with the military community. . . . And I believe that we owe them the [AUMF] debate."[58] Similarly, Republican Chris Stewart, a former Air Force officer, said that members of the military "notice that we don't have the courage to debate this and to give them the authority to go [to war]."[59] Notably, this view was at odds with the Trump administration's position that the 2001 AUMF gave it all the authority it needed to carry out US military operations against ISIS. A House Republican foreign policy aide observed: "The Trump White House had zero interest in any AUMF debate. They said they want no endless wars, but they love having the authority to use special forces."[60] Nevertheless, prodded by Lee and the House Republican military veterans calling for repeal, the Republican-led committee approved the Lee amendment by voice vote.

But the Republican leadership of the GOP-controlled House prevented Lee's amendment from advancing further, stripping it from the appropriations bill before the legislation went to the House floor.[61] Speaker of the House Paul Ryan commented, "An appropriations bill I don't think is the right way to deal with [the AUMF issue]. What matters to me is that we don't undercut the military."[62] A Democratic congressional aide bemoaned, "At the [House Republican] leadership level, they don't want their members lining up against the Trump White House in an AUMF debate."[63]

Around the same time, the Senate considered an amendment to the National Defense Authorization Act introduced by Rand Paul that would repeal the 2001 and 2002 AUMFs in six months.[64] On the Senate floor, Paul argued: "Realize that, if we do not force these authorizations to expire, this war could go on forever."[65] Paul and several Democratic supporters of the amendment, including Senators Ben Cardin and Christopher Murphy, argued that repealing the earlier AUMFs would force Congress to debate and vote on a new AUMF tailored to current threats. Emphasizing the constitutional responsibilities of lawmakers, Murphy added, "It is very easy for the US Congress to just step back and say that authorizing military force is too hard. . . . That is not what the Founding Fathers imagined."[66]

But other members of both parties sharply criticized Paul's amendment. Republican Senator John McCain said, "Repealing the 2001 and 2002 AUMFs without simultaneously passing a new authorization would be premature, it would be irresponsible, it would threaten US national security."[67] Democratic Senator Jack Reed argued similarly, "Without [a new] AUMF, we are going to cause confusion and we are going to cause disruption among our forces and our allies."[68] In September 2017, the Senate rejected Paul's amendment by a vote of 36-61, with 33 Democrats and 3 Republicans voting for it and 48 Republicans and 13 Democrats voting against it.[69] This vote underscored the persistence of cross-partisanship on the AUMF issue, as well as the difficulty of marshaling a majority in support of any particular legislative option.

The Senate's rejection of Paul's amendment also suggested that the Flake-Kaine proposal represented the best prospect for advancing AUMF legislation. At an October 2017 SFRC hearing on the issue, Secretary of State Rex Tillerson and Secretary of Defense Jim Mattis reiterated the Trump administration's position that a new AUMF was unnecessary but said that if Congress did seek to approve a new AUMF, it must ensure that the new AUMF not have any time limits, geographic constraints, or restrictions on the use of ground troops.[70] Some Republicans on the committee strongly endorsed this administration view. For instance, Senator Ron Johnson noted that Congress did not place any restrictions on the use of force when it declared war against Germany and Japan in World War II, and he argued that Congress should not do so with respect to terrorist groups either.[71] But Flake challenged the administration's unwillingness to accept any temporal restrictions on military action, observing that the lack of any sunset provision in the 2001 AUMF had enabled that authorization to still be serving as the basis for US military actions 16 years later.[72]

Subsequently, Corker sought to accommodate the administration by developing a new resolution that largely mirrored the Flake-Kaine proposal but dropped its sunset provision, instead just creating a process for a quadrennial congressional review of the use of force authorization.[73] Nevertheless, after Corker introduced the new bipartisan resolution with Senators Kaine, Flake, Coons, Young, and Bill Nelson in April 2018, the administration reacted coolly to it, simply commenting that a new AUMF was not needed.[74] The proposal also generated criticism from many Senate Democrats for not adequately restraining presidential authority. For instance, Chris Murphy argued that its authorization was "over-broad," and Ben Cardin stated that any new AUMF must have a sunset provision.[75] In this context, Corker opted not to bring the resolution forward for a committee vote before he resigned from the Senate at the end of 2018. In an interview, Corker commented: "We expended a lot of effort trying to modify the 2001 AUMF. On the Republican side, this was tough because Republicans were generally happy with the policies that were being carried out—using military force to deal with ISIS and Al Qaeda. On the Democratic side, this was tough because Democrats were unwilling to allow the kind of flexibility an administration needs to be able to react quickly to evolving circumstances."[76]

Public and elite opinion

Public opinion only weakly constrained the positions of members of Congress in the AUMF debates discussed in this chapter and offered lawmakers little incentive to prioritize the issue.[77] In a series of polls, majorities of Democrats and Republicans among the American public consistently backed the use of force against ISIS, though Republicans favored more aggressive action than Democrats. Despite this broad support for intervention against ISIS, voters in both parties considered AUMF legislation a low priority.

Most Democratic and Republican members of the public supported military action against ISIS under both Obama and Trump. During the Obama administration, an average of 68% of Republicans and 62% of Democrats said they supported the US military campaign against ISIS across five Pew polls.[78] Nine months into Donald Trump's presidency, the percentage of Republicans supporting the campaign increased further, to 82%, while 63% of Democrats continued to back the campaign.[79] (See Table 5.1.)

Yet a left-right split was evident in the extent to which Democrats and Republicans favored more aggressive action against ISIS. Upward of 60% of Republicans supported the use of ground troops in the fight against ISIS, while only about 30% of Democrats backed that approach (see Table 5.2.) This difference was consistent with the general tendency of conservatives to be more hawkish than liberals.[80]

There was less polling regarding public attitudes on the AUMF dimension of the US approach to ISIS, most likely because the issue was less salient.

Table 5.1 Public approval of military campaign against ISIS

Survey date	Democrats approving	Democrats disapproving	Republicans approving	Republicans disapproving
October 2014	54%	36%	68%	24%
February 2015	58%	N/A	71%	N/A
July 2015	64%	N/A	67%	N/A
December 2015	67%	N/A	69%	N/A
April 2016	65%	28%	66%	30%
October 2017	63%	N/A	82%	N/A

Note: The table presents data from all public opinion surveys by the Pew Research Center conducted between October 2014 and December 2020 that asked the following question: "Overall, do you approve or disapprove of the US military campaign against Islamic militants in Iraq and Syria?" Table entries indicating "N/A" represent survey results that Pew did not report.

WAR POWERS AUTHORITIES   107

Table 5.2 Public opinion on use of ground troops against ISIS

Survey date	Democrats favoring	Democrats opposing	Republicans favoring	Republicans opposing
October 2014	28%	66%	57%	39%
July 2015	31%	63%	63%	32%
December 2015	33%	64%	66%	28%
April 2016	31%	65%	68%	28%

Note: The table presents data from all public opinion surveys by the Pew Research Center conducted between October 2014 and December 2020 that asked the following question: "Would you favor or oppose the US sending ground troops to fight Islamic militants in Iraq and Syria?"

During the Obama and Trump presidencies, I found only three surveys that asked whether respondents favored the approval of an AUMF against ISIS. Two of these were conducted in February 2015, shortly after Obama had sent his AUMF proposal to Congress. One of these surveys, by NBC News/Marist, described Obama's proposal in some detail and then asked respondents whether they wanted their member of Congress to vote for or against it. Sixty percent of Democrats and 52% of Republicans said they wanted their representative to vote for it.[81] The second, by CBS News, simply asked respondents whether Congress should authorize the use of force against ISIS. Seventy-one percent of Democrats and 65% of Republicans said yes.[82]

The third survey was conducted by Morning Consult during the Trump administration in October 2017. This survey presented respondents with four options regarding an AUMF. Among Democratic respondents, 27% favored passing a new AUMF, 33% favored allowing the 2001 AUMF to remain, 14% favored revoking any AUMF, and 26% said they didn't know or had no opinion. Among Republican respondents, 33% favored passing a new AUMF, 43% favored allowing the 2001 AUMF to remain, 4% favored revoking any AUMF, and 20% said they didn't know or had no opinion.[83]

While the first two surveys might suggest that members of Congress would have an incentive to vote for an AUMF against ISIS, this third survey reveals that much of the public had weak preferences on the issue and that, when presented with options other than just approving a new AUMF or doing nothing, there did not exist majority support for any single option. This dispersal of opinion underscores the challenge lawmakers faced trying to generate consensus around any particular approach to the issue. At the same time, the sizable percentage of respondents saying they didn't know or lacked an opinion suggests that much of the public was not following the AUMF debate closely.

Indeed, congressional officials involved in the AUMF debate felt little public pressure to take action. Jeff Flake observed about the debate in 2017: "Members of Congress are not feeling the heat. The lack of [congressional] backbone is simply a function of 'you're not hearing it from your constituents, and so you can afford to just let it go.' "[84] Ilan Goldenberg, who was involved in the debate as director of the Middle East Security Program at the Center for a New American Security, bemoaned in a 2018 interview: "We can't get the public or members of Congress excited about [AUMF legislation]. So even if it gets out of committee, it's unlikely we can get it on the floor."[85]

Moreover, lawmakers faced political risks if they did vote on the issue. A senior House Republican aide who handled the issue said in an interview: "There were members who didn't want to vote on the record on this because they saw how the previous [2002 Iraq] AUMF was used as a campaign issue. They wanted to be silent on this or just criticize the previous AUMF."[86] Tommy Ross, who served as a senior defense and intelligence advisor to Senate Majority Leader Harry Reid, commented in a similar vein: "[The AUMF debate] is a conversation that needs to be had, and nobody wants to have it because it's too hard politically. Because who is going to go back to their constituents and say, 'Yeah, I'm going to authorize war in 16 different countries.' "[87]

While many foreign policy elites had stronger preferences about the issue, their attitudes on it also broke down partly, but not entirely, along left-right lines. Prominent conservative hawks argued against restricting the authority of the commander-in-chief.[88] By contrast, progressive experts urged repealing the earlier AUMFs or cautioned against enacting a new AUMF that would hand war-making authority to the president.[89] Progressives were joined in expressing this point of view by libertarian intellectuals, whose small government philosophy led them to favor restrictions on presidential power.[90] In a reflection of this ideological alignment of progressives and libertarians on war powers issues, some members of the House, led by Democrat Ro Khanna and Republican Andy Biggs, formed in 2019 a new War Powers Caucus with the mission of "restoring Congress's constitutionally-mandated authority over matters of war and peace."[91] Noting how far apart he and Khanna were on many other issues, Biggs commented of their partnership on war powers: "Sometimes you go all the way around the circle."[92] At the same time, some Trump-aligned conservatives who are not necessarily libertarians have also backed AUMF repeal. Reid Smith, director for Foreign Policy at Stand Together, which has advocated for repeal, commented: "Trump slaughtered some sacred cows when he attacked Jeb Bush for his brother's interventionism. . . . Many of the Republicans who support repeal are the iconoclasts within the party."[93]

Advocacy group activity

The interest group landscape also provided lawmakers with little incentive to enact a new AUMF and made compromise on the issue more difficult, but advocacy groups helped forge the cross-partisan coalitions in Congress that pushed for restrictions on presidential authority. While the AUMF debate was characterized by relatively limited advocacy, those groups that did engage Congress tended to advocate major restrictions, rather than the kind of modest constraints contained in proposals advanced by lawmakers such as Kaine, Flake, and Corker. This context was not conducive to advancing measures designed to balance congressional and presidential prerogatives but provided an added impetus to lawmakers who favored greater constraints on military action. Jamil Jaffer, who handled the issue as a senior SFRC aide to Corker, said, "The positions taken by the antiwar groups were untenable in Congress, except for some very liberal Democrats and very libertarian Republicans. You had little room in the middle for a consensus view that would have combined presidential authority with some restrictions on the use of force."[94]

A variety of human rights, civil liberties, antiwar, libertarian, and conservative groups urged Congress to repeal the 2001 and 2002 AUMFs and if a new AUMF were enacted, ensure that it sharply circumscribed the president's use of force authority. For instance, after Obama proposed a new AUMF in February 2015, the American Civil Liberties Union, Friends Committee on National Legislation, MoveOn.org, Win Without War, and other progressive groups issued statements opposing the proposal on the grounds that it gave the president too much leeway for waging war.[95] In a representative comment, the antiwar group Peace Action stated, "While we oppose any AUMF because the war is not working, we encourage members of Congress to push for tighter restrictions than what President Obama proposes should an AUMF move forward."[96]

These and other like-minded groups continued to advocate scaling back the president's use of force authority after Trump took office. For example, as senators were developing new AUMF proposals in 2017, 10 organizations with missions focused on human rights, civil liberties, or government accountability wrote a letter to senators stating that "vague and overbroad war authorizations undermine accountability, frustrate effective oversight, invite mission creep, and risk embroiling the nation in unauthorized or perpetual wars that threaten human rights and the rule of law."[97] After Corker and Kaine introduced their revised AUMF proposal in 2018, an expanded group of 23 organizations sharply criticized the proposal in a new letter to senators, arguing that the proposal would "cede breathtaking and unnecessary powers to the president" and urging Congress instead to "meaningfully rein in the Executive Branch's misuse of the 2001 and 2002 AUMFs."[98] Rita Siemion of Human Rights First also testified to Congress in opposition to the Corker-Kaine proposal, arguing that the proposal would make it easy for the president to place the United States at war with a large array of groups.[99] Some left-leaning think tanks, including the Center for American Progress and New America, advocated for the repeal of the earlier AUMFs or cautioned against enacting a new AUMF on similar grounds.[100]

Organizations committed to libertarian and small-government principles joined in some of this advocacy, forming a strange bedfellows coalition with groups on the left. The Charles Koch Institute, committed to limited government, asserted that Congress's unwillingness to mandate restrictions on presidential war-making authority had allowed "the staggering expansion of executive powers and the calcification of a permanent war posture, unbound by spatial or temporal boundaries."[101] Freedom Works, which promotes lower taxes and a smaller government, signed the 2018 letter opposing the Corker-Kaine proposal mentioned above. Some conservative organizations have also supported veterans groups, such as Concerned Veterans for America, that favor restricting US military involvement overseas.[102]

In an effort to amplify their influence, many of the left-leaning and right-leaning pro-repeal groups have cooperated on advocacy strategy. Heather Brandon-Smith, the legislative director for Militarism and Human Rights at the Quaker-affiliated Friends Committee on National Legislation, noted: "It's been easy to work across ideological boundaries. I think there is also a recognition that a broad array of backgrounds and perspectives is needed if we're going to be successful. If it was just a bunch of progressive groups lobbying on the issue, we wouldn't have gotten this far."[103]

At the same time, some experts outside government sought to build consensus in support of a new AUMF. Notably, a group of Democratic and Republican national security law experts agreed on guiding principles for a new AUMF that represented a middle ground between the proposals of progressives and hawks. These principles—outlined in several articles and blog posts—called for including a sunset provision and requirements for executive branch reporting to Congress, but not for restrictions on the use of ground troops.[104] While these experts were highly respected among national security and legal professionals, they lacked the political influence necessary to overcome the countervailing headwinds described above.

Lobbying data also illustrate how the advocacy landscape was unfavorable to approval of a new AUMF. Among the five legislative proposals for a new AUMF considered by Congress between 2014 and 2018 and discussed in this chapter, the Open Secrets lobbying database indicates that only the American Civil Liberties Union, Human Rights First, Friends Committee on National Legislation, and Project on Government Oversight engaged in direct lobbying in connection with any of the proposals.[105] Notably, these organizations, which seek to promote civil liberties, human rights, peace, and government accountability, all opposed the new AUMF proposals on the grounds that they did not sharply circumscribe presidential use of force authority.[106] The lack of any direct lobbying in support of the AUMF proposals suggests that lawmakers did not experience much pressure to enact the legislation.

Indeed, congressional staff noted in interviews that there was little pressure from groups for Congress to act on the AUMF issue. A Democratic congressional aide involved in the issue commented in 2017: "A lot of groups want any AUMF to have constraints on the president, but they're not advocating directly for an AUMF. They're just saying that if Congress does pass an AUMF, it should have these constraints. No one is asking us to pass this."[107]

The Yemen and Iran war powers debates

While some lawmakers continued to press for repealing or replacing the 2001 and 2002 AUMFs during the latter part of the Trump administration, congressional activity on war powers became more focused then on legislative efforts to prohibit US military action in Yemen and Iran. I briefly recap these debates here to show that cross-partisanship marked them too. However, as with the earlier repeal or replace debates, congressional Democrats were generally more willing than congressional Republicans to constrain the president in these cases. This pattern reflected both the stronger opposition of most liberals than of most conservatives to military action abroad as well as the differing partisan incentives facing lawmakers under a Republican president.

Restricting the use of force in Yemen

In 2015, the United States had begun providing military support to a coalition of Persian Gulf countries led by Saudi Arabia that were waging war in Yemen against Houthi rebels aligned with Iran. These military contributions included intelligence sharing, logistical support, weapons sales, and midair refueling of warplanes.[108] By 2018, widespread civilian casualties and a growing humanitarian catastrophe caused by the bombing and blockade of Yemen by the Saudi-led coalition triggered growing congressional concern about the war. In February 2018, a motley crew of three senators—Democratic Socialist Bernie Sanders, libertarian Republican Mike Lee, and progressive Democrat Chris Murphy—introduced a resolution directing the removal within 30 days of US armed forces from hostilities in Yemen, except for forces engaged in operations against Al Qaeda or its associates. The resolution also specified that "hostilities" included in-flight refueling of aircraft conducting missions over Yemen.[109]

Debate on the Sanders-Lee-Murphy resolution broke down along similar lines as the ISIS AUMF debate, encountering resistance from most, but not all, Republicans and support from most, but not all, Democrats. Senate Majority Leader Mitch McConnell argued that withdrawing US support would increase the risk of civilian casualties in Yemen and "signal that we are not serious about containing Iran or its proxies."[110] Bob Menendez, the top Democrat on the SFRC, commented similarly that withdrawal of military support would weaken US influence over the conflict in Yemen, while allowing Iran "to expand its proxy power."[111] In March 2018, the Senate voted to table the Sanders-Lee-Murphy resolution by a vote of 55-44, with 45 Republicans and 10 Democrats voting against taking up the resolution, and 39 Democrats and five Republicans voting for the Senate to consider it.[112]

The resolution gained new life, however, after the killing by the Saudi government of Jamal Khashoggi in October 2018, which intensified congressional concerns in both parties about the behavior of Saudi Crown Prince Mohammed bin Salman (commonly known as MBS). Reid Smith, who has overseen foreign policy initiatives and advocacy at the Charles Koch Institute and Stand Together since 2016, observed: "There was a visceral reaction by many members of Congress after the assassination of Khashoggi that perhaps our partners in Saudi Arabia weren't the best partners for us."[113]

In this context, support rose for cutting off US military involvement in the Yemen war, as well as for taking other steps to convey US dissatisfaction with Saudi Arabia, such as sanctioning officials responsible for Khashoggi's death and cutting off arms sales to Saudi Arabia.[114] In December, the Senate approved the same Sanders-Lee-Murphy resolution by a vote of 56-41, with seven Republicans joining all Democrats in support of the measure.[115] Jeff Flake, one of the senators who had voted to table the resolution in March but voted for it in December, explained the shift in an interview two days before the latter vote: "There is information coming out of that war that you just can't ignore—that our involvement is not what was claimed, is not making the war more humane. And then you pair that with the bloom coming off of the rose of MBS."[116] In a reference to the Constitution, Flake added, "And I do think there are more Republicans who are seeing the importance of the article one branch reasserting itself."[117]

Although the Republican-controlled House did not act on the resolution before the end of the 2017–2018 Congress, Sanders, Lee, and Murphy reintroduced it at the beginning of 2019.[118] In March, the Senate approved it by a vote of 54-46, with seven Republicans again joining all Democrats in support of it.[119] In April, the now Democratic-controlled House approved it by a vote of 247-175, with 16 Republicans joining all Democrats to send the legislation to Trump.[120] Trump subsequently vetoed the resolution, accompanying his rejection with a forceful defense of presidential prerogatives: "This resolution is an unnecessary, dangerous attempt to weaken my constitutional authorities, endangering the lives of American citizens and brave service members, both today and in the future."[121] In May, the Senate failed to override the veto, with the same seven Republicans joining all Democrats in support of the override—leaving the effort well short of the two-thirds supermajority needed for it.[122]

Although proponents of ending the war in Yemen were unable to achieve enactment of the resolution, legislative efforts on the issue were still consequential. As the resolution and other legislative proposals to distance the United States from Saudi Arabia gained momentum in Congress in late 2018, the Trump administration announced that the United States would no longer refuel Saudi or other aircraft involved in the war. Congress later cemented this policy shift by enacting a law prohibiting in-flight refueling of any aircraft involved in hostilities in Yemen.[123] The congressional pressure may also have influenced a 2019 decision by the United Arab Emirates to restrict its military involvement in Yemen.[124]

Restricting the use of force against Iran

Yet another war powers debate occurred as the United States and Iran engaged in a tit-for-tat series of aggressive actions following Trump's 2018 withdrawal from the Joint Comprehensive Plan of Action with Iran (which I discuss in detail in Chapter 7). Based on concern that the two countries might approach the brink of war, in July 2019 the House approved an amendment introduced by Democratic Representative Ro Khanna, a leading progressive, and Republican Representative Matt Gaetz, a staunch conservative, that prohibited the use of federal funds for any use of military force in or against Iran unless Congress authorized the military action. Twenty-seven Republicans joined 223 Democrats in voting for the amendment, while seven Democrats joined 163 Republicans in voting against it.[125] But Senate Republicans opposed to the measure blocked it from being enacted into law at the end of 2019.[126]

Lawmakers revived this effort after Trump ordered the killing of Qasem Soleimani, head of the Iranian Revolutionary Guards' Quds Force, in January 2020. Ryan Costello, policy director of the National Iranian American Council, which advocated for legislation prohibiting military action against Iran, recalled of this period, "When we went to congressional offices, we were knocking on an open door. Many people on Capitol Hill thought Trump was nuts and were worried that he would go to war."[127]

Tim Kaine took the lead in marshaling bipartisan support for a new resolution that would prohibit military action against Iran.[128] In February, eight Senate Republicans joined all Senate Democrats in voting for Kaine's proposal to prohibit the use of force against Iran "or any part of its government or military" unless authorized by Congress.[129] The following month, the House approved the measure, with all but six Democrats voting for it and all but six Republicans voting against it.[130]

Remarkably, this was just the second time that Congress had acted under the 1973 War Powers Resolution to prohibit a president from using military force.[131] The first time was the previous year, when Congress had passed the aforementioned resolution restricting the president's authority to take military action in Yemen.[132] As he had done with the Yemen resolution, Trump vetoed the Iran measure. Seven Senate Republicans then joined all Democrats in an unsuccessful effort to achieve the two-thirds majority needed to override the president's veto.[133]

Although this veto override effort failed, the resolution's approval by both chambers of Congress had clearly signaled that there existed little appetite in Congress for a war with Iran—a signal that might, despite Trump's veto of the legislation, have led Trump to think twice before taking any additional military steps against Iran. Kaine noted, "Our feeling is when Congress stands up and acts . . . even if he chooses to veto it and we can't override, the will of both bodies and the public that they represent, that is something that could well be a factor in his decision-making."[134]

Conclusion

Overall, congressional war powers debates under Obama and Trump further illustrate the prevalence of cross-partisanship in foreign policy and show how cross-partisanship is facilitated when an issue is not highly salient and does not pit party-affiliated groups against each other. Bipartisan coalitions could form in the debates to repeal or replace the 2001 and 2002 AUMFs in part because they carried relatively low political stakes and the advocacy landscape associated with them itself brought together strange bedfellows. However, the greater hawkishness of most conservatives than of most liberals made it very difficult to forge broad consensus across the two parties.

The dogged efforts of some lawmakers in both parties during these years to restrict presidential war-making authority also highlight the institutional concerns about congressional prerogatives that can contribute to inter-branch clashes on foreign policy. But the war powers debates show too how institutional prerogatives can be outweighed by electoral concerns in congressional decision-making. For the vast majority of lawmakers, who did not place a high priority on the protection of congressional war powers, the electoral risks associated with AUMF votes made them content to leave the president in the driver's seat when it came to military action against ISIS and other terrorist groups.

6

Sanctions on Russia

As a presidential candidate in 2016, Donald Trump repeatedly called for more cooperation between the United States and Russia.[1] After being elected that year, he suggested that he was thinking about lifting sanctions on Russia, which included an array of penalties that the Obama administration and Congress had imposed in response to Russian human rights violations, aggression in Ukraine, and interference in the election. Shortly before his January 2017 inauguration, Trump told a reporter: "Let's see if we can make some good deals with Russia . . . Russia's hurting very badly right now because of sanctions, but I think something can happen that a lot of people are gonna benefit."[2] Soon after Trump took office, the White House directed agencies to prepare plans for removing sanctions on Russia, and National Security Council officials informed congressional staff that the administration was getting ready to lift all of them.[3]

Trump's plans prompted strong bipartisan pushback from lawmakers. In a characteristic comment, Republican Senator Rob Portman said, "I am deeply concerned about reports suggesting that sanctions imposed on Russia may be lifted without resolving the unacceptable and hostile actions that caused the sanctions to be imposed by the US and our allies."[4] Portman was one of 10 Republican and 10 Democratic senators to sign on to a bill introduced that month by Ben Cardin, the senior Democrat on the Senate Foreign Relations Committee, and Republican John McCain that directed the imposition of new sanctions on Russian officials, institutions, and businesses in response to its election interference.[5] Cardin also joined with Republican Senator Lindsey Graham in February to introduce a bill that gave Congress the power to review and block an executive branch effort to lift any preexisting sanctions on Russia.[6]

The Trump administration urged Congress not to advance these proposals, arguing that they would hinder negotiations with Russia and place unconstitutional restrictions on presidential power.[7] Nevertheless, after the proposals

Bipartisanship and US Foreign Policy. Jordan Tama, Oxford University Press. © Oxford University Press 2024.
DOI: 10.1093/oso/9780197745663.003.0006

were merged and coupled with measures imposing new sanctions on Iran and North Korea, the House and Senate approved the legislation by votes of 419-3 and 98-2, respectively.[8] This rebuke of Trump's Russia policy was all the more remarkable considering that Trump's Republican Party controlled both the House and Senate at the time. Trump signed the legislation, as his aides said that he had little choice but to accept it given the veto-proof majorities backing it in Congress.[9] Nonetheless, Trump vented about the legislation in a signing statement: "By limiting the Executive's flexibility, this bill makes it harder for the United States to strike good deals for the American people."[10]

Trump's positive attitude toward Russian President Vladimir Putin made him an outlier in American politics, where the prevailing view in both parties saw Putin as an adversary of the United States. In conjunction with the charges that emerged during and after the 2016 campaign of collusion between the Trump campaign and Russian officials, resulting in a panoply of investigations, Trump's unusual view of Russia brought an idiosyncratic dimension to Russia debates during his presidency.

But anti-presidential bipartisanship also characterized a major Russia sanctions debate during the Obama administration, and some fundamental features of the politics of Russia policy have remained constant across recent presidencies. Congressional proposals to penalize Russia for objectionable actions have repeatedly generated broad bipartisan support on Capitol Hill and triggered White House concerns that the legislation might undermine international cooperation. In 2012, Congress enacted the Magnitsky Act, which sanctioned Russian government officials who had committed gross violations of human rights. Much like Trump's calculus in the summer of 2017, Obama worried that the legislation would make it harder to work with Russia but acquiesced given its strong bipartisan backing in Congress. In 2014, nearly all Democratic and Republican lawmakers agreed on the imposition of a new set of sanctions on Russia in response to its invasion of Ukraine and annexation of Crimea. In this instance, Congress was mainly on the same page as the Obama administration, which favored penalizing Russia for its aggression and was largely in the driver's seat in US policymaking. But inter-branch tension was not absent from this debate either, as the administration resisted more far-reaching congressional proposals that would have tied the president's hands and threatened US coordination with European allies. As I discuss in Chapter 10, a similar dynamic marked the US response to Russia's invasion of Ukraine in 2022.

In this chapter, I explain why several Russia sanctions debates under Obama and Trump were marked by anti-presidential bipartisanship. I show that disagreement between the president and lawmakers in both parties over Russia sanctions reflected their differing institutional incentives, with lawmakers generally more willing to take a strong stand against troubling behavior by a powerful country and the president more concerned with fostering diplomatic cooperation and maintaining policymaking flexibility. At the same time, a favorable ideological and advocacy landscape facilitated bipartisanship within Congress on Russia sanctions. Most American voters and elites across the political spectrum viewed actions by the Russian government with concern and favored penalizing it for perceived wrongdoing. While Democrats became more anti-Russia than Republicans in the Trump era, attitudes toward Russia remained negative within both parties throughout the period. Meanwhile, the strongest advocacy in these debates occurred on the pro-sanctions side, by human rights and Eastern European diaspora groups. Although the business community sometimes weighed in against sanctions, the intensity of its advocacy was limited by the relatively small size of the US-Russia economic relationship. This context made it easier for lawmakers in both parties to back sanctioning Russia repeatedly.[11]

Sanctioning Russian human rights violators

The first major Russia sanctions debate during the Obama years focused on holding Russian government and law enforcement officials accountable for gross violations of human rights.[12] This debate was triggered by a set of abuses targeting Sergei Magnitsky, a Russian tax attorney. In 2007, Magnitsky had discovered that Russian government officials had carried out a $230 million tax fraud. After Magnitsky testified publicly about this fraud, he was arrested by Russian officials, tortured in a Russian detention facility, and denied essential medical care, resulting in his death.[13]

This whistle-blowing and abuse came to the attention of Democratic Senator Ben Cardin and Democratic Representative Jim McGovern—two legislators with a long-standing commitment to the protection of human rights—through hearings that they chaired on human rights conditions in Russia.[14] In response, McGovern and Cardin drafted legislation to place sanctions, in the form of a visa ban and freeze of financial assets, on any individuals determined by the State Department to have been responsible for Magnitsky's mistreatment and death.[15] Soon after introducing the legislation, which became known as the Magnitsky Act, McGovern and Cardin gained several Republican cosponsors of it, including Senator John McCain.

The Obama administration opposed the Magnitsky Act because it threatened to undermine the administration's "reset" policy toward Russia, which aimed to build cooperative ties with the country.[16] This policy had facilitated the New START nuclear arms control agreement between the United States and Russia, along with Russian assent to UN Security Council sanctions on Iran and the transportation of US troops through Russia to Afghanistan, at a time when Dmitry Medvedev was serving as the Russian president. For senior administration officials, concern about jeopardizing such cooperation outweighed any desire to take a stand against human rights violations. One Obama administration official involved in internal deliberations over the Magnitsky Act recalled, "Some people within the administration wanted to embrace [the legislation]. But the prevailing view was that we should stiff arm the congressional cosponsors because it would complicate our relations with Russia."[17] In July 2011, the State Department conveyed to congressional officials the administration's rationale for opposing the bill in an informal memo:

> The passage of the legislation as written could have foreign policy implications that could hurt our international sanctions efforts in countries like Iran, North Korea and Libya, and jeopardize other areas of cooperation, including transit to Afghanistan. . . . Senior Russian government officials have warned us that they will respond asymmetrically if this legislation passes. Their argument is that we cannot expect them to be our partner in supporting sanctions against countries like Iran, North Korea, and Libya, and sanction them at the same time.[18]

Despite the administration's opposition to the legislation, Cardin and McGovern introduced new versions of it in 2011 and 2012 that heightened the administration's concern by expanding the legislation's scope.[19] These new versions applied a visa ban and financial asset freeze not only on individuals implicated in the Magnitsky case but also on any other individual in Russia who was determined by the State Department to have committed a gross violation of human rights.

The desire of McGovern and Cardin to keep pushing the issue reflects the pattern highlighted in this book: lawmakers are more willing than executive branch officials to take a principled stand even if it might antagonize an important foreign government. In May 2012, McGovern said, "Threats from Russian officials should not deter us from enacting a law that holds human rights violators accountable and strengthens human rights defenders."[20] McGovern later commented in an interview: "I think there are some nervous nellies in the administration who are saying, 'What's Putin going to do next if we publish a list [of people to be sanctioned]? But we have to demonstrate that we're serious about human rights."[21] Along similar lines, Cardin said in an interview, "We can't let a great power like Russia take these kinds of actions without repercussions. The State Department—God bless them, they're very devoted to their cause—they want peace, and they will throw out accountability to get it. But I think we need to hold accountable those people that don't respect human rights."[22]

The new versions of the Magnitsky Act eventually accumulated 61 Republican and 56 Democratic congressional cosponsors in the two chambers, demonstrating its broad backing. This growing bipartisan support for the legislation was aided by events in Russia that increased concern about the country on Capitol Hill. After Russia's December 2011 parliamentary elections, independent monitors reported that the elections were accompanied by large-scale fraud, including evidence of widespread ballot stuffing, which triggered a series of major demonstrations in Moscow.[23] The Russian government cracked down harshly on the protest movement, and as Vladimir Putin returned to the Russian presidency after the March 2012 election, the Russian government enacted a series of repressive laws, including measures restricting the work of nongovernmental organizations and imposing fines of 300,000 rubles (9000 US dollars) for participation in unsanctioned demonstrations.[24] In addition, as the Syrian civil war intensified, the Russian government had begun providing heavy military aid to the Assad government in an effort to prop up a friendly regime and bolster Russian influence in the Middle East.

The Magnitsky Act became the vehicle for legislators to act on concerns about all of these developments. In June 2012, the House Foreign Affairs Committee and Senate Foreign Relations Committee unanimously approved the bill.[25] During the House committee's debate, Republican Representative Ileana Ros-Lehtinen, the committee's chairwoman, echoed the views of McGovern and Cardin in dismissing Russian objections to the legislation: "The Kremlin has threatened that if Congress dares to pass this simple piece of legislation, if Congress dares to defy its commands, it will retaliate.

So let our committee send a clear and unmistakable message to the Kremlin by passing this bill unanimously and demonstrate to the corrupt rulers of Russia that they cannot threaten us into silence."[26]

Around the same time, the administration determined that enactment of the Magnitsky Act would probably be necessary in order to gain congressional approval of Permanent Normal Trade Relations (PNTR) status for Russia, in conjunction with Russia's 2012 entrance into the World Trade Organization (WTO).[27] The granting of PNTR to Russia was being held up by a nearly 40-year-old US measure called the Jackson-Vanik amendment, which required the president to deny normal trade relations status to any country that did not allow its citizens to freely emigrate from that country.[28] The Jackson-Vanik amendment had been motivated by Soviet restrictions on Jewish emigration, and many lawmakers credited the amendment with leading the Soviet Union to allow more Jews to leave the country—although data on Jewish emigration levels from the Soviet Union suggest that the amendment may not have had this positive effect.[29] Even though the amendment had become outdated in that Russia's post-Soviet government did not restrict emigration, some of these lawmakers were reluctant to take the measure off the books because they saw it as the only US law that held Russia accountable for behavior related to human rights.[30] But according to WTO rules, Russia would be able to maintain higher tariffs on US imports if the United States did not extend unconditional nondiscriminatory trade treatment to it. The Obama administration and US business associations therefore wanted Congress to extend PNTR to Russia—which would also entail repealing the Jackson-Vanik amendment—to ensure that US firms would not be disadvantaged in the Russian market.[31]

However, the concerns of members of Congress about human rights conditions in Russia and foreign policy actions by Russia meant that legislation extending PNTR to Russia could not pass the House and Senate unless it was coupled with a bill that addressed some of those concerns. As the debate unfolded, a number of prominent senators and representatives in both parties stated that they would oppose the granting of PNTR to Russia unless it was accompanied by enactment of the Magnitsky Act.[32] In June, Representative Sander Levin, the senior Democrat on the House Ways and Means Committee, commented, "I think it's now clear that without a human rights provision, it will be difficult for PNTR [for Russia] to pass the Senate and the House."[33] Seeing this political landscape, congressional supporters of PNTR for Russia chose to attach the Magnitsky Act to the PNTR bill. A senior

House Democratic aide involved in the issue noted that Democratic Senator Max Baucus and Republican Representative Dave Camp—the chairmen of the Senate Finance Committee and House Ways and Means Committee, which had jurisdiction over the trade bill—would have preferred to keep the bill free of non-trade provisions, but they realized that merging it with the Magnitsky Act was necessary to achieve its enactment.[34]

The attachment of the Magnitsky Act to the PNTR bill softened the administration's opposition to the human rights measure. Nevertheless, the administration lobbied congressional officials to weaken the sanctions provisions.[35] In response, McGovern, Cardin, and other key legislators agreed to an administration request to allow the executive branch to list individuals designated for the sanctions only in a classified document if the executive branch determined that it was vital to do so for national security reasons. However, the legislators rejected administration requests to turn the legislation into a nonbinding "sense of the Congress" bill.

The Magnitsky-PNTR package was approved by the House in November by a vote of 365-43 and approved by the Senate in December by a vote of 92-4, with the no votes cast mainly by Democrats who did not support the trade liberalization portion of the package.[36] Eight days later, President Obama signed the bill into law, even though he opposed the sanctions components.[37] A *New York Times* article noted that with "such overwhelming support in Congress" for the sanctions, "the White House has had little leverage to press its case."[38] Amanda Sloat, who served at the time as senior advisor to the assistant secretary of state for European and Eurasian Affairs, commented along similar lines, "Politically it's hard to argue with punishing human rights abusers in Russia. . . . There's legislation you don't like, and there's legislation you can't live with. This was legislation that Obama didn't like but could live with."[39]

Even though the Obama administration did not support the Magnitsky Act, the legislation has influenced US-Russian relations and served as the model for other important human rights laws. When the bill began gaining momentum in Congress in 2011, the administration imposed a visa ban on some Russian officials who were responsible for Magnitsky's death in an effort to preempt congressional action on the legislation.[40] The bill also affected diplomacy with Russia before its enactment. A State Department official noted that whenever a government-to-government working group with Russia met while the Magnitsky Act was being considered in Congress, Russian officials issued threats of retaliation over it.[41]

After the legislation was enacted, the Russian government followed through on its retaliation threats by restricting imports of US meat products and prohibiting Americans from adopting Russian children.[42] The Obama administration, for its part, implemented the law by imposing the visa ban and asset freeze on at least 44 Russian individuals, even though the law grants the secretary of state and secretary of the treasury the authority to waive the application of the sanctions if they determine that such a waiver is in the national security interests of the United States and provide Congress a justification for the waiver.[43] The strong bipartisan support for the sanctions influenced the administration's decisions to apply the penalties despite this grant of discretion. Daniel Fried, the State Department coordinator for sanctions policy at the time, explained: "The answer to 'Why did we implement it?' is 'It's the law.' And when it is the law, you can find ways of resisting and dragging your feet and screaming and yelling, but that would've meant a constant fight with Congress."[44]

Indeed, on the one occasion when the Obama administration met a reporting requirement under the law by informing Congress that it had not added anyone to the "Magnitsky list" of sanctioned individuals, legislators in both parties sharply criticized the decision. McGovern commented to a *Washington Post* reporter, "The lack of new names on the list is very disappointing."[45] In a similar vein, Bob Corker, the senior Republican on the Senate Foreign Relations Committee, wrote in a letter to Secretary of State John Kerry: "The Magnitsky Act was passed by Congress and signed into law by President Obama. We are all, therefore, obligated to ensure its full implementation."[46] The Obama administration appeared to get the message, as it imposed sanctions on additional Russian officials in conjunction with each subsequent reporting deadline under the law.

The Magnitsky Act has also provided a model for additional sanctions laws that have been adopted by the United States and other countries. After the law's enactment, Cardin and McGovern joined with McCain and Republican Representative Chris Smith to introduce a new bill that authorizes the executive branch to impose the same travel ban and asset freeze stipulated by the Magnitsky Act on individuals who have committed gross violations of human rights anywhere in the world. This legislation, known as the Global Magnitsky Act, was approved by Congress and signed by Obama in December 2016.[47] During the Trump administration, the State Department and Treasury Department imposed these sanctions on at least 94 people and 102 institutions from 24 countries.[48]

A number of other countries, including Canada, the United Kingdom, Australia, Estonia, Latvia, and Lithuania, have enacted their own versions of the Magnitsky Act or Global Magnitsky Act since the enactment of the US laws.[49] Like the US versions, each of these laws is named after Magnitsky and centers on a travel ban and asset freeze for human rights violators. The author of Canada's Magnitsky law noted that it was "modeled on the US initiative."[50]

While the Magnitsky Act is a landmark human rights bill, it also contributed, along with Putin's return to the Russian presidency, Russia's support for the Assad government, and Russia's 2014 invasion of Ukraine (discussed below), to a deterioration in US-Russian relations following the hopeful period of the early Obama presidency. Matthew Rojansky, the president and CEO of the US Russia Foundation, said that the law was "a major blow to the US-Russian relationship. . . . It was one more nail in the coffin of a very productive agenda that had been developed since 2008."[51] In an unexpected twist, the law also contributed to the scandal about possible links between Trump's 2016 presidential campaign and Russia, as a lawyer linked to the Russian government lobbied Trump's son and other Trump advisors to advocate for the law's repeal during the campaign.[52] Despite this lobbying campaign and Trump's stated desire to improve relations with the Russian government, the Trump administration followed the example set by the Obama administration in choosing to implement the law, adding five more people to the Magnitsky list in December 2017 and six additional people in May 2019.[53] Given Trump's attitude regarding Russia and his general lack of concern with human rights violations, it is certain that the administration would not have taken these steps without the law.[54] With this variety of follow-on effects, the Magnitsky Act represents one of the more consequential initiatives of anti-presidential bipartisanship of recent years.

Public and elite opinion

Public and elite opinion in the United States regarding Russia and human rights was conducive to bipartisan congressional support for the Magnitsky Act. I could not find any surveys that asked Americans specifically about the act, but various survey data from the years surrounding the Magnitsky Act debate suggest that a broad cross-section of Americans would have supported legislation along these lines. In a 2005 survey by the Chicago Council on Foreign Relations[55] and Program on International Policy Attitudes, 70% of

Americans said they favored placing diplomatic pressure on the Russian government to respect human rights.[56] In a 2012 Chicago Council on Global Affairs public opinion survey, 69% of Democrats and 59% of Republicans said they considered the placement of sanctions on countries that violate international law to have been very or somewhat effective in achieving the foreign policy goals of the United States.[57] In a 2014 study, 79% of Americans said they considered the use of economic sanctions in response to human rights violations to be acceptable.[58] In a 2014 Chicago Council survey of foreign policy experts and decision-makers, 95% of Democrats and 84% of Republicans said that promoting and defending human rights in other countries should be a very or somewhat important foreign policy goal of the United States.[59] While none of these surveys directly concern the Magnitsky Act, they point toward bipartisan support at both the public and elite levels for taking a stand against human rights violations by other governments.

Indeed, the Magnitsky Act attracted support from think tanks and thought leaders across the ideological spectrum, including from the conservative Heritage Foundation, neoconservative Foreign Policy Initiative, centrist Bipartisan Policy Center, and left-of-center Truman National Security Project.[60] Rachel Kleinfeld, then-CEO of the Truman National Security Project, wrote in the *Huffington Post* as the legislation began advancing in the House, "I don't often agree with [neoconservative and former Reagan and George W. Bush administration official] Elliot Abrams against the Obama Administration—but the Magnitsky bill creates strange bedfellows."[61] A diverse set of major newspapers also endorsed the legislation. The *Washington Post*'s left-leaning editorial page wrote that passing the bill would "send Mr. Putin and his cadres the message that their lawless behavior will have consequences,"[62] while the *Wall Street Journal*'s conservative editorial page called the Magnitsky Act "the most consequential piece of human-rights legislation since Jackson-Vanik, and a worthy successor."[63] This public and elite opinion landscape made supporting the Magnitsky Act a natural position for most Democratic and Republican members of Congress to take.

Advocacy group activity

The advocacy landscape was also conducive to bipartisan congressional support for the Magnitsky Act. The bill attracted support from groups with links to both parties and generated minimal interest group opposition.

Unsurprisingly, it was backed by major human rights NGOs. These groups included Human Rights Watch and Human Rights First, which have close ties to Democratic elected officials,[64] and Freedom House, which has close ties to Republican elected officials.[65] Tom Malinowski, at the time the Washington director of Human Rights Watch, and David Kramer, then the president of Freedom House, were particularly vocal in advocating for the legislation on Capitol Hill.[66] Some Eastern European diaspora groups that possessed non-partisan reputations, such as the Joint Baltic American National Committee, also lobbied lawmakers on behalf of the Magnitsky Act.[67]

At the same time, the Magnitsky Act generated little interest group opposition. Prior to the merging of the legislation with the PNTR bill, no groups publicly opposed it.[68] After the bills were combined, just one small labor union publicly opposed the legislative package, while more than 100 firms and business associations endorsed it.[69] While major labor unions largely stayed on the sidelines of the Russia PNTR debate because they had bigger priorities and trade with Russia did not threaten many blue-collar American jobs, the business community generally accepted the Magnitsky Act as a means of advancing PNTR.[70]

Enactment of the Magnitsky Act was also greatly aided by the dogged advocacy of an individual, Bill Browder, who developed ties with congressional officials in both parties. Browder had been CEO of an investment fund that employed Magnitsky. After Magnitsky died, Browder commented that his "inability to protect" his former employee was a "curse that rattled around" his brain.[71] Browder responded to the tragedy by making his mission in life the imposition of sanctions on the people responsible for Magnitsky's death.[72] He used his own considerable resources to raise media awareness about the case and repeatedly flew to Washington to urge lawmakers to take action on the issue. His persistent advocacy, in conjunction with that of human rights groups, played a critical role in building bipartisan support for the legislation on Capitol Hill.

Sanctioning Russia over its 2014 Ukraine invasion

Another sanctions debate emerged in the United States following Russia's military intervention in Ukraine and annexation of Crimea in early 2014. In this case—unlike the Magnitsky case—the president favored penalizing Russia for its actions. Obama used his executive authority to put in place many sanctions in the months after the invasion and annexation, in coordination with European allies. As a result, the president was the lead actor in shaping Ukraine sanctions. Margaret Taylor, who served at the time as deputy chief counsel on the Democratic staff of the Senate Foreign Relations Committee (SFRC), noted, "Congress was pretty much on the same page as the administration. The administration was geared up to be pretty aggressive itself."[73] Charles Kupchan, who served as senior director for European Affairs on the National Security Council from 2014 to 2017, commented, "Policy was generally coming out of the White House. Congress played a supporting role, but not a driving role."[74]

However, lawmakers in both parties helped ensure a forceful US response to Russia's aggression. Kupchan noted, "Congress applied pressure to stiffen the policy."[75] On February 28, the day after pro-Russian gunmen began taking control of key facilities in the Crimean capital, six Democrats and six Republicans on SFRC wrote a letter to Obama urging the use of sanctions as part of the US response.[76] In subsequent days, some lawmakers went a step further, arguing that the United States should aim to weaken the Russian economy severely. Ed Royce, the chairman of the House Foreign Affairs Committee, called for "crippling sanctions" on Russia, while Senator Chris Murphy, a Democrat on SFRC, said the United States needed to show Russia that its "entire country will suffer consequences" for its government's actions.[77]

Initial action by Congress on the issue was strongly bipartisan but relatively modest. On March 5, Republican Representative Hal Rogers and Democratic Representative Nita Lowey, the chairman and senior Democrat of the House Appropriations Committee, introduced a bill that provided economic and security aid to Ukraine, and mandated asset freezes and visa bans on any Russian individuals who were involved in or responsible for violations of Ukraine's territorial integrity.[78] The bill also granted the administration flexibility in the form of authority to waive the imposition of the stipulated sanctions based on a determination that doing so was in the national security interest of the United States. The administration was developing similar targeted sanctions on the issue during this time and, with flexibility built into the legislation, did not object to the bill.[79] Obama signed the legislation in early April after it was approved by a vote of 385-23 in the House and by voice vote in the Senate.[80]

Around the same time, other lawmakers began developing more far-reaching sanctions legislation, leading the administration to grow more concerned about congressional activity. Generally, the administration wanted Congress to stay on the sidelines, so it would be able to calibrate sanctions carefully—thereby maintaining unity with European partners— and remove sanctions quickly if Russia reversed its aggression.[81] The administration therefore had a strong incentive to forestall Congress from acting more forcefully on sanctions by showing it was taking strong action on its own, which it did through a series of executive orders and regulations imposing a range of sanctions on Russian officials, institutions, and companies between March and December 2014.[82] Although the administration would have taken most of these steps regardless of congressional activity, the prospect of further legislative action prompted the administration to accelerate and expand its sanctioning activity. David Kramer, who had served as a deputy assistant secretary of state for European and Eurasian Affairs during the George W. Bush administration and was heavily involved in discussions about sanctioning Russia in 2014, commented, "Sanctions [after the Ukraine invasion] came in several waves from the administration, and those waves would have been smaller if there wasn't pressure from Congress."[83]

The administration also urged lawmakers during these months to scale back legislative sanctions proposals and add more flexibility to them. In May, Bob Corker, then the senior Republican on SFRC, introduced a bill directing the president to impose financial, trade, and diplomatic sanctions against a wide range of Russian government institutions and firms, including the entire Russian energy sector, while giving the president no discretion regarding implementation of the sanctions.[84] The bill triggered strong resistance from the administration. Dan Fried, who served as the State Department's point person on the issue, recalled that "the administration went to the Hill and argued that mandatory sanctions along these lines would create an instant breach between the United States and Europe, and would thereby help Putin."[85] Corker then engaged in talks with SFRC Chairman Bob Menendez, a Democrat, that resulted in a softer bipartisan bill.[86]

In September, Menendez and Corker introduced their sanctions bill with seven other Senate Democrats and six other Republican senators signed on as cosponsors.[87] The bill maintained most of the sanctions stipulated in the original Corker bill, but incorporated much more flexibility regarding the bill's implementation. In particular, the Menendez-Corker bill made the legislation's most controversial sanctions—on Russia's energy sector— permissive, rather than mandatory, meaning that the bill authorized, but did not require, the president to apply the sanctions. The new bill also allowed the president to waive the application of most of its other stipulated sanctions for purposes of US national security and terminated most of the sanctions upon the president's certification to Congress that Russia was no longer undermining the peace, sovereignty, or territorial integrity of Ukraine. Kyle Parker, who covered Russia policy at the time as a senior Democratic aide on the House Foreign Affairs Committee, noted that Russia hawks on Capitol Hill were willing to grant the administration these types of flexibility regarding the implementation of sanctions because the administration was already taking steps to counter Russia's aggression: "Here you had an administration response that was serious enough and was leading the way and was bringing the Europeans in line."[88]

Although the revised bill incorporated more flexibility into it, the administration continued to express concerns that the broad scope of its sanctions provisions would alienate European allies and fragment the transatlantic coalition that the administration had worked hard to establish on the issue. Shortly before the Senate was scheduled to vote on the bill, Obama said at a meeting of a trade advisory group:

> There may be some movement out of Congress for us to get out ahead of Europe further. We have argued that that would be counterproductive. . . . The notion that we can simply ratchet up sanctions further and further and further, and then, ultimately, Putin changes his mind I think is a miscalculation. What will ultimately lead to Russia making a strategic decision is if they recognize that Europe is standing with us and will be in it for the long haul and we are, in fact, patient.[89]

Nevertheless, the Republican-controlled House and Democratic-controlled Senate approved the bill in December without objection and by voice vote, respectively, and Obama signed the legislation.[90] A *New York Times* article noted, "The Congress passed the bipartisan measure without opposition, making a veto politically untenable, and administration officials said they were satisfied that enough discretion was incorporated into the bill to give the president room to maneuver."[91]

Although this law was far-reaching, its permissive, rather than mandatory, character, diminished its impact.[92] Nevertheless, the leverage provided to the executive branch by the law made it consequential. For instance, although the administration did not apply the law's sanctions on investors in Russia's energy sector, Fried noted that the possibility of such action dissuaded another country from proceeding with an important deal involving Russia.[93] Fried did not identify this country in our interview, but the media reported soon after the law's enactment that Chinese banks were no longer willing to go forward with financing a project to build three pipelines to transport natural gas from Russia to China.[94]

Public and elite opinion

Public and elite opinion in the United States facilitated bipartisan congressional support for sanctioning Russia over Ukraine. Voters and elites in both parties viewed Russia negatively and were concerned about Russian actions in the wake of the country's invasion of Ukraine and annexation of Crimea. In the spring and summer of 2014, Chicago Council on Global Affairs surveys asked the public and foreign policy elites to rate their feelings toward Russia on a scale of zero to 100, with zero representing a very cold feeling, and 100 representing a very warm feeling. Responses revealed that the Democratic public, the Republican public, Democratic foreign policy elites, and Republican foreign policy elites all viewed Russia coolly, reporting average feelings of 33, 32, 33, and 29, respectively.[95] The Chicago Council survey of foreign policy elites also found that 84% of Democrats and 94% of Republicans saw Russia's territorial ambitions as an important or critical threat to the vital interest of the United States in the next 10 years, while a Pew public opinion survey that summer found that 75% of Americans considered Russia to be an adversary or a serious problem.[96] Such views persisted as the Ukraine crisis continued to unfold. In February 2015, Pew found that 76% of Republicans and 69% of Democrats had an unfavorable view of Vladimir Putin.[97]

With respect to sanctions specifically, large majorities of voters in both parties favored penalizing Russia for its actions involving Ukraine. Across all polls I could find from 2014 and 2015 that asked Americans their opinion on the issue and which broke down the data by party affiliation, an average of 64% of Democrats and 64% of Republicans said they supported sanctioning Russia based on its behavior regarding Ukraine.[98] (See Table 6.1.)

Moreover, the bipartisan support for sanctions did not come only from Democrats and Republicans near the middle of the political spectrum. A March 2014 ABC News/Washington Post poll found that 68% of liberal Democrats and 69% of conservative Republicans supported sanctioning

Table 6.1 Public opinion on sanctioning Russia over Ukraine

Pollster	Survey period	Democrats in support	Democrats opposed	Republicans in support	Republicans opposed
ABC/Wash[a]	March 2014	63%	N/A	62%	N/A
CNN/ORC[b]	March 2014	65%	34%	67%	31%
Quinnipiac[a]	March 2014	70%	19%	69%	22%
Pew[c]	April 2014	58%	33%	55%	31%
Pew[c]	February 2015	62%	N/A	64%	N/A
Chicago Council[c]	May-June 2015	67%	30%	68%	29%

Note: The table includes all public opinion polls I could find during 2014 and 2015 that asked respondents whether they supported imposing or increasing sanctions on Russia in connection with its actions in Ukraine and provided a partisan breakdown of the responses. Table entries indicating "N/A" represent survey results that the pollster did not report.

[a] "Overall, do you support or oppose the United States and its European allies imposing economic sanctions on Russia for its actions involving Ukraine?"

[b] "Here are some actions which the United States and its allies might take to try to force Russia to remove its troops from the Crimean Peninsula and to make sure Russia does not send troops into other parts of Ukraine. Which of these actions do you favor and which do you oppose [Imposing economic sanctions on Russia]?"

[c] "In response to the situation involving Russia and Ukraine, would you support or oppose the United States increasing economic and diplomatic sanctions on Russia?"

Russia over Ukraine, while a CNN/ORC survey that same month found that 54% of liberals, 64% of moderates, and 59% of conservatives backed sanctioning Russia.[99] These attitudes underscore the extent to which attitudes on Russia sanctions did not break down on a left-right ideological spectrum. In this context, congressional Democrats and Republicans were likely to favor sanctioning Russia themselves, and the electoral incentives stemming from voter preferences only reinforced that tendency.

Advocacy group activity

Legislation to sanction Russia over Ukraine generated supportive advocacy from groups with bipartisan links and only a modest amount of lobbying in opposition. Supportive advocacy came mainly from Ukrainian-Americans and other Americans of Eastern European descent. Around the time of the Ukraine sanctions debate, the number of Americans who were born in Ukraine or possessed Ukrainian heritage neared 1 million—or about .3%

of the US population.[100] Although these figures are relatively small, the Ukranian-American community has been mobilized enough to generate bipartisan links to Congress. As of December 2021—before Russia's 2022 invasion of Ukraine—the Senate Ukraine Caucus, an informal grouping of senators interested in Ukraine, included nine Democrats and seven Republicans, while its House counterpart included 26 Democrats and 14 Republicans.[101] Ukrainian diaspora groups, including the US-Ukraine Foundation and the Ukrainian Congress Committee of America, advocated directly sanctioning Russia in 2014.[102] In one indication of the reach of this advocacy, then-National Security Council official Charles Kupchan recalled, "Some members of Congress called to tell me that they had Ukrainian-Americans in their district who were very concerned with what was going on in Ukraine."[103]

The much larger community of Americans with ties to other Eastern European countries amplified the reach of Ukrainian-American advocacy. The Central and East European Coalition, which represents Americans from more than a dozen countries, in April 2014 called for "expanding economic sanctions on Russia to include not only individuals within Putin's inner circle, but major sectors of Russia's economy."[104] Later in 2014, the Joint Baltic American National Committee, which represents Americans of Latvian, Estonian, and Lithuania descent, lobbied lawmakers to support the Menendez-Corker bill.[105] Kyle Parker, the senior Democratic aide handling Russia policy at the time on the House Foreign Affairs Committee, observed, "There was significant advocacy from Ukrainian-American diaspora groups, Eastern Europeans, Baltics. They pushed as hard as they could."[106]

On the other side of the issue, some oil and gas companies, including Exxon Mobil and Chevron, lobbied lawmakers not to enact sanctions on Russia's energy sector.[107] This advocacy contributed to the softening of the legislation—in particular, by incorporating more implementing flexibility into the energy sanctions—as it advanced through Congress. But the business community as a whole was not mobilized strongly enough against sanctioning Russia to block the legislation entirely. Parker noted, "Business was here doing the rounds on the bill. But their opposition wasn't that strong. American businesses have a minimal footprint in Russia. It's only a few companies that really have a stake in this."[108] As a result, the pro-sanctions and anti-Russia attitudes of policy elites and those portions of the public that did care about the issue largely carried the day. Since such views did not break down along partisan lines, the debate featured strong bipartisanship in Congress despite the involvement of some corporations with close ties to Republicans.

Sanctioning Russia over election interference

Many of the patterns in the Magnitsky and Ukraine sanctions debates also marked the Trump-era debate about sanctioning Russia over its interference in the 2016 US election. This debate was rooted in the accumulation of evidence during and after the election campaign that Russia had used illegal cyber activities and social media trolls to sow political discord in the United States and boost Trump's election prospects. These Russian efforts included hacking into Clinton campaign and Democratic Party email accounts and leaking the stolen emails through WikiLeaks; posting fake and divisive information on Facebook, Twitter, and YouTube; and organizing political rallies in the United States. In January 2017, the US Office of the Director of National Intelligence released a declassified version of the intelligence community's assessment of the interference, which concluded:

> We assess Russian President Vladimir Putin ordered an influence campaign in 2016 aimed at the US presidential election. Russia's goals were to undermine public faith in the US democratic process, denigrate Secretary Clinton, and harm her electability and potential presidency. We further assess Putin and the Russian Government developed a clear preference for President-elect Trump. We have high confidence in these judgments.[109]

Evidence also emerged starting in 2016 of a variety of contacts between Trump campaign officials and Russian officials and agents. In response to the emerging evidence, the Federal Bureau of Investigation opened an investigation in July 2016 of possible coordination between the Trump campaign and Russia, and the House and Senate intelligence committees launched their own probes early the next year.[110] After Trump fired FBI Director James Comey in May 2017, Deputy Attorney General Rod Rosenstein appointed a special counsel, Robert Mueller, to conduct an independent investigation. Mueller's report, completed in March 2019, endorsed the intelligence community's assessment that Russia had sought to aid Trump's election through its interference in the election; detailed untoward conversations between Trump advisors and representatives of the Russian government, including about the disclosure of information designed to discredit Clinton's campaign; and documented numerous efforts by Trump to hinder government investigations of the issue.[111] The special counsel's probe also resulted between 2017 and 2019 in the filing of criminal charges against 25 Russian nationals and six Trump advisers and associates.[112] The Senate Intelligence Committee further documented Russian interference efforts in a series of bipartisan reports based on its own investigation, while the House Intelligence Committee's investigation largely devolved into a partisan effort by Trump loyalists, led by Committee Chairman Devin Nunes, to defend the president.[113]

Debate over sanctioning Russia in response to its election interference developed in parallel to these investigations. In December 2016, the Obama administration ordered the departure of 35 Russian government officials posted in the United States who the administration believed served as spies; revoked Russian government access to compounds that Russia owned in Maryland and New York; and imposed sanctions on some Russian agencies, officials, and firms that were responsible for interference.[114] Following this step, key lawmakers in both parties called for more expansive sanctions. Ben Cardin, who had become the top Democrat on the SFRC, endorsed the administration's action but said that it was insufficient, adding, "The executive branch has acted, but it is imperative the legislative branch now pick up the ball and move it forward."[115] Republican Senators Lindsey Graham and John McCain commented more sharply that the administration's sanctions were "a small price for Russia to pay for its brazen attack on American democracy," and said they intended to "lead the effort in the new Congress to impose stronger sanctions on Russia."[116] Addressing suggestions by Trump that Russia might not have been responsible for the election interference, Graham said, "There are 100 United States senators. I would say that 99 of us believe the Russians did this and we're going to do something about it."[117]

Republican leaders on Capitol Hill also joined Democrats in urging Trump not to remove preexisting sanctions on Russia following reports that he was considering doing so. Senate Majority Leader Mitch McConnell said in January 2017, "I'm against lifting any sanctions on the Russians. Those sanctions were imposed because of their behavior in Crimea, eastern Ukraine and now we know they've been messing around in our elections as well. If there's any country in the world that doesn't deserve sanctions relief, it's Russia."[118]

In February, as White House officials indicated that the administration was moving toward lifting Russia sanctions, Graham and Cardin introduced legislation designed to prevent such a step. The bill stipulated that the president could not lift any sanctions that were in place on Russia without the action first being reviewed by Congress, with expedited procedures established for House and Senate votes on whether to approve or disapprove the sanctions removal.[119] This proposal departed from the standard balance of power between Congress and the president on sanctions, in that under prior sanctions laws the president could typically remove sanctions that had been imposed through executive action by a new executive action, without any congressional review required. In addition to Graham and Cardin, 18 Senate Democrats and four Senate Republicans signed on to the bill. House Minority Whip Steny Hoyer, a Democrat, introduced the same bill in the House, where 31 Democrats and 15 Republicans signed on as cosponsors.[120]

At the same time, Cardin and McCain gained bipartisan support for a bill that prohibited US recognition of Russian sovereignty over Crimea and directed the president to impose sanctions against any Russian institution or individual that undermines cybersecurity; conducts business with the Russian defense or intelligence sector; or invests in the Russian energy sector.[121] The bill also expanded some preexisting Ukraine-related sanctions and converted others into mandatory, rather than discretionary, penalties. Margaret Taylor, who served then as Democratic chief counsel on the SFRC, explained how Cardin sought to maintain bipartisanship on the bill, whose 20 Senate cosponsors included an equal mix of Democrats and Republicans: "We told Democrats, 'you can only get on the bill if you find a Republican to get on the bill,' so that it wouldn't get politicized."[122]

In June, after the Graham-Cardin and Cardin-McCain bills were combined, the Senate voted by a 97-2 margin to add the measures to an Iran sanctions bill, with only libertarian Republicans Rand Paul and Mike Lee voting against the amendment.[123] During the debate over the Russia sanctions provisions on the Senate floor, Senate Minority Leader Chuck Schumer cited the bipartisan cooperation in the development of the legislation as an "example of how we can work together on issues we agree on."[124] McConnell said similarly, "I think this is a good example of the Senate at its best. We all know this has been a period of rather partisan sparring back and forth on a variety of different things, but both sides were able to put that aside."[125]

This Senate action came despite the Trump administration's opposition to the legislation. The morning before the Senate vote on the measure, Secretary of State Rex Tillerson commented on it at an SFRC hearing: "[We] have some channels that are open [with Russia] where we are starting to talk, and I think what I would not want to do is close the channels off with something new."[126] The next day, Tillerson said at a House Foreign Affairs Committee hearing: "Essentially, we would ask for the flexibility to turn the heat up [on Russia] when we need to, but also to ensure that we have the ability to maintain a constructive dialogue."[127] Subsequently, the administration lobbied House Republicans to weaken the legislation by removing the limitation on the president's authority to lift preexisting sanctions and reducing the scope of the new sanctions.[128]

Nevertheless, after softening the legislation's provisions targeting the Russian energy sector, House Republican leaders brought the bill to the floor, resulting in its approval in both chambers with a total of just five representatives and senators voting against it. Trump decided to acquiesce in the legislation despite his strong dissatisfaction with it.[129] The *Wall Street Journal* noted, "The overwhelming majority showed the president that there was enough strength in Congress to override a veto should he choose to block the legislation."[130] Trump complained on Twitter, "It's very sad that Republicans, even some that were carried over the line on my back, do very little to protect their President."[131] The Russian government retaliated against the law's enactment by seizing two US facilities in Russia and ordering the United States to reduce the number of staff serving at its missions in Russia by 755 people.[132]

Subsequently, lawmakers in both parties pressured the administration to carry out the law.[133] This pressure, which was reinforced by some of Trump's advisors, was only partially successful. The administration opted not to implement some of the law's key provisions. For instance, it did not apply authority the law granted it to sanction firms involved in the construction of Russian energy export pipelines. But the administration did apply some other major parts of the law. In March, June, August, and December 2018, the administration imposed sanctions on several Russian institutions and more than two dozen Russian individuals implicated in election interference and other cyberattacks.[134] In response, Russia's government expanded its own list of Americans prohibited from visiting or doing business in Russia.[135]

In September 2018, the Trump administration took another step to implement the law, applying its provision targeting entities that conduct business with the Russian defense or intelligence sector by sanctioning a Chinese government institution for purchasing Russian combat aircraft and surface-to-air missile system equipment. In addition, the administration warned other governments that they too could be sanctioned under the law if they went forward with purchases of Russian arms.[136] Christopher Ford, the assistant secretary of state for International Security and Nonproliferation, noted in 2019 that this threat of sanctions based on the law had allowed the administration "to shut down billions in Russian arms sales that would likely otherwise have taken place."[137]

Trump himself strongly opposed taking these sanctions actions against Russia, but some of his advisors convinced him that the steps would help insulate the president from criticism that he was too soft on Russia and ward off the possible enactment by Congress of additional sanctions legislation targeting Russia.[138] At the same time, the 2017 law and the strong rhetorical pushback from leading lawmakers against the removal of Russian sanctions helped deter Trump from lifting preexisting penalties.[139]

Public and elite opinion

Opinion data from the Trump era show a striking divergence between attitudes regarding the investigation of possible wrongdoing by Trump or his associates in connection with Russia and attitudes regarding the imposition of sanctions against the country. Whereas views on Russia-related probes broke down sharply along partisan lines, sanctioning Russia continued to be broadly popular among voters and elites.

A Quinnipiac poll taken soon after Trump's inauguration found that 87% of Democrats and just 28% of Republicans favored investigations into potential links between some of Trump's campaign advisers and the Russian government.[140] In a similar partisan split, a May–June 2017 Quinnipiac poll revealed that 88% of Democrats and only 21% of Republicans believed that Trump did something illegal or unethical with respect to Russia.[141] This enormous partisan gap, stoked by a constant drumbeat of heated rhetoric from Trump about the issue and the issue's huge electoral stakes, helps explain why Congress was heavily polarized on Russia investigation matters.

But most voters and elites in both parties retained negative attitudes toward the Russian government, saw Russia as a threat, and backed the imposition of additional sanctions on Russia after Trump took office. A June–July 2017

Chicago Council public opinion survey indicated that 97% of Democrats and 61% of Republicans saw Russian influence in American elections as a critical or important threat to the vital interest of the United States in the next 10 years, while 96% of Democrats and 92% of Republicans viewed Russian military power as such a threat.[142] Democrats and Republicans also shared negative perceptions of Vladimir Putin. In a June 2017 Gallup public opinion survey, just 4% of Democrats and 24% of Republicans said they had a favorable view of Putin.[143] These negative attitudes were even more pronounced among foreign policy elites in both parties. A 2018 Chicago Council survey found that 0% of Democratic foreign policy elites and 8% of Republican foreign policy elites had a favorable view of Putin.[144]

With respect to sanctions specifically, majorities of the publics in both parties favored increasing sanctions on Russia after the 2016 election. In a January 2017 Quinnipiac public opinion poll, 87% of Democrats and 54% of Republicans said they supported imposing additional sanctions on Russia, while just 7% of Democrats and 27% of Republicans said they opposed doing so.[145] Americans in both parties also opposed lifting sanctions on Russia. A July 2017 Chicago Council survey found that just 17% of Democrats and 16% of Republicans supported decreasing or stopping sanctions on Russia, whereas 81% of Democrats and 79% of Republicans backed increasing sanctions or keeping them the same.[146] Broad support for sanctioning Russia persisted beyond 2017. In an April 2018 ABC News/Washington Post public opinion poll, 74% of Democrats and 68% of Republicans said they favored placing tougher sanctions on Russia.[147]

Statements about Russia by foreign policy elites provide additional evidence of the limited relationship between left-right ideological divisions and attitudes toward Russia. A study analyzing comments by members of Congress during the 2017 sanctions debate found that the vast majority of lawmakers in both parties described Putin's government as a threat to the United States.[148] Andrew King, a former deputy chief of staff to Senator Lindsey Graham, noted, "Congress has historically been very tough on Russia. Congress thinks we should have diplomacy, but we still need to punish bad actors. A new presidential direction on Russia wasn't going to change that."[149]

Such elite consensus was also evident in the positions of leading experts outside government. For instance, in July 2017, Laura Rosenberger, who had served as Hilary Clinton's foreign policy advisor during the 2016 presidential campaign, and Jamie Fly, who had served as Marco Rubio's foreign policy advisor during that campaign, launched the Alliance for Securing Democracy, a bipartisan think tank initiative centered on protecting the United States and other democracies from interference by Russia and other unfriendly countries.[150]

In addition to a favorable ideological landscape, potential electoral fallout from the Trump-Russia scandal may have contributed to the decision of some Republican lawmakers to challenge Trump on sanctions at the same time as they defended him from charges of collusion with Russia. Kyle Parker, who handled the issue as a senior Democratic House Foreign Affairs Committee aide, commented about the 2017 sanctions law, "Most Republicans thought this was good policy. But it's also good politics for them. Now Republicans can go back to their districts and say, 'we just voted for and passed the strongest sanctions package ever on Russia,' and use it as a foil against all the other Russia baggage around the administration."[151]

Advocacy group activity

The advocacy landscape, for its part, provided lawmakers in both parties with political leeway to support the sanctions legislation advanced in Congress under Trump, while influencing Republican efforts to weaken provisions targeting the Russian energy sector. On the pro-sanctions side, some of the human rights and diaspora groups that had backed the Magnitsky Act or Ukraine sanctions advocated the Trump-era sanctions legislation too.[152] But in a context where Russia's interference in the 2016 election had a very high degree of national salience, this advocacy was less consequential than the views of lawmakers and voters. A senior House Democratic congressional aide commented on the 2017 law, "I don't think anyone pushed this through because the Ukrainian-American Chicago chapter was putting pressure on them, for instance. This didn't require a significant push from the outside."[153]

Republican lawmakers did get lobbied rather heavily to water down parts of Russia sanctions legislation by some major corporations with which they were closely aligned. In particular, in 2017, oil and gas companies successfully pressed the House Republican leadership to increase a threshold for the share of Russian investment in an energy project that would lead participants in the project to be sanctioned under the legislation and to incorporate more flexibility into provisions targeting construction of the Nord Stream 2 pipeline that would transport gas from Russia to Germany through the Baltic

Sea.[154] But the 2017 bill's many other new sanctions and its restrictions on presidential authority remained largely unchanged as the bill advanced through the legislative process, as business community opposition was not strong enough to outweigh the principled and political motivations for Republicans to support the landmark legislation.

Conclusion

Stepping back to consider the full set of congressional sanctions initiatives discussed in this chapter, what stands out is the extent to which Democratic and Republican lawmakers repeatedly cooperated to advance the application of pressure on Russia—even in the face of presidential resistance. Congressional bipartisanship in these debates was enabled by elite and public attitudes across the ideological spectrum that backed a tough stance toward Putin's government, as well as by a favorable advocacy landscape. At the same time, the inter-branch clashes over Russia sanctions reflected the greater incentive of presidents than of lawmakers to prioritize the cultivation of close diplomatic ties with other governments, and therefore to be warier of measures that might antagonize foreign leaders. While lawmakers accommodated some presidential concerns about the bills, they refused to accommodate others and used the broad support for Russia sanctions to induce Obama and Trump to institute sanctions that they would not have otherwise imposed. In this way, these debates illustrate the continued capacity of Congress to exercise legislative authority in foreign policy despite the intense polarization of contemporary American politics.

7

Sanctions on Iran

Snapshots of two Obama-era debates regarding the use of sanctions against Iran point to remarkable variation in political alignments on Iran policy in recent years, from anti-presidential bipartisanship to strong polarization. In 2011, a time when Iran appeared to be developing the capacity to produce nuclear weapons, Democratic Senator Bob Menendez and Republican Senator Mark Kirk introduced an amendment that would penalize any country or firm that conducted business with Iran's central bank. Although the Obama administration had itself sought to apply economic pressure on Iran in response to Iran's nuclear pursuits, it argued to Congress that the Menendez-Kirk proposal went too far. In particular, the administration worried that cutting off all international transactions with Iran's central bank would drive up the global price of oil and create a wedge between the United States and its overseas allies.[1] Despite the administration's efforts to urge Congress not to pass the measure, the Senate adopted it by a vote of 100-0 in December 2011.[2] In the face of this overwhelming bipartisan support for the legislation, Obama decided to sign it, while venting in a signing statement that the sanctions interfered with his "constitutional authority to conduct foreign relations."[3]

Just four years later, Congress considered the Joint Comprehensive Plan of Action (JCPOA), an agreement negotiated by Obama with Iran and other major powers after Hassan Rouhani was elected president of Iran and responded positively to Obama's overtures for talks. Under the JCPOA, Iran agreed to a variety of constraints on its nuclear activities, and the United States agreed to lift an array of sanctions on Iran. In the congressional debate over the JCPOA, lawmakers split largely along partisan lines. In the key Senate vote, 40 Democrats voted to block consideration of a proposal to forbid the lifting of legislative sanctions under the agreement, while four Democrats and all 54 Republicans voted to bring the proposal to the Senate floor—leaving the opponents of lifting sanctions two votes short of being able to overcome a filibuster and allowing the agreement to go into effect.[4]

Bipartisanship and US Foreign Policy. Jordan Tama, Oxford University Press. © Oxford University Press 2024.
DOI: 10.1093/oso/9780197745663.003.0007

These votes illustrate broader patterns in recent Iran debates. From the 1990s through the election of Rouhani in 2013, Democrats and Republicans joined forces to impose a series of powerful sanctions on Iran, often despite presidential concerns that the sanctions would antagonize foreign partners or harm the US economy. Even since the negotiation of the JCPOA, Congress has acted in a bipartisan manner to impose new sanctions on Iran in connection with issues other than its nuclear program. But debates over lifting nuclear sanctions on Iran in return for Iranian concessions have been far more polarized, with most Democrats supporting diplomatic give-and-take and most Republicans maintaining that the United States should only accept complete Iranian capitulation to US demands. Just as lawmakers split mainly along party lines when debating whether the United States should lift sanctions and enter the JCPOA in 2015, many Republicans cheered and Democrats universally denounced Donald Trump's decision to reimpose sanctions and pull out of the JCPOA in 2018. However, Trump's JCPOA withdrawal also triggered intra-party Republican division, as some GOP lawmakers argued that the United States would be shooting itself in the foot by pulling out of a deal with which Iran was complying.

The analytical framework of this book highlights how ideology, advocacy groups, and institutional differences influence political alignments in Washington, DC. In this chapter, I explore how and to what extent those factors shaped the bipartisanship and polarization that have marked different phases of Iran sanctions debates over the past few decades. I find that, from Bill Clinton's presidency through Obama's first term, strong congressional bipartisanship on Iran sanctions was facilitated by negative attitudes toward Iran and concern about its nuclear program that were widely shared by Americans across the ideological spectrum, as well as by intensive advocacy from an influential advocacy group—the American Israel Public Affairs Committee (AIPAC)—that possessed strong ties to both parties. The anti-presidential character of much of this bipartisanship was driven by the greater concern of presidents than of lawmakers with the potential effects of sanctions on the US economy and important diplomatic relationships.

By contrast, the strong polarization associated with debates related to the JCPOA was fueled by a different ideological and advocacy landscape, as well as the higher political stakes of these debates. As the focus of Iran policy shifted from imposing sanctions on Iran to lifting sanctions as part of an international agreement, the general left-right ideological divide over multilateral cooperation pushed Democrats and Republicans further apart. A gradual long-term shift in the partisan breakdown of attitudes toward the Middle East, in which Republicans have become more pro-Israel than Democrats, also contributed to this polarization. Nevertheless, the continued influence of AIPAC in both parties, along with broadly shared concern among Democrats and Republicans about non-nuclear aspects of Iran's behavior, facilitated strong bipartisan support for new sanctions legislation targeting Iran's ballistic missile programming and financing of terrorism after the JCPOA went into effect.

The centrality of Iran policy to the foreign policy agenda of Obama and Trump further contributed to polarization with respect to the lifting or re-imposition of sanctions in connection with the JCPOA. For Obama, the JCPOA was a signature achievement, which gave congressional Democrats a strong incentive to support it and Republicans a strong incentive to oppose it. Conversely, pulling out of the JCPOA was a high-profile decision by Trump, which generated the opposite set of incentives for Democrats and Republicans on Capitol Hill.[5]

Sanctioning Iran before the JCPOA

Inter-branch tensions between Congress and the president over Iran policy date back at least to the 1970s, when members of Congress attempted to block the Ford administration from negotiating an agreement with Iran that would involve the transfer of civilian nuclear technology to the country.[6] More recently, from the 1990s through 2012, based mainly on concern that Iran might be developing the capacity to produce nuclear weapons, members of Congress in both parties repeatedly advanced sanctions proposals targeting Iran that presidents considered too blunt and far-reaching. While Congress often accommodated some presidential concerns about the bills, public opinion and advocacy activity gave Congress a strong hand in these inter-branch disagreements, and presidents ultimately accepted numerous sanctions provisions that they considered excessive and undesirable. This pattern spanned Democratic and Republican presidencies, periods of Republican and Democratic control of Congress, and periods of unified and divided party control of the presidency and Congress, indicating that it was not dependent on any particular constellation of party affiliations among national leaders.

The Clinton and Bush years

During the Clinton administration, Congress began to consider the imposition of new sanctions on Iran after Iran and Russia signed a contract in 1995 to construct a nuclear power plant in Iran. Subsequently, Republican-controlled Congresses enacted two significant sanctions laws concerning Iran under Clinton. In 1996, Congress mandated certain sanctions on foreign companies that invested more than $40 million in Iran's (or Libya's) energy sector.[7] In 2000, Congress authorized a set of sanctions on foreign governments or entities that provided Iran with goods or technology that could contribute to Iran's acquisition of nuclear, chemical, biological, or advanced conventional weapons.[8] The House and Senate approved each of these laws in unanimous or unanimous consent votes.[9]

Clinton resisted the 1996 law out of concern that it would strain ties with US allies that had considerable investments in Iran, but he signed it after Congress narrowed the scope of some of its sanctions provisions.[10] Clinton also resisted the 2000 law, out of concern that it would damage relations with Russia and reduce Russia's cooperation with the United States in nonproliferation efforts concerning Iran.[11] In 1998, Clinton vetoed an early version of this legislation based on concern about its potential effects both on relations with Russia and relations with the reformist Iranian government of Mohammad Khatami, which had been elected in 1997 and with which Clinton hoped to pursue a diplomatic opening.[12] However, Clinton signed the legislation after Congress revised it to authorize but not mandate sanctions.[13]

Inter-branch tensions continued to characterize Iran sanctions debates during the George W. Bush presidency. When the 1996 law came up for reauthorization in 2001, Bush pressed Congress to extend the law for only two, rather than five, years, in order to minimize the displeasure of foreign governments.[14] But the Republican-controlled House and the Democratic-controlled Senate voted almost unanimously to extend the law for five years, and Bush signed the reauthorization into law.[15]

In 2006, Iran announced that it had enriched uranium for the first time and that it would no longer cooperate with certain International Atomic Energy Agency inspections.[16] In response, lawmakers in both parties advanced new legislation that would take away the president's authority to waive the imposition of sanctions on firms that invested in Iran's energy sector.[17] Bush opposed this legislation, worried that it would split the United

States from European allies and make it more difficult for the United States to gain backing from other countries for multilateral sanctions on Iran.[18] The House, where Democrats now held a majority, nevertheless green-lighted the bill by a vote of 397-16.[19] After Bush threatened to veto the legislation, leaders of the Democratic-controlled Senate opted not to bring it to the floor.[20]

The Obama years

Bipartisan congressional coalitions also repeatedly challenged the president on Iran policy during Obama's first term, both when the Democratic Party controlled Congress in 2009–2010 and after the Republican Party gained control of the House in 2011. Obama initially sought to engage Iran's government diplomatically, while preparing to pursue multilateral sanctions on Iran if it did not show a willingness to rein in its nuclear program. As the diplomatic track yielded little apparent progress, legislators expressed impatience with the administration's approach. For instance, Democratic Senator Bob Menendez stated in October 2009, "We cannot weather endless rounds of fruitless negotiations while the Iranian regime surreptitiously advances its nuclear ambitions."[21]

In this context, legislators began to advance unilateral sanctions legislation. In November 2009, the House Foreign Affairs Committee approved a bill introduced by Howard Berman, the committee's Democratic chairman, and Ileana Ros-Lehtinen, the committee's senior Republican, that imposed new sanctions on governments, companies, or individuals that invested in Iran's energy sector or sold Iran gasoline or other refined petroleum products, while Democratic Senator Christopher Dodd introduced a similar bill in the Senate.[22]

The Obama administration conveyed strong concerns to lawmakers about these bills. In December 2009, Deputy Secretary of State James Steinberg urged senators not to move forward with a vote on the Dodd bill, stating that the legislation "might weaken rather than strengthen international unity and support for our efforts [on the Iran nuclear issue]."[23] Nevertheless, the House passed its version of the bill with the support of all but 12 representatives, and the Senate approved its version by unanimous consent.[24] By early 2010, Iran policy expert and advocate Trita Parsi notes, "Congress was coming at the Obama administration like a steamroller."[25]

With strong momentum behind the legislation, the administration adjusted its political strategy. Dennis Ross, who served at the time as Obama's principal White House advisor on Iran policy, commented, "We first tried to forestall the legislation and then tried to carve out waiver authorities to give us greater leeway regarding diplomacy."[26] Lawmakers responded by revising the legislation to allow more presidential discretion regarding the application of some of the sanctions, but they refused to remove the main substantive provisions to which the administration objected.

Democratic congressional leaders did, however, delay advancing the legislation to give the administration more time to achieve approval of new multilateral sanctions against Iran at the United Nations Security Council. In an interview, Howard Berman noted, "I didn't move the bill to Obama's desk right away because I wanted to give Obama a chance to make diplomacy work. Coordinating with [UN Ambassador] Susan Rice, I held up the bill until the Security Council voted for sanctions. It was a purposeful strategy on my part to not have a unilateral US approach."[27] Two weeks after the UN Security Council approved the new multilateral sanctions in June 2010, the Senate and House approved the final version of the legislation by votes of 99-0 and 408-8, respectively.[28] Obama signed it into law even though he considered the sanctions excessive.[29]

The political dynamics on Iran sanctions did not change much after the Republican Party took control of the House at the beginning of 2011. Later that year, Menendez and Republican Senator Mark Kirk advanced their proposal to sanction any country or entity that conducted transactions with Iran's central bank. The administration told lawmakers that this measure risked "fracturing the international coalition that has been built up over the last several years to bring pressure to bear on Iran," and it argued instead for pursuing voluntary action among countries against Iran's central bank.[30] Nevertheless, as described in the opening to this chapter, Obama signed legislation that included the Menendez-Kirk amendment after the Senate approved the amendment unanimously.

In 2012, Congress advanced additional bipartisan Iran sanctions bills that went further than the Obama administration wanted. One of these bills, advanced by Ros-Lehtinen and Berman, required the placement of Iranian oil sale revenues into escrow accounts maintained in the countries that bought the oil, and it mandated that Iran could only spend the revenues on certain types of goods.[31] The administration was concerned that this measure would further antagonize allies and partners that did business with Iran.[32] After lawmakers increased the number of goods on which money in the escrow accounts could be spent, the House and Senate approved the legislation in overwhelming bipartisan votes and Obama signed it.[33]

A few months later, lawmakers and the administration disagreed over another Menendez-Kirk proposal, which imposed further restrictions on transactions involving Iran's energy, port, shipping, and shipbuilding sectors. Regarding this proposal, a White House spokesperson said, "As we focus with our [international] partners on effectively implementing [Iran sanctions], we believe additional authorities now threaten to undercut these efforts."[34] The administration also argued that new sanctions should only be imposed on Iranian entities that directly aided Iranian nuclear and military programs, rather than on broad sectors of the Iranian economy. After members of Congress scaled back some aspects of the legislation, the measure was approved unanimously in the Senate and signed into law by Obama.[35]

Although lawmakers softened some provisions of these bills to gain presidential acquiescence to them, the bipartisan legislative activity added greatly to the scope and intensity of economic pressure on Iran.[36] Richard Nephew, who handled Iran sanctions on the National Security Council from 2011 to 2013 and at the State Department from 2013 to 2015, noted: "Congressional pressure knocked us out of our comfort zone and made us make choices that we weren't inclined to make.... The administration wouldn't have gone as far without Congress, and there wouldn't have been as much pressure on Iran without Congress."[37]

Differences in the foreign policy incentives and responsibilities of lawmakers and the president contributed to the pattern of anti-presidential bipartisanship on Iran sanctions throughout these years. Mark Dubowitz, the chief executive of the Foundation for Defense of Democracies, which advocated for many Iran sanctions bills, commented, "The administration has lots of equities at play, Congress has fewer. If you are a member of Congress, you don't have the same plethora of concerns regarding various diplomatic relationships."[38] Along similar lines, Colin Kahl, who handled Iran issues from 2009 to 2011 as deputy assistant secretary of defense for the Middle East, said, "The administration is more worried [than Congress] about economic blowback and diplomatic blowback.... The preference of any administration is to not rock the boat in diplomatic relations."[39]

Public and elite opinion

American public opinion was highly conducive to bipartisan support for sanctioning Iran prior to the negotiation of the JCPOA. Throughout these years, Gallup surveys consistently found that more than three-quarters of Americans had a very or mostly unfavorable opinion of Iran.[40] While I was unable to find public opinion surveys before 2006 that asked Americans specifically about Iran's nuclear program or the use of sanctions on Iran, data from the period when Iran accelerated its nuclear activities indicate that most Americans were concerned about this issue and favored placing penalties on Iran. A 2006 Fox News/Opinion Dynamics public opinion survey found that 78% of Democrats and 89% of Republicans thought Iran sought to enrich uranium for military, rather than civilian, purposes; 70% of Democrats and 82% of Republicans were very or somewhat concerned that Iran would attack the United States if it obtained nuclear weapons; and 88% of Democrats and 98% of Republicans were very or somewhat concerned that Iran would supply nuclear weapons to terrorists if it possessed them.[41] Gallup surveys that year also found that the vast majority of Americans thought Iran was attempting to develop nuclear weapons and were worried that Iran would use them aggressively if it obtained them.[42] A 2012 Chicago Council on Global Affairs public opinion survey found in a similar vein that 75% of Republicans and 61% of Democrats viewed Iran's nuclear program as a critical threat.[43]

Surveys conducted between 2006 and 2012 also found broad public support for sanctioning Iran based on its nuclear program. A 2006 ABC News/Washington Post poll found that 71% of Americans favored imposing sanctions on Iran to try to prevent it from acquiring nuclear technology.[44] A 2009 Pew survey found that 81% of Republicans and 72% of Democrats supported imposing tougher sanctions on Iran.[45] Other surveys conducted in 2009 and 2012 found similarly that about three in four Americans backed sanctioning Iran in an effort to prevent it from developing nuclear weapons.[46] (See Table 7.1.)

Given these public attitudes, supporting the imposition of sanctions on Iran was clearly a safer choice politically for Democratic and Republican lawmakers than opposing the use of sanctions. As a congressional aide involved in the issue noted, "There's no percentage in members going back to their home state and saying anything other than, 'I want the toughest sanctions in place.'"[47]

Table 7.1 Public opinion on sanctioning Iran over its nuclear program

Pollster	Survey period	Total in support	Total opposed	Democrats in support	Republicans in support
ABC/Wash Post[a]	January 2006	71%	26%	N/A ·	N/A
Pew[b]	Sept–Oct 2009	78%	12%	72%	81%
CNN/Opinion Research[c]	Oct 2009	77%	21%	N/A	N/A
ABC/Wash Post[d]	Oct 2009	78%	18%	N/A	N/A
ABC/Wash Post[d]	March 2012	74%	21%	N/A	N/A

Note: The table includes all public opinion polls I could find from 1996 to 2012 that asked respondents whether they supported imposing or increasing sanctions on Iran in connection with its nuclear program. Table entries indicating "N/A" reflect survey results that the pollster did not report.

[a] "Iran says it is refining uranium to use in nuclear power plants. Other countries are concerned Iran may also use this uranium in nuclear weapons. To try to prevent Iran from developing nuclear technology, would you support or oppose imposing international economic sanctions against Iran?"

[b] "Would you approve or disapprove of tougher international economic sanctions on Iran?"

[c] "Would you favor or oppose imposing economic sanctions on Iran in an attempt to prevent Iran from developing nuclear weapons?"

[d] "To try to prevent Iran from developing nuclear weapons, would you support or oppose increasing international economic sanctions against Iran?"

Although I could not find any surveys of foreign policy decision-makers or experts that asked whether they favored sanctioning Iran over its nuclear program, related survey data suggest that support for such sanctions would probably not have broken down along left-right lines among elites either. A 2016 Chicago Council survey of foreign policy professionals found that 79% of Democrats and 81% of Republicans thought preventing the spread of nuclear weapons should be a very important goal of the United States, while a 2018 Chicago Council survey of foreign policy professionals found that 81% of Democrats and 73% of Republicans favored sanctioning non-democracies.[48]

Advocacy group activity

The advocacy landscape also facilitated bipartisanship on Iran sanctions during this period. Many of the major Iran sanctions bills were strongly backed by the American Israel Public Affairs Committee (AIPAC), which Washington insiders have repeatedly rated as one of the most influential advocacy groups on Capitol Hill.[49] AIPAC possessed close ties to lawmakers in both parties throughout the period in which Congress was very active in sanctioning Iran.[50] AIPAC took a particularly strong interest in Iran policy because of the threat that Iran could pose to Israel. AIPAC provided input to legislative offices on the drafting of many Iran sanctions bills and lobbied members of Congress to support them.[51] Other hawkish or pro-Israel groups also shaped and advocated Iran sanctions bills. In particular, the Foundation for Defense of Democracies urged lawmakers to adopt a variety of sanctions and exercised outsized influence among Iran hawks on Capitol Hill.[52]

Meanwhile, interest group opposition to Iran sanctions bills was relatively limited and muted. Business associations typically represent the most important interest group opponents of sanctions, since sanctions curtail economic and financial exchange. But the business community generally did not make it a priority to block Iran sanctions bills.[53] This decision reflected both the limited scale of US economic interests in Iran and the difficulty of blocking legislation that had such strong support. One congressional aide said that the business community largely stayed on the sidelines because it saw that "AIPAC-pushed bills are usually juggernauts, and it's not worth trying to stop them."[54]

The result of this advocacy landscape was that lawmakers with large pro-Israel constituencies or close ties to AIPAC had a particularly strong incentive to advance Iran sanctions bills, while other lawmakers generally had more reason to support than to oppose the bills. Studies of interest groups have shown that groups often exercise influence by working closely with legislative allies.[55] Pro-Israel groups shaped Iran sanctions legislation mainly in this way. At the same time, pro-Israel groups regularly conducted outreach to nearly every congressional office in an effort to gain the broadest possible support for the bills.[56] Given the strong public backing for sanctioning Iran and the weak interest group opposition to Iran sanctions, the path of least political resistance for most lawmakers was to support the sanctions measures.

Lifting sanctions under the JCPOA

For the first part of 2013, congressional bipartisanship on Iran sanctions remained strong. Early in the year, Representatives Ed Royce and Eliot Engel, the new Republican and Democratic leaders of the House Foreign Affairs Committee, introduced a bill designed to expand further the US list of blacklisted Iranian companies and block Iran's access to foreign bank assets held in euros, while Menendez and Kirk introduced a similar bill in the Senate.[57] This legislation was approved by the House by a vote of 400-20 and gained 17 Democratic and 43 Republican cosponsors in the Senate.[58]

However, this legislation's momentum weakened after the May 2013 election of Hassan Rouhani, who supported diplomatic engagement with the United States, as Iranian president. Under Rouhani, talks between US and Iranian officials, which had been taking place secretly since 2012, began making more substantial progress.[59] These talks resulted in the signing in November 2013 of an interim nuclear agreement between the United States, several other countries, and Iran in which Iran agreed to accept some restrictions on its nuclear activities in exchange for some sanctions relief.[60]

Perhaps most importantly for Obama, the interim agreement's achievement suggested that a more comprehensive final agreement with Iran might be within reach. In that context, Obama lobbied Congress intensively and publicly not to impose new sanctions on Iran. Between November 2013 and January 2014, Obama called and met personally with many Democratic legislators on the issue to urge them not to support the sanctions bill.[61] Obama also used his January 2014 State of the Union address to issue a high-profile veto threat: "If this Congress sends me a new sanctions bill now that threatens to derail these talks, I will veto it. For the sake of our national security, we must give diplomacy a chance to succeed."[62] This presidential activity made it very clear that preventing the enactment of new sanctions on Iran was a top priority for Obama, giving the issue greater political stakes for the Democratic and Republican Parties.

In this context, Senate Democratic support for the Menendez-Kirk bill diminished considerably. In December 2013, 10 Democratic chairs of Senate committees sent a letter to Senate Majority Leader Harry Reid asking him to hold off bringing the bill to the Senate floor because the enactment of such legislation would cause the Iranians to abandon negotiations.[63] Some other Democratic senators who had previously supported the Menendez-Kirk bill also said they no longer favored advancing the bill because the Iranians had come to the bargaining table and the president needed room to pursue diplomacy.[64] Reid signaled that he shared this view and decided not to bring the Menendez-Kirk bill to the Senate floor.[65] A congressional aide involved in the issue commented, "The president made a forceful policy argument that new sanctions now would be a big mistake. Democratic senators found that argument persuasive."[66]

Meanwhile, congressional Republicans sharply criticized the interim agreement and continued to support imposing further sanctions on Iran—resulting in a polarization of congressional positions on the issue.[67] In February 2014, House Majority Leader Eric Cantor said, "The United States must remain firm. Already, the limited sanctions relief provided by the interim deal has undermined the perception of international pressure so critical to convincing the Iranians to change course."[68] When Kirk and Menendez reintroduced their sanctions bill in January 2015, the bill garnered 44 Republican and just eight Democratic cosponsors—a notable change from 2013, when the legislation had attracted 43 Republican and 17 Democratic cosponsors.[69]

Obama again urged Congress not to advance new sanctions legislation in his January 2015 State of the Union address, stating that "new sanctions passed by this Congress, at this moment in time, will all but guarantee that diplomacy fails. . . . And that's why I will veto any new sanctions bill that threatens to undo this progress."[70] As the United States and Iran moved closer to a final agreement, congressional positions polarized further. In March 2015, 47 Republican senators signed a letter to Iranian leaders circulated by Senator Tom Cotton noting that any agreement reached between Obama and the Iranian government could be revoked by a future US president or modified by the US Congress.[71] This letter, which did not have any Democratic signatories, was a clear effort to undermine the US-Iran negotiations, and it was sharply criticized by both the White House and congressional Democrats.[72]

Polarization continued after Obama, Iran, and other world leaders finalized the JCPOA, under which Iran accepted far greater restrictions on its nuclear program than those contained in the interim agreement, in return for much more sanctions relief.[73] As described in the introduction of this chapter, congressional voting on the provision of sanctions relief to Iran under the JCPOA broke down almost entirely along party lines. Given this polarization, the JCPOA only went into effect because Obama had signed it as an executive agreement, rather than a treaty. Whereas a two-thirds supermajority in the Senate is needed to ratify a treaty, an executive agreement does not require congressional approval.

With the JCPOA treated as an executive agreement, opponents of the deal could only block it by enacting legislation that prohibited the lifting of sanctions under it.[74] Since Obama was certain to veto any such legislation, in practice this meant that opponents of the agreement needed the support of two-thirds of representatives and senators—the share required to over-ride a presidential veto—in order to torpedo the deal. As a result, Obama only needed to gain the backing of most Democratic lawmakers in order for the JCPOA to go into effect, which he was able to achieve. But instituting the JCPOA as an executive agreement, rather than a Senate-approved treaty, made it easier for Trump to later withdraw from the agreement.

Public and elite opinion

In contrast to the broad public support for sanctioning Iran prior to the election of Rouhani, public attitudes regarding the JCPOA were strongly polarized. On the one hand, across 10 public opinion surveys conducted during the two-month period between the signing of the JCPOA and the key Senate vote related to the agreement, an average of 54% of Democrats supported the agreement, while an average of just 22% of Democrats opposed it. On the other hand, in the same set of polls, an average of only 17% of Republicans favored the agreement, while an average of 68% of Republicans opposed it.[75] (See Table 7.2.)

Although I could not find a survey that asked foreign policy leaders or experts about the agreement during this two-month period, a survey from an adjacent period reveals polarization on this issue at the elite level too. A 2014 Chicago Council survey of foreign policy professionals found that 97% of Democrats and 45% of Republicans favored the 2013 interim deal with Iran, while 3% of Democrats and 55% of Republicans opposed it.[76]

Public and elite polarization on the JCPOA was consistent with the ideological divide that separates liberals and conservatives on issues involving multilateralism and international cooperation. As discussed in Chapter 3, liberals are generally more supportive than conservatives of international agreements. Ilan Goldenberg, who handled Middle East issues as a Democratic aide on the Senate Foreign Relations Committee, noted: "The Iran deal conveyed a message of, 'We can do diplomacy instead of war,' which is an important message for a lot of Democrats."[77] In a similar vein, Lester Munson, who served as the Republican staff director on the Senate Foreign Relations Committee during the JCPOA debate, observed: "This was a multilateral arms control agreement. If you're a Wilsonian, this is exactly the type of international agreement that you'd support."[78]

Table 7.2 Public opinion on Iran nuclear deal, 2015

Pollster	Survey period	Democrats in support	Democrats opposed	Republicans in support	Republicans opposed
YouGov[a]	July 14–16	60%	13%	28%	55%
Pew[b]	July 14–20	59%	25%	14%	75%
ABC/Wash Post[c]	July 16–19	69%	25%	41%	54%
NBC/Wall St Journal[d]	July 26–30	58%	8%	15%	60%
CBS[e]	July 29–Aug 2	32%	15%	6%	58%
Monmouth[f]	July 30–Aug 2	41%	14%	13%	55%
CNN/ORC[g]	Aug 13–16	70%	28%	15%	83%
Quinnipiac[h]	Aug 20–25	46%	25%	4%	87%
Pew[b]	Sept 3–7	42%	29%	6%	78%
CNN/ORC[g]	Sept 4–8	64%	33%	23%	74%

Note: The table includes all public opinion polls I could find that asked respondents whether they supported or opposed the Joint Comprehensive Plan of Action between the signing of the JCPOA on July 14, 2015, and the key Senate vote on the agreement on September 10, 2015.

[a] "Several world powers, including the United States, have reached an international agreement that will limit Iran's nuclear activity in return for the lifting of major economic sanctions against Iran. Do you support or oppose this agreement?"

[b] "From what you know, do you approve or disapprove of this agreement?"

[c] "As you may know, the US and other countries have announced a deal to lift economic sanctions against Iran in exchange for Iran agreeing not to produce nuclear weapons. International inspectors would monitor Iran's facilities, and if Iran is caught breaking the agreement economic sanctions would be imposed again. Do you support or oppose this agreement?"

[d] "As you may know, an agreement has been reached between Iran and a group of six other nations, including the US. The agreement attempts to prevent Iran from developing a nuclear weapon by limiting Iran's ability to produce nuclear material and allowing inspections into Iran's nuclear sites in exchange for reducing certain economic sanctions that are currently in place. Do you support or oppose this agreement or do you not know enough to have an opinion?"

[e] "Recently, Iran and a group of six countries led by the United States reached an agreement to limit Iran's ability to make nuclear weapons for more than a decade in return for lifting economic sanctions against Iran. From what you've heard or read so far, do you approve or disapprove of the recent agreement with Iran, or don't you know enough about it yet to say?"

[f] "Should Congress vote to approve or not approve this agreement, or are you not sure?"

[g] "Do you think Congress should approve or reject the deal with Iran?"

[h] "Do you support or oppose the nuclear deal with Iran?"

By contrast, conservatives tend to place less trust in pledges by foreign governments, particularly adversaries.[79] It was therefore natural that Republicans would be warier than Democrats of making concessions to Iran in return for Iranian commitments. A House Republican aide involved in

Middle East policy observed: "Many Republicans thought the JCPOA was a bad idea because they didn't trust the Iranian regime."[80] The partisan incentive of most Republicans to oppose a potential legacy achievement by a Democratic president and of most Democrats to support such an accomplishment only added to this impetus for polarization on the trading of sanctions relief for Iranian nuclear commitments.

Advocacy group activity

The advocacy landscape on Iran policy, for its part, grew more complicated as the JCPOA debate unfolded. Whereas AIPAC had dominated discussions of earlier Iran sanctions bills, it was challenged during this debate by a variety of left-leaning and pro-peace groups who favored the agreement. These groups neutralized AIPAC's influence among Democratic lawmakers and, in conjunction with the political incentive of Democrats to support an international agreement negotiated by their party's standard-bearer, led most Democrats to back the deal even though AIPAC strongly opposed it.

AIPAC did lobby aggressively against the JCPOA, spending tens of millions of dollars on advertising against the agreement, flying legislators' constituents to Washington so they could lobby their representatives against the deal, and threatening to back primary challengers to lawmakers who supported it.[81] But an array of other groups were also very active in advocacy on the JCPOA, both in opposition and in support. In addition to AIPAC, opponents of the agreement included other conservative and pro-Israel groups, the Foundation for Defense of Democracies, and the Israeli and Saudi ambassadors. On the other side of the debate, the deal was backed by the pro-Israel and pro-peace group J Street; other peace organizations, such as Win Without War and the Quaker-affiliated Friends Committee on National Legislation; arms control NGOs, such as the Ploughshares Fund and the Arms Control Association; the National Iranian American Council; various progressive groups; and European ambassadors.[82] While the pro-JCPOA coalition did not spend as much money on advertising as the anti-JCPOA coalition did, it lobbied Democratic lawmakers intensively on Capitol Hill, coordinating hundreds of thousands of phone calls and emails from constituents to congressional offices.[83] A former House Democratic aide noted that "members got pummeled by groups from both sides" on the issue, adding that the progressive left was "mobilized hard-core" on it.[84]

The ability of the pro-JCPOA coalition to counter the influence of AIPAC was aided by the tarnishing of AIPAC's standing among many Democrats due to the group's close alignment with the conservative Israeli government of Benjamin Netanyahu, whose hawkish policies toward Palestinians and vociferous opposition to diplomacy with Iran alienated many Democrats.[85] In an event that infuriated many Democrats, Netanyahu, with the support of AIPAC and at the invitation of Republican congressional leaders, had lambasted Obama's Iran policy in an address to a joint session of Congress in March 2015, telling lawmakers that the prospective agreement with Iran was "a very bad deal."[86] Ryan Costello, policy director of the National Iranian American Council, which advocated for the JCPOA, noted that in the wake of Netanyahu's speech, "AIPAC seemed more like a partisan group, and J Street became more influential among Democrats."[87]

Obama's own intensive lobbying of members of Congress on the issue also contributed to the strong backing of Democratic lawmakers for the deal. Obama called dozens of Democratic representatives and senators to urge them to support the deal and met with many others in the White House.[88] An administration official involved in the issue described one such two-and-a-half-hour meeting in August between Obama and 20 House Democrats: "Obama went around the room and answered the most difficult, technical questions each of these members had about the agreement. . . . We left the meeting with almost all the members saying, 'I was on the fence, but I'm with you right now.' "[89] Other senior administration officials also spent countless hours making the case for the agreement to members of Congress.[90]

The administration's lobbying of Democratic lawmakers also included old-fashioned deal-making and arm-twisting. Margaret Taylor, who served as Democratic chief counsel and deputy staff director on the Senate Foreign Relations Committee during the JCPOA debate, noted: "The administration was telling Democrats they'd protect them when their reelect comes up in fifteen months."[91] Another senior Democratic congressional aide commented that the White House said to some members, "We're going to make life hard for you if you oppose us on this."[92] This aide added that, in the end, Democratic lawmakers "didn't fear AIPAC as much as they feared the White House or feared a progressive backlash."

Trump's JCPOA withdrawal

As a presidential candidate, Trump lambasted the JCPOA, calling it "the worst deal ever negotiated," and pledging to dismantle it.[93] After taking office, Trump, for a time, heeded the advice of some of his advisors to hold off on exiting the agreement. H. R. McMaster, who served as Trump's national security advisor from February 2017 to March 2018, notes in his memoir that he argued to Trump that the United States would have more leverage vis-à-vis Iran by staying in the agreement than by exiting it.[94] But in May 2018, Trump formally withdrew from the JCPOA and began imposing an array of punishing sanctions on Iran as part of a campaign that his administration called "maximum pressure."[95] The sanctions included ones that the Obama administration had lifted under the JCPOA, as well as others that went beyond pre-JCPOA penalties, such as the denial of waivers to all countries that purchased Iranian oil.[96]

Congressional reactions to Trump's withdrawal from the agreement broke down partly, but not entirely, along party lines. Unsurprisingly, congressional Democrats uniformly opposed the withdrawal.[97] Even the handful of Democrats who had not supported the agreement in 2015 argued that it would be counterproductive to pull out of a deal with which Iran was complying.[98] Senator Ben Cardin commented: "President Trump has breathed air into Tehran's inevitable argument to the international community: We kept our end of the deal, but America is not good for its word and cannot be trusted."[99]

Conversely, many Republican lawmakers praised the withdrawal. House Majority Leader Kevin McCarthy commented that "we must oppose bad deals that give our enemies a pathway to a nuclear bomb, which is why I applaud the President's actions."[100] Other leading Republican hawks, such as Senators Tom Cotton and Marco Rubio, as well as numerous rank-and-file GOP lawmakers, also strongly endorsed the pullout.[101] One compendium of Republican congressional reactions to Trump's withdrawal listed endorsements of the withdrawal by 22 lawmakers and criticisms of it by just four lawmakers.[102]

But several prominent congressional Republicans, including House Foreign Affairs Committee Chairman Ed Royce, Senate Foreign Relations Committee Chairman Bob Corker, and House Armed Services Committee Chairman Mac Thornberry, said that the United States should focus on enforcing the agreement vigorously and strengthening it through diplomacy, rather than exiting it.[103] A House Republican aide involved in Middle East policy explained the rationale of these Republicans: "We'd already lost all our negotiating power with Iran. So why abandon what little leverage we had left? We were never going to be able to re-create all of the international sanctions. And withdrawing would make people question the word of the United States."[104] Political considerations may also have shaped the thinking of Republican opponents of withdrawal, in that pulling out of the agreement could make the Republican Party appear responsible for any subsequent crisis with Iran.[105]

These differences of view regarding JCPOA withdrawal coexisted under Trump with continued strong bipartisanship in support of sanctioning Iran over non-nuclear issues. In June 2017, the Senate passed by a vote of 98-2 a bill that mandated new sanctions on Iran based on its ballistic missile program and support for terrorism.[106] This legislation was subsequently enacted into law after also being approved with overwhelming bipartisan support in the House.[107] Importantly, missile and terrorism sanctions did not conflict with US commitments under the JCPOA, which only involved nuclear sanctions. A Senate Democratic foreign policy aide noted in 2017: "Sanctions are a safe space for Republicans and Democrats on Iran if the sanctions don't threaten the JCPOA."[108] Less charitably, a House Republican foreign policy aide commented: "The fig leaf the Democrats took to cover themselves on the JCPOA was to say, 'We are still going to push Iran on ballistic missiles and financing terrorism.'"[109]

Public and elite opinion

Public and elite opinion data from 2017 and 2018 reveal broad agreement among Democrats but disagreement among Republicans over whether the United States should withdraw from the JCPOA. While Democrats overwhelmingly opposed withdrawal, about half of Republicans backed pulling out of the agreement.

I found three public opinion surveys that asked Americans whether they supported withdrawing from the Iran nuclear deal between US entry into the agreement and Trump's withdrawal decision. The first of these surveys, conducted by CNN in October 2017, found that 13% of Democrats and 47% of Republicans favored withdrawal.[110] The second poll, conducted by

Table 7.3 Public opinion on withdrawing from Iran nuclear deal, 2016–2018

Pollster	Survey period	Democrats in support	Democrats opposed	Democrats unsure	Republicans in support	Republicans opposed	Republicans unsure
CNN[a]	Oct 12–15, 2017	13%	80%	N/A	47%	48%	N/A
CNN[a]	May 2–5, 2018	10%	84%	N/A	51%	43%	N/A
CBS[b]	May 3–6, 2018	10%	26%	64%	39%	12%	48%

Note: The table includes all public opinion polls I could find that asked respondents whether they supported or opposed withdrawing from the Joint Comprehensive Plan of Action prior to Trump's decision to withdraw from the agreement on May 8, 2018. Table entries indicating "N/A" reflect survey results that the pollster did not report.

[a] "As you may know, the United States and five other countries entered an agreement with Iran aimed at preventing Iran from developing nuclear weapons. Do you think the US should or should not withdraw from that agreement?"

[b] "Do you think the United States should remain in the 2015 Iran nuclear deal, or do you think United States should leave the 2015 Iran nuclear deal, or don't you know enough about it to say?"

CNN during the week before Trump announced his decision in May 2018, found similarly that 10% of Democrats and 51% of Republicans backed withdrawal.[111] The third survey, conducted by CBS around the same time, gave respondents a "don't know enough about it to say" option, in addition to support and oppose options. This survey revealed that many Americans were unsure about the issue. While 10% of Democrats and 39% of Republicans said they backed withdrawal in this survey, 64% of Democrats and 48% of Republicans said they didn't know enough about it to say.[112] (See Table 7.3.)

A pair of Chicago Council surveys conducted soon after Trump's withdrawal decision further show that elite and public opinion on the issue broke down similarly. In a July 2018 public opinion survey, the Chicago Council found that 82% of Democratic members of the public and 53% of Republican members of the public thought the United States should participate in the Iran nuclear agreement.[113] In a survey of foreign policy professionals conducted from August to October of 2018, the Chicago Council found that 100% of Democrats and 46% of Republicans thought the United States should participate in the accord.[114]

Collectively, these data reveal both a large partisan gap and considerable division within the Republican Party. Whereas Republicans were overwhelmingly opposed to entry into the JCPOA in 2015, they were more split over whether to pull out of an agreement with which Iran was in compliance.

At the same time, much of the public was relatively uninformed about the issue and did not have a strong position on it. These conditions were conducive to uniform opposition from Democratic lawmakers to withdrawal, along with intra-party division among Republican elected officials. But the importance of the issue to Trump gave Republican lawmakers a partisan incentive to back the president on the issue, leading most congressional Republicans to do so.

Advocacy group activity

The advocacy landscape was also conducive to the combination of Democratic unity and Republican division that characterized the debate over JCPOA withdrawal. Whereas the debate over joining the agreement featured vigorous lobbying on both sides of the issue, with conservative pro-Israel and hawkish groups lined up against an array of progressive and pro-peace groups, advocacy activity in the withdrawal debate was more one-sided. In particular, whereas a variety of think tanks and left-leaning organizations argued for remaining in the agreement,[115] few critics of the deal advocated exiting the agreement. This context only bolstered the inclination of congressional Democrats to oppose a JCPOA pullout, while giving congressional Republicans less reason to support a withdrawal than they had to oppose entering into the agreement in the first place.

AIPAC did continue to highlight what it saw as shortcomings of the JCPOA. But it stopped short of calling for a withdrawal from the agreement, instead urging the Trump administration to strengthen the deal by making it permanent and incorporating into it stronger provisions for international inspections of Iranian military sites.[116] AIPAC's calls to strengthen, rather than tear up, the agreement were motivated in part by the group's desire to avoid fraying further its ties to Democrats.[117] Middle East policy expert Ilan Goldenberg noted during the withdrawal debate: "2015 was traumatic for AIPAC. They want bipartisan action that preserves the JCPOA and is tough on Iran's other behavior."[118]

Some other prominent critics of the JCPOA outside government also argued for strengthening, rather than dismantling, the agreement. Michael Singh, the managing director of the Washington Institute for Near East Policy, a pro-Israel think tank, had testified to Congress in 2015 against entering the agreement, but he testified in 2017 that the United States should seek to improve the deal through diplomacy instead of jettisoning it.[119] Mark Dubowitz, the most well-known Iran hawk in Washington and the head of the Foundation for Defense of Democracies, also favored the negotiation of new side agreements that would place tighter reins on Iran rather than setting the deal aside.[120]

In short, Republicans faced little pressure from advocacy groups to back withdrawal from the JCPOA and were even advised by some trusted groups and experts that a better alternative to withdrawal existed. It was therefore easier politically for Republicans to oppose withdrawal than it was for Republicans to support entry into the agreement in 2015, contributing to the greater intra-party division in the withdrawal debate. But Republicans did have a political incentive to support their party's leader on one of his top foreign policy priorities, which largely explains why most Republican lawmakers endorsed Trump's decision.

Conclusion

Taken together, the debates over Iran sanctions and related issues discussed in this chapter reveal both the possibilities and limits of foreign policy bipartisanship. Before Iran policy achieved very high salience during Obama's nuclear negotiations with Iran, congressional Democrats and Republicans repeatedly worked together to mandate a series of major sanctions on Iran, often despite presidential resistance to their efforts. These inter-branch clashes were fueled by the differing incentives of lawmakers and the president. While the positions of members of Congress reflected the support of most voters and influential advocacy groups for a tough stance toward Iran, presidents worried about the economic and diplomatic repercussions of sanctioning Iran and its international partners so heavily.

But partisan incentives largely overwhelmed these favorable conditions for bipartisanship when the debate over Iran policy became centered on a diplomatic agreement with the potential to become a landmark achievement for Obama, leading more members of Congress to see Iran policy primarily through the lens of how it would affect the national standing of the two parties. These partisan incentives, along with the greater support of liberals than of conservatives for multilateral agreements, fueled a sharp polarization of the Iran policy debate during the later years of Obama's presidency. This polarization softened a bit when the debate shifted to Trump's withdrawal from the JCPOA, as withdrawal threatened to create new political problems for Republicans down the line. But the pull of partisan loyalty remained quite strong on an issue that was a high priority for Trump, just as it was for Obama, leading most Republican members of Congress to back Trump's replacement of the JCPOA with a new set of punishing sanctions on Iran.

8

The Trans-Pacific Partnership and international trade

In October 2015, the United States and 11 other countries—Australia, Brunei, Canada, Chile, Japan, Malaysia, Mexico, New Zealand, Peru, Singapore, and Vietnam—reached agreement on the Trans-Pacific Partnership (TPP), a landmark agreement to reduce a variety of barriers of trade. The TPP countries, scattered across the fast-growing Pacific rim region, represented about 40% of the world's GDP (gross domestic product).[1] In announcing the agreement, Obama said, "This partnership levels the playing field for our farmers, ranchers, and manufacturers by eliminating more than 18,000 taxes that various countries put on our products."[2]

Obama's negotiation of the TPP had been facilitated by the approval by Congress earlier in 2015 of trade promotion authority (TPA). Like most congressional votes on trade in recent decades, the House and Senate votes on TPA had featured cross-partisanship, with most Republicans and a substantial minority of Democrats voting to streamline the process for congressional approval of trade agreements.[3] This political alignment reflected the long-standing ideological and advocacy landscape on trade. Liberals and conservatives do not differ from each other consistently in their attitudes regarding trade liberalization, as pro-trade and protectionist positions coexist on both sides of the left-right ideological spectrum.[4] While advocacy groups aligned with the Republican Party back trade agreements much more than groups aligned with the Democratic Party do—with major business associations typically lining up against labor unions and environmental groups—support for trade liberalization also tends to vary greatly across economic sectors. As a result, lawmakers representing different parts of the country have varying incentives with regard to their positions on trade, regardless of their political party.[5]

Congressional reactions to the TPP revealed divisions within both parties on the agreement. A few Republican and Democratic lawmakers voiced unreserved enthusiasm about the TPP. Republican Senator John McCain, of

Bipartisanship and US Foreign Policy. Jordan Tama, Oxford University Press. © Oxford University Press 2024.
DOI: 10.1093/oso/9780197745663.003.0008

Arizona, said the agreement would "keep American companies competitive in one of the most economically vibrant and fastest-growing regions in the world," while Democratic Representative Ron Kind, of Wisconsin, called it a "historic 21st century agreement" that would "set the trading rules for this region."[6] But Republican members of Congress with close ties to the pharmaceutical and tobacco industries, which were dissatisfied with certain TPP provisions, criticized the agreement. Republican Senator Thom Tillis, representing the tobacco-producing state of North Carolina, commented, "I will not only vote against the TPP, but actively work to help defeat its ratification in the Senate."[7] At the same time, pro-labor and progressive Democrats charged that the agreement would result in a race to the bottom on labor and environmental standards. Democratic Senator Debbie Stabenow, of Michigan, said: "We want to export products and not jobs."[8]

On top of these standard perspectives and concerns regarding trade, the particular character of the 2016 presidential election campaign added a major obstacle to advancing legislation that Congress needed to pass in order to allow US participation in the TPP to go into effect. As Donald Trump emerged as the Republican Party's standard-bearer, he made protectionism one of the central planks of his campaign, making it harder politically for pro-trade Republican lawmakers to support the agreement publicly.[9] In this context, Republican congressional leaders, who had strongly backed TPA in 2015, adopted a lukewarm stance toward the TPP in 2016, and Congress did not vote on the agreement before Obama left office.[10] Trump then promptly withdrew from the agreement soon after taking office. Many Democratic members of Congress applauded Trump's withdrawal, while key Republican lawmakers offered a muted response to it, torn between their pro-trade orientation and their partisan loyalty on a top presidential priority.[11]

In this chapter, I focus on the TPP debate and the political dynamics that influenced it. An examination of the attitudes of the public and elites, the activity of advocacy groups, and the positions of elected officials highlights the political pressures that contributed to cross-partisanship on the issue across the Obama and Trump presidencies. Toward the end of the chapter, I more briefly examine two key subsequent trade debates under Trump—regarding the imposition of tariffs on other countries and the replacement of the North American Free Trade Agreement (NAFTA) with the United States-Mexico-Canada Agreement (USMCA). The tariff debate featured similar alignments as the TPP debate, with Trump's tariffs generating opposition from much of the business community and Republican congressional leaders, along with support from major labor unions and many Democrats in Congress. The USMCA, on the other hand, represents a case of pro-presidential bipartisanship, fueled by a rare convergence of positions in support of a trade agreement among the most powerful business and labor groups.

The launch of TPP talks

Obama inherited from George W. Bush a nascent initiative to negotiate the Trans-Pacific Partnership. This initiative began in 2007 as an effort among Brunei, Chile, New Zealand, Singapore, and the United States to reduce barriers to trade, and it expanded in 2008 to include Australia, Peru, and Vietnam.[12] In late 2009, the Obama administration announced that it would pick up the negotiations, which expanded in 2010 to include Malaysia, in 2012 to include Canada and Mexico, and in 2013 to include Japan.

The Bush administration's rationale for launching the TPP negotiations was that a major agreement with countries in the Asia-Pacific region was needed to ensure that the United States would not be excluded from new economic arrangements taking form in the region, many of which were driven by China.[13] The Obama administration saw the need for the TPP in similar terms. When announcing his desire to negotiate the TPP, Obama said, "As an Asia-Pacific nation, the United States expects to be involved in the discussions that shape the future of this region and to participate fully in appropriate organizations as they are established and evolve."[14] More broadly, the Obama administration saw the TPP as a centerpiece of its "pivot" or "rebalance" to Asia—a strategy designed to ensure continued US leadership and influence in a region that would only become more important during the 21st century.[15] These rationales of the Bush and Obama administrations align with the political incentive of presidents to support policies that advance overall welfare and broad national interests.

Consistent with the greater support for free trade of interest groups aligned with the Republican Party than of groups aligned with the Democratic Party, congressional Republicans largely reacted positively to the launch of TPP negotiations, while reactions from congressional Democrats were mixed. When Obama announced his intention to pursue the talks, Representatives Dave Camp, the senior Republican on the Ways and Means Committee, and Kevin Brady, the senior Republican on the Ways and Means Subcommittee on Trade, applauded the step.[16] Brady also echoed some of the administration's rationale for the TPP: "Negotiations with the TPP countries . . . can help counter efforts by our competitors to move ahead aggressively and leave American workers and exporters behind."[17]

Some key congressional Democrats endorsed the negotiations too. Senate Finance Committee Chairman Max Baucus highlighted the likely benefits of the TPP for American workers and exporters, while Senate Foreign Relations Committee Chairman John Kerry emphasized the need to participate more vigorously in the Asia-Pacific region.[18] Other Democrats sounded notes of caution about the TPP negotiations, however, expressing a variety of concerns. Representatives Charles Rangel, the Democratic chairman of the Ways and Means Committee, and Sander Levin, the Democratic chairman of that committee's trade subcommittee, noted the potential promise of the TPP, but they highlighted the importance of "gaining real access for US farmers, workers and businesses, and incorporating international labor and environmental standards."[19] Some Democrats also voiced concerns about practices by countries involved in the negotiations that might be inconsistent with American values or place US firms and workers at a disadvantage, including restrictions by Vietnam on political freedoms and the use by Japan of non-tariff trade barriers that made it difficult for American automakers to be successful in the Japanese market.[20] Michigan Senator Debbie Stabenow, representing a state that hosted many auto industry jobs, expressed alarm at "a situation where we have a country [Japan] involved that has spent 80 years blocking our auto industry from fully participating in trade."[21]

The Trade Promotion Authority debate

The debate over the TPP intensified as the trade negotiations advanced, particularly after Obama formally asked Congress to grant him TPA in July 2013.[22] Formerly known as fast-track authority, TPA is a legislative device designed to facilitate the negotiation and approval of trade agreements while preserving a large congressional role in the process. Under TPA, the executive branch must pursue certain trade negotiation objectives that are stipulated by the TPA legislation and consult with the relevant congressional committees during any trade negotiations. The House and Senate, in turn, are required to take up and vote on any agreement negotiated under TPA no more than 90 legislative business days after the date on which the president submits the agreement to Congress, without amending the agreement.

If Congress does not vote on the agreement within that timeframe, it goes into effect.

The rationale behind these rules is that they prevent Congress from sending the United States and other parties to an agreement back to the negotiating table as a result of amendments and ensure that inaction by Congress will not hold up an agreement's implementation. TPA should therefore give other countries more confidence that negotiating an agreement with the United States is worthwhile. In the view of critics, however, TPA short-circuits Congress's constitutional authority to regulate international trade.[23] Congress had last approved TPA in 2002, during the presidency of George W. Bush, with most Republicans and a minority of Democrats voting for it.[24] But the legislation had lapsed in 2007.

The Obama administration considered TPA essential to complete the TPP negotiations, and the positions of lawmakers in the TPA debate largely mirrored their positions on the TPP. Then-US Trade Representative Michael Froman observed: "It was clear to everyone that the vote for TPA was a proxy vote for TPP."[25] As Congress began considering Obama's request for TPA, a faction of Tea Party Republicans joined progressive and pro-labor Democrats in mobilizing against both TPA and the TPP.[26] In November 2013, 151 Democratic members of the House signed a letter circulated by Representatives Rose DeLauro and George Miller—two leading progressives—that argued the approval of TPA would exclude Congress from having a "meaningful role in the formative stages of trade agreements and throughout negotiating and approval processes."[27] Progressives also took their case against the TPA and TPP to the House floor. In January 2014, members of the House Progressive Caucus devoted a full hour of floor time to explaining why TPA and the TPP would be bad for America. Representative Barbara Lee, another leader among progressive Democrats, said the TPP "would sacrifice the well-being of working Americans for the wealth of multinational corporations."[28]

On the other side of the aisle, 23 House Republicans signed a letter circulated by Representative Walter Jones, a libertarian, that echoed some of the concerns of progressives, stating, "We do not agree to cede our constitutional authority to the executive through an approval of a request for 'Fast Track' Trade Promotion Authority."[29] Some Tea Party and Freedom Caucus members further argued that the TPP negotiations did not include enough transparency and that the TPP threatened the American way of life.[30]

With Senate Majority Leader Harry Reid, a Democrat, also opposing TPA, pro-trade lawmakers did not begin to advance TPA legislation until the Republican Party gained control of the Senate at the beginning of 2015, placing both chambers of Congress in Republican hands. In April 2015, House Ways and Means Committee Chairman Paul Ryan, Senate Finance Committee Chairman Orrin Hatch, and Ron Wyden, the senior Democrat on the Senate Finance Committee, introduced TPA legislation along the lines that Obama had requested.[31] In a response to some of the key concerns voiced by lawmakers about trade agreements, the legislation required that in order for a US trade agreement to be considered under TPA, parties to the agreement must adopt internationally recognized labor, environmental, and human rights standards, and avoid manipulating exchange rates to gain an unfair competitive advantage.[32] In a further effort to build support for TPA among congressional Democrats, Republican backers of TPA agreed to pair its approval by Congress with approval of trade adjustment assistance, a form of economic aid to workers that have lost their jobs as a result of international trade.[33]

A fierce debate over TPA ensued over the next few months. At congressional hearings in April and May, the administration and pro-trade lawmakers argued that TPA was necessary to unlock the advantages of trade and strengthen the US position in Asia, while opponents maintained that the TPA legislation's negotiating objectives remained insufficient to ensure that the TPP or other agreements negotiated under TPA would adequately address their concerns. Administration officials testified that the enactment of TPA would enable the achievement of trade agreements, including the TPP, that would give American workers, farmers, ranchers, and businesses greater access to key markets and enhance the ability of the United States to compete with China for access to those markets.[34] Republican and Democratic congressional backers of TPA made similar arguments. Ryan, who would become speaker of the House later in 2015, said: "In the first 10 years of the century, the countries of East Asia negotiated 48 trade agreements. . . . And the US has been a party to 2 in the region. . . . And while we are sitting on the sidelines, guess what? China is negotiating agreements all around the world."[35] Gregory Meeks, a Democrat representing a district in New York City, commented: "We only represent 5% of the world's population. So if we are going to create jobs we have got to do it outside of here and that is what this is all about."[36]

But most congressional Democrats and some Republicans remained opposed to TPA. In comments representative of the position of many

Democrats, Chuck Schumer, then chairman of the Senate Democratic Policy Committee, voiced skepticism about the significance of the standards outlined in the TPA legislation: "With every trade agreement, we talk about enforcement, and we get virtually none. None. We do not get labor enforcement, we do not get environmental enforcement."[37] Other senators in both parties, including Ohio Democrat Sherrod Brown, Pennsylvania Democrat Bob Casey, Pennsylvania Republican Rob Portman, and Stabenow, called for requirements in TPA and the TPP that countries face trade penalties if they maintain their currency at a value that advantages their exports.[38] Some Democratic and Republican lawmakers, including Democratic Senator Ben Cardin and Republican Representative Chris Smith, also objected to TPA and the TPP on human rights grounds, highlighting the poor record of Vietnam in terms of treatment of its own people.[39]

In late April 2015, the Senate Finance Committee and Ways and Means Committee approved TPA by votes of 20-6 and 25-13, respectively. In the Senate committee vote, 13 of 14 Republicans and 7 of 12 Democrats voted for TPA.[40] In the House committee vote, all 23 Republicans and just two of 15 Democrats voted for TPA.[41] In its majority report on the legislation, Ways and Means Committee Republicans, led by Ryan, said that TPA would enable the negotiation of trade agreements that would create US jobs and stimulate the economy.[42] Sander Levin, the committee's senior Democrat, attached a dissenting opinion on behalf of the minority arguing that the TPA negotiating instructions on issues including labor standards, environmental standards, and currency manipulation were not sufficiently enforceable.[43]

The full House and Senate subsequently approved TPA and trade adjustment assistance (TAA) in cross-partisan votes in June, sending both bills to Obama for his signature. In the House, TPA was approved by a vote of 218-208, with 79% of Republicans and 15% of Democrats voting for it.[44] In the Senate, it was approved by a vote of 60-38, with 90% of Republicans joining 30% of Democrats in voting yes.[45] Soon after passing TPA, the House and Senate also approved TAA in conjunction with an Africa trade bill by votes of 286-138 and 76-22, respectively, with 111 Republican representatives and 30 Republican senators joining nearly all Democrats in voting for the package.[46] Obama then signed the bills into law.[47]

After the votes, in a rare public display of bipartisanship by the Senate majority leader, Mitch McConnell praised Obama for working closely with Republicans on the issue: "Republicans were glad to accept President Obama's support in advancing a principle we've long believed in—that we ought to show our support for American workers by knocking down unfair foreign trade barriers. . . . We are grateful for the President's efforts to help us move this idea forward."[48] Obama also highlighted the bipartisanship on the issue after the congressional action: "I applaud the Democrats and Republicans in Congress who came together to give the United States the chance to negotiate strong, high-standard agreements for free and fair trade that protect American workers and give our businesses the opportunity to compete."[49]

The debate over the TPP

With this boost from Congress, the United States and the 11 other parties to the TPP talks reached agreement on the accord in October 2015. The final agreement eliminated or reduced tariffs and many other barriers to trade on an array of industrial and agricultural products among the 12 countries and included compromises on a variety of sensitive issues.[50] For instance, the United States and other countries had disagreed about the number of years of intellectual property protection to accord cutting-edge pharmaceutical drugs known as biologics. While the United States pushed for 12 years of protection, other countries, such as Chile and Peru, pressed for much shorter monopoly periods.[51] The final agreement stipulated that this period could be no longer than eight years. In another compromise, Japan and the United States agreed to large reductions in agricultural and automobile tariffs but with the reductions phased in over many years.[52]

The agreement also featured provisions designed to strengthen labor and human rights practices by parties to the agreement. For instance, it required all parties to adopt and maintain labor standards set by the International Labor Organization; prohibited Vietnam from becoming a full party to the agreement until the United States determined that it had enacted reforms that allowed independent trade unions, enhanced protections against employment discrimination, and increased penalties for forced labor; and created mechanisms to monitor whether Malaysia and Brunei were implementing their own commitments concerning labor rights and human trafficking.[53] The TPP countries also signed a side agreement in which they pledged to avoid manipulating their exchange rate to gain an unfair trade advantage.[54]

Independent analyses by the US International Trade Commission and the Peterson Institute for International Economics found that the agreement would produce a modest overall boost to US GDP and employment, with the US agriculture and services sectors experiencing gains from the agreement and the US manufacturing sector experiencing losses from it.[55] In addition to highlighting the TPP's economic benefits and labor protections, the administration continued to make a geostrategic argument when touting it. US Trade Representative Michael Froman said the agreement could make the difference between "cementing our leadership in the region or handing it over to China."[56]

Initial congressional reactions to the agreement mainly reflected the same divisions that had been evident in the TPP and TPA debates for several years but included some worrisome signs for TPP supporters. Although some pro-trade Republicans and Democrats expressed strong support for the deal, several key congressional Republicans who had backed TPA did not commit to supporting the TPP. Senate Majority Leader McConnell just said the Senate would review the TPP and "determine if it meets the high standards Congress and the American people have demanded," while Speaker of the House Ryan stated, "I am reserving judgment until I am able to review the final text, and consult with my colleagues and my constituents."[57] In subsequent months, McConnell and Ryan remained noncommittal about the agreement.[58]

Some of the lukewarm Republican reception was rooted in dissatisfaction in parts of the business community with certain terms of the agreement. Nasim Fussell, who served at the time as the Republican trade counsel on the Trade Subcommittee of the House Ways and Means Committee, observed that the agreement "fell short of some of the ambitious outcomes that we'd sought on investor-state dispute settlement and intellectual property— pharma, in particular."[59] Senator Orrin Hatch, who had played a central role in shepherding the approval of TPA as Finance Committee chairman, said the TPP fell "woefully short," maintaining that the United States should have negotiated a 12, rather than an eight, year period of monopoly protection for biologic drugs.[60] Although experts argued that such an outcome was not achievable given the positions of other TPP countries, Hatch was a close ally of the pharmaceutical industry, which had advocated intensively for a 12-year period.[61] Some congressional Republicans also gave voice to concerns of the tobacco and financial services industries that the agreement did not allow companies to sue countries that restrict smoking and did not do enough to facilitate cross-border financial data flows.[62]

The withholding of support by some Republican lawmakers was influenced by the emergence of Donald Trump as the leading Republican candidate in the 2016 presidential election. By August 2015, Trump had established a sub-stantial lead in the Republican nominating contest, which he would maintain for the remainder of the primary season.[63] As part of his protectionist plat-form, Trump sharply criticized the TPP throughout the presidential cam-paign, calling it a "bad deal" that would "squeeze our manufacturing sector" and "send even more jobs overseas."[64] In that context, it became more diffi-cult for Republican lawmakers to support the TPP publicly.[65]

At the same time, Bernie Sanders's strong challenge to Hillary Clinton in the Democratic presidential primary made it harder for Democratic politicians to back the agreement. Like Trump, Sanders regularly castigated the TPP, calling it a "disastrous" agreement that would "hurt consumers and cost American jobs."[66] Pressure on the issue from Sanders led Clinton to come out against the agreement, even though she had played a central role in the early stages of its negotiation as secretary of state. Two days after the agreement was reached, Clinton said, "As of today, I am not in favor of what I have learned about it," adding that it did not adequately address currency manipulation and that it appeared to privilege pharmaceutical companies over patients and consumers (the opposite concern as that of Hatch).[67] This stance by Clinton, who had long supported trade liberalization, suggested that few Democratic lawmakers would be likely to vote for the agreement.

In January 2016, three months after the 12 countries had reached agree-ment on the TPP, Obama and his 11 counterparts signed it.[68] But with the leading presidential candidates in both parties opposing the TPP, the prospects for its congressional approval during the election season were dim. Michael Froman noted: "As the Republican and Democratic primaries progressed, passing the TPP became harder and harder."[69] At a March 2016 hearing on trade policy, most members of the Senate Finance Committee, which has historically been a bastion of pro-trade sentiment on Capitol Hill, avoided taking a direct position on the TPP.[70]

Nor did any supporters of the TPP take to the floor of Congress in 2016. The only members of Congress to speak about the TPP on the House or Senate floor that year were Jeff Sessions, a protectionist Republican aligned with Trump, and a handful of progressive Democrats. These lawmakers argued that the TPP would cause a loss of hundreds of thousands of manufacturing jobs, and the progressives further charged that the agreement would cause a race to the bottom on labor and environmental standards.[71] Democratic Senator Sherrod Brown, of Ohio, said: "We have had 25 years of trade policy that has cost jobs in places like Lorain, OH, Cleveland, OH, and Dayton, OH.

We know these trade agreements pull down worker safety standards, environmental rules and protections, and food safety laws and rules."[72]

The upshot was that political conditions were not ripe for advancing the TPP in 2016. As Susan Rice, Obama's national security advisor at the time, commented, "We worked really hard to get TPA, and to whip all those votes—to get Republican support and some Democratic support. That was a success. Then the election came around, and nobody would touch it with a ten-foot pole."[73] John Murphy, senior vice president for international policy at the US Chamber of Commerce, noted similarly: "With the emergence of Donald Trump as the Republican nominee and his positions on trade, it wasn't really possible to take the TPP up during the election year."[74] However, the very close votes on TPA the previous year suggest that gaining congressional approval of the TPP would have been difficult even if Trump (and Sanders) had not gained so much traction during the presidential campaign.

Once it became clear that Congress would not approve the TPP before the election, the Obama administration urged congressional leaders to take it up during the "lame duck" period between the election and the close of the 114th Congress at the end of the year. But by the fall of 2016, at least five of the 60 senators who had voted for TPA had come out against TPP, and marshaling a majority in support of the TPP in the House would have proven even harder.[75] A few days after the election, congressional leaders told the White House that they would not advance the agreement during the lame-duck period.[76] An Obama administration legislative affairs official recalled, "The Republican leadership didn't think they had the votes [needed to pass the agreement]."[77] Some congressional Republicans may also have calculated that Trump would adjust his stance once he took office and thereby enable the TPP to get approved then. A former senior House Democratic aide involved in the issue said, in describing the thinking of some Republicans, "Why not wait and let Trump come in and make some tweaks to the TPP and then take credit for it?"[78]

Reaction to Trump's withdrawal from the TPP

Instead, just three days into his presidency, Donald Trump announced his withdrawal from the TPP, stating that dealing "directly with individual countries on a one-on-one (or bilateral) basis" would better enable him to "create fair and economically beneficial trade deals" that help American workers.[79] In a reflection of the importance the White House placed on the action, Stephen Bannon, Trump's chief strategist and a strong proponent of Trump's brand of economic nationalism, called the withdrawal "one of the most pivotal moments in modern American history."[80] Obama administration officials also highlighted the significance of the withdrawal, though in a more negative way. Obama administration chief trade negotiator Michael Froman noted, "There's no doubt that this action will be seen as a huge, huge win for China."[81]

Yet congressional reaction to the move was muted. Democrats largely backed the withdrawal, while urging Trump to take additional steps to assist American workers. Schumer, who had become the Senate minority leader, noted, in a reflection of the cross-partisanship that characterized the debate, that his views on trade were "probably closer to President Trump's than they were to President Obama."[82] Schumer also pressed Trump to go further by labeling China a currency manipulator and ordering his own companies to produce all of their products in the United States.[83] In another comment typical of Democratic reactions, Representative Chellie Pingree, a member of the House Progressive Caucus, said, "While I can't say I agree with all of the actions the President took today—including crippling reproductive health around the world by reinstating the global gag rule—TPP is certainly one of the areas where we agree."[84] But a few Democratic lawmakers criticized the withdrawal. Representative Ron Kind said at a Ways and Means Committee hearing, "I may be in the minority . . . within my own party, but I happen to believe that our withdrawal from the Trans-Pacific Partnership trade agreement will go down as one of the great strategic mistakes that we made in the 21st century."[85]

Only a few congressional Republicans criticized Trump's move directly. Senate Agriculture Committee Chairman Pat Roberts called the withdrawal "a missed opportunity."[86] In a more scathing comment, John McCain said the withdrawal was a "serious mistake" that "will forfeit the opportunity to promote American exports, reduce trade barriers, open new markets, and protect American invention and innovation."[87]

Most Republican legislators, including long-time supporters of liberalized trade, reacted quietly to the move. Speaker of the House Paul Ryan simply noted that Trump had "followed through on his promise to insist on better trade agreements."[88] Ways and Means Committee Chairman Kevin Brady, who had backed the TPP and urged Trump to renegotiate rather than withdraw from it, gently flagged his concern about reducing economic engagement abroad, "I believe the TPP agreement contains considerable benefits for the US economy—but it fell short in other ways. It's important that America not abandon the Asia-Pacific region because American companies and workers will lose out."[89]

The largely muted congressional response to Trump's TPP withdrawal reflected the fact that the agreement had more support from lawmakers in Trump's own party than from congressional Democrats. Whereas Democrats on Capitol Hill would have been quick to rebuke Trump for a decision that departed from their own preferences, most Republican lawmakers were reluctant to sharply criticize a major decision by Trump on one of his top policy priorities.[90]

However, pro-trade Republican lawmakers and governors urged Trump in private to reconsider his decision. In conjunction with continued pro-trade advocacy by major business associations, this lobbying appeared to bear some fruit in April 2018, when Trump told a group of lawmakers and governors from states with large agricultural industries that he was open to rejoining the TPP if it was modified.[91] The following day, he emphasized the importance of adjusting the agreement, while leaving the door open to reentering it, tweeting, "Would only join TPP if the deal were substantially better than the deal offered to Pres. Obama."[92]

Trump's flirtation with rejoining the TPP was short-lived, though, and his administration never seriously pursued rejoining the agreement. Several days after suggesting he was open to reentering it, Trump gave voice once again to his protectionist impulses, tweeting, "While Japan and South Korea would like us to go back into TPP, I don't like the deal for the United States. Too many contingencies and no way to get out if it doesn't work. Bilateral deals are far more efficient, profitable, and better for OUR workers."[93] In the meantime, the other parties to the agreement went forward with implementing the agreement without the United States under the new name Comprehensive and Progressive Agreement for Trans-Pacific Partnership (CPTPP).[94]

Public and elite opinion

Public opinion on trade has facilitated cross-partisanship among elected officials on the TPP and other trade issues. Neither party's electorate adheres to an ideological orthodoxy on trade. Instead, pro-trade and anti-trade sentiments coexist within each of the two electorates, providing space for politicians in both parties to support or oppose trade agreements.[95] At the same time, public attitudes regarding trade have fluctuated in response to economic conditions and national political developments. Pro-trade positions have been more prevalent during good economic times, while a partisan gap emerged in attitudes regarding trade agreements after Trump became the Republican Party's standard-bearer in 2016. Foreign policy elites in both parties have remained strong supporters of trade, however, further facilitating cross-partisan behavior in Congress.

For more than two decades, Gallup has been asking Americans whether they see international trade more as an opportunity for economic growth through increased exports or as an economic threat from foreign imports. Across a set of 13 Gallup public opinion surveys conducted during the George W. Bush and Obama presidencies, an average of 51% of Democrats and 50% of Republicans said that they saw trade more as an opportunity than as a threat.[96] (See Table 8.1.) However, the share of voters responding this way was lower during the 2008–2009 financial crisis and higher as the post-crisis economic recovery gained steam. At the same time, in a reflection of the effect of partisan identities on policy positions, more Republicans than Democrats tended to see trade as an opportunity during the Bush presidency, whereas more Democrats than Republicans tended to see it as an opportunity during the Obama presidency. For instance, 36% of Democrats and 46% of Republicans saw it more as an opportunity than as a threat in 2008, whereas 63% of Democrats and 50% of Republicans did so in 2016.

Counterintuitively, given Trump's protectionist rhetoric and policies, even more voters in each party saw trade positively during his presidency. Across the four years of his presidency, an average of 78% of Democrats and 71% of Republicans saw trade more as an opportunity than as a threat. For Democratic voters, the increase in support for trade under Trump was likely driven by the combination of continued growth in the US economy and Trump's unpopularity, as voters who disapproved of Trump would have been more likely to reject his policies. For Republican voters, the bump in support may have been driven by the strong economy and a view that Trump had adjusted trade policy such that it had become more beneficial for the United States. John Murphy of the US Chamber of Commerce noted, "When you have your guy as president, you feel more trusting in trade."[97]

While these data suggest that public attitudes regarding trade have been more favorable than recent trade debates in Washington would suggest, other data show that many Americans have concerns about the effect

Table 8.1 Trade—Economic opportunity or threat?

Year	Democrats opportunity	Republicans opportunity	Total opportunity	Total threat
2001	51%	55%	51%	37%
2002	47%	57%	52%	39%
2003	50%	54%	49%	41%
2005	38%	56%	44%	48%
2006	45%	50%	44%	48%
2008	36%	46%	41%	52%
2009	43%	45%	44%	47%
2011	47%	48%	45%	45%
2012	55%	41%	46%	46%
2013	66%	51%	57%	35%
2014	57%	52%	54%	38%
2015	61%	51%	58%	53%
2016	63%	50%	58%	34%
2017	80%	66%	72%	23%
2018	71%	68%	70%	25%
2019	79%	70%	74%	21%
2020	82%	78%	79%	18%

Note: This table reports responses to public opinion surveys by Gallup asking the following question: "Do you see foreign trade more as an opportunity for economic growth through increased US exports or a threat to the economy from foreign imports?" Gallup did not report percentages of Democrats or Republicans answering "threat." Totals include responses by Independents and others who do not affiliate with one of the two parties.

of trade on US jobs. The 2016 Chicago Council on Global Affairs public opinion survey found that just 47% of Democrats and 34% of Republicans thought trade was good for the creation of jobs in the United States, and only 41% of Democrats and 30% of Republicans thought it was good for the job security of American workers.[98] (See Table 8.2.) Additional Chicago Council data point to continued concern about links between trade and jobs among both publics during Trump's presidency. In 2018, 49% of Democrats and 77% of Republicans said they thought the United States should restrict imported foreign goods to protect US jobs.[99] The upshot is that most Americans in both electorates think trade benefits the United States but worry about the economic dislocations that it creates. This constellation of views has provided room for a diversity of positions on trade among politicians in each party.

Table 8.2 Trade—Public and elite views

	Democrat public	Democrat elites	Republican public	Republican elites
Good for US economy	68%	93%	51%	88%
Good for American companies	65%	91%	50%	99%
Good for consumers like you	75%	99%	66%	93%
Good for own standard of living	72%	95%	60%	92%
Good for creating jobs in US	47%	64%	34%	61%
Good for job security for American workers	41%	30%	30%	45%

Note: This table reports responses of "good" to a 2016 survey of the public by the Chicago Council on Global Affairs and a 2016 survey of foreign policy elites by the Chicago Council on Global Affairs and Texas National Security Network asking the following six questions: "Overall, do you think international trade is good or bad for [the US economy] [American companies] [consumers like you] [your own standard of living] [creating jobs in the United States] [the job security of American workers]?"

Regarding free-trade agreements specifically, public opinion data show a diversity of opinion within each party, while elite opinion data show nearly universal support. (See Table 8.3.) From 2009 to 2015, Pew polls found on average that a little more than one-half of the public in each party thought free-trade agreements had generally been good for the United States, while slightly more than one-third of the public in each party thought they had generally been bad for the United States.[100] Public attitudes regarding free-trade agreements grew more polarized after the rise of Trump, though, with Pew polls between 2016 and 2018 finding an average of 61% of the Democratic public and 35% of the Republican public saying free-trade agreements had generally been good for the United States.[101]

Public opinion surveys show a similar trend with regard to the TPP. (See Table 8.4.) In the spring of 2015—before Trump had launched his presidential campaign—Pew found that 51% of Democrats and 43% of Republicans thought the TPP would be a good thing for the United States, whereas just 26% of Democrats and 34% of Republicans thought it would be a bad thing.[102] In August 2016—a month after the Republican Party nominated Trump for the presidency—Pew found that Democratic support for the TPP remained relatively strong, with 55% of Democrats considering it good for the United States and just 24% considering it bad.[103] But Republican support

Table 8.3 Free-trade agreements—Good or bad for US?

Date	Democrats good	Democrats bad	Republicans good	Republicans bad	Total good	Total bad
March–April 2009	53%	34%	57%	31%	52%	34%
Feb–March 2011	51%	39%	42%	48%	48%	41%
Feb–March 2014	60%	30%	55%	36%	59%	30%
May 2015	58%	33%	53%	35%	58%	33%
March 2016	56%	34%	38%	53%	47%	43%
August 2016	58%	34%	32%	61%	50%	42%
October 2016	56%	31%	24%	68%	40%	52%
April 2017	67%	26%	36%	58%	52%	40%
April–May 2018	67%	19%	43%	46%	56%	30%

Note: This table reports responses to surveys by the Pew Research Center between 2009 and 2018 asking the following question: "In general, do you think that free trade agreements between the US and other countries have been a good thing or a bad thing for the United States?" Totals include responses by Independents and others who do not affiliate with one of the two parties.

for the TPP cratered by that time, with 17% of Republicans considering it good and 58% considering it bad.[104]

The drop in Republican backing for the TPP after the rise of Trump, as well as Trump's ability to win the Republican nomination on a protectionist agenda, points to the fluidity of positions on trade. Indeed, in most opinion surveys about the TPP, substantial shares of Americans—as much as 45% in one Morning Consult survey—answered "don't know" or "no opinion," or refused to provide an answer.[105] This lack of certainty in the opinions of many Americans regarding a key trade agreement underscores the absence of party orthodoxies regarding trade.

At the same time, support among Democratic and Republican foreign policy elites for trade has been consistently strong. In a survey conducted by the Chicago Council and the Texas National Security Network in 2016, 93% of Democratic foreign policy professionals and 88% of Republican foreign policy professionals said trade was good for the US economy.[106] (See Table 8.2.) In the same survey two years later, 100% of Republican foreign policy elites and 97% of Democratic foreign policy elites responded in this way.[107] These data suggest that when elected officials pursue protectionist policies, they are doing so based not on the preferences of policy practitioners and

Table 8.4 Trans-Pacific Partnership—For or against?

Date	Pollster	Democrats for	Democrats against	Republicans for	Republicans against	Total don't know
Feb–March 2014	Pew[a]	59%	N/A	49%	N/A	20%
April 2014	Chicago Council[b]	70%	22%	66%	29%	7%
Spring 2015	Pew[a]	51%	26%	43%	34%	22%
March 2016	Morning Consult[c]	32%	23%	24%	34%	45%
June 2016	Chicago Council[b]	76%	24%	58%	42%	N/A
August 2016	Morning Consult[c]	43%	N/A	30%	N/A	43%
August 2016	Pew[a]	55%	24%	17%	58%	24%
July 2018	Chicago Council[d]	76%	19%	45%	49%	7%

Note: This table reports all public opinion survey results I could find that provided a partisan breakdown of views of the TPP between 2009 and 2018. Table entries indicating "N/A" represent survey results that the pollster did not report. Figures in the last column represent the total number of respondents indicating that they did not know or did not have an opinion or who refused to answer.

[a] "As you may know, the United States is negotiating a free trade agreement with 11 countries in Asia and Latin America called the Trans-Pacific Partnership, or TPP. Do you think this trade agreement would be a good thing for our country or a bad thing?"

[b] "As you may know, the United States is negotiating a free trade agreement with 12 Pacific nations called the Trans-Pacific Partnership (or TPP). Based on what you know, do you strongly support, somewhat support, somewhat oppose or strongly oppose this free trade agreement?"

[c] "Do you support or oppose the free trade agreement with eleven countries in Asia and Latin America called the Trans-Pacific Partnership?"

[d] "Based on what you know, do you think the United States should or should not participate in the . . . Comprehensive and Progressive Agreement for Trans-Pacific Partnership (or CPTPP), a trade agreement among 11 Pacific nations based on the Trans-Pacific Partnership (PPP) trade agreement?"

experts, but rather based on the views of voters or pressure from advocacy groups.

All this said, it is important to recognize the limitations of survey data for understanding how the attitudes of Americans influence US trade policy. Opinion surveys usually do not give a full picture of how public attitudes might shape the positions of elected officials because they do not take into account variation across voters in the extent to which they care about an issue. Only a relatively small share of voters care enough about trade to vote based on candidates' trade positions.[108] Importantly, these voters tend to be more protectionist than other Americans. Neil Newhouse, a Republican pollster and strategist, has noted that "the intensity and energy on the issue is all on the anti-trade side. . . . Those who support free trade are more 'lukewarm.' For them it's not a voting issue."[109] These different levels of intensity help explain why so many politicians in both parties have adopted anti-trade positions, despite the relatively pro-trade views of most Americans and the staunchly pro-trade views of Democratic and Republican elites.

Advocacy group activity

Trade policy debates have long featured intensive advocacy by economic interest groups, particularly business associations and labor unions. The lion's share of business associations, led by the US Chamber of Commerce, have consistently favored trade liberalization. However, businesses have adopted varying positions on trade deals depending on their economic characteristics. In particular, industries and firms that are export oriented or possess many global links have tended to be more supportive of trade liberalization than import-sensitive or domestically focused sectors and corporations. Labor unions and environmental groups, for their part, have typically opposed free-trade agreements based on concerns that reducing barriers to trade would lead corporations to move jobs to countries with lower labor costs and weaker environmental standards.[110]

Given the close ties between major business associations and the Republican Party, on the one hand, and among major labor unions, environmental groups, and the Democratic Party, on the other hand, this advocacy landscape has been a key driver of the greater support among Republican members of Congress than among Democratic members of Congress for trade agreements over the past several decades.[111] At the same time, the varying economic characteristics of states and congressional districts have incentivized cross-partisanship in most trade debates, since some Democratic lawmakers represent constituencies that stand to benefit more from liberalization, whereas some Republican lawmakers represent constituencies that are more threatened by it.[112] Everett Eisenstadt, who served as the chief international trade counsel on the Senate Finance Committee's Republican staff from 2011 to 2017, noted: "Somebody from the industrial belt in Ohio is going to look at trade differently than someone from Miami whose district is closely linked to Latin America."[113]

Lobbying on the TPP largely conformed to the advocacy patterns that have characterized most US trade debates in recent decades. Most major business associations backed the TPP. The Business Roundtable, a group representing CEOs of major corporations, spent about $6.5 million lobbying for TPA in 2015 and organized pro-TPP events in more than 120 congressional districts in 2016.[114] In a statement typical of the messaging of much of corporate America on the issue, Thomas Donohue, president and CEO of the US Chamber of Commerce, testified to the Senate Finance Committee in 2015: "The Trans-Pacific Partnership agreement would open the dynamic Asia-Pacific markets to American goods and services. It is critical that we do so, because nations across the Pacific are clinching their own trade agreements that exclude the United States, denying American exporters access to these very important markets."[115] The US agriculture sector was among the most enthusiastic supporters of the agreement, based on an expectation that it would boost US agricultural exports to countries along the Pacific rim.[116] The US technology and service sectors also largely supported the TPP.[117]

A few industries opposed the TPP based on concerns about certain provisions, including the pharmaceutical industry, which wanted the agreement to provide more years of intellectual property protection for biologics, and the tobacco industry, which was upset that the agreement would allow countries to regulate tobacco products more aggressively.[118] The financial services sector was also upset that it was not included in provisions designed to facilitate cross-border data flows.[119] Nilmini Rubin, who handled the TPP as a Republican aide on the House Foreign Affairs Committee, said that such concerns weakened support for the agreement among Republican lawmakers: "Many House and Senate Republicans were willing to push it forward until the text was released, and they saw major problems with it."[120] But a former Obama administration legislative affairs official who dealt with Congress on the issue said, "Pharma and tobacco weren't happy with the agreement, but Republicans are deflecting blame by trying to blame Obama for negotiating a bad deal. If you had a big pharma or tobacco constituency, you weren't happy with the deal. But if you were an [agricultural] state, you loved it."[121]

Major labor unions, for their part, opposed the TPP. An AFL-CIO statement in 2015 asserted, "The TPP is a corporate rights agreement that threatens good jobs and wages in the US while allowing worker abuses abroad to continue unabated."[122] Leo W. Gerard, the international president of the United Steelworkers, used more colorful language in a 2015 article, calling the TPP "a big fat dead rat."[123] Leading environmental groups, such as the Sierra Club and National Resources Defense Council, also opposed the agreement, based on concern that it would not ensure compliance among member countries with international environmental standards and could allow corporations to challenge US environmental standards in courts outside the United States.[124] This concern that trade rules could result in a weakening of environmental protections has also led environmental groups to oppose other trade agreements in recent years, making environmental organizations increasingly important actors in trade debates.[125]

Unions, environmental organizations, and other progressive groups engaged in intensive anti-TPP advocacy, funding a large advertising campaign against the agreement, organizing "Rock against the T.P.P." concerts across the country, and sending blimps with anti-TPP messages flying over the offices of some members of Congress.[126] Council on Foreign Relations trade policy expert Edward Alden said: "Labor unions pulled out all the stops to fight the TPP. They said they'd sponsor primary challenges against Democrats who voted for it. It was the most intense union campaign I'd ever seen against a trade deal."[127] Then-House Republican aide Nilmini Rubin commented: "I knew TPP was in trouble when I saw the Rayburn House Office Building flooded with labor activists wearing T-shirts advocating against TPP."[128]

Trump's tariffs and the United States-Mexico-Canada Agreement

The remainder of Trump's first term in office featured two other major trade debates: over Trump's imposition of tariffs on various sets of imported goods, and his negotiation of the United States-Mexico-Canada Agreement (USMCA). Like the TPP debate, these debates did not break down sharply along partisan lines, but political alignments on them varied. On the one hand, Trump's heavy use of tariffs prompted more opposition than support in Congress, with congressional Republicans expressing the most concern about it even though Trump was their party's leader. The USMCA, on the other hand, generated broad bipartisan support in Congress. These differing alignments reflected differing interest group landscapes on these issues. Pro-Republican business groups strongly opposed the tariffs while pro-Democratic labor unions offered qualified support for them, but the business community and major unions came together in support of the USMCA.

Tariffs

In March 2018, Trump began to use tariffs aggressively as an instrument of international economic policy, announcing the placement of a 25% tariff on imported steel and a 10% tariff on imported aluminum.[129] The move represented only the beginning of a series of protectionist actions by Trump, including a set of decisions in 2018 and 2019 to impose tariffs on hundreds of billions of dollars of imports from China.[130]

Some senior Republicans on Capitol Hill criticized Trump's use of tariffs. After Trump announced the steel and aluminum tariffs, Speaker of the House Paul Ryan commented, "I disagree with this action and fear its un-intended consequences," while Senate Majority Leader Mitch McConnell said, "There is a lot of concern among Republican senators that this could sort of metastasize into a larger trade war."[131] Reaction from congressional Democrats was more mixed. Senate Majority Leader Charles Schumer said, "The president and I may agree on trade—we may be closer on this issue than I've been with either the Bush or Obama administrations—but the slapdash way these tariffs were constructed has few of us cheering, even those who really wanted to go after China long before politics was a gleam in President Trump's eye."[132] West Virginia Senator Joe Manchin offered stronger backing for the tariffs, stating, "I'm glad we are finally standing up for ourselves, and I applaud President Trump's leadership and willingness to hold places like China accountable for the damage they've done to our economy."[133]

These congressional positions were consistent with the stances of major interest groups aligned with each of the parties. Aside from the steel and aluminum sectors, the US business community strongly opposed the tariffs, worried that they would increase production costs for a wide array of products and trigger economic retaliation by other countries against US goods.[134] The US Chamber of Commerce launched a public campaign on the issue with the headline, "Trade Works. Tariffs Don't."[135] The Chamber's John Murphy said, "Our perspective was, 'Why impose tariffs on every country in the world when the problem is China, not Canada or other NATO allies? . . . American businesses and consumers pay the tariffs."[136] But the

AFL-CIO, the leading US labor union, endorsed some of the tariff actions, calling them necessary to protect American jobs.[137]

Some members of Congress in both parties tried to block Trump from using tariffs without the input of Congress. In June 2018, Bob Corker, the Republican chairman of the Senate Foreign Relations Committee, introduced legislation, with eight Democratic and eight Republican senators cosponsoring it, to restrict the president's authority to impose tariffs.[138] The bill stipulated that the president could not adjust imports based on national security grounds, which Trump had invoked in imposing the aluminum and steel tariffs, without Congress passing a resolution approving the step. In introducing the bill, which would have applied retroactively to the aluminum and steel tariffs that Trump had already imposed, as well as to any future presidential tariff proposals, Corker said, "Making claims regarding national security to justify what is inherently an economic question not only harms the very people we all want to help and impairs relations with our allies but also could invite our competitors to retaliate."[139] North Dakota Senator Heidi Heitkamp, a Democrat, added, "Huge economic policy decisions like tariffs shouldn't be taken lightly, and Congress should serve as a need to check to make sure we aren't losing out in the end."[140] A variety of business associations endorsed the bill.[141]

However, in a clear example of the power of partisan incentives on a top presidential priority, most Senate Republicans were unwilling to challenge Trump on tariffs, and McConnell refused to bring the legislation to the Senate floor.[142] In an interview, Corker said: "Traditionally you'd be able to get almost all the Republicans in the Senate to push back against tariffs. But Republicans weren't interested in pushing back on Trump on this."[143] Similarly, Republican Senator Jeff Flake, a staunch supporter of free trade who strongly criticized the tariffs, bemoaned in an interview that "there are too few Republicans who are willing to cross the president on tariffs."[144] In the end, the Republican-led Congress did little to restrain Trump's aggressive and unilateral use of tariffs despite the reservations of many Republicans about them.[145]

The USMCA

The debate over the USMCA also featured substantial bipartisanship, but in this case bipartisanship took the pro-presidential form. After Trump took office, lawmakers in both parties were concerned that Trump might pull out of the North American Free Trade Agreement (NAFTA) and backed the president's decision to renegotiate it as a preferable alternative to a unilateral withdrawal. A former senior House Democratic aide noted, "There was pretty widespread concern on the Hill about withdrawing from NAFTA. Getting rid of it would have had very severe economic consequences for the United States, particularly in border states."[146] Well aware of Trump's deep hostility to NAFTA, lawmakers called for revising it, rather than pulling out.[147]

The process of negotiating the USMCA was a model of inter-branch bipartisan cooperation. Led by US Trade Representative Robert Lighthizer, the Trump administration worked closely with congressional Democrats in negotiating the agreement. Lighthizer had long-standing close ties to Democrats on Capitol Hill, having often been called by Democrats as a hearing witness before his appointment by Trump. Nasim Fussell, who served as the Republican chief counsel for international trade on the Senate Finance Committee from 2018 to 2020, commented: "Ambassador Lighthizer came in with a perspective that resonated with Democrats who had been skeptical of trade."[148] Edward Alden of the Council on Foreign Relations observed of the USMCA negotiations: "Lighthizer was very sympathetic toward what Democrats wanted and very respectful of them. He went back to Democrats on Ways and Means again and again and asked them, 'What do you need?'"[149] Lighthizer also worked closely with major unions in negotiating the agreement.[150]

This effort resulted in the most progressive trade agreement in US history, a remarkable outcome considering that it occurred during a Republican administration. The USMCA includes an array of new labor standards—for instance, requiring Mexico to establish independent labor courts and requiring 40% of the value of a car to be manufactured by workers who make at least $16 per hour.[151] The agreement also eliminated investor-state dispute settlement mechanisms that gave companies more legal standing under NAFTA to challenge consumer safety, environmental, and workplace protections.[152]

The AFL-CIO endorsed the agreement, which provides for on-site monitoring of compliance with its terms and penalties if a country fails to follow through on commitments, stating: "For the first time, there truly will be enforceable labor standards—including a process that allows for the inspections of factories and facilities that are not living up to their obligations."[153] Democratic support for the agreement was further bolstered by Mexico's enactment of a law enhancing the collective bargaining rights of independent unions, as well as by the Trump administration's decision to strip from the agreement a provision that would have provided pharmaceutical companies with 10 years of patent protection for biologics.[154]

Although major business associations disliked these provisions, on balance the USMCA included more elements that the business community liked than elements that it disliked. For instance, the agreement promised to boost US dairy exports and modernize trade rules on digital trade and services.[155] Perhaps more importantly, the highly unattractive alternative of the United States leaving NAFTA without instituting a replacement for it provided a strong incentive for all economic actors with a stake in US trade with Mexico and Canada to support the USMCA—an incentive strengthened by the close integration of numerous supply chains linking the economies of the three countries. John Murphy of the US Chamber of Commerce, which urged Congress to approve the agreement, commented, "The business community looked at the outcome and said, 'It could have been worse.' In a context where the administration's threat to withdraw from NAFTA never went away, it made sense for business to support the USMCA."[156] Everett Eissenstat, who served from 2018 to 2021 as senior vice president of Global Public Policy at General Motors, noted: "The threat of withdrawal [from NAFTA] brought the business community on board the USMCA. So many businesses were so integrated with the Mexican economy that they'd take an imperfect USMCA over no USMCA."[157]

In pro-presidential bipartisan votes, large majorities of representatives and senators in both parties—83% of House Democrats, 82% of Senate Democrats, 99% of House Republicans, and 98% of Senate Republicans— voted for the USMCA in December 2019 and January 2020, respectively. Strikingly, both parties could hail the achievement as a victory. Democratic Representative Rosa DeLauro, a long-time leader of progressive critics of trade deals, explained her support for the agreement after its approval by Congress: "This is a celebration of what Democrats were able to secure. We secured positive changes on environmental standards, labor standards and access to medicine."[158]

Despite the strong bipartisanship on the USMCA, Trump only invited Republican lawmakers to witness him sign the implementing legislation in the midst of the Senate's trial regarding his impeachment. But US Trade Representative Robert Lighthizer thanked "the members of Congress, Republicans and Democrats, who worked so hard on this agreement," adding that they "were involved every step of the way" and "made this a bipartisan success."[159]

Conclusion

It remains to be seen whether the pro-presidential bipartisanship that marked the USMCA debate will be replicated in future trade debates, but the broader pattern of political dynamics on trade in recent decades suggests that the degree of unity associated with the USMCA debate is anomalous. As shown in Chapter 2, cross-partisanship is the norm on international economic issues. In trade debates specifically, the limited alignment between policy positions and liberal or conservative ideology opens the door for people across the ideological spectrum to support or oppose trade agreements, providing a favorable condition for intra-party splits. At the same time, economic constituencies typically develop positions on trade based more on the particular ways they are affected by trade than on their party affiliations, further facilitating the formation of bipartisan coalitions. However, the long-standing close links between business associations and the Republican Party, on the one hand, and between labor unions and the Democratic Party, on the other hand, usually lead more Republican than Democratic members of Congress to back trade liberalization. Collectively, these conditions tend to make it very difficult to build consensus in Washington on trade policy, contributing to the small number of trade agreements instituted by the United States in recent years.

9

Spending on foreign aid and diplomacy

Soon after taking office in 2017, President Donald Trump asked lawmakers to cut the US international affairs budget—which funds the State Department (State), the Agency for International Development (AID), and other non-military foreign assistance programs—by 31% in the next fiscal year. Even though Trump's Republican Party controlled the House of Representatives and Senate, Congress rejected Trump's proposal and increased the international affairs budget slightly instead. This story largely repeated itself in each of the subsequent three years, including after the Democratic Party gained control of the House in 2019. Each year, Trump asked Congress to cut between 22% and 25% of the international affairs budget. In response, Congress maintained or slightly increased the core budget for diplomacy and foreign aid every time, while appropriating billions of additional dollars that Trump had not requested for international COVID relief after the global pandemic broke out in early 2020. The upshot was that, rather than undergoing a large retrenchment, total US civilian foreign policy spending actually grew over the course of Trump's presidency.[1]

This sequence of events is remarkable for multiple reasons. First, given the high level of overall polarization in contemporary American politics, it may seem surprising that Republican and Democratic lawmakers would band together to reject Trump's proposals so decisively. Second, presidents generally have stronger incentives than members of Congress to support internationalist policies.[2] It might therefore seem puzzling that lawmakers would depart from the president by moving US foreign policy in a more internationalist direction.[3] Third, conservatives generally favor reducing government spending on social welfare programs.[4] One might therefore expect that Republican lawmakers would be enthusiastic about cutting civilian foreign assistance. However, anti-presidential bipartisanship on the international affairs budget is consistent with a broader pattern in which lawmakers tend to be more assertive on spending matters than in other areas of foreign policy.[5]

In this chapter, I briefly review the political dynamics in debates over the international affairs budget under Obama and then examine in more

Bipartisanship and US Foreign Policy. Jordan Tama, Oxford University Press. © Oxford University Press 2024.
DOI: 10.1093/oso/9780197745663.003.0009

detail the politics of international affairs spending under Trump. I find that congressional bipartisanship on the issue has been enabled by its low salience, the support of an ideologically diverse advocacy coalition for diplomatic and development spending, and the absence of concerted interest group opposition to it. Since international affairs spending is rarely the subject of public debate, lawmakers have relatively little incentive to use the issue to gain partisan advantage and considerable leeway to follow their own compass on it. The issue's low salience also means that many new lawmakers join Congress without strongly held preexisting positions on it, creating an opening for internationalist advocacy groups to influence their views.

A strange bedfellows coalition of development and humanitarian aid NGOs, major corporations, retired military officers, and faith-based leaders has taken advantage of these favorable conditions by working together to build support for diplomatic and foreign aid spending on Capitol Hill. While many policymakers would assume that development and humanitarian aid NGOs favor civilian foreign assistance, the business, military, and religious members of this coalition have served as powerful external validators of the importance of diplomacy and foreign aid. These validators have been particularly important in building support among Republican legislators for the international affairs budget given that Republicans tend to hold business, military, and faith-based leaders in high regard, yet conservative ideology would otherwise suggest a preference for reducing government spending on foreign aid.

Since lawmakers usually have weaker incentives than presidents to support internationalist policies, the advocacy efforts of this coalition have usually been focused on urging Congress to adopt the president's position when it comes to spending levels on diplomacy and foreign aid. Under Trump, however, the president's "America first" philosophy led to a different dynamic, with the president proposing to slash the international affairs budget and the advocacy coalition lobbying Congress to resist the president's proposed cuts. In this way, Trump's nationalist agenda created an impetus for advocacy on the issue during his presidency to take an anti-presidential form. In this context, the politically diverse character of the advocacy coalition helped enable supporters of the international affairs budget to build and maintain bipartisan support despite Trump's opposing position. The issue's low salience also facilitated anti-presidential bipartisanship under Trump by making it easier for Republicans in Congress to buck their party leader.

This chapter's findings support the book's argument that bipartisanship is facilitated when advocacy groups with close ties to both parties favor the same policies, and bipartisanship is likely to take an anti-presidential form when such advocacy is at odds with the president's positions. The chapter also illustrates how public opinion and partisan incentives take on less weight in congressional decision-making when an issue has limited salience and relatively low political stakes. In these circumstances, it is easier for elected officials to cooperate across the aisle, creating an opening for advocacy groups seeking to forge bipartisan coalitions. For scholars of interest groups, a key takeaway from the chapter is therefore that advocacy groups can have considerable influence on policy decisions, but they are more likely to exercise influence when they form politically diverse coalitions and when voters are not mobilized in support of a different position.

Maintaining international affairs spending under Obama

Before turning to action on the international affairs budget under Trump, I review here how Democrats and Republicans aligned on diplomatic and foreign aid spending under Obama. In keeping with the historical pattern of the president being more internationalist than Congress, Congress provided less funding for diplomacy and international development in every year of the Obama presidency than the administration had requested, including when both chambers of Congress were controlled by the Democrats, when the House was Republican controlled and the Senate was Democratic controlled, and when both chambers were Republican controlled. But congressional cuts to Obama's international affairs spending proposals were remarkably limited when the Republicans controlled one or both chambers, even in a broader federal budget context under which Congress forced large spending cuts across the US government, pointing to the effectiveness of the pro-aid advocacy coalition.

After Republicans took control of the House in January 2011, with many newly elected lawmakers representing the anti-government Tea Party movement, congressional Republicans pressed for deep cuts in most areas of federal spending. Although the Obama administration resisted these cuts, Republicans managed later that year to achieve the enactment of legislation, called the Budget Control Act, which mandated 5% reductions in federal government spending from the prior year level and then capped spending at that lower level for the next decade.[6] In that context, known as sequestration, the outlook for the international affairs budget appeared particularly bleak given the more limited public support for that portion of the federal budget than for many other federal programs.

With encouragement from the pro-aid advocacy community, however, key Republican lawmakers worked with congressional Democrats and the Obama administration to maintain a relatively constant level of spending for diplomacy and development. Throughout 2011, prominent NGOs, corporations, and retired military officers urged Congress not to slash international affairs spending sharply. In March, a letter from 70 retired US generals and admirals coordinated by the US Global Leadership Coalition (USGLC), a major umbrella group that backs robust levels of diplomatic and foreign aid spending, urged lawmakers "to support a strong and effective International Affairs Budget and oppose disproportionate cuts to this vital account."[7] The letter added that "addressing today's challenges with civilian tools costs far less than it does to send in the military in dollars and, more importantly, in terms of the risks to the lives of our men and women in uniform."[8] In June, a USGLC-coordinated letter from leaders of 51 major corporations and business associations urged members of Congress to support a "strong and effective International Affairs Budget," asserting that the budget "is vital for achieving a more prosperous future for American workers and businesses."[9]

Some key Republican lawmakers expressed similar points of view. At a November 2011 USGLC event in South Carolina featuring local military, business, and faith-based leaders, Lindsey Graham, the top Republican on the Senate appropriations subcommittee responsible for diplomatic and foreign aid spending, stated, "The foreign operations account is national security in another form, and the funds are an essential piece in protecting our own nation."[10] Kay Granger, the chairwoman of the corresponding House appropriations subcommittee, also defended the international affairs budget. Regarding aid to Mexico, she argued in April 2012, "That's our southern border. Don't we want our neighbor to be safe, to have a good economy? There are some that say, 'That's their problem.' I say, 'Well, I completely disagree with that.'"[11]

With internationalists like Graham and Granger driving Republican policy on the international affairs budget on the Hill, the budget escaped major cuts under sequestration. Between fiscal year (FY) 2011 and FY 2017 spending on diplomacy and development increased in some years and

Table 9.1 The international affairs budget under Obama

	FY 2010	FY 2011	FY 2012	FY 2013	FY 2014	FY 2015	FY 2016	FY 2017
Administration request	52.2	56.8	59.7	54.9	51.8	52.2	52.9	52.8
Congressional appropriation	48.9	48.3	53.5	53.5	49.2	52.0	52.8	52.1
Difference	−6.3%	−14.9%	−10.3%	−2.6%	−5.2%	−0.5%	−0.2%	−1.3%

Note: Amounts in billions of dollars. Data compiled from 2010–2017 editions of *CQ Almanac.*

decreased in others, but it changed relatively little on the whole. (See Table 9.1.) In fact, the gap between the administration's request for the international affairs budget and the congressional appropriation in this area was larger on average during the first two years of the Obama administration— when the Democrats controlled both chambers of Congress—than it was during the subsequent six years. One should not make too much out of that pattern given that administration budget requests are developed, in part, based on what the administration expects Congress is willing to fund. But in an indication of the maintenance of congressional support for the international affairs budget following the rise of the Tea Party, an executive branch official involved in foreign aid policy commented in 2013, "In many ways, our best allies in Congress are Republicans."[12]

Granger and Graham, in collaboration with Representative Nita Lowey and Senator Patrick Leahy, the top Democrats on the key appropriations subcommittees, played particularly important roles in working to ensure that left-right disagreements over certain kinds of foreign assistance did not derail the overall spending bill. Their subcommittees regularly split along partisan lines when debating aid for family-planning services overseas or efforts to combat climate change—issues marked by ideological polarization and intensive advocacy by party-affiliated groups.[13] But they collaborated to limit the effect of such disputes and maintain bipartisan support for the broader budget. Former Graham Deputy Chief of Staff Andrew King commented on the approach of Graham and Leahy: "They work extremely well together. They have disagreements over issues like the Mexico City policy [which prohibits US aid to groups that provide abortion services overseas], but they've never let that stand in the way of the larger bill."[14]

Jamie Curtis, who served on Granger's subcommittee staff from 2011 to 2014, noted similarly that Granger and Lowey shared a "practical outlook on wanting to get the bill done" and "recognized the need to address certain political issues in order to get it passed."[15] Granger commented at a 2012 hearing of the subcommittee: "Mrs. Lowey and I have a unique relationship. While we do not agree on everything, we do have a strong working relationship and we are both invested in the important work of this Subcommittee. It is a pleasure to work with her and I respect her very much."[16]

Graham and Granger also sought to build support among other Republican lawmakers for the international affairs budget. Andrew King noted, "Senator Graham has put a lot of time into making the case to his colleagues on why this is necessary. He would regularly take a group of Republican senators to Africa, to show them how transformational PEPFAR [President's Emergency Plan for AIDS Relief] and MCC [Millennium Challenge Corporation] have been."[17] In 2012, for instance, in conjunction with the ONE Campaign, which advocates addressing global poverty, Graham led a group of six Republican senators on an eight-day trip to Africa that included visits to a hospital, a school, and other programs funded by the US government.[18] Graham also defended the international affairs budget during Senate debates. After Senator Rand Paul introduced a proposal to cut foreign aid spending by 50% in 2015, Graham said: "To those who constantly demagogue foreign aid as being the root of our financial problems, please stop, because you don't know what the hell you're talking about. . . . This account, I believe, is the smartest use of federal dollars of any place within the federal government."[19] Other key Republican congressional leaders also backed international affairs spending. Mitch McConnell, the top Senate Republican during the Obama presidency, had resisted efforts by Republican colleagues to slash the foreign aid budget when he served as chairman of the foreign operations appropriations subcommittee in the 1990s, and he continued to support the budget as a Republican Party leader.[20]

The international affairs budget, moreover, was not the only locus of bipartisanship on foreign aid during the Obama presidency. During the last year of the Obama administration, with the House and Senate under Republican control, Congress and the president enacted into law important foreign aid reform legislation as well as major bills designed to advance global food security and promote affordable electricity across sub-Saharan Africa.[21] Each of these bills entailed support for foreign aid programming while requiring private sector partnerships and the use of performance metrics, approaches that appealed to Republicans with pro-business attitudes who were skeptical of the efficiency of government programs.

Pushing back against Trump

While the story of the Obama presidency on international affairs spending was largely one of pro-presidential bipartisanship, anti-presidential bipartisanship became the norm on diplomatic and foreign aid spending under Trump. Backed by aid supporters in the NGO, business, military, and faith communities, internationalist lawmakers in both parties repeatedly stymied Trump administration efforts to slash this part of the federal budget or avoid spending appropriated foreign aid funds.

Five weeks after Trump took office, the administration leaked plans to request a 37% cut to international affairs spending in its first budget request to Congress.[22] As news of the administration's budget plans broke, 121 retired three- and four-star US generals and admirals sent a letter to the Democratic and Republican leaders of Congress arguing that a robust international affairs budget was needed to protect national security. The former military leaders stated that "elevating and strengthening diplomacy and development alongside defense are critical to keeping America safe," adding:

> As Secretary James Mattis said while Commander of US Central Command, "If you don't fully fund the State Department, then I need to buy more ammunition." The military will lead the fight against terrorism on the battlefield, but it needs strong civilian partners in the battle against the drivers of extremism—lack of opportunity, insecurity, injustice, and hopelessness. . . . Now is not the time to retreat.[23]

In subsequent weeks, faith-based and business leaders added their voices to the retired military leaders' calls for protecting funding for diplomacy and foreign aid. In March, 106 Christian leaders—many of them representing prominent evangelical or Catholic faith-based institutions—wrote to congressional leaders arguing for foreign aid spending on moral and humanitarian grounds: "Today, there are 65 million displaced people, the most since World War II, and 795 million people still go to bed hungry every night. Matthew 25 tells us when we serve the least of these, we are serving the Lord. As people of faith, we cannot turn our back on those in desperate need."[24]

In May, 225 leaders of US-based corporations—from General Electric to Walmart—made their own case for diplomacy and foreign aid in a public letter to Secretary of State Rex Tillerson: "America's diplomats and development experts help build and open new markets for US exports by doing what only government can do: fight corruption, strengthen the rule of law, and promote host country leadership to create the enabling environment for private investment. . . . American companies depend on robust US engagement overseas, especially in the fast growing markets in the developing world."[25]

The reach of these letters was amplified by coverage of them in major media outlets.[26] In addition, many other civil society leaders and groups—from Bill Gates to numerous humanitarian NGOs, such as CARE, Oxfam, and ONE—spoke out against the proposed cuts and lobbied lawmakers directly to maintain the international affairs budget.[27] During the first nine months of 2017, USGLC members contacted congressional offices via in-person meetings, phone calls, or letters nearly 900,000 times.[28]

As this wide-ranging advocacy campaign was getting underway, leading Democratic and Republican foreign policy voices on Capitol Hill denounced the administration's planned cut to the international affairs budget.[29] While Democratic congressional opposition to a Trump budget cut proposal should not have been surprising, the intensity of Republican congressional opposition was striking. Lindsey Graham said that the proposed 37% cut would be a "disaster" for national security and referenced the letter from the 121 retired generals and admirals in describing his national security concerns.[30] Graham later highlighted the letter again in a subcommittee hearing on the issue, adding, in a reflection of the credibility associated with military officers, "If you don't believe me, listen to the generals."[31]

Other prominent lawmakers also underscored the national security benefits of aid and echoed the argument of the retired military officers in explaining their opposition to the administration's planned cut. Senate Majority Leader Mitch McConnell said, "I don't think these reductions at the State Department are appropriate because many times diplomacy is a lot more effective—and certainly cheaper—than military engagement."[32] Republican Representative Harold Rogers, chairman of the House appropriations foreign operations subcommittee, commented along similar lines, "There [are] two sides to fighting the problem that we're in: There is military and then there's diplomatic. And we can't afford to dismantle the diplomatic half of that equation."[33]

Some lawmakers also highlighted their agreement across the aisle when touting the national security benefits of diplomacy and foreign assistance. Republican Senator Marco Rubio tweeted, "Foreign Aid is not charity. We must make sure it is well spent, but it is less than 1% of budget & critical to our national security." In response, Democratic Senator Chris Murphy tweeted, "Well said, Marco. An emerging bipartisan consensus that cutting State Dept., USAID, makes us less safe."[34]

In response to the bipartisan outcry against the cuts, the administration trimmed the proposed cut from 37% to 31% when it issued its official budget proposal in May.[35] But this modest change still left a huge gap between the administration and both parties in Congress. When Secretary of State Tillerson testified before the Senate appropriations foreign operations subcommittee in June, Senators Graham and Leahy lambasted the proposed budget. Leahy echoed some of the language used by the retired generals and admirals in arguing that the budget represented a US "retreat" from international leadership, and added, "Why would we give up that influence? . . . We can't build a Fortress America."[36] The Republican-controlled Senate Appropriations Committee subsequently issued a report that further rebutted the administration's proposal: "Battlefield technology and fire-power cannot replace diplomacy and development. The administration's apparent doctrine of retreat . . . serves only to weaken America's standing in the world."[37] The committee report also highlighted testimony the committee had received from 16 retired four-star generals and admirals asserting that "the severe cuts to the State Department and USAID that the Administration has proposed will make America less safe."[38] Several months later, Congress approved and Trump signed into law an appropriation of $55.9 billion for the FY 2018 international affairs budget—a figure 38% above the administration's proposal.[39] (See Table 9.2.)

Similar sequences of events characterized debates over the international affairs budget in each of the remaining years of Trump's presidency. For FY 2019, Trump requested $42.2 billion for diplomacy and development—a figure 25% lower than the level enacted into law for FY 2018.[40] A diverse set of groups again quickly sprang into action opposing the proposed cuts. For instance, the ONE Campaign called on its 9 million members to urge Congress to ignore the administration's proposal,[41] while more than 1,200 veterans from all 50 states sent a letter to congressional leaders in both parties explaining why they considered investments in State and AID to be "essential" to national security.[42]

Table 9.2 The international affairs budget under Trump

	FY 2018	FY 2019	FY 2020	FY 2021
Administration request	40.5	42.2	43.3	43.9
Congressional appropriation	55.9	56.1	56.6	71.0*
Difference	+38%	+33%	+31%	+62%

Note: Amounts in billions of dollars. Data compiled from US Global Leadership Coalition and Congressional Research Service reports.

* Includes emergency funding for international COVID-19 relief.

Congressional foreign policy leaders in both parties also denounced the new proposal. House Foreign Affairs Committee (HFAC) Chairman Ed Royce, a Republican, said, "A strong, bipartisan coalition in Congress has already acted once to stop deep cuts . . . that would have undermined our national security. This year, we will act again."[43] Representative Eliot Engel, the senior Democrat on HFAC, called the proposed cuts "draconian."[44] A few months later, congressional negotiators reached agreement on an FY 2019 international affairs appropriation of $56.1 billion, an amount slightly above the enacted FY 2018 level and 33% above the administration's FY 2019 proposal.[45] As he did the previous year, Trump signed the legislation even though its international affairs budget bore little resemblance to his request.[46]

The pattern remained the same after the Democratic Party gained control of the House at the start of 2019. The administration's FY 2020 budget proposal included just $43.3 for the international affairs budget, a 23% cut from the enacted FY 2019 level.[47] As news of the proposal broke, 14 former US combatant commanders released a statement arguing that "diplomacy and development are essential to combating threats before they reach our shores" and urging Congress to "protect resources for America's International Affairs Budget."[48] The following day, 10 major development and humanitarian NGOs issued a statement asserting, "Now is not the time to slash effective, life-saving programs that help create a safer and more secure world."[49]

Lawmakers in both parties also sharply criticized the proposal. Representative Nita Lowey, the new chairwoman of the House Appropriations Committee and its subcommittee on State and foreign operations, commented, "Our nation's security cannot afford a budget that does not adequately fund our diplomatic and development programs, or life-saving humanitarian assistance."[50] Michael McCaul, the senior Republican on HFAC, highlighted the long-term costs of the cuts to national security and cited the aforementioned statement by former Secretary of Defense Jim Mattis, "If you don't fund the State Department fully, then I need to buy more ammunition."[51]

Lowey worked with Representatives Granger and Rogers, the senior Republicans on the House appropriations committee and subcommittee, to develop a more robust budget for diplomacy and development for FY 2020. When the spending bill went to the House floor, Lowey and Rogers cooperated to defeat several amendments introduced by Republican lawmakers to cut the legislation's funding levels by amounts ranging from 1% to 34%, with scores of House Republicans joining with nearly all Democrats to reject each of these proposed cuts.[52] Congress ultimately enacted an international affairs budget for FY 2020 that increased funding by 1% from the FY 2019 level and by 31% from Trump's request. This appropriation included 24% more funding than Trump had requested for humanitarian assistance, 43% more for global health, and 38% more for international peacekeeping.[53]

The Trump administration tried yet again in 2020, this time requesting a 22% cut international affairs spending from the enacted FY 2020 level.[54] Remarkably, even though the coronavirus had already spread to 28 countries by the time the administration released its budget request, the proposal included a 34% cut in global health funding, among other cuts.[55] As in previous years, leading congressional foreign policy voices in both parties immediately criticized the proposal. Eliot Engel said, "If this draconian budget were enacted, it would weaken our security and leadership around the world."[56] McCaul offered a comment that is worth quoting at some length for the extent to which it departed from Trump's "America first" foreign policy approach:

> While I welcome the President's efforts to cut wasteful government spending, we must ensure that cuts don't result in higher costs to taxpayers down the road. This includes efforts to: target the root causes of instability; prioritize critical security and development programs in Central America and West Africa; and support vital global health and food security programs. Successful diplomacy is cost effective—fully funding our foreign assistance programs will ultimately save taxpayer dollars, military resources and protect the homeland.[57]

For the fourth consecutive year, Congress resoundingly rejected the administration's proposal. In addition to preserving the base budget for diplomacy and development again, Congress appropriated $16.1 billion in additional emergency international COVID relief aid in late 2020 and early 2021. The result was a gap between the Trump request and the total amount of foreign aid approved by Congress for FY 2021 of a whopping 62%.[58]

In addition to repeatedly rejecting Trump's proposed budget cuts, Democrats and Republicans in Congress banded together to push back successfully against an administration plan to avoid spending appropriated international affairs funds. In 2018, journalists reported that the administration's Office of Management and Budget (OMB) was considering carrying out a plan in which more than $3 billion in FY 2018 foreign aid funding that had not yet been spent by State or AID would be sent back to the US Treasury, under a process known as a "rescission," at the end of the fiscal year.[59]

Advocacy groups and members of Congress in both parties pushed back against this rescission plan. The ONE Campaign spearheaded 13,000 letters from its members to congressional offices protesting the idea.[60] Some lawmakers voiced particular displeasure at the prospect of the executive branch defying the will and authority of Congress. Bob Corker, the Republican chairman of the Senate Foreign Relations Committee, said that the proposed rescission did not appear to be legal and would be a "breach of trust," adding that his office would look for ways to counter the move if it was carried out.[61] Bob Menendez, the top Democrat on SFRC, threatened that if the administration went forward with the plan, "We'll have to push back, or retaliate by holding up all [executive branch] nominations."[62] In response to this pushback, the administration dropped the plan. Reuters highlighted the role of lawmakers in this shift: "Secretary of State Mike Pompeo urged the administration at a meeting on Tuesday to abandon the plan in the face of congressional opposition, several sources with knowledge of the situation said."[63]

Congress pushed back successfully against an administration rescission plan again in 2019. In August of that year, OMB ordered State and AID to freeze most unspent foreign aid funding from FY 2019, laying the groundwork for between $2 billion and $4 billion of funds to be returned to the US Treasury at the end of the fiscal year.[64] As they did the previous year, advocacy groups and members of Congress in both parties strongly criticized the move. USGLC President and CEO Liz Schrayer called the step "reckless and irresponsible,"[65] while more than 90 NGOs sent a letter to congressional leaders urging them to reject the rescission proposal.[66] In a defense of institutional prerogatives, Eliot Engel said, "When Congress decides how much we spend on foreign assistance, it isn't a suggestion. It's the law, backed up by the Constitution."[67] In a joint letter to Trump, Graham and Harold Rogers also issued a veiled threat: "Not only do these cuts have the potential to undermine significant national security and antiterrorism efforts of our diplomats and international partners overseas, but we fear such a rescission package could complicate the ability of the administration and Congress to work constructively on future appropriations deals."[68]

In the face of this strong congressional pushback, the Trump administration again abandoned its plan to not spend appropriated funds.[69] In an effort to prevent any future executive branch attempt to carry out such a plan, Congress also included in the FY 2020 international affairs appropriations act provisions requiring certain funds to be spent within 60 days and requiring the executive branch to notify and consult Congress before carrying out programmatic or funding changes.[70]

Public and elite opinion

Bipartisanship on the budget for diplomacy and foreign aid is counterintuitive because liberals and conservatives generally have different views regarding social welfare spending, stemming from core left-right differences over the role of government in society. In domestic affairs, liberals favor higher levels of government spending than conservatives on programs designed to improve human welfare. Since economic and humanitarian assistance to other countries also represents a form of government spending designed to improve human well-being, liberals naturally also support higher levels of such international spending than do conservatives. This difference is evident in public opinion surveys, which show higher levels of support for foreign aid spending among Democrats than among Republicans. However, this left-right ideological gap has not resulted in strong polarization in Washington over the international affairs budget because the issue's low salience has reduced the influence of public attitudes on the positions of lawmakers on the issue and because the pro-aid advocacy coalition has managed to persuade many Republican lawmakers that spending on diplomacy and foreign assistance is worthwhile.

In general, most Americans think the United States should make a "measured contribution" to development and relief efforts overseas,[71] but they do not consider it a high priority. More specifically, most voters believe the

United States should provide aid to promote economic growth and address basic needs in other countries, with the highest levels of support associated with humanitarian assistance.[72] But most voters also think the United States is spending too much money on foreign aid, though they greatly overestimate the percentage of the US budget devoted to this policy area.[73] When presented with accurate figures representing current US spending on aid and other policy areas, just as many Americans support increasing humanitarian aid spending as support reducing it, but a majority of Americans favors cutting development aid.[74]

There also exists a left-right split in attitudes about foreign assistance. As scholars Helen Milner and Dustin Tingley note: "Foreign aid is government intervention into the (international) marketplace. Republicans in the United States are much less likely to support the use of economic aid than are Democrats."[75] Indeed, when asked in public opinion surveys, in 2010 and 2017 by the Chicago Council on Global Affairs, whether they supported humanitarian, agricultural, or development assistance to people in needy countries, Democrats were more likely than Republicans to support each of these kinds of aid by amounts ranging from 13% to 21%.[76] (See Table 9.3.)

This left-right split is also evident in other opinion data. The 2017 Chicago Council public opinion survey found that 36% of the Democratic public supported cutting back economic aid to other countries, while 68% of Republicans endorsed such cuts. (See Table 9.4.)[77] In another indication of the left-right split, when asked in a 2018 Chicago Council public opinion survey how much of $100 in their own tax money they would spend on economic foreign aid if they could make the decision, Democrats answered $6

Table 9.3 Support for types of foreign assistance

	Democrats (2010)	Republicans (2010)	Democrats (2017)	Republicans (2017)
Food and medical aid	82%	68%	89%	72%
Agricultural aid	83%	67%	84%	71%
Development aid	73%	52%	77%	56%

Note: This table reports responses to Chicago Council on Global Affairs public opinion surveys asking respondents whether they favored or opposed the following types of foreign aid: food and medical assistance to people in needy countries; aid to help farmers in needy countries become more productive; and aid that helps needy countries develop their economies. Table cells represent the percentage of respondents answering "favor."

Table 9.4 Opinion on economic aid to other countries

	Democratic public	Republican public	Democratic elites	Republican elites
Expand	17%	5%	52%	14%
Cut back	36%	68%	6%	38%
Keep about the same	40%	22%	42%	47%
Not sure	7%	5%	0%	1%

Note: This table reports percentages of respondents indicating whether they thought economic aid to other nations should be expanded, cut back, or kept about the same, in a 2017 survey of the public by the Chicago Council on Global Affairs and a 2018 survey of foreign policy elites by the Chicago Council on Global Affairs and Texas National Security Network.

on average, but Republicans answered just $3 on average.[78] This partisan gap was somewhat smaller with regard to diplomatic spending, with Democrats allocating $5 and Republicans allocating $4 on average out of an imagined $100 in tax money to diplomatic programs.[79] A separate 2017 public opinion survey by the University of Maryland's Program for Public Consultation found that, when told how much money the United States currently spends on diplomacy and development, Democrats favored keeping the amount roughly constant, but Republicans supported cutting it by about 25%.[80]

The attitudes of elites regarding foreign aid spending also reveal a left-right gap, though elites in both parties support higher spending levels than their co-partisan publics. Six percent of Democratic foreign policy elites and 38% of Republican foreign policy elites supported cutting back economic aid to other countries in a 2018 Chicago Council/Texas National Security Network survey.[81] (See Table 9.4.) Support for diplomacy attracts bipartisan support among foreign policy decision-makers and experts, however. In the same 2018 survey, just 5% of Democratic elites and 3% of Republican elites backed cutting back diplomatic programs, whereas 69% of Democratic elites and 47% of Republican elites favored expanding them.[82] (See Table 9.5.)

While public attitudes would seem to suggest that elected officials—particularly those representing more conservative states or districts—would have more of an electoral incentive to cut than to increase foreign aid spending, politicians usually have considerable leeway on the issue because it has low public salience.[83] This low salience has been evident in recent US election cycles. During the 2016 cycle, the USGLC tracked references to foreign aid in congressional campaign statements

Table 9.5 Opinion on diplomatic spending

	Democratic elites	Republican elites
Expand	69%	47%
Cut back	5%	3%
Keep about the same	27%	51%
Not sure	0%	0%

Note: This table reports percentages of respondents indicating whether they thought spending on diplomatic programs to promote US policies abroad should be expanded, cut back, or kept about the same in a 2018 survey of foreign policy elites by the Chicago Council on Global Affairs and Texas National Security Network. (The Chicago Council has not asked this question in its recent public opinion surveys.)

and communications. In a post-election recap, it reported: "Out of several hundred television ads focused on foreign policy, Senator Rand Paul (R-KY) was the only candidate that ran anti-foreign assistance ads."[84] The USGLC found a similar pattern during the 2018 election cycle, despite the executive-legislative clash over the international affairs budget that marked the first two years of the Trump presidency: "Following the trend of most election cycles, foreign assistance largely remained out of the spotlight and was rarely mentioned during the vast majority of the 2018 campaign. In reviewing thousands of campaign ads, only one candidate—who lost in the primary—specifically mentioned cutting foreign assistance."[85]

The low salience of the international affairs budget means that lawmakers are unlikely to be rewarded or punished by voters for supporting or opposing changes to it. Diana Ohlbaum, a former senior Democratic aide responsible for foreign aid policy on HFAC, observed: "Foreign aid is an open area for members. Few constituents care enough about it to vote on it. Members get some letters [from constituents] opposing aid, but they're few in number, and there's not an organized opposition to aid. So there's freedom for members in how they vote."[86]

Advocacy group activity

The relatively weak public and electoral pressures facing members of Congress on international affairs spending also give advocacy groups an opening to influence congressional views. As I argue in Chapter 3, the influence of advocacy groups on Capitol Hill is limited on issues where voters are themselves highly mobilized, but their influence can be considerable if they do not face countervailing opposition from other important groups or the public. If the groups form a politically diverse coalition, they can also be well positioned to cultivate congressional bipartisanship. These favorable conditions have marked the political landscape on the international affairs budget in recent decades.

The advocacy coalition supporting international affairs spending includes four key sets of actors: development and humanitarian NGOs, businesses, military leaders, and faith-based leaders.[87] It is intuitive that development and humanitarian aid NGOs back foreign aid spending. Since Democrats generally favor governmental action to address social needs, Democratic policymakers tend also to be predisposed to support foreign assistance and to be receptive to the arguments of such NGOs. However, the small-government ideology of conservatives makes it more difficult for pro-aid advocates to persuade Republicans to support diplomatic and development spending. Given these realities, NGO leaders recognized over two decades ago that building and maintaining support for the international affairs budget among Republican officials required other actors to be involved in advocacy efforts. They therefore made a strategic decision to develop and institutionalize an advocacy coalition that includes groups that tend to be highly regarded among Republicans and have close ties to Republican leaders.

This strategic decision was rooted in the end of the Cold War and the Republican Party's winning of House and Senate majorities in the November 1994 election, a pair of events that weakened congressional support for robust US international engagement. Soon after the 1994 election, incoming SFRC Chairman Jesse Helms even pejoratively likened foreign aid programs to sending money down "foreign ratholes."[88] In this context, US spending on foreign assistance declined from $27 billion in FY 1991 to $19.5 billion in FY 1997 in constant dollars.[89]

In an effort to counter this shift, in 1995 a group of NGOs formed the USGLC with the single goal of advocating for higher overall US international affairs spending.[90] Liz Schrayer, who had served previously as the national political director of the American Israel Public Affairs Committee, was the driving force behind this step. John Glenn, USGLC's policy director, explained:

Liz Schrayer saw that, after the Cold War, everyone was fighting for a slice of the shrinking federal budget on Capitol Hill, and that we might be more successful if we worked together on behalf of overall international affairs spending. A diverse set of actors should be able to come together around supporting the overall budget but would likely fracture if the focus was on specific spending priorities. Her insight was to bring in not just the traditional actors in the foreign assistance community, but others who you wouldn't necessarily expect to be advocating for foreign assistance, such as the business community.[91]

The USGLC has carried out this strategy by developing and coordinating a network of NGOs, businesses, and military leaders who endorse a robust international affairs budget. This network spans over 500 organizations ranging from American Airlines to the American Red Cross. The organization also draws on advisory councils that include former secretaries of state in both parties and over 200 retired three- and four-star generals and admirals, as well as a network of more than 30,000 veterans who support its mission.[92]

The organization seeks to persuade elected officials that they should support the international affairs budget by demonstrating the breadth of backing for diplomacy and development. In addition to organizing joint statements and letters from its members, USGLC regularly brings three of its members—typically, a business executive, a military figure, and, depending on the congressional office, an NGO or faith-based leader—to meet with individual lawmakers on Capitol Hill and discuss with them how foreign assistance matters.[93]

USGLC also hosts events in lawmakers' states or districts at which locally respected figures explain why diplomacy and development are beneficial. Glenn said of such events: "We're trying to demonstrate to members of Congress that there is support for these issues among their constituents and 'grass-tops' actors—business leaders, faith-based leaders, people who are influential in their communities. These influential voices can give members of Congress additional cover to support development and diplomacy."[94]

In interviews, Democratic and Republican foreign aid practitioners gave a great deal of credit to the pro-aid advocacy coalition—and particularly USGLC—for building and maintaining bipartisan congressional support for international affairs spending. Former HFAC Democratic aide Diana Ohlbaum said that USGLC changed "the whole playing field by creating a powerful coalition behind aid."[95] Dafna Rand, who has served as a senior foreign policy official in Democratic administrations as well as a senior official at Mercy Corps, a major humanitarian aid NGO, noted: "Using military and business leaders to complement the NGO community was a very smart move politically."[96]

Republican practitioners offered similar takes. Nilmini Rubin, a former senior Republican aide handling foreign aid issues on HFAC, commented that USGLC is very effective with Republicans because it "highlights the economic and national security benefits of aid."[97] Mark Lagon, a former State Department official in the George W. Bush administration and Republican aide on the Senate Foreign Relations Committee, added that USGLC has been particularly good at "using different validators to tailor its message differently to conservative Republicans than to progressive Democrats."[98]

USGLC is not the only organization that has developed bipartisanship with respect to the international affairs budget. The anti-poverty ONE Campaign—co-founded by Bono—has also become a heavyweight in aid debates, particularly with regard to global health programs. Its organizational model is centered around individual, rather than institutional, members, and it boasts over 9 million members worldwide. Importantly, it has also made a concerted effort to engage Republicans and bring them on board its campaign.[99] Its board of directors includes Republicans Kelly Ayotte, a former US senator, and Joshua Bolten, who served as White House chief of staff under President George W. Bush.[100] A Democratic Senate foreign policy aide noted (in a remark intended positively), "USGLC and ONE have gone out of their way to focus on Republicans."[101]

Some prominent evangelical leaders and faith-based organizations have also played important roles in building Republican support for humanitarian aid to save lives and address other basic needs in impoverished countries. Scholar Mark Amstutz notes: "Because of their core moral values—such as the sanctity of human life, the priority of families and the well-being of children, religious liberty, and poverty reduction—[evangelicals] have challenged the US government to be more concerned with issues such as human trafficking, religious persecution, and humanitarian relief."[102] For instance, evangelical groups have been central to the mobilization and maintenance of support for the President's Emergency Plan for AIDS Relief, a major program developed during the George W. Bush administration to address the HIV/AIDS epidemic in developing countries, particularly in Africa.[103]

The pro-aid coalition has been further boosted in recent years by the creation of 150PAC, a political action committee founded in 2016 by a bipartisan group of former congressional staff, which provides campaign contributions to members of Congress who strongly support the international affairs budget, which is known in the congressional appropriations process as the "150 account." Josh Bolten and former Clinton White House Chief of Staff Mack McLarty serve as the honorary co-chairs of 150PAC. Across the 2016 and 2018 election cycles, about 64% of its $42,500 in campaign contributions went to Republican lawmakers, while 36% of its contributions went to Democratic lawmakers.[104]

The impact of the pro-aid coalition has been enhanced by a lack of concerted advocacy against the international affairs budget. To be sure, some prominent public intellectuals and foreign policy analysts have argued that foreign aid is wasteful or counterproductive.[105] But these anti-aid voices are far fewer than the many voices across the foreign policy establishment who highlight the benefits of diplomacy and development, and they are not reinforced by groups that represent major segments of American society or the US economy. Diana Ohlbaum observed, "No one pulls together a coalition to cut aid."[106] This lack of significant anti-aid advocacy reflects the fact that no segment of American society is significantly harmed by spending on international affairs. Put another way, the costs of the spending are too small and diffuse to register politically.

Shaping congressional views

In addition to providing political cover for Republicans to support international affairs spending, the pro-aid advocacy coalition has influenced the views of some lawmakers who have come to Congress without strong pre-existing views about the international affairs budget. In particular, USGLC has made a concerted effort to engage the most conservative members of Congress.[107]

This outreach has borne fruit. Consider the cases of Republican Representatives Ted Yoho and Tom Emmer. Yoho, who represented a conservative district in Florida from 2013 to 2021, entered the House after running for office as a Tea Party conservative committed to shrinking the size of the federal government.[108] Yoho joined the House Freedom Caucus and became a reliably conservative member of the House, particularly with respect to government spending.[109] Yet he also became a supporter of the international affairs budget, in conjunction with becoming a congressional leader of foreign aid reform efforts as co-chair of the Caucus for Effective Foreign Assistance. He explained this evolution in 2017:

> I came up here [to Congress] with the attitude, "I'm going to do whatever I can to get us out of foreign aid." But then it was a short study when you start diagnosing the problem. If we pull out of a country and another country goes in there, that is not favorable to the US. We've just made our situation worse, and our goal is to help these countries become self-sufficient on their own and wean them off of foreign aid so they're sovereign nations that are strong allies of America. . . . We can help these countries improve their living standards and by doing that they're better off, we're better off and hopefully we'll all benefit.[110]

Emmer, for his part, was elected to the House from a conservative district in Minnesota in November 2014 after running for office with the backing of the Tea Party. He did not come to Congress planning to focus on foreign policy but chose to invest time in educating himself about international issues after being assigned by the House leadership to the Foreign Affairs Committee.[111] Just a few months into his term, he went with USGLC CEO Liz Schrayer, former Marine Corps Commandant Mike Hagee, and Republican Representative Adam Kinzinger on a USGLC-funded trip to Ethiopia and Kenya, where the group met with local farmers and entrepreneurs. After returning to the United States, Immer said the trip turned him into a supporter of foreign aid:

> I know the attitude, and I've been guilty of it myself: "Why would you invest over there instead of building bridges, building schools, doing stuff here?" It is all about economics and national security . . . I'm learning in even more detail that our national defense and our diplomacy are intertwined. . . . You could make a choice certainly to spend it . . . on bombs, bullets, and boots on the ground or you could help these emerging countries on imparted knowledge and technical support and experience to allow them to improve their economic status. If these programs keep raising people's economic situation, their quality of life, their standard of living, it actually results in a direct benefit to us. Because they don't want anything to do with Al-Shabab.[112]

The evolution and learning illustrated by these examples is enabled by the fact that many lawmakers enter Congress without strongly held beliefs about foreign assistance and do not face strong pressures from constituents to maintain certain positions on foreign aid. Former HFAC Republican aide Nilmini Rubin noted: "When members [of Congress] first come to the Hill, they don't usually have foreign policy backgrounds, but as they learn more, they see the importance of aid. If you sit down with members and talk to them one-on-one, you can really shift minds."[113]

Using reform to build bipartisanship

The advocacy community has sought to further strengthen support for the international affairs budget by strategically promoting reforms designed to make US foreign aid programs more efficient and effective, particularly when the aid budget has been under threat. Former SFRC Democratic aide Steven Feldstein commented, "The efficiency argument is one that many in the aid community see as a way to get Republicans interested in supporting foreign aid."[114] Indeed, given the skepticism inherent in conservative ideology about large government programs, reform initiatives designed to promote greater efficiency naturally appeal to many Republicans. Conservative thought leaders make up a core component of the Consensus for Development Reform, an NGO influential in Republican circles that espouses a commitment both to "US leadership in global development" and "improvement of our foreign assistance's effectiveness."[115]

But pro-reform advocacy has also been deeply bipartisan. The Modernizing Foreign Assistance Network (MFAN), an NGO backed by the USGLC and led by a mix of Democratic and Republican former officials and experts, has served as a key node for advancing many recent reform initiatives.[116] Former SFRC Republican Staff Director Lester Munson highlighted an additional political effect of these initiatives: "Reform efforts go through Congress, so pursuing aid reform makes Congress a stakeholder in the program."[117]

The aid community was particularly active in promoting reform after the Republican Party's takeover of control of the House of Representatives in January 2011, which presented the prospect of steep cuts to the international affairs budget. Later that year, the Center for American Progress and Center for Global Development joined with other pro-aid think tanks and advocacy groups to form a bipartisan working group on diplomatic and foreign aid programs, which produced a major report outlining reform ideas.[118] MFAN also supported the formation in May 2011 of the bipartisan Congressional

Caucus for Effective Foreign Assistance,[119] and it advocated persistently through reports and meetings on Capitol Hill for legislative action on particular reform items.[120]

The Obama administration contributed heavily to this reform movement too. Under Obama, AID Administrator Raj Shah supported reform initiatives in Congress and directed efforts within the agency to increase the transparency and evaluation of aid programs, in part to build congressional support for the agency in the context of Republican control of the House.[121] As an executive branch official involved in foreign aid policy noted in 2013, "Shah has cultivated support in Congress by cracking down on waste, fraud, and abuse; focusing on data and metrics; and emphasizing that USAID is run as a business and as an enterprise, not as a charity."[122] Lawmakers and foreign aid experts credited such initiatives, along with intensive personal outreach to conservative members of Congress by Shah, with strengthening Republican support for foreign aid during the Obama years.[123]

The aid reform movement also contributed to the enactment of reform legislation with strong bipartisan support. In 2011, MFAN began working with Republican Representative Ted Poe, a conservative, on the development of legislation designed to institutionalize more independent evaluation and public disclosure of data with regard to aid programs.[124] This legislation gained support from key Democrats and Republicans in Congress, and it was approved by the House in a voice vote and in the Senate by unanimous consent before being signed into law by President Obama in 2016.[125]

Donald Trump's proposals to slash foreign aid provided a further impetus to the pro-aid community to advance reform. During the first half of the Trump administration, MFAN, the ONE Campaign, the Center for Global Development, and other NGOs and business groups worked with a bipartisan coalition of lawmakers to develop and promote a major reform bill entitled the Better Utilization of Investments Leading to Development (BUILD) Act. This legislation, which was enacted into law in 2018, replaced the Overseas Private Investment Corporation with a new International Development Finance Corporation designed to increase the agility and transparency of US programs that facilitate private sector investments in developing countries.[126]Legislative approval of these aid reform initiatives helped strengthen support for the foreign aid budget among congressional Republicans, contributing to the series of bipartisan actions by Congress to push back successfully against Trump's proposed cuts.

Conclusion

Congressional action to maintain the international affairs budget under Trump represents one of the most important examples of anti-presidential bipartisanship on foreign policy in recent years. Across the four years of Trump's presidency, Congress enacted into law budgets for diplomacy and foreign assistance that exceeded the president's requests by an average of about 40%. This remarkable bipartisan pushback against the president would have been unnecessary were it not for Trump's distinct "America first" agenda. But the close cooperation of Democratic and Republican lawmakers on the issue—under both Obama and Trump—was facilitated by the issue's low salience and by the sustained efforts of the pro-aid advocacy coalition to influence attitudes and develop close ties with elected officials in both parties. The effectiveness of this advocacy coalition points to some important lessons for citizens and groups seeking to foster bipartisanship, which I discuss in Chapter 10.

PART 3
CONCLUSIONS

10

Implications and bipartisanship
under Biden

In his 2021 presidential inaugural address, Joe Biden argued that, more than anything else, the United States needed unity in order to address an array of pressing challenges. Biden used the word "unity" and synonyms of it, such as "togetherness," a remarkable 19 times in the speech.[1] While his inaugural address was unusual in emphasizing this theme quite that much, many presidents have called on the country to come together or pledged to lead on behalf of all Americans. The notion of unity aligns with the classic conception of bipartisanship, in which nearly all Democrats and Republicans join hands in support of a policy decision or initiative. Leaders and pundits have considered this type of unity to be particularly important in foreign policy, as indicated by the oft-expressed notion that politics should stop at the water's edge.

The rarity of unity in recent years has led many scholars and analysts to consider foreign policy bipartisanship to be all but dead. But the research presented in this book shows that bipartisanship remains prevalent in contemporary US foreign policy, just in different forms than the classic conception. Democrats and Republicans are rarely fully unified, but subsets of elected officials regularly form substantial bipartisan coalitions. In some cases, moreover, bipartisanship within Congress is paired with disagreement between lawmakers and the president. In short, political alignments on foreign policy are more varied and nuanced than either the classic conception of bipartisanship or perceptions of constant polarization would suggest.

In this book, I've tried to enhance understanding of the politics of US foreign policy by highlighting the character of different political alignments, investigating the frequency of these alignments in important policy debates, and examining factors that influence decisions by elected officials to line up with or against members of the other party. The data I presented on important congressional votes over the past three decades showed that strong polarization remains the exception, rather than the norm, on foreign policy,

Bipartisanship and US Foreign Policy. Jordan Tama, Oxford University Press. © Oxford University Press 2024.
DOI: 10.1093/oso/9780197745663.003.0010

with pro-presidential bipartisanship, anti-presidential bipartisanship, and cross-partisanship all occurring regularly. Moreover, although polarization has been increasing on both domestic and international issues, this increase has been more gradual in the latter domain. In short, foreign policy bipartisanship is very much alive, though certainly not as robust as proponents of unity would hope.

The book's case studies further demonstrated some of the conditions that facilitate or impede types of bipartisanship. Several of the cases, including the debates over military intervention in Syria, the repeal or replacement of the 2001 and 2002 authorizations for use of military force (AUMF), and the Trans-Pacific Partnership (TPP), were marked by cross-partisanship. In the Syria intervention debate, the absence of a left-right ideological fault line or of advocacy campaigns by influential partisan groups gave Democrats and Republicans considerable political leeway to adopt either pro-intervention or anti-intervention positions, resulting in bipartisan coalitions on both sides of the issue. In the AUMF repeal or replace debates, a strange bedfellows coalition of progressives and libertarians, backed by a diverse set of outside groups, pushed to sharply rein in presidential authority, but they were opposed by some centrist lawmakers in both parties and hawkish Republicans. On the TPP, the ideological fluidity of trade policy positions facilitated intra-party divisions, while the backing of business associations and opposition of labor unions led to more support among Republicans than among Democrats for the agreement on Capitol Hill.

In each of these cases, the intra-party divisions also made it more difficult for Congress to act. On intervention in Syria, Congress was not sufficiently unified to take many consequential steps. On repealing or replacing the AUMF, the splits within and between the parties, coupled with electoral disincentives to prioritize the issue, prevented the House or Senate from approving legislation. On the TPP, Donald Trump's strongly anti-trade rhetoric strengthened the protectionist wing of the Republican Party and impeded congressional endorsement of the deal before Trump withdrew from it.

Collectively, these cases highlight how cross-partisanship tends to limit the influence of Congress by making it harder to marshal legislative majorities behind policy measures. At the same time, they show that cross-partisanship can hamper the president's ability to carry out foreign policy effectively by making it more difficult for the president to gain congressional approval of important initiatives. Cross-partisanship can also reduce the informal influence of Congress by making it harder for lawmakers to send clear signals to

the media, the public, the president, or foreign governments regarding congressional preferences.[2] Given the prevalence of cross-partisanship in contemporary foreign policy debates, these effects may be an underappreciated
contributor to the overall decline in recent decades in the capacity of Congress
to shape foreign policy. The limited support within Congress for efforts to repeal or replace the AUMFs further suggests that electoral motivations tend to
outweigh institutional prerogatives in the calculus of legislators when electoral and institutional concerns come into conflict with each other.

Some of the other cases discussed in the book were marked by broader
bipartisan agreement on Capitol Hill, facilitated by favorable public and elite
attitudes or by supportive outside advocacy. In debates over sanctioning
Russia and Iran, widely shared concerns across the ideological spectrum
about the behavior of those countries led large majorities of elites and the
public to favor placing a series of sanctions on them. This favorable ideological context was reinforced by the advocacy landscape, as many of the
proposed sanctions on Russia and Iran were backed by groups with links to
both parties. At the same time, in examples of anti-presidential bipartisanship, the greater concern of presidents than of members of Congress with
preserving flexibility and limiting diplomatic and economic costs resulted
in frequent inter-branch clashes over the use of sanctions against the two
countries.

On Iran, however, congressional bipartisanship diminished sharply as
Obama negotiated the 2015 Joint Comprehensive Plan of Action, which ac-
tivated the left-right ideological divide over multilateral agreements. In the
context of this major diplomatic achievement by the president, members of
Congress also gained a strong partisan incentive to either support or attack
the agreement, depending on their party identity. This sequence of events
illustrates how partisan motivations tend to take on greater weight relative to
the personal policy preferences of elected officials when an issue carries large
political stakes, thereby generating greater polarization.

The book's final case, regarding international affairs spending, provides
particularly powerful evidence of the importance of advocacy groups in
fostering polarization or bipartisanship. On this issue, the ideological context alone suggests that Congress should have been polarized, given that
liberals are much more supportive than conservatives of non-military foreign aid. But the concerted advocacy of a pro-aid coalition spanning groups
with close ties to both parties fostered bipartisan backing for the international affairs budget on Capitol Hill, leading to strong anti-presidential

bipartisanship when Trump sought to slash the budget dramatically. This case also highlights further the importance of an issue's salience, as its relatively low political stakes made it easier for Republicans to buck Trump on it.

The sanctions and international affairs spending cases show too that Congress still sometimes wields considerable influence on foreign policy. Indeed, congressional influence is at its peak when Democrats and Republicans band together to reject a presidential proposal or push policy in a direction that the president does not favor. Bipartisan congressional pressure on the president can also sometimes paradoxically strengthen the president's hand in international negotiations by enabling the president to tell foreign counterparts that if they don't make greater concessions to the United States, lawmakers will penalize them or reject an agreement.[3] In addition, anti-presidential bipartisanship can strengthen the effectiveness of US foreign policy in instances where the president is pursuing a misguided policy. But in cases where the president's preferred course of action is more sound than that of Congress, anti-presidential bipartisanship can be harmful to the United States.

Overall, the book's findings advance knowledge about the drivers of polarization and bipartisanship in important ways. Much of the literature on polarization is premised on the idea that policy debates can be mapped on a left-right spectrum, with liberal positions pitted against conservative ones. The book's data and cases show that many foreign policy debates do not break down sharply along left-right lines and that this ideological fluidity opens up opportunities for Democratic and Republican elected officials to form coalitions with each other. This reality suggests a need to distinguish among issues when making claims about the relationship between ideology and polarization. In short, ideology polarizes voters and elites on many issues but does not do so across-the-board.

Relatedly, the book suggests an important addendum to the long-standing scholarly debate about the relative importance of ideology and partisanship in fueling polarization. Rather than seeing one of these factors as being consistently more important than the other, it may be more fruitful to see their relative importance as varying depending on an issue's ideological content and salience. In particular, ideology is likely to contribute most to polarization in debates that involve very distinct liberal and conservative positions, while partisanship is likely to fuel polarization the most on highly salient issues.

The book's analysis also underscores the importance of taking advocacy groups more heavily into account in analyses of polarization and bipartisanship. Although a rich literature exists on the influence of interest groups, much of the polarization literature pays relatively little attention to them. As with ideology, a key takeaway of the book is that the advocacy landscape is not uniform; rather, it varies considerably across issues, sometimes fostering polarization and sometimes facilitating bipartisanship. Taken together, these insights also reveal that forces contributing to polarization and bipartisanship operate at multiple levels of politics and society, from the bottom-up pressures generated when voters have strong preferences, to the top-down pressures created when elected officials have strong views, to the outside-in pressures triggered when advocacy groups push for certain courses of action.

Foreign policy bipartisanship under Biden

While the book's core data and case studies only run through the Trump presidency, a quick look at the first two years of the Biden presidency reveals the continuing applicability of the book's themes. Overall, partisan polarization in American politics has been quite high under Biden, extending the decades-old trend. But Democrats and Republicans in Congress have joined together under Biden on many foreign policy issues in a range of bipartisan constellations.

Public opinion polls and political alignments on major domestic issues point to the high levels of overall polarization under Biden. Gallup polls in 2021 found, on average, an eighty-three percentage-point gap between the share of Democrats approving of Biden's performance and the share of Republicans approving of it—the highest such gap in the first year of any presidency since Gallup began measuring this 70 years ago.[4] Many highly salient domestic policy debates have also been strongly polarized during Biden's presidency. When the House and Senate approved a $1.9 trillion pandemic relief and economic stimulus bill in March 2021, all but one Democratic member of Congress voted for the bill and every Republican member of Congress voted against it.[5] Later in the year, the leading legislative proposal to protect voting rights and election integrity was backed by all Democrats and opposed by all but one Republican in key House and Senate votes.[6] In the spring of 2022, just three Senate Republicans joined all Senate Democrats in voting to confirm Ketanji Brown Jackson to the Supreme Court.[7] On a measure concerning climate change and a variety of domestic issues, every Democrat in Congress supported and every Republican in Congress opposed legislation providing for large investments in green energy programs, capping the cost of prescription drugs, strengthening the tax enforcement capacity of the Internal Revenue Service, and raising some corporate taxes.[8]

One major exception to this pattern of strong polarization in domestic affairs during the first two years of Biden's presidency involved infrastructure spending legislation, which generated cross-partisanship. In August 2021, the Senate approved a $550 billion infrastructure spending package by a vote of 69-30, with 19 Republicans joining all 50 Democrats in support.[9] Three months later, the House approved the bill by a vote of 228-206, with 13 Republicans and six Democrats voting against their party's majority.[10] The decision of 32 congressional Republicans to cross party lines on the issue was facilitated by the ideological and advocacy landscapes on it. Public opinion surveys showed that, across the ideological spectrum, most Americans favored infrastructure investments, while many businesses and labor unions took the same position in advocating for the spending.[11] The cross-party cooperation on this infrastructure bill underscores that bipartisanship still marks even some highly salient domestic issues.[12]

In foreign policy, bipartisanship has marked many debates during Biden's presidency. Most strikingly, Democrats and Republicans came together in support of major steps to counter Russia and support Ukraine after Russia invaded Ukraine in February 2022. This bipartisanship, which reinforced Biden's approach to the war in Ukraine, involved both symbolic acts of unity and concrete policy actions. When Biden delivered his State of the Union address five days after the invasion, Democratic and Republican members of Congress repeatedly stood in unison to applaud as Biden emphasized the importance of US support for Ukraine.[13] More importantly, Congress repeatedly bolstered the US response to the war by passing pro-Ukraine legislation with strong bipartisan support. Through a series of laws enacted in March, May, September, and December 2022, Congress appropriated a total of more than $75 billion in military, financial, and humanitarian aid to Ukraine.[14] Congress also mandated new penalties on Russia, approving legislation that revoked Russia's permanent normal trade relations status and codified a ban that Biden had imposed on imports of Russian oil, gas, and coal.[15]

Bipartisanship has characterized other important foreign policy debates under Biden too. On China, Biden has pursued a set of policies that are similar in key respects to those of Trump and that reflect the solidification in both parties of a view that the United States should act firmly to counter Chinese actions and influence. For instance, Biden has kept in place various tariffs that Trump had imposed on Chinese imports and continued to send warships through the South China Sea in defiance of Chinese claims that the waters belong to China. Foreign policy commentator Josh Rogin observed in early 2022, "Restraining China is now a multi-administration bipartisan strategy."[16] At the same time, bipartisan coalitions in Congress have successfully advanced China-related legislation during the Biden administration. In 2021, the Senate approved by voice vote and the House passed with just one vote in opposition a bill restricting imports of goods produced using forced labor in the Xinjiang province of China.[17] In the summer of 2022, on an issue that involves both foreign and domestic policy, 24 Republican representatives and 17 Republican senators joined nearly all Democrats in approving legislation designed to enhance US economic competitiveness with China by making extensive investments in the US production of semiconductors.[18]

Some other Biden-era foreign policy debates have also generated strong bipartisanship or cross-partisanship on Capitol Hill. As worry increased in the summer of 2021 about likely Taliban reprisals in the wake of a US withdrawal from Afghanistan, the Senate and House approved, by votes of 416-11 and 98-0, a large increase in the number of visas available to Afghans who had worked for or with the US military in Afghanistan, along with funding for their relocation to the United States.[19] In August 2022, the Senate cleared the admission of Sweden and Finland to NATO by a vote of 95-1.[20] The following month, 21 Senate Republicans joined 46 Senate Democrats in approving a global treaty backed by a coalition of major environmental and industry groups that phases out the use of hydrofluorocarbons, a major greenhouse gas pollutant.[21] This approval, like the congressional rejection of Trump's proposals to slash the budget for diplomacy and foreign aid, points to the influence of politically diverse advocacy coalitions. Even though positions on a global climate change treaty would tend to map onto a left-right ideological spectrum, the support of Republican-leaning business groups for this treaty brought many Senate Republicans on board.[22]

Democrats and Republicans even worked together to claw back a bit of foreign policy authority from the executive branch early in the Biden administration, enacting legislation mandating that State Department special envoys be subject to Senate confirmation and imposing administrative penalties on any State Department officials who do not comply with inspector general requests for documents or interviews.[23] But on another issue of foreign policy authority, intra-party division continued to stymie congressional action. In June 2021, 219 House Democrats and 49 House Republicans voted to green-light legislation repealing the 2002 authorization for use of military force against Iraq, but Senate Minority Leader Mitch McConnell blocked the measure from being approved in the Senate.[24]

While the Biden administration supported many of these foreign policy measures, bipartisan coalitions in Congress directly challenged the administration's policies on other international issues. In April 2021, after Biden chose not to impose sanctions on Saudi Arabian Crown Prince Mohammed bin Salman for ordering the murder of Saudi dissident Jamal Khashoggi, the House voiced its displeasure with the decision by approving a bill limiting US arms sales to Saudi Arabia in a vote of 350-71.[25]

Democrats and Republicans in Congress also banded together to press the administration to go further than it considered advisable in penalizing Russia and supporting Taiwan. In July 2022, the Senate unanimously passed a resolution urging the secretary of state to designate Russia a state sponsor of terrorism, despite the Biden administration's argument that the action would be counterproductive in forcing the administration to sanction US allies that do business with Russia and precluding any possibility of diplomatic engagement with the country.[26] After the administration continued to decline to label Russia a state sponsor of terrorism, a bipartisan set of senators introduced legislation in September 2022 that would require the administration to do so.[27]

On Taiwan, lawmakers in both parties pushed for major steps to strengthen US ties with the island, despite objections from the Biden administration that the steps would escalate tensions with China. In August 2022, Speaker of the House Nancy Pelosi traveled to Taiwan, defying administration requests to Pelosi not to go forward with the visit.[28] As Pelosi met with Taiwanese leaders, Mitch McConnell and 25 other Senate Republicans released a statement expressing support for her trip.[29] The following month, the Senate Foreign Relations Committee approved by a vote of 17-5 a bill elevating the diplomatic status of Taiwan, bolstering US military support to Taiwan, and designating Taiwan a major non-NATO ally. The administration urged lawmakers not to support this measure based on concern that it would inflame China and could lead to war.[30]

Still other foreign policy debates took on a more partisan character during the first part of Biden's presidency. Most notably, many Republicans sharply attacked Biden's handling of the US withdrawal from Afghanistan. For instance, Mike Rogers, the senior Republican on the House Armed Services Committee, called the withdrawal an "unmitigated disaster."[31] While some Democrats also found fault with the way the administration carried out the withdrawal, they largely defended the decision to leave Afghanistan and accused Republicans of playing politics with the issue.[32] The partisan dimension of this debate reflected the issue's high degree of salience and Biden's political vulnerability on it. Many congressional Republicans also strongly criticized Biden's effort to negotiate a new nuclear agreement with Iran, continuing the pattern of polarization around nuclear diplomacy with Iran dating back to 2015.[33] Overall, though, foreign policy bipartisanship has remained common under Biden, suggesting that the arguments and findings of this book remain highly relevant.

Fostering bipartisanship

Looking ahead, bipartisanship will be an essential ingredient for an effective US foreign policy in the coming years. This is not to say that broad agreement is always better than contention. Achieving bipartisan support for a bad policy does more harm than good, and the United States is usually best served when important decisions are made after vigorous debate.[34] Strong consensus can also generate a dangerous temptation for the United States to push a policy too far. As Council on Foreign Relations Senior Fellow Christopher Tuttle notes, "Partisan criticism often provides an important check on ambition, and when that check is absent, oversteering becomes harder to resist."[35] But on balance, US foreign policy is more successful and sustainable when it involves some degree of bipartisanship. Among other effects, bipartisanship strengthens America's ability to address global challenges, send clear signals to adversaries, uphold international commitments, maintain a reputation for reliability, and learn from foreign policy failures.[36] So, what lessons can we take from this book's findings and other research regarding ways of fostering bipartisanship?

Other scholars and experts have developed a wide array of ideas for facilitating bipartisanship. Some of these ideas focus on reforms of the US electoral system designed to encourage the election of more leaders who are predisposed to pursue bipartisanship. Such proposals include the institution of open primaries that are not restricted to voters in a particular party, campaign-finance rules that give less influence to big donors that possess extreme views, non-partisan redistricting commissions that reduce the role of partisanship in the drawing of congressional lines, and ranked-choice voting procedures that make more than two candidates competitive in elections.[37]

Some other ideas for reducing polarization focus more on how the House and Senate operate. Over a period of decades, congressional party leaders have instituted a variety of rules and procedures that have contributed to polarization on Capitol Hill.[38] Steps such as giving the minority party more say in the legislative process, scheduling regular member meetings that include lawmakers from both parties, increasing the number of days per year in which Congress is in session, electing the speaker of the House by supermajority vote, and increasing the staffing capacity of congressional committees would give members more incentive and ability to reach across the aisle.[39]

While structures, rules, and procedures can enable or impede bipartisanship, individual people ultimately need to cooperate with each other in order for bipartisanship to come about. In this regard, the trend in recent decades of Democratic and Republican legislators socializing with each other less often makes it harder for members to develop the trust-based relationships that are often a key foundation for cooperation.[40] As Republican Senator Susan Collins has noted, "It's far harder to demonize someone you've broken bread with."[41] Recognizing this reality, a number of institutions, including the Bipartisan Policy Center, Brookings Institution, Council on Foreign Relations, Hewlett Foundation, Lugar Center, New America, Partnership for a Secure America, R Street, and Woodrow Wilson Center, have designed programs that regularly bring lawmakers or congressional staff from the two parties together to get to know each other or discuss policy issues.[42]

This type of private relationship building is particularly important because leaders can often engage more meaningfully with counterparts in the other party when they are not in the public eye. Indeed, private or secret deliberations frequently aid the forging of compromise and agreement by making it easier politically for officials to make concessions to each other.[43] As a result, bipartisanship is often facilitated when congressional leaders negotiate with each other privately or when congressional committees hold closed-door sessions.[44]

This book's findings point to some additional takeaways with respect to the fostering of bipartisanship on particular issues. *First, bipartisanship is more feasible in debates that do not revolve around clashing liberal and conservative commitments.* A standard approach to bipartisanship is to build consensus at the center of the ideological spectrum, and then try to move outward toward the left and right to pick up additional support. For instance, Danielle Thomsen highlights the importance of moderates serving in Congress, and Matthew Yglesias and Stephen Teles call for moderates in both parties to form a bipartisan bloc on Capitol Hill.[45] The creation of bipartisan "gangs" in the Senate often follows this model of building coalitions from the center out.[46] Implicit in this model is the notion that issues break down on a left-right spectrum, with centrists serving as the key bridge for bringing together liberals and conservatives.

Many policy debates do break down in this way, and bipartisanship would certainly get a big boost if more moderates held elected office and worked together to build coalitions from the center out. But ideological centrists do not always need to be the focal points for bipartisan coalitions. As shown in this book, many foreign policy debates are conducive to strange bedfellow coalitions or other bipartisan constellations. For instance, in debates over intervention to stop mass atrocities, Republican national security hawks and Democratic humanitarians often find common ground in favoring forceful action, while in war powers debates, progressives and libertarians routinely join hands in seeking to limit the president's war-making authority. In such debates, the same policy stance can resonate with people who are typically on opposite ends of the ideological spectrum, facilitating cross-partisanship.[47] On still other issues, such as the use of sanctions against countries engaged in objectionable behavior, a policy option may be popular among liberals, conservatives, and centrists, facilitating broad bipartisan agreement. Recognizing how the ideological landscape varies across issues can enable a more fine-grained understanding of the prospects for bipartisanship in different debates.

Second, politically diverse advocacy coalitions can play critical roles in developing bipartisanship. Admittedly, the raison d'être of some advocacy groups is the advancement of partisan goals. Such groups are not likely to be interested in working across party lines. But for the many groups driven by policy, rather than partisan, commitments, the creation of advocacy coalitions spanning politically diverse sets of organizations can help prompt Democratic and Republican elected officials to adopt common positions.[48] The impact of the US Global Leadership Coalition on congressional stances on foreign aid vividly shows how significant this influence can be. Diverse advocacy coalitions can be particularly well positioned to foster bipartisanship on issues that are not very salient, as elected officials are less likely to have strong preexisting commitments of their own on such issues or to have strong electoral incentives to engage in partisan warfare on them.

Third, people at different levels of society can be forces for bipartisanship. Bipartisanship can be generated from the top-down, bottom-up, and outside-in. The agency of individual leaders should not be minimized or overlooked. Even in today's highly polarized environment, some elected officials make it a priority to cultivate relationships across the aisle, as evidenced by the many examples in this book of congressional Democrats and Republicans working together on important legislative initiatives. Outside institutions can encourage such bipartisanship by giving recognition to members of Congress who engage in it, as the Lugar Center does by publishing a bipartisan index that ranks members of Congress based on how often they work across party lines.[49]

Yet the behavior of elected officials is often influenced and constrained by voters and advocacy groups. When it comes to bipartisanship, voters send mixed messages to politicians overall. In general, voters indicate that they value bipartisanship and want leaders to compromise with each other.[50] On specific issues, however, many voters often prefer that leaders fight for the adoption of their party's policy goals rather than make concessions that would be needed to achieve a compromise.[51]

When thinking about whether to reach across the aisle on an issue, elected officials are likely to be influenced less by general voter professions of support for bipartisanship than by the views of voters on that particular issue. If a majority of voters in both red and blue jurisdictions favor a certain policy stance, Democratic and Republican elected officials will have a strong incentive to adopt it, facilitating bipartisanship. If there does not exist a prevailing view on an issue among either party's electorate, conditions should be ripe for cross-partisanship. But if Democratic voters see an issue differently than Republican voters, elected officials will feel pressure to take opposite sides in the debate. Pushing for bipartisanship on issues where the electorate itself is not already polarized will therefore tend to be more fruitful than pressing for it on issues where it is.

Overall, when one looks beyond the high-profile issues that dominate public debate, the prospects for bipartisanship look better than one might expect. To be sure, the landscape of contemporary American politics is bleak in many ways. The pernicious effects of rising polarization have only been compounded by the poisonous rhetoric and anti-democratic actions of Donald Trump and other demagogues. But even during this time of intense partisan disagreement and hostility, Democrats and Republicans have continued to cooperate under the radar on many important international issues. In the years ahead, new opportunities for foreign policy bipartisanship will emerge. Elected officials, voters, and advocacy groups will jointly determine whether and how Democrats and Republicans work together to address the array of global challenges facing the United States.

Notes

Chapter 1

1. Nick Corasaniti, "Republicans Attack House Democrats on Impeachment, and Democrats Change the Subject," *New York Times* (December 17, 2019); Connor O'Brien, "Senate Democrat Blasts Republicans' 'Blind Partisan Loyalty' to Trump," *Politico* (October 6, 2019).
2. House Votes 695 and 696, Articles I and II of H.Res. 755, Impeaching President Donald John Trump, President of the United States, for high crimes and misdemeanors (December 18, 2019); Senate Votes 33 and 34, Articles of impeachment against President Donald John Trump (February 5, 2020).
3. Aaron Blake, "4 Takeaways from the Impeachment of President Trump," *Washington Post* (December 18, 2019).
4. House Vote 701 and Senate Vote 14 on H.R. 5430, United States-Mexico-Canada Implementation Act (December 19, 2019, and January 16, 2020).
5. Senate approval by unanimous consent and House Vote 635 on S. 1838, Hong Kong Human Rights and Democracy Act of 2019 (November 19, 2019, and November 20, 2019).
6. House Vote 672 and Senate Vote 400 on S. 1790, National Defense Authorization Act for Fiscal Year 2020 (December 11, 2019, and December 17, 2019).
7. Ibid.
8. US Global Leadership Coalition, "Congress Finalizes FY20 Spending: International Affairs Budget Sees Small Increase as Global Challenges Grow" (December 20, 2019).
9. On cross-partisanship, see Cooper and Young 1997; Gibson 2000. Hurlburt and Polimédio 2016 use the term "transpartisanship" to describe this political constellation. See also Lantis and Homan 2019.
10. Martin 2000; Schultz 2001; Howell and Pevehouse 2007; Kupchan and Trubowitz 2007; Schultz 2017; Jervis et al. 2018; Myrick 2022.
11. Drutman 2020, 90–91.
12. Karol 2019, 5; Klein 2020, 5.
13. McCarty, Poole, and Rosenthal 2006; Sinclair 2006; Theriault 2008; Jacobson 2013; Abramowitz 2018; Rosenfeld 2018; McCarty 2019; Thomsen 2020.
14. Voteview, "Congress at a Glance: Major Party Ideology" (n.d.), voteview.com/parties/all.
15. Brookings Institution, *Vital Statistics on Congress: Data on the U.S. Congress* (updated November 2022), Table 8.3; Shawn Zeller, "No Quarter for Centrists in House: 2020 Vote Studies," *Roll Call* (March 3, 2021).

16. Voteview, "117th Congress (2021–2023)—Senators: DW-Nominate plot," voteview.com/congress/senate; Voteview, "117th Congress (2021–2023)—Representatives: DW-Nominate plot," voteview.com/congress/house; Voteview, "Congress at a Glance: Major Party Ideology," voteview.com/parties/all (all no date available).

17. For an overview of recent research on polarization and foreign policy, see Friedrichs and Tama 2022.

18. Destler, Gelb, and Lake 1984; Meernik 1993; Prins and Marshall 2001; Peake 2002; DeLaet and Scott 2006. See also Krebs 2015 for a different periodization of foreign policy consensus and disagreement.

19. Lee 2009; Snyder, Shapiro, and Bloch-Elkon 2009.

20. McCormick and Wittkopf 1990; Kupchan and Trubowitz 2007; Lapinski 2013; Jeong and Quirk 2019; Bendix and Jeong 2021. See also Hurst and Wroe 2016, which highlights fluctuations in foreign policy polarization between 1970 and 2012, and Wagner 2020, which shows that congressional voting on foreign policy was also highly polarized before World War II.

21. Howell and Pevehouse 2007; Kriner 2010; Flores-Macías and Kreps 2013; Hildebrandt et al. 2013; Kriner and Shen 2014; Schultz 2017, 11–14.

22. Jeffrey M. Jones, "Last Trump Job Approval 34%; Average Is Record Low 41%," Gallup (January 18, 2021).

23. Ruth Igelnik, Scott Keeter, and Hannah Hartig, "Behind Biden's 2020 Victory," Pew Research Center (June 30, 2021).

24. Iyengar et al. 2019.

25. Pew Research Center, "Partisan Antipathy: More Intense, More Personal" (October 10, 2019).

26. Charles Homans and Alyce McFadden, "Today's Politics Divide Parties, and Friends and Families, Too," *New York Times* (October 18, 2022).

27. Iyengar and Westwood 2015; Abramowitz and Webster 2016.

28. Mason 2018; Barker and Suhay 2021.

29. Mason 2018, 14.

30. Mansbridge and Martin 2016, 1.

31. Klein 2020, xix.

32. Carl Hulse, "After Stimulus Victory in Senate, Reality Sinks in: Bipartisanship Is Dead," *New York Times* (March 6, 2021); Jack Shafer, "'Bipartisanship' Is Dead in Washington. That's Fine," *Politico* (May 28, 2021).

33. Kupchan and Trubowitz 2021, 92.

34. Drezner 2019b, 10.

35. Smeltz, Busby, and Tama 2018.

36. Curry and Lee 2020.

37. Harbridge 2015.

38. Chaudoin, Milner, and Tingley 2010.

39. Friedman 2022.

40. Kertzer, Brooks, and Brooks 2021.

41. Fowler 2015, 173.

42. Collier 2011, 9.

43. Fowler 2015, 173.

44. Crabb 1957, 44–81; Zelizer 2010, 60–80.

45. Johnson 2006, 31–88.

46. Melanson 2005; Zelizer 2010. See also Krebs 2015.

47. Garcia 2009; Andrew Hanna, "Senate Votes Overwhelmingly to Admit Montenegro to NATO," *Politico* (March 28, 2017); Ellen Mitchell, "Senate Votes for North Macedonia to Join NATO," *The Hill* (October 22, 2019); Diego Areas Munhoz and Nancy Ognanovich, "US Senate Ratifies NATO Membership for Finland and Sweden," Bloomberg (August 3, 2022).

48. Senate Vote 281 and House Vote 342, S.J. Res. 23, Authorization for Use of Military Force (September 14, 2001).

49. House Vote 158 and Senate Voice Vote on H.R. 1298, United States Leadership Against HIV/AIDS, Tuberculosis, and Malaria Act of 2003 (May 1, 2003, and May 16, 2003).

50. House Vote 701 and Senate Vote 14 on H.R. 5430, USMCA.

51. Jordain Carney, "Congress Cuts Deal For $13.6 Billion for Ukraine Aid in Funding Bill," *The Hill* (March 9, 2022); Mike DeBonis, "Congress Passes Pair of Bills Punishing Russia," *Washington Post* (April 8, 2022); Catie Edmondson and Emily Cochrane, "House Passes $40 Billion More in Ukraine Aid, with Few Questions Asked," *New York Times* (May 10, 2022); Marianna Sotomayor and Jacob Bogage, "Biden Signs Bill to Fund Government, Hours Before a Shutdown Deadline," *Washington Post* (September 30, 2022).

52. Other studies have examined congressional activism or assertiveness but without necessarily focusing on the extent to which efforts to challenge an administration or initiate policy change attract bipartisan support. See Ripley and Lindsay 1993; Johnson 2006; Carter and Scott 2009; Scott and Carter 2014; Lantis 2019a; Peck and Jenkins 2020.

53. Zelizer 2010, 104.

54. Franck and Weisband 1979; Howell and Pevehouse 2007.

55. Walldorf 2008, 112–143; Søndergaard 2020, 164–214.

56. Tama 2020.

57. Daugirdas and Mortensen 2017.

58. Fisher 2015.

59. Trubowitz and Harris 2019; Coons 2020; Chaudoin, Milner, and Tingley 2021; Tama 2021.

60. U.S. Senate, "Vetoes by President Donald J. Trump" (n.d.), https://www.senate.gov/legislative/vetoes/TrumpDJ.htm.

61. Congressional Quarterly 1935.

62. Deibel 2002.

63. House Roll Call Vote 186 on H.R. 1591, U.S. Troop Readiness, Veterans' Care, Katrina Recovery, and Iraq Accountability Appropriations Act (March 23, 2007).

64. House Roll Call Vote 477 on H.R. 2454, American Clean Energy and Security Act (June 26, 2009).

232 NOTES

NOTES

65. Senate Vote 325 and House Roll Call Vote 420 on H.R. 5376, Inflation Reduction Act of 2022 (August 7, 2022, and August 12, 2022).
66. Senate Vote 264 on Cloture on Senate Amendment 2640 to H.J. Res. 61 (September 10, 2015).
67. Kriner and Schickler 2016.
68. Karol 2000; Hiscox 2002; Destler 2005; Guisinger 2017.
69. Gibson 2000, 104.
70. House Roll Call Vote 374 on the Motion to Concur in the Senate Amendment with Amendment to H.R. 2146, To amend the Internal Revenue Code of 1986 to allow Federal law enforcement officers, firefighters, and air traffic controllers to make penalty-free withdrawals from governmental plans after age 50, and for other purposes (June 18, 2015); Senate Roll Call Vote 219 on the Motion to Concur in the House Amendment to the Senate Amendment to H.R. 2146 (June 24, 2015). See also Lantis and Homan 2019, 167–171.
71. McCormick and Black 1983; Krutz and Peake 2011, 108–121.
72. Auerswald 2012; Kreps, Saunders, and Schultz 2018; Lee 2019.
73. House Vote 494 on H.R. 2278, To limit the use of funds appropriated to the Department of Defense for United States Armed Forces in support of North Atlantic Treaty Organization Operation Unified Protector with respect to Libya, unless otherwise specifically authorized by law (June 24, 2011).
74. Lee 2009; Theriault 2013; Lee 2016.
75. Curry and Lee 2020.
76. Adler and Wilkerson 2012.
77. Mueller 1970; Baker and Oneal 2001; Baum 2002.
78. David W. Moore, "Bush Job Approval Highest in Gallup History," Gallup News Service (September 24, 2001).
79. Chaudoin, Milner, and Tingley 2010, 92; Hicks, Lauter, and McElhinny 2018.
80. In closely related research, Helen Milner and Dustin Tingley have found that public opinion and interest groups are key influences on the president's power relative to Congress in foreign policy. See Milner and Tingley 2015.
81. Baldassarri and Gelman 2008, 429; Noel 2013, 81. Some domestic policy debates, on issues such as good government causes or disaster relief, also do not feature ideological polarization. See Lee 2009, 56–59.
82. Erikson, MacKuen, and Stimson 2002, 196; Baldassarri and Gelman 2008, 423–429.
83. Smeltz et al. 2017.
84. In this book, I generally use the terms "advocacy groups" and "interest groups" interchangeably, but I mainly employ the former term since it is more commonly understood to encompass a wide array of corporate and nonprofit organizations. While the term "interest groups" is also sometimes applied to the full gamut of organizations that engage in advocacy on public policy issues, it is often associated solely with business interests.
85. Bonica 2013, 306; Hafner-Burton, Kousser, and Victor 2015.
86. Karol 2009; Milner and Tingley 2015.
87. Howell and Pevehouse 2007; Lee 2009; Kriner 2010.

88. For an exception, see Peck and Jenkins 2020.

89. Krasner 1978; Meernik and Oldmixon 2008; Howell, Jackman, and Rogowski 2013.

90. Mayhew 2004; Davidson et al. 2018, 316–317.

91. Sinclair 2016; Davidson et al. 2018; Curry and Lee 2020.

92. Hertzke 2004; Carter and Scott 2009; Snyder 2013; Gagnon 2018.

93. Bresolin 2014.

94. This legislation built on an earlier Magnitsky Act, enacted in 2012, that imposed sanctions only on Russian officials who had committed gross violations of human rights. See Tama 2018a.

95. Goldgeier and Saunders 2018.

96. Hicks, Lauter, and McElhinny 2018, 7.

97. Binder and Lee 2015.

98. Peake 2002; Binder 2003; Lapinski 2013; Thurber and Yoshinaka 2015; Barber and McCarty 2016.

99. Binder 2017, 237.

100. Fowler 2015; Chergosky and Roberts 2018; LaPira, Drutman, and Kosar 2020.

101. Alduncin, Parker, and Theriault 2017.

102. Mann and Ornstein 2006, 2012; LaPira, Drutman, and Kosar 2020; Jentleson 2021.

103. Hicks 2017; Jervis et al. 2018; Trubowitz and Harris 2019.

104. Martin 2000; Kelley and Pevehouse 2015; Schultz 2017; Coons 2020; Myrick 2022. See also Peake, Krutz, and Hughes 2012; Lee 2019.

105. Howell 2003; Lewis 2003. But see also Christenson and Kriner 2020; Reeves and Rogowski 2022.

106. Fowler 2015; Carter and Scott 2021b; Marshall and Haney 2022.

107. Martin 2000; Trubowitz and Harris 2019.

108. Schultz 2017, 19.

109. Hinckley 1994; Weissman 1995; Kosar 2020.

110. Fisher 2000; Rudalevige 2006; Hendrickson 2015; Murray 2015; Edelson 2016; Burns 2020; Crouch, Rozell, and Sollenberger 2020; Warburg 2021.

111. Caruson and Farrar-Myers 2007.

112. Adams and Murray 2014.

113. Zegart 2011; Fowler 2015; Glennon 2015; Fowler 2021; Warburg 2021.

114. Goldgeier and Saunders 2018, 156. See also Binder, Goldgeier, and Saunders 2020.

115. Lindsay 1994; Carter and Scott 2009; Auerswald and Campbell 2012; Kronlund and Mäkinen 2015; Milner and Tingley 2015; Carter and Scott 2021a.

116. Lindsay 1994; Milner and Tingley 2015.

117. Destler 2005.

118. Lavelle 2011a.

119. Martin 2000; Auerswald and Maltzman 2003; Krutz and Peake 2011; Kreps, Saunders, and Schultz 2018.

120. Forsythe 1987; Snyder 2013; Søndergaard 2020.

121. Milner and Tingley 2015; Carcelli 2022.

122. Tama 2020.

123. Auerswald 2000; Howell and Pevehouse 2007; Kriner 2010; Auerswald and Campbell 2015; Recchia 2016.

124. Many of the interviews were conducted on a not-for-attribution basis based on the preference of the interview subject.

Chapter 2

1. Trubowitz and Mellow 2005; Jochim and Jones 2013; Harbridge 2015; Hurst and Wroe 2016; Wagner 2020. But see Jeong and Quirk 2019.

2. McCormick and Wittkopf 1992; Meernik 1993; Prins and Marshall 2001.

3. I am grateful to Balazs Martonffy, James Bryan, Harrison Brooks, and Gabriel Exposito for their excellent work on the data set. For a related analysis of the data set, see Bryan and Tama 2022.

4. For instance, see Flynn 2014; Harbridge 2015; Kriner and Schickler 2016.

5. Mayhew 2005, 202–203.

6. Including these additional votes from *CQ Almanac*, rather than only including the CQ key votes, greatly expands the size of the data set, allowing richer analysis. Although the additional votes were probably not quite as consequential on average as the CQ key votes, it is reasonable to assume that they were also important since *CQ Almanac* only covers significant legislative debates. *CQ Almanac* articles typically list important votes in a text box labeled "Box Score." The data set includes any votes directly referenced in one of these box scores. For articles lacking a box score, the data set includes any votes directly referenced in the body of the article. I included votes highlighted in *CQ Almanac* articles from every third year, rather than every other year or every fourth year, to avoid possible overrepresentation or underrepresentation of presidential or congressional election years, which might feature different patterns of bipartisanship than non-election years. The tabulations presented in this chapter incorporate all votes highlighted in *CQ Almanac* articles from 1992, 1995, 1998, 2001, 2004, 2007, 2010, 2013, 2016, and 2017. (The last year is 2017, rather than 2019, because *CQ Almanac* stopped publishing these types of articles after 2017. Since 2017 is close chronologically to 2019 and both years were not election years, I substituted the 2017 votes for the unavailable 2019 votes.)

7. The exclusion of voice votes and unanimous consent votes from voting analyses can result in significant underestimations of the prevalence of bipartisanship in Congress. See Mayhew 2005, 222. When presenting data that include voice votes and unanimous consent votes, I treat these votes as involving majorities of both parties voting together because these voting procedures are typically used only for legislation that has broad bipartisan support. See Harbridge 2015, 75. But I drop voice votes and unanimous consent votes when presenting more fine-grained measures of bipartisanship since precise vote totals are not available for them. See also Carrubba et al. 2006; Thierse 2016.

8. Unless otherwise noted, differences in all comparisons highlighted in this chapter are statistically significant at the 5% level, meaning there is less than a 5% chance

that the difference does not reflect an actual difference between the two categories. I determined the statistical significance of differences for dichotomous measures using chi-square tests. I determined the statistical significance of differences for continuous measures using t-tests.

9. Dropping the immigration votes from comparisons of foreign and domestic policy votes could be sensible because many of the immigration votes concern both cross-border and domestic dimensions of immigration policy. But I keep the immigration votes in the foreign policy category in most of the tabulations presented in this chapter since immigration policy is widely considered an element of foreign policy.

10. The rates of bipartisanship that I report in this chapter are broadly comparable to rates of bipartisan voting reported in other studies of the US Congress. Sean Theriault's analysis of congressional voting on important legislation from 1973 to 2004 finds average gaps between the percentage of Democrats and the percentage of Republicans voting for legislation of about .5. See Theriault 2008, 34, 167. Laurel Harbridge's study of House roll call votes during the same time period finds that a majority of Democrats and a majority of Republicans voted together in about half of all votes and about four-fifths of final passage votes. See Harbridge 2015, 28. Using a measure somewhat akin to my strength of bipartisanship score, Wolfgang Wagner finds average levels of agreement on foreign policy of .66 in the House and .62 in the Senate from 1941 to 2014. See Wagner 2020, 47–48.

11. Baumgartner et al. 2009.

12. Ryan 2019.

13. *CQ Almanac* lists votes on which the president took a clear public position in tables entitled "Presidential Position Votes."

14. Cameron 2000; Canes-Wrone 2006.

15. Wildavsky 1966; Sigelman 1979; Fleisher et al. 2000; Canes-Wrone, Howell, and Lewis 2008; Cohen 2019.

16. This finding is also consistent with other work finding that Congress challenges the president more often on use of force decisions when the opposition party has more power on Capitol Hill and that members of the opposition party are more likely than members of the president's party to act as foreign policy entrepreneurs. See Howell and Pevehouse 2007; Carter and Scott 2009.

17. This finding contrasts with the finding in a previous study that congressional polarization did not increase on foreign policy between 1947 and 2001 when the data were limited to votes on the final passage of legislation. See Chaudoin, Milner, and Tingley 2010.

18. These percentages do not add up to 100 because of rounding.

19. Senate Vote 314 on S. Amdt. 1046 to H.R. 3116, Department of Defense Appropriations Act for Fiscal Year 1994 (October 15, 1993); House Vote 544 on S. 2845, Intelligence Reform and Terrorism Prevention Act of 2004 (December 7, 2004); Senate Vote 259 on S. 3930, Military Commissions Act of 2006 (September 28, 2006); and House Vote 452 on H. Con. Res. 105, Prohibiting the President from deploying or maintaining United States Armed Forces in a sustained combat role in Iraq without specific, subsequent statutory authorization (July 25, 2014).

20. Senate Vote 139 on S. Amdt. 2665 to S. Amdt. 2664, FREEDOM Support Act (July 1, 1992); House Vote 362 on H. Amdt. 319 to H. Amdt. 318, Foreign Operations, Export Financing, and Related Programs Appropriation Act for Fiscal Year 1998 (September 4, 1997); House Vote 411 on H.R. 5682, Henry J. Hyde United States and India Nuclear Cooperation Promotion Act of 2006 (July 26, 2006); and House Vote 427 on H.R. 850, Nuclear Iran Prevention Act of 2013 (July 31, 2013).

21. Some sanctions bills are listed by CRS as foreign trade and international finance legislation, while others are listed as international affairs legislation.

22. Senate Vote 142 on H.R. 2212, United States-China Act of 1991 (July 23, 1991); House Vote 575 on H.R. 3450, North American Free Trade Agreement Implementation Act (November 17, 1993); Senate Vote 292 on S. 1269, Reciprocal Trade Agreements Act of 1997 (November 4, 1997); and House Vote 608 on H.R. 6156, Russia and Moldova Jackson-Vanik Repeal and Sergei Magnitsky Rule of Law Accountability Act of 2012 (November 16, 2012).

23. Senate Vote 394 on S. 2205, DREAM ACT of 2007 (October 24, 2007); Senate Vote 168 on S. 744, Border Security, Economic Opportunity, and Immigration Modernization Act (June 27, 2013); House Vote 94 on H.J. Res. 46, Relating to a national emergency declared by the President on February 15, 2019 (February 26, 2019).

24. Twenty-two of the 36 immigration votes in the data set occurred between 2007 and 2020.

25. Wong 2006; Citrin and Sides 2008; Facchini, Mayda, and Mishra 2011; Milner and Tingley 2011; Freeman and Tendler 2012; Peters 2015; Hammer and Kafura 2019.

26. Milner 1999; Baldwin and Magee 2000; Hiscox 2002; Fordham and McKeown 2003; Guisinger 2017.

27. McCormick and Wittkopf 1992; Meernik 1993; Prins and Marshall 2001.

28. This finding departs from a study that found the opposite pattern from 1953–1998. See Prins and Marshall 2001.

Chapter 3

1. Lee 2009; Theriault 2013; Baker 2015.
2. Lee 2016.
3. Baumgartner et al. 2009; Lee 2009.
4. Lavelle 2011a; Baker 2015.
5. Adler and Wilkerson 2012; Curry and Lee 2020; Harbridge-Yong 2020b.
6. Trubowitz and Mellow 2011.
7. Mayhew 2004.
8. Fenno 1973.
9. Noel 2013, 40, 41.
10. Cronin and Fordham 1999, 969.
11. Ellis and Stimson 2012, 15–17; Lewis 2019, 32.
12. For overviews of knowledge of elite politics and the relationship between elites and the public, see Kertzer 2020; Saunders 2022.

13. Souva and Rohde 2007.
14. Fenno 1973.
15. Author's interview of Bob Corker (June 29, 2022).
16. Noel 2013.
17. Ellis and Stimson 2012, 10. Some scholars instead employ a typology of ideology that decouples economic and social views, generating four, instead of two, ideologies: liberalism, conservativism, libertarianism, and populism. See Carmines and D'Amico 2015.
18. Fiorina and Abrams 2008; Levendusky 2009; Abramowitz 2010; Lelkes 2016. But see also Grossman and Hopkins 2016 for an analysis showing that ideological sorting has been greater among Republicans than among Democrats.
19. Pew Research Center, "In a Politically Polarized Era, Sharp Divides in Both Partisan Coalitions" (December 17, 2019), 111–112.
20. This fit is analogous to the R-squared statistic in standard quantitative models. Noel 2013, 74–82; email correspondence with Hans Noel (April 10, 2020).
21. Baldassarri and Gelman 2008, 423–428.
22. Baldassarri and Gelman 2008, 429. See also Cronin and Fordham 1999.
23. These data are based on my tabulations of ANES data from all questions listed in the "Public Opinion on Public Policy Issues" section of the ANES Guide to Public Opinion and Electoral Behavior that ask respondents for their view on a governmental policy issue. I follow the issue categories in the ANES Guide in classifying questions as involving military and foreign policy issues or domestic policy issues. American National Election Studies, "The ANES Guide to Public Opinion and Electoral Behavior," http://electionstudies.org/resources/anes-guide/.
24. Erikson, MacKuen, and Stimson 2002, 196. See also McCormick 2014.
25. Kertzer, Brooks, and Brooks 2021.
26. Kertzer et al. 2014; Rathbun et al. 2016.
27. Murray, Cowden, and Russett 1999; Murray 2002; Rathbun 2007; Nincic and Ramos 2010.
28. Wittkopf 1990; Holsti 2004; Rathbun 2004; Kupchan and Trubowitz 2007; Dueck 2010; Rathbun 2012; Gries 2014; Nau 2015; Jeong and Quirk 2019; Wenzelburger and Böller 2019; Raunio and Wagner 2020; Wagner 2020; Bendix and Jeong 2022; Böller 2022; Fordham and Flynn 2022.
29. Busby, Kafura, Smeltz, et al. 2020. The Chicago Council surveys of foreign policy elites poll executive branch and congressional officials, think tank experts, interest group leaders, professors, and other senior professionals whose work concerns international issues.
30. Busby, Kafura, Monten, et al. 2020, 126.
31. Gries 2014, 235–262; Smeltz, Busby, et al. 2015, 15; Busby, Kafura, Smeltz, et al. 2020, 8.
32. Gries 2014, 108–115; Milner and Tingley 2015, 393; Smeltz, Busby, et al. 2015, 17.
33. Broz 2011.
34. American National Election Studies, "ANES Guide."
35. Busby, Kafura, Smeltz, et al. 2020.

36. Busby, Kafura, Smeltz, et al. 2020, 5. At the same time, there was some movement in public attitudes on NATO during the Trump era, as pro-NATO attitudes became more dominant among Democrats and less dominant among Republicans. Goldgeier 2019.
37. Busby, Kafura, Smeltz, et al. 2020, 6, 11.
38. Smeltz et al. 2019, 34.
39. Noel 2016; Rathbun 2016; Guisinger and Saunders 2017; Boucher and Thies 2019; Friedrichs 2022.
40. Smeltz and Kafura 2022.
41. Texas National Security Review 2018; Dueck 2020; Smeltz and Tama 2021.
42. Carol Giacomo, "One Thing They Can Agree on—They Need to Listen," *New York Times* (January 18, 2018); Susan B. Glasser, "Laura Rosenberger and Jamie Fly: The Full Transcript," *Politico* (February 26, 2018); Anthony J. Blinken and Robert Kagan, "'America First' Is Only Making the World Worse. Here's A Better Approach," *Washington Post* (January 1, 2019); Alliance for Securing Democracy 2020.
43. Chollet and Lindberg 2008, 2.
44. Lagon and Schulz 2012; Gries 2014, 114–115; Kertzer et al. 2014; Maxey 2020.
45. Author's interview of Russell Feingold (May 13, 2021).
46. Haesebrouck and Mello 2020; Homan and Lantis 2020; Wagner 2020.
47. Pew Research Center, "Beyond Red vs. Blue: The Political Typology" (June 26, 2014), 66.
48. Rathbun 2016.
49. Intra-party divisions and cross-partisanship can also be fueled by splits within both parties between elected officials who favor working within the system to develop compromises and antiestablishment politicians who privilege ideological purity over bridge building. See Noel 2016; Wagner 2020.
50. Zaller 1992; Groeling and Baum 2008; Berinsky 2009; Kriner 2010; Saunders 2015; Zingher and Flynn 2016; Guisinger and Saunders 2017; Kriner 2018; Saunders 2022.
51. Zaller 1992. At the same time, different types of elites can exercise more or less influence in different circumstances. If public attitudes on an issue are already polarized, the public is likely to respond more to cues from partisan elites than from expert elites. But if public views on the issue are not already polarized, the public will be more likely to be influenced by expert opinion. See Guisinger and Saunders 2017.
52. Dante Chinni, "Democrats, GOP Move in Opposite Directions on Russia Views," NBCNews.com (December 8, 2019).
53. Hurwitz and Peffley 1987; Murray 2002; Gries 2014; Rathbun et al. 2016; Kertzer and Zeitzoff 2017.
54. Busby, Kafura, Smeltz, et al. 2020, 7.
55. Guisinger and Saunders 2017, 432.
56. Drezner 2008, 60–62; Bardes and Oldendick 2017, 262–263; Guisinger 2017, 7.
57. Page and Bouton 2006. But see also Kertzer 2020, who shows that elite-public gaps are smaller when controlling for other demographic variables.
58. Miller and Stokes 1963; Lipset 1966; Jacobs and Page 2005.
59. Bartels 1991; Hartley and Russett 1992; Wlezien 1996.
60. Overby 1991.

61. Sobel 2001; Baum 2004; Hildebrandt et al. 2013. But see also Kreps 2018.
62. Aldrich, Brinegar, et al. 2006.
63. Christenson and Kriner 2020.
64. Aldrich, Gelpi, et al. 2006, 494.
65. Brady 2011; Foyle 2012.
66. Kull and Destler 1999; Bishin 2010; Miler 2014.
67. Kull and Destler 1999.
68. Broockman and Skovron 2018.
69. Author's interview of Lee Hamilton (October 25, 2017).
70. As noted in Chapter 1, I use the terms "advocacy groups" and "interest groups" interchangeably, though some readers may associate the latter term only with business interests.
71. Berry and Wilcox 2009; Leech 2011; Heaney 2012; Rozell, Wilcox, and Franz 2012.
72. Baumgartner et al. 2009.
73. Gilens and Page 2014.
74. Grossman 2012.
75. Adams 1981; Thorpe 2014.
76. Stark 2021.
77. Milner 1997; Baldwin and Magee 2000.
78. Destler and Henning 1989; Broz and Hawes 2006; Lavelle 2011a.
79. Snyder 2018.
80. Busby 2007; Amstutz 2014.
81. Smith 2000; Kandel 2010; DeWind and Segura 2014; Thurber, Campbell, and Dulio 2018.
82. Fordham 1998.
83. Garrett 1978; Tierney 1993; Newhouse 2009; Lavelle 2011b; Hatipoglu 2014.
84. Lee 2005.
85. Mahoney 2007; Baumgartner et al. 2009.
86. Bonica 2014, 381.
87. Baumgartner et al. 2009; Berry and Wilcox 2009; Grossman 2009; Heaney 2012; Rozell, Wilcox, and Franz 2012; Karol 2015; Skocpol and Hertel-Fernandez 2016; Karol 2019.
88. Layman et al. 2010; Bawm et al. 2012; Baylor 2017.
89. Matt Grossman and David Hopkins show that the Democratic Party largely represents a coalition of party-affiliated groups, while the Republican Party largely represents a conservative ideological movement. See Grossman and Hopkins 2016.
90. Heaney 2012; Karol 2015.
91. Trubowitz 2011; Flores-Macías and Kreps 2013.
92. Smith 2000; Ambrosio 2002; Karol 2009; McCormick 2012.
93. Hafner-Burton, Kousser, and Victor 2015, Figure 8.
94. Bonica 2013, 306.
95. Center for Responsive Politics, "Business Associations," n.d., https://www.opensecr ets.org/industries/totals.php?cycle=2020&ind=N00, and Center for Responsive Politics, "Labor," OpenSecrets.org, n.d., https://www.opensecrets.org/industries/

totals.php?cycle=2020&ind=P. The weaker Republican tilt of business associations in 2020 than in 2016 reflected tensions between Trump Republicans and parts of the business community. It is also worth noting that not all industry sectors are characterized by a pro-Republican tilt. Tory Newmyer and Aaron Gregg, "Chamber Faces Backlash from Republican Allies," *Washington Post* (May 24, 2021); Gimpel, Lee, and Parrott 2014.

96. Destler 2005.
97. Center for Responsive Politics, "Defense," n.d., https://www.opensecrets.org/ind ustries/totals.php?cycle=2020&ind=D; Center for Responsive Politics, "Pro-Israel," n.d., https://www.opensecrets.org/industries/totals.php?cycle=2020&ind=Q05.
98. Hertzke 2004; Busby 2007; Berry and Wilcox 2009, 107; Amstutz 2014, 159–165.
99. Drezner 2019a.
100. LegBranch Team, "Broad Coalition Calls for Congress to Reclaim Its National Security Powers," LegBranch (March 18, 2020); Katrina Manson, "Has America Had Enough of War?," *Financial Times* (May 7, 2021).
101. Wildavsky 1966; Canes-Wrone, Howell, and Lewis 2008, 5–6.
102. Milner and Tingley 2015.
103. Tierney 1993; Milner and Tingley 2015.
104. Zegart 1999, 24–25.
105. Baumgartner and Leech 2001, 1208. See also Canes-Wrone, Howell, and Lewis 2008, 5–6 for a discussion of this pattern.
106. Karol 2009.
107. Krasner 1978, 63–64; Lake 1988; Canes-Wrone, Howell, and Lewis 2008, 5; Meernik and Oldmixon 2008, 187; Howell, Jackman, and Rogowski 2013, 37–39; Milner and Tingley 2015, 32.
108. Howell and Moe 2021, 117.
109. On presidential incentives to preserve flexibility, see Ingber 2020.
110. Wood 2009; Trubowitz 2011; Kriner and Reeves 2015. See also Dearborn 2021 for an analysis of change over time in prevailing ideas about the extent to which the president represents the overall interests of the country.
111. Jervis et al. 2018; David 2020.
112. Yasmeen Abutaleb and Josh Dawsey, "Trump's Praise of Xi Alarms Advisers," *Washington Post* (February 17, 2020).
113. Tama 2021.
114. Mayhew 2004; Davidson et al. 2018, 316–317.
115. Jentleson 1992.
116. Wittkopf 1987; Page and Barabas 2000, 357–359; Holsti 2004.
117. Lindsay 1994; Hertzke 2004; McCormick and Mitchell 2007; Carter and Scott 2009; Cutrone and Fordham 2010; Snyder 2018; Lantis 2019a; Søndergaard 2020; Lupton 2021.
118. Fenno 1973; Deering and Smith 1997.
119. Tama 2020.
120. Kaempfer and Lowenberg 2000; Smith 2000; Walldorf 2008; Hufbauer et al. 2009; McCormick 2012; Hatipoglu 2014.

121. Lindsay 1986; Whang 2011.
122. Smeltz, Daalder, et al. 2015.
123. Arnold 1990; Mayhew 2004.
124. Busby et al. 2020.
125. Martin 1992, 105–110; Hertzke 2004; Søndergaard 2020; Tama 2020.
126. Author's interview of David Kramer (August 3, 2017).
127. Tama 2020.
128. Mayhew 2000, 216–222; Kriner and Schickler 2016; Peck and Jenkins 2020.
129. Jordain Carney, "Senate Overwhelmingly Approves Iran Review Bill in 98-1 Vote," *The Hill* (May 7, 2015).
130. Coons 2020; Ryan 2020; Chaudoin, Milner, and Tingley 2021; Tama 2021.
131. Mayhew 2000.
132. Peck and Jenkins 2020, 257–260.
133. Fowler 2015.
134. Carter and Scott 2021a, 195.
135. Wittkopf 1990; Holsti 2004; Gries 2014; Milner and Tingley 2015.
136. Lindsay 1986; Whang 2011.
137. Mayda and Rodrik 2005; Rathbun 2016.
138. Milner and Tingley 2015.
139. Baldwin and Magee 2000; Destler 2005.
140. Smith 2000; Walldorf 2008; McCormick 2012; Hatipoglu 2014.
141. Snowball sampling is a standard technique for interview-based research. See Esterberg 2002; Tansey 2007.
142. This is a standard approach for elite interviewing. See Aberbach and Rockman 2002.

Chapter 4

1. S.J. Res. 21, Authorization for the Use of Military Force Against the Government of Syria to Respond to Use of Chemical Weapons (113th Cong.).
2. Hearing Before the U.S. Senate Committee on Foreign Relations, "The Authorization of Use of Force in Syria," S. Hrg. 113–479 (September 3, 2013).
3. U.S. Senate Committee on Foreign Relations, Business Meeting (September 4, 2013), https://www.foreign.senate.gov/hearings/2013/09/04/business-meeting.
4. Wilson Andrews, Aaron Blake, Darla Cameron, and Kennedy Elliott, "Where Congress Stands on Syria," *Washington Post* (last updated September 13, 2013).
5. Michael R. Gordon, "U.S. and Russia Reach Deal to Destroy Syria's Chemical Arms," *New York Times* (September 14, 2013).
6. Hendrickson 2015, 55–70; Böller and Müller 2018, 650–654.
7. Jennifer M. Freedman, "UN to Investigate Syrian Human-Rights Violations, Overriding Russia, China," Bloomberg (August 23, 2011).
8. James Doubek, "More Than 3,700 People Were Killed in Syria's Civil War This Year," NPR.org (December 4, 2021).

9. S. Res. 180, A resolution expressing support for peaceful demonstrations and universal freedoms in Syria and condemning the human rights violations by the Assad regime (112th Cong.).

10. Executive Order 13573, "Blocking Property of Senior Officials of the Government of Syria," *Federal Register* 76, 98 (2011), 29143–29146.

11. S. 1472, Syria Sanctions Act of 2011 (112th Cong.).

12. Executive Order 13582, "Blocking Property of the Government of Syria and Prohibiting Certain Transactions with Respect to Syria," *Federal Register* 76, 162 (2011), 52209–52211.

13. President Barack Obama, "Statement on the Situation in Syria" (August 18, 2011).

14. Scott Wilson and Joby Worrick, "Assad Must Go, Obama Says," *Washington Post* (August 18, 2011).

15. Author's interview of Robert Ford (November 1, 2017).

16. S. Res. 370, A resolution calling for democratic change in Syria (112th Cong.).

17. Office of Senator Marco Rubio, "Senators Casey and Rubio Introduce Syria Resolution," Press release (February 10, 2012).

18. Josh Rogin, "Debate over Syria Intervention Takes Shape," *The Cable* (March 7, 2012); Emily Cadei, "Trying to Get Off the Sidelines," *CQ Weekly* (April 16, 2012).

19. Josh Rogin, "Top Democrat: We Shouldn't Do Anything in Syria Right Now," *The Cable* (March 1, 2012).

20. Hearing Before the U.S. Senate Committee on Foreign Relations, "Syria: U.S. Policy Options," S. Hrg. 112-495 (April 19, 2012), 4.

21. John T. Bennett, "Mixed Messages on Syria," *U.S. News and World Report* (March 2, 2012); Hrg., SFRC, "Syria: U.S. Policy Options."

22. SFRC, Business Meeting.

23. S. Res. 424, A resolution condemning the mass atrocities committed by the Government of Syria and supporting the right of the people of Syria to be safe and to defend themselves (112th Cong.); Emily Cadei, "On Syria, Looking for a Plan of Action," *CQ Weekly* (June 11, 2012).

24. Jonathan Broder, "Rebel Gains Bring Call for U.S. Action on Syria," *CQ Weekly* (December 3, 2012).

25. Senate Roll Call Vote 220 on S. Amdt. 3262 to S. 3254, National Defense Authorization Act for Fiscal Year 2013 (December 4, 2012).

26. Panetta 2014.

27. Anne Gearan and Karen DeYoung, "Obama Unlikely to Reconsider Refusal to Arm Rebels in Syria," *Washington Post* (February 9, 2013); Clinton 2014, 462–464; Chollet 2016, 140–143; Rhodes 2018, 197–198; Burns 2019, 327–328.

28. Arms Control Association, "Timeline of Syrian Chemical Weapons Activity, 2012–2022" (n.d.), https://www.armscontrol.org/factsheets/Timeline-of-Syrian-Chemical-Weapons-Activity.

29. H.R. 1327, Free Syria Act of 2013 (113th Cong.).

30. Josh Rogin, "Democrats and Republicans Unite Around Calls for More Aggressive Syria Policy," *The Cable* (March 21, 2013).

31. Hearing Before the U.S. Senate Committee on Armed Services, "Update on the Situation in Syria," S. Hrg. 113-110 (April 17, 2013), 23; McCain and Salter 2018, 182.
32. Hearing Before the U.S. House Committee on Foreign Affairs, "Crisis in Syria: The U.S. Response," Serial No. 113-10 (March 20, 2013), 4.
33. Hrg., Senate Committee on Armed Services, "Update on the Situation in Syria," 17.
34. S. 960, Syria Transition Support Act (113th Cong.).
35. Cristina Marcos, "U.S. Could Aid Syrian Rebel Groups Under Bill Approved by Senate Panel," CQ Weekly (June 3, 2013).
36. Quoted in Jennifer Rubin, "Iran and Congress Rebuke Obama's Syria Policy," Washington Post (May 22, 2013).
37. Office of Senator Tom Udall, "Udall on Syria: Intervening in Another Middle Eastern Civil War Is Not in U.S. Interests," Press release (June 17, 2013).
38. U.S. Senate Committee on Foreign Relations, "Syria Transition Support Act of 2013," S. Rept. 113-79 (July 24, 2013).
39. Jennifer Rubin, "Iran and Congress Rebuke Obama's Syria Policy," Washington Post (May 22, 2013)
40. Author's interview of Ilan Goldenberg (January 16, 2018).
41. Mark Mazzetti, Michael R. Gordon, and Mark Landler, "U.S. Moves to Supply Weapons to Syrian Rebels," New York Times (June 15, 2013); Karen DeYoung and Anne Gearan, "U.S., Citing Use of Chemical Weapons by Syria, to Provide Direct Military Support to Rebels," Washington Post (June 14, 2013).
42. Reuters, "U.S. Concludes Assad's Forces Used Chemical Weapons in Syria" (June 13, 2013); Rhodes 2018, 224.
43. Author's interview of Dafna Rand (June 6, 2018); author's interview of Amanda Sloat (July 24, 2017).
44. Author's interview of Amanda Sloat (July 24, 2017).
45. Author's interview of Susan Rice (June 13, 2019).
46. Quoted in Niels Lesniewski, "Levin, McCain, Menendez: Arming Syrian Rebels Won't Be Enough," The Hill (June 18, 2013).
47. Quoted in Karen DeYoung, "Divisions on Hill Stall Syria Plan," Washington Post (July 11, 2013).
48. Quoted in Donna Cassata and Bradley Klapper, "Congress Scattered on Foreign Policy: Party Lines Blurred in Disputes over U.S. Role in Syria, Egypt," St. Louis Post-Dispatch (July 24, 2013).
49. Joby Warrick, "More Than 1,400 Killed in Syrian Chemical Weapons Attack, U.S. Says," Washington Post (August 30, 2013); The White House, "Government Assessment of the Syrian Government's Use of Chemical Weapons on August 21, 2013" (August 30, 2013).
50. The White House, "Remarks by the President to the White House Press Corps" (August 20, 2012).
51. Hadas Gold, "McCain Wants Syria Intervention," Politico (August 22, 2013).
52. Bedford Daily Voice, "Report: Westchester Rep. Eliot Engel Urges Action Against Syria" (August 26, 2013).

53. Alan Cowell, Steven Erlanger, and Rick Gladstone, "Momentum Builds for Military Strike in Syria," *New York Times* (August 27, 2013).
54. Chollet 2016, 1–7; Rhodes 2018, 226–237.
55. The White House, "Statement by the President on Syria" (August 31, 2013), https://obamawhitehouse.archives.gov/the-press-office/2013/08/31/statement-presid ent-syria.
56. Howell 2013; Kriner 2014; Goldberg 2016; Rhodes 2018, 235, 240; Burns and Stravers 2020.
57. Author's interview of Robert Ford (November 1, 2017).
58. Christenson and Kriner 2020, 184–191.
59. Philip Rucker and Ed O'Keefe, "Obama Lobbies Hard on Syria," *Washington Post* (September 6, 2013); Chollet 2016, 13–16; Kerry 2018, 134–135.
60. Author's interview of Susan Rice (June 13, 2019).
61. Author's interview of Jamil Jaffer (April 20, 2020).
62. Author's interview of Margaret Taylor (April 30, 2020).
63. Paul Kane and Ed O'Keefe, "Approval by Congress Far from a Guarantee," *Washington Post* (September 1, 2013).
64. David A. Fahrenthold and Paul Kane, "In Congress, Unlikely Allies Against Strike," *Washington Post* (September 7, 2013).
65. SFRC, Business Meeting; Paul Singer and Aamer Madhani, "Syria Sell Begins," *USA Today* (September 3, 2013).
66. Ed O'Keefe, "On Syria, Assessing the Splits on Syria," *Washington Post* (September 2, 2013); Jonathan Broder, "Damned if You Do . . . ," *CQ Weekly* (September 9, 2013).
67. Andrews et al., "Where Congress Stands on Syria."
68. NPR, "Should the U.S. Choose Sides in Syria? A Democrat Says 'Yes,'" Weekend Edition (February 22, 2014); Remarks of Senator John S. McCain, 160 Cong. Rec. S3256–S3259 (May 22, 2014).
69. S. 2410, Carl Levin National Defense Authorization Act for Fiscal Year 2015 (113th Cong.).
70. U.S. Senate Committee on Armed Services, "Carl Levin National Defense Authorization Act for Fiscal Year 2015: Report to Accompany S. 2410," S. Rept. 113-176 (June 2, 2014), 459.
71. Carl Levin and Howard P. "Buck" McKeon National Defense Authorization Act for Fiscal Year 2015, Public Law 113-291 (113th Cong.).
72. President Barack Obama, "Remarks by the President at the United States Military Academy Commencement Ceremony" (May 28, 2014).
73. Chollet 2016, 140–143.
74. Steve Holland and Patricia Zengerle, "Obama Seeks $500 Million from Congress to Help Moderate Syrian Rebels," Reuters (June 26, 2014); Karen DeYoung, "Obama Seeks Funds to Train Syrian Rebels," *New York Times* (June 27, 2014)
75. Chollet 2016, 143.
76. House Roll Call Vote 507 on H. Amdt. 1141 to H. J. Res. 124, Continuing Appropriations Resolution, 2015 (September 17, 2014); Senate Vote 270 on H. J. Res.

124, Continuing Appropriations Resolution, 2015 (September 18, 2014). The legislation was enacted as Public Law 113-164.

77. John Hudson, "Congress Approves Arming of Syrian Rebels," *Foreign Policy* (September 18, 2014).

78. Michael D. Shear, Helene Cooper, and Eric Schmitt, "Obama Administration Ends Effort to Train Syrians to Combat ISIS," *New York Times* (October 9, 2015).

79. Pew Research Center, "Public Says U.S. Does Not Have Responsibility to Act in Syria" (December 14, 2012).

80. Pew Research Center, "Public Remains Opposed to Arming Syrian Rebels" (June 17, 2013).

81. Smeltz 2012; Smeltz, Daalder, and Kafura 2014; Pew Research Center, "Public Remains Opposed to Arming Syrian Rebels"; Peter Brown, "American Voters Say 2-1 Stay Out of Syria, Quinnipiac University National Poll Finds," Quinnipiac University (July 11, 2013); Scott Clement, "Most in U.S. Oppose Syria Strike, Post-ABC Poll Finds," *Washington Post* (September 4, 2013).

82. Smeltz 2012; Smeltz, Daalder, and Kafura 2014; ABC News/Washington Post Poll: "Few Back U.S. Military Role in Syria—But Support Jumps in Specific Cases," Press release, Langer Research (December 20, 2012).

83. Smeltz, Busby, et al. 2015.

84. Dieck 2014.

85. Pew Research Center, "Public Opinion Runs Against Syrian Airstrikes" (September 3, 2013); Scott Clement, "Most in U.S. Oppose Syria Strike, Post-ABC Poll Finds," *Washington Post* (September 3, 2013); Andrew Dugan, "U.S. Support for Action in Syria Is Low vs. Past Conflicts," Gallup (September 6, 2013); Dana Blanton, "Fox News Poll: Despite Chemical Weapons, Voters Oppose US Action in Syria," FoxNews. com (September 9, 2013); Sarah Dutton, Jennifer De Pinto, Anthony Salvanto, and Fred Backus, "Majority Opposes Military Attack on Syria, Poll Says," CBSNews.com (September 9, 2013); Scott Clement, "More Americans Against Airstrike, Survey Finds," *Washington Post* (September 10, 2013).

86. Adam Berinsky details a similar process of voter attitudes changing based on the party identity of the president during the Iraq war. See Berinsky 2009.

87. Anna Palmer, "Libertarians, Liberals Unite Against Syria Strike," *Politico* (September 4, 2013).

88. Karen Tumulty and Peter Wallstein, "Obama Is Making Little Headway with Congress on Syria," *Washington Post* (September 6, 2013).

89. Quoted in Corey Boles, "President Is Opposed by Unlikely Alliance in Congress," *Wall Street Journal* (August 31–September 1, 2013).

90. Author's interview of Ilan Goldenberg (January 16, 2018).

91. Author's interview of Tommy Ross (July 2, 2018).

92. Lantis 2021.

93. See, e.g., Human Rights Watch 2015.

94. Author's interview of Jamil Jaffer (April 20, 2020).

95. Kaufman 2019; Mallory Simon and Kate Bolduan, "He Smuggled War Crimes Evidence and Begged the US for Help. Now Congress Is Finally Acting and Set to Sanction Syria," CNN.com (December 17, 2019).

96. Author's interview of Robyn Lieberman (August 7, 2017).

97. Hearing Before the U.S. House of Representatives Tom Lantos Human Rights Commission, "The Human Rights Crisis in Syria" HRG-2012-HOR-0003 (March 27, 2012), 28.

98. Testimony of Suzanne Nossel, Executive Director, Amnesty International, Hrg., Tom Lantos Human Rights Commission; Human Rights First, "Blueprint Details Steps for U.S. to Cut Ties with Russian Arms Dealer at Heart of Syrian Atrocities," Press release (July 23, 2013); Amnesty International, "Syria: Possible International Armed Intervention After Alleged Chemical Weapons Attack" (August 29, 2013).

99. Author's interview of Tommy Ross (July 2, 2018).

100. Testimony of Radwan Ziadeh, Hrg., Tom Lantos Human Rights Commission; Susan Cornwell, "Syrian Opposition Group Organizes to Send Funds to Rebel Army," Reuters (August 10, 2012); Mohammed Alaa Ghanem and Jason T. Hunt, "Syria: A Clear Path," Coalition for a Democratic Syria (April 2013); Syrian Emergency Task Force, "Supporters of a Democratic Syria Are Encouraged to Write Letter to the Editors" (May 2, 2013), http://www.syriantaskforce.org/supporters-of-a-democra tic-syria-are-encouraged-to-write-letter-to-the-editors/; Christina Wilkie, "Syrian Rebels Lobby Washington Behind the Scenes," HuffPost (May 4, 2013).

101. Author's interview of Radwan Ziadeh (April 24, 2020); Wilkie, "Syrian Rebels Lobby Washington."

102. Legistorm, "Friends of a Free, Stable and Democratic Syria Caucus" (n.d.), legistorm. com/organization/summary/144081/Friends_of_a_Free_Stable_and_Democratic_ Syria_Caucus.html.

103. Author's interview of House Republican foreign policy aide (April 2020).

104. Author's interview of Robert Ford (November 1, 2017); Steve Strunsky, "Syrian-Americans Divided over U.S. Military Strike," NJ.com (September 10, 2013).

105. Author's interview of Radwan Ziadeh (April 24, 2020).

106. Author's interview of human rights advocate (August 2017).

107. Zong 2015, 4.

108. Anne-Marie Slaughter, "How to Halt the Butchery in Syria," *New York Times* (February 23, 2012).

109. Foundation for Defense of Democracies, "Policy Experts Urge President Obama to Take Immediate Action to Establish Safe Zones in Syria," Press release (July 24, 2012).

110. Hrg., SFRC, "Syria: U.S. Policy Options," 16–17.

111. Kagan 2013.

112. Andrew J. Tabler, "Assad Must Be Forced to Allow Peaceful Assembly," Washington Institute for Near East Policy (April 18, 2012); Andrew J. Tabler, Jeffrey White, and Simon Henderson, "Field Reports on Syria and the Opposition," Washington Institute for Near East Policy (March 12, 2013); Testimony of Michael Singh, Hearing Before the U.S. Senate Foreign Relations Subcommittee on Near Eastern

and South and Central Asian Affairs, "Syria's Humanitarian Crisis," S. Hrg. 113-134 (March 19, 2013); Testimony of Dennis Ross, Hearing Before the U.S. Senate Committee on Foreign Relations, "U.S. Policy Toward Syria," S. Hrg. 113-197 (April 11, 2013).

113. Author's interview of congressional foreign policy aides (August 2017); author's interview of Dafna Rand (June 6, 2018).

114. Author's interview of House Democratic foreign policy aide (August 2017).

115. This includes the various Casey-Rubio, Levin-McCain, Engel-Rogers, and Menendez-Corker bills discussed above: S. Res. 370 (112th Cong.), S. Res. 424 (112th Cong.), H.R. 1327 (113th Cong.), and S. 960 (113th Cong.). MapLight, "Bill Positions" data set, www.maplight.org.

116. I searched for any organization in the Center for Responsive Politics databases with the word "Syria" or "Syrian" in its title. Data available at https://www.opensecrets.org/.

117. See Human Rights Watch and Human Rights First campaign contribution data available at Center for Responsive Politics, https://www.opensecrets.org/.

118. Matt Kibbe, "Key Vote NO on the Syria War Resolution," FreedomWorks (September 6, 2013); Juliet Eilperin, "MoveOn.org Lobbies Against Syria Resolution, While OFA Stays Neutral," *Washington Post* (September 5, 2013); Frank James, "Opponents of Syria Strikes Gain Edge in Lobbying Fight," NPR.org (September 6, 2013).

119. Nick Berning, "MoveOn's 8 Million Members Vote Overwhelmingly to Oppose Military Action in Syria," MoveOn.org (September 4, 2013); Kibbe, "Key Vote NO on the Syria War Resolution."

120. AIPAC, "AIPAC Statement on Syria Resolution," Press release (September 3, 2013); Jodi Rudoren and Isabel Kershner, "Lobbying Group for Israel to Press Congress on Syria," *New York Times* (September 9, 2013).

121. Mark Katkov, Jessica Taylor, and Tom Bowman, "Trump Orders Syria Air Strikes After 'Assad Choked out the Lives' of Civilians," NPR.org (April 6, 2017).

122. Alicia Parlapiano, Anjali Singhvi, Jon Huang, and Thomas Kaplan, "Where Top Lawmakers Stand on Syria: Now and in 2013," *New York Times* (April 7, 2017).

123. Foran 2017.

124. Office of Nancy Pelosi, "Pelosi Statement on U.S. Airstrikes in Syria," Press release (April 6, 2017).

125. Andrew Prokop, "Syria Strike Reactions: What Top Republicans and Democrats in Congress Are Saying," *Vox* (April 6, 2017).

126. Office of Marco Rubio, "Rubio Statement on U.S. Airstrikes in Syria," Press release (April 6, 2017).

127. Snow and Haney 2018, 163–164.

128. Ken Thomas and Richard Lardner, "Trump's Military Action Unnerves GOP Libertarians, Dems," AP (April 7, 2017).

129. Ibid.

130. Tweet by Thomas Massie (April 7, 2017), https://twitter.com/RepThomasMassie/status/850360924020101120.

131. Hearing Before the U.S. House of Representatives Committee on Foreign Affairs, "Syria After the Missile Strikes: Policy Options," Serial No. 115-27 (April 27, 2017), 2.
132. Ibid., 2–3.
133. Ibid., 45.
134. Nicholas Fandos, "Divided on Strikes, Democrats and Republicans Press for Clearer Syria Strategy," *New York Times* (April 14, 2018).
135. Cathleen Decker, "As U.S. Attacks Syria, Congress Stays on the Sidelines," *Los Angeles Times* (April 15, 2018).
136. Author's interview of former Senate foreign policy aide (June 2018).
137. Author's interview of Ilan Goldenberg (January 16, 2018).
138. Tweet by President Donald Trump (December 19, 2018), https://twitter.com/real DonaldTrump/status/1075528854402256896.
139. Ibid.
140. Bergen 2019; Bolton 2020; Mark Landler, Helene Cooper, and Eric Schmitt, "Trump to Withdraw U.S. Forces from Syria, Declaring 'We Have Won Against ISIS,'" *New York Times* (December 19, 2018).
141. Lantis 2021.
142. Howard LaFranchi, "Policy or Politics? Trump's Sudden Syria Move Kicks up a Storm," *Christian Science Monitor* (December 20, 2018).
143. Office of Senator Jeanne Shaheen, "Shaheen Statement on President Trump's Decision to Withdraw Troops from Syria" (December 19, 2018); Remarks by Senator Robert Menendez, 164 Cong. Rec., S7976 (December 20, 2018).
144. Senate Vote 14 on S. Amdt. 65 to S. 1, Strengthening America's Security in the Middle East Act of 2019 (February 4, 2019).
145. Mark Landler and Helene Cooper, "In Latest Shift, Trump Agrees to Leave 400 Troops in Syria," *New York Times* (February 22, 2019).
146. Office of Mitch McConnell, "McConnell Statement on Turkey and U.S. Partners in Syria," Press release (October 7, 2019).
147. House Vote 560 on H.J. Res. 77, Opposing the decision to end certain United States efforts to prevent Turkish military operations against Syrian Kurdish forces in northern Syria (October 16, 2019).
148. Lolita C. Baldor, "US May Now Keep Some Troops in Syria to Guard Oil Fields," AP (October 21, 2019).

Chapter 5

1. S.J. Res. 59, Authorization for Use of Military Force of 2018 (115th Cong.).
2. U.S. Senate Committee on Foreign Relations, "Senators Propose Legislation to Update Authorities Used to Fight Terror Abroad," Press release (April 16, 2018).
3. Hearing Before the U.S. Senate Committee on Foreign Relations, "Authorizing the Use of Military Force: S.J. 59" (May 16, 2018).
4. Ibid.
5. Ibid.

6. John Bennett, "White House Has Tepid Response to Corker-Kaine AUMF," *Roll Call* (April 17, 2018).

7. On the history of presidential assertions of executive power under the 2001 AUMF, see Murray 2015.

8. John Bresnahan, "Senators Discuss Revising 9/11 Resolution," *Politico* (May 7, 2013).

9. Roll Call Vote 410 on Amendment No. 73 to H.R. 2397, Department of Defense Appropriations Act of 2014 (July 24, 2013).

10. Peter Baker, "Obama, with Reluctance, Returns to Action in Iraq," *New York Times* (August 7, 2014).

11. President Barack Obama, "Statement by the President on ISIL" (September 10, 2014).

12. Rice 2019, 418–423.

13. Amanda Sakuma, "Kurdish-Led Forces Stomp Out Final ISIS Stronghold in Syria," *Vox* (March 23, 2019).

14. Böller and Müller 2018, 654–657; Kreps 2018, 175–178.

15. Pew Research Center, "Bipartisan Support for Obama's Military Campaign Against ISIS" (September 15, 2014); Pew Research Center, "Support for U.S. Campaign Against ISIS; Doubts About Its Effectiveness, Objectives" (October 22, 2014).

16. Jonathan Weisman, Mark Landler, and Jeremy W. Peters, "As Obama Makes Case, Congress Is Divided on Campaign Against Militants," *New York Times* (September 8, 2014).

17. Hearing Before the U.S. Senate Committee on Foreign Relations, "United States Strategy to Defeat the Islamic State in Iraq and the Levant," S. Hrg. 113-668 (September 17, 2014), 16; Hearing Before the U.S. House of Representatives Committee on Foreign Affairs, "The ISIS Threat: Weighing the Obama Administration's Response," Serial No. 113-219 (September 18, 2014), 27.

18. Mark Landler, "Asking Congress to Back ISIS Strikes in Syria Is Tricky for Obama," *New York Times* (August 29, 2014); Jake Sherman and John Bresnahan, "Hill Leaders Duck ISIL," *Politico* (September 8, 2014); Josh Rogin, "Republicans Offer Obama ISIS War Authorization He Doesn't Want," *Daily Beast* (September 9, 2014); Christina Marcos, "House Members Call for New Vote on Authorizing Military Force," *The Hill* (September 19, 2014).

19. Marcos, "House Members Call for New Vote on Authorizing Military Force."

20. S.J. Res. 44, Authorization for Use of Military Force Against the Islamic State in Iraq and the Levant (113th Cong.).

21. Office of Senator Tim Kaine, "Kaine Discusses Urgent Need for a Debate and Vote on an Authorization for Use of Military Force Against ISIL at Woodrow Wilson Center Event," Press release (November 12, 2014).

22. Hearing Before the U.S. Senate Committee on Foreign Relations, "Authorization for the Use of Military Force Against ISIL," S. Hrg. 113-699 (December 9, 2014), 2.

23. Ibid., 36.

24. Author's interview of Jeff Flake (December 11, 2018).

25. Paul Waldman, "Why White House and Congress Don't Want Vote on Military Action," *Washington Post* (September 9, 2014).

26. James Downie, "Obama Can't Let Congress Cower over Islamic State Strikes," *Washington Post* (September 11, 2014).

27. Author's interviews of Democratic congressional aides and Obama administration legislative affairs officials (August–September 2017); Jonathan Weisman, Mark Landler, and Jeremy W. Peters, "As Obama Makes Case, Congress Is Divided on Campaign Against Militants," *New York Times* (September 8, 2014).

28. S.J. Res. 47, Authorization for the Use of Military Force Against the Islamic State of Iraq and the Levant (113th Cong.).

29. Hrg., SFRC, "Authorization for the Use of Military Force Against ISIL," 34–35.

30. Ibid., 48.

31. Ibid., 8.

32. U.S. Senate, "A Joint Resolution to Authorize the Limited Use of United States Armed Forces Against the Islamic State of Iraq and the Levant, Report Together with Minority Views," S. Rept. 113-323 (December 13, 2014).

33. Author's interview of Margaret Taylor (April 30, 2020).

34. Author's interview of Obama administration legislative affairs official (August 2017).

35. Karen DeYoung and Ed O'Keefe, "Obama to Seek Congressional Authorization to Fight Islamic State," *Washington Post* (February 10, 2015).

36. Author's interview of Obama administration official (August 2017).

37. Author's interview of senior Democratic congressional aide (August 2017).

38. Wolfensberger 2018, 98–99.

39. The White House, "Message from the President of the United States Transmitting a Draft Authorization for the Use of Military Force Against the Islamic State of Iraq and the Levant," House Document 114-9 (February 11, 2015).

40. Hearing Before the U.S. Senate Committee on Foreign Relations, "The President's Request for Authorization to Use Force Against ISIS: Military and Diplomatic Efforts," S. Hrg. 114-90 (March 11, 2015), 32.

41. Peter Baker and Ashley Parker, "Congress Shows a Lack of Enthusiasm for Giving More Powers to Obama," *New York Times* (February 13, 2015).

42. Hearing Before the U.S. House of Representatives Committee on Armed Services, "Outside Perspectives on the President's Proposed Authorization for the Use of Military Force Against the Islamic State of Iraq and the Levant," Serial No. 114-13 (February 26, 2015), 1.

43. Hearing Before the U.S. House of Representatives Committee on Foreign Affairs, "The Administration's Strategy to Confront ISIS," Serial No. 114-52 (March 26, 2015), 3.

44. Hrg. SFRC, "The President's Request," 3–4, 21.

45. S. 1587, Authority for the Use of Military Force Against the Islamic State of Iraq and the Levant Act (114th Cong.).

46. Author's interview of Obama administration legislative affairs official (August 2017); Hrg., SFRC, "Authorization for the Use of Military Force Against ISIL," 14.

47. Letter from 35 members of the House to Speaker of the House Paul Ryan (November 6, 2015), https://mcgovern.house.gov/sites/mcgovern.house.gov/files/nov%202 015%20bipartisan%20letter%20to%20speaker%20ryan%20on%20aumf%20fi nal.pdf.

48. Karoun Demirjian, "Despite Ryan's Attention, Deal on ISIS Fight Authorization Still Elusive," *Washington Post* (January 8, 2016).
49. Author's interview of senior Democratic congressional aide (August 2017).
50. S.J. Res. 43, Authorization for Use of Military Force Against Al-Qaeda, the Taliban, and the Islamic State of Iraq and Syria (115th Cong.).
51. Hearing Before the U.S. Senate Committee on Foreign Relations, "Reviewing Congressional Authorizations for the Use of Military Force," S. Hrg. 115-711 (June 20, 2017), 18.
52. Ibid., 22.
53. Ryan Goodman, "Exclusive: Draft Military Force Authorization Against ISIL—By House Foreign Affairs Committee, Ranking Member Rep. Engel," Just Security (June 19, 2017).
54. Discussion Draft, H.J. Res X, "To amend the 2001 Authorization for Use of Military Force with respect to the use of force against the Islamic State of Iraq and the Levant (ISIL) and associated forces of ISIL, and for other purposes," https://www.justsecurity.org/wp-content/uploads/2017/06/ENGEL_Discussion-Draft-AUMF-2017.pdf.
55. Author's interview of Democratic congressional aide (September 2017).
56. Hearing Before the U.S. House of Representatives Committee on Foreign Affairs, "Authorization for the Use of Force and Current Terrorist Threats," Serial No. 115-62 (July 25, 2017), 55.
57. H.R. 1229, Repeal of the Authorization for Use of Military Force (115th Cong.).
58. Bryan Bender and Jennifer Scholtes, "House Panel Votes to Force New Debate on Terror War," *Politico* (June 29, 2017).
59. Ibid.
60. Author's interview of House Republican foreign policy aide (April 2020).
61. Austin Wright, "Ryan Tries to Control Growing Movement to Re-Open War Debate," *Politico* (July 12, 2017).
62. Bender and Scholtes, "House Panel Votes to Force New Debate on Terror War."
63. Author's interview of senior Democratic congressional aide (August 2017).
64. S. Amdt. 871 to S. Amdt. 1003 to H.R. 2810, National Defense Authorization Act for Fiscal Year 2018 (115th Cong.).
65. Remarks by Senator Rand Paul, 163 Cong. Rec. S5257 (September 13, 2017).
66. Remarks by Senator Chris Murphy, 163 Cong. Rec. S5255 (September 13, 2017).
67. Remarks by Senator John McCain, 163 Cong. Rec. S5258 (September 13, 2017).
68. Remarks by Senator Jack Reed, 163 Cong. Rec. S5257 (September 13, 2017).
69. Senate Roll Call Vote 195 on S. Amdt. 871 to S. Amdt. 1003 to H.R. 2810, National Defense Authorization Act for Fiscal Year 2018 (September 13, 2017).
70. Hearing Before the U.S. Senate Committee on Foreign Relations, "The Authorizations for the Use of Military Force: Administration Perspective," S. Hrg. 115-639 (October 30, 2017), 6–10.
71. Ibid., 13–16.
72. Ibid., 17–19.
73. S.J. Res. 59 (115th Cong.).
74. Bennett, "White House Has Tepid Response to Corker-Kaine AUMF."

75. Hrg., SFRC, "Authorizing the Use of Military Force: S.J. 59."

76. Author's interview of Bob Corker (June 29, 2022).

77. Kreps 2018, 175–178.

78. Pew Research Center, "Support for U.S. Campaign Against ISIS; Doubts About Its Effectiveness, Objectives" (October 22, 2014); Pew Research Center, "Growing Support for Campaign Against ISIS—And Possible Use of U.S. Ground Troops" (February 24, 2015); Pew Research Center, "A Year Later, U.S. Campaign Against ISIS Garners Support, Raises Concerns" (July 22, 2015); Pew Research Center, "Views of Government's Handling of Terrorism Fall to Post-9/11 Low" (December 15, 2015); Pew Research Center, "Public Uncertain, Divided over America's Place in the World" (May 5, 2016).

79. Pew Research Center, "Partisans Have Starkly Different Opinions About How the World Views the U.S." (November 9, 2017).

80. Wittkopf 1990; Holsti 2004; Gries 2014.

81. Marist College Institute for Public Opinion, "Obama's Request for Military Action Against ISIS Receives Majority Support," Press release (February 12, 2015).

82. Sarah Dutton, Jennifer De Pinto, Anthony Salvanto, and Fred Backus, "How Americans Are Feeling About the Fight Against ISIS, Economy," CBS News (February 19, 2015).

83. Cameron Easley, "Critics Say Public's Tepid Response to War Debate Is Congress' Failure," *Morning Consult* (November 1, 2017).

84. Remarks by Jeff Flake, Panel on "Updating the AUMF (Authorization to Use Military Force): Will Congress Act?," Woodrow Wilson Center (July 27, 2017).

85. Author's interview of Ilan Goldenberg (January 16, 2018).

86. Author's interview of former House Republican foreign policy aide (April 2020).

87. Author's interview of Tommy Ross (July 2, 2018).

88. John Yoo, "Say No to the AUMF," *National Review* (February 12, 2015); Hrg., SFRC, "Reviewing Congressional Authorizations for the Use of Military Force"; Jim Talent, "An AUMF Debate Is Unlikely to Be Productive in This Political Climate," *National Review* (October 27, 2017).

89. Alyssa Sims, "Repeal the AUMF," New America (January 5, 2017); Ken Gude and Kate Martin, "Preventing Endless War Requires Real Congressional Oversight— Not New War Authority," Center for American Progress (December 14, 2018).

90. Cato Institute 2017, 279–283.

91. Juliegrace Brufke, "Biggs, Khanna Launch Bipartisan War Powers Caucus," *The Hill* (June 18, 2019).

92. Ibid.

93. Author's interview of Reid Smith (July 5, 2022).

94. Author's interview of Jamil Jaffer (April 22, 2020).

95. Win Without War, "Members of Congress, Experts, and Organizations Oppose the Proposed AUMF," Press release (February 13, 2015).

96. Ibid.

97. Letter from the Constitution Project, Council on American-Islamic Relations, Human Rights First, Just Foreign Policy, National Religious Campaign Against

Torture, OpenTheGovernment, Peace Action, US Labor Against the War, Win Without War, Women's Action for New Directions to Senators Bob Corker and Ben Cardin (June 19, 2017), https://www.humanrightsfirst.org/resource/coalition-let ter-aumf.

98. Letter from American Civil Liberties Union, Brennan Center for Justice, Campaign for Liberty, Center for Constitutional Rights, Coalition for Peace Action, Common Defense, Defending Rights & Dissent, Defense Priorities, Demand Progress, Free the People, FreedomWorks, Friends Committee on National Legislation, Government Information Watch, Human Rights Clinic (Columbia Law School), Human Rights First, Indivisible, Interfaith Network on Drone Warfare, Just Foreign Policy, National Religious Campaign Against Torture, OpenTheGovernment, Peace Action, Project on Government Oversight, Public Citizen, Win Without War to Senators Bob Corker and Bob Menendez (May 15, 2018), https://www.pogo.org/let ter/2018/05/civil-society-urges-senate-not-to-authorize-expanded-presidential-war-powers.

99. Hrg., SFRC, "Authorizing the Use of Military Force: S.J. 59."

100. Sims, "Repeal the AUMF"; Gude and Martin, "Preventing Endless War Requires Real Congressional Oversight."

101. Charles Koch Institute, "The Problem with a Perpetual AUMF" (July 21, 2016).

102. Author's interview of Reid Smith (July 5, 2022).

103. Author's interview of Heather Brandon-Smith (June 24, 2022).

104. Jack Goldsmith, Ryan Goodman, and Steve Vladeck, "Five Principles That Should Govern Any U.S. Authorization of Force," *Washington Post* (November 14, 2014); Benjamin Wittes and Jennifer Daskal, "The Intellectual—But Not Political—AUMF Consensus," Just Security and Lawfare (March 2, 2015); Heather Brandon-Smith, "An ISIS AUMF: Where We Are Now, Where to Go Next, and Why It's So Important to Get It Right," Just Security (May 5, 2017).

105. See the lobbying data for the following resolutions available at OpenSecrets.org: S.J. Res. 44 (113th Cong.); S.J. Res. 47 (113th Cong.); S. 1587 (114th Cong.); S.J. Res. 43 (115th Cong.); S.J. Res. 59 (115th Cong.).

106. For instance, they were among the 23 signatories of the May 2018 letter to Senators Bob Corker and Bob Menendez opposing the Corker-Flake AUMF proposal.

107. Author's interview of Democratic congressional aide (September 2017).

108. Safi 2018; Malley and Pomper 2021.

109. S.J. Res. 54, A joint resolution to direct the removal of United States Armed Forces from hostilities in the Republic of Yemen that have not been authorized by Congress (115th Cong.).

110. Office of Senator Mitch McConnell, "Sanders Resolution on Yemen Would Harm Allies, Embolden Iran," Press release (March 20, 2018).

111. Remarks by Senator Robert Menendez, 164 Cong. Rec., S1809 (March 20, 2018).

112. Senate Vote 58 on the Motion to Table the Motion to Discharge S. J. Res. 54, A joint resolution to direct the removal of United States Armed Forces from hostilities in the Republic of Yemen that have not been authorized by Congress (March 20, 2018).

113. Author's interview of Reid Smith (July 5, 2022).

114. Tama 2018b.
115. Senate Vote 266 on S.J. Res. 54 (as Amended), A joint resolution to direct the removal of United States Armed Forces from hostilities in the Republic of Yemen that have not been authorized by Congress (December 13, 2018).
116. Author's interview of Jeff Flake (December 11, 2018).
117. Ibid.
118. S.J. Res. 7, A joint resolution to direct the removal of United States Armed Forces from hostilities in the Republic of Yemen that have not been authorized by Congress (116th Cong.).
119. Senate Vote 48 on S.J. Res. 54 (as Amended), A joint resolution to direct the removal of United States Armed Forces from hostilities in the Republic of Yemen that have not been authorized by Congress (March 13, 2019).
120. House Vote 153 on S.J. Res. 54 (April 4, 2019).
121. The White House, "Presidential Veto Message to the Senate to Accompany S.J. Res. 7" (April 16, 2019).
122. Senate Vote 94 on Overriding the Veto of S.J. Res. 54 (May 2, 2019).
123. U.S. House of Representatives, "National Defense Authorization Act for Fiscal Year 2020—Conference Report to Accompany S. 1790," H. Rept. 116-333 (December 9, 2019), 504.
124. Stark 2021.
125. Joe Gould, "House Votes to Curb Trump's War Powers, Challenging Senate to Act," *Defense News* (July 12, 2019).
126. Emily Stewart and Li Zhou, "Could a Congressional Amendment Have Stopped Trump from Striking Against Iran?," *Vox* (January 3, 2020).
127. Author's interview of Ryan Costello (June 30, 2022).
128. Jenna Portnoy, "With Iran War Powers Resolution, Kaine Finds New Way to Push His Signature Issue," *Washington Post* (January 9, 2020).
129. Senate Vote 52 on S.J. Res. 68, A joint resolution to direct the removal of United States Armed Forces from hostilities against the Islamic Republic of Iran that have not been authorized by Congress (February 13, 2020).
130. House Vote 101 on S.J. Res. 68, A joint resolution to direct the removal of United States Armed Forces from hostilities against the Islamic Republic of Iran that have not been authorized by Congress (March 11, 2020).
131. Binder 2020.
132. Senate Vote 48 and House Vote 153 on S. J. Res. 7, A joint resolution to direct the removal of United States Armed Forces from hostilities in the Republic of Yemen that have not been authorized by Congress (March 13 and April 4, 2019). Trump vetoed the legislation on April 6, 2019. Seven Senate Republicans then joined all Senate Democrats in voting on May 2, 2019 (Senate Vote 94) to override the veto, but this was not enough to gain the needed two-thirds support for a veto override.
133. Senate Vote 84 on S.J. Res. 68, A joint resolution to direct the removal of United States Armed Forces from hostilities against the Islamic Republic of Iran that have not been authorized by Congress (May 7, 2020).
134. Karoun Demirjian, "Senate Seeks to Restrict Trump Action on Iran," *Washington Post* (February 13, 2020).

Chapter 6

1. Andrew Kaczynski, Chris Massie, and Nathan McDermott, "80 Times Trump Talked About Putin," CNN.com (March 2017).

2. Michael Gove, "Donald Trump: 'Brexit Will Be a Great Thing . . . You Were So Smart,'" *The Times of London* (January 16, 2017).

3. Tweet by Susan Glasser (January 26, 2017), https://twitter.com/sbg1/status/824 734913790349313; Peter Baker, "Trump Meets Theresa May of Britain as He Weighs Lifting Russia Sanctions," *New York Times* (January 27, 2017); author's interview of senior Senate Democratic foreign policy aide (April 2020).

4. Office of Senator Rob Portman, "Portman Statement on Reports Suggesting Sanctions on Russia May Be Lifted," Press release (January 27, 2017).

5. S. 94, Countering Russian Hostilities Act of 2017 (115th Cong.).

6. S. 341, Russia Sanctions Review Act of 2017 (115th Cong.).

7. Julie Hirschfeld Davis and Matt Flegenheimer, "White House Tries to Get G.O.P. to Water Down Russia Sanctions Bill," *New York Times* (June 21, 2017); Mike DeBonis and John Wagner, "White House Will Step Up Lobbying Against Stalled Russia Sanctions Bill," *Washington Post* (June 24, 2017).

8. House Vote 413 and Senate Vote 175 on H.R. 3364, Countering America's Adversaries Through Sanctions Act (July 25, 2017, and July 27, 2017).

9. Peter Baker and Andrew Higgins, "White House Signals Acceptance of Russia Sanctions Bill," *New York Times* (July 23, 2017); Natalie Andrews, "Trump to Sign Russia Sanctions Bill," *Wall Street Journal* (July 28, 2017).

10. The White House, "Statement by President Donald J. Trump on Signing the 'Countering America's Adversaries Through Sanctions Act'" (August 2, 2017).

11. For another analysis of congressional activity regarding Russia during much of this period, see Hicks, Lauter, and McElhinny 2018, 87–123.

12. I worked on the legislation discussed in this section as a fellow on the Tom Lantos Human Rights Commission, where I served as a senior aide to Representative Jim McGovern, from January to August 2012. In that role, I negotiated aspects of the legislation with other congressional offices and discussed the legislation with administration officials on McGovern's behalf. The case study draws in part on my firsthand knowledge and notes regarding these events.

13. Browder 2015; European Court of Human Rights, "Case of Magnitskiy and Others v. Russia," Judgment (August 27, 2019).

14. Hearing Before the U.S. Commission on Security and Cooperation in Europe, "The Medvedev Thaw. Is It Real? Will It Last?" CSCE 111-1-4 (June 23, 2009); Hearing Before the U.S. House of Representatives Tom Lantos Human Rights Commission, "Human Rights in Russia: An Overview" HRG-2010-HOR-0006 (May 6, 2010).

15. H.R. 6365 and S. 3881, The Justice for Sergei Magnitsky Act of 2010 (111th Cong.).

16. The White House, "U.S.-Russian Relations: 'Reset' Fact Sheet" (June 24, 2010); Burns 2019, 272–292.

17. Author's interview of administration official (March 2013).

18. U.S. Department of State, "Administration Comments on S. 1039 Sergey Magnitsky Rule of Law," Memo (July 2011), https://www.scribd.com/doc/60996722/Adminis tration-Comments-on-S1039-Final.

19. S. 1039, The Sergei Magnitsky Rule of Law Accountability Act of 2011(112th Cong.); H.R. 4405, The Sergei Magnitsky Rule of Law Accountability Act of 2012 (112th Cong.).

20. Remarks by Representative James McGovern, "U.S.-Russia Trade Relations and Human Rights," Bipartisan Policy Center event, Rayburn House Office Building (May 9, 2012). On file with author.

21. Author's interview of Jim McGovern (February 15, 2013).

22. Author's interview of Ben Cardin (April 1, 2014).

23. BBC News, "Russian Election: Biggest Protests Since Fall of USSR" (December 10, 2011).

24. David M. Herszenhorn, "New Russian Law Assesses Heavy Fines on Protesters," *New York Times* (June 8, 2012); Reuters, "Russia's Putin Signs NGO Foreign Agents Law" (July 21, 2012).

25. Markup Before the U.S. House of Representatives Foreign Affairs Committee, "Various Bills and Resolutions," Serial No. 112-175 (June 7, 2012); U.S. Senate, "Sergei Magnitsky Rule of Law Accountability Act of 2011: Report to Accompany S. 1039," Senate Rept. 112-191 (2012).

26. U.S. House Foreign Affairs Committee, "Various Bills and Resolutions," 106.

27. McFaul 2018.

28. For a detailed account of the origins of Jackson-Vanik amendment, see Stern 1979.

29. Snyder 2018, 36.

30. Author's communications with congressional aides (March–August 2012). Notes on file with author.

31. McFaul 2018.

32. Josh Rogin, "More Senators Oppose Lifting Trade Sanctions on Russia," *Foreign Policy* (March 16, 2012).

33. Hearing Before the U.S. House of Representatives Committee on Ways and Means, "Russia's Accession to the World Trade Organization and Granting Russia Permanent Normal Trade Relations," Serial No. 112-125 (June 20, 2012), 26.

34. Author's interview of senior House Democratic aide (February 2013).

35. Author's communications with State Department and congressional officials (June–July 2012). Notes on file with author.

36. House Roll Call Vote 608 and Senate Roll Call Vote 223 on H.R. 6156, The Russia and Moldova Jackson-Vanik Repeal and Magnitsky Rule of Law Accountability Act of 2012 (November 16, 2012, and December 6, 2012).

37. Public Law 112-208.

38. Jeremy W. Peters, "U.S. Senate Passes Russian Trade Bill, with a Human Rights Caveat," *New York Times* (December 6, 2012).

39. Author's interview of Amanda Sloat (July 24, 2017).

40. Author's interview of State Department official (September 2013); U.S. Department of State, "Administration Comments on S. 1039 Sergey Magnitsky Rule of Law

Accountability Act." McGovern and Cardin viewed this visa ban as insufficient because the administration did not indicate the number of people being sanctioned in this way, did not publicly identify any of the sanctioned individuals, and did not freeze the assets of the sanctioned individuals.

41. Author's interview of State Department official (March 2013).

42. Ellen Barry, "Russia Announces Barriers on Imports of U.S. Meat," *New York Times* (December 8, 2012); Masha Lipman, "What's Behind the Russian Adoption Ban?," *New Yorker* (December 21, 2012).

43. U.S. Department of State, "Background Briefing on the Administration's Implementation of the Sergei Magnitsky Rule of Law Accountability Act of 2012" (April 12, 2013), U.S. Department of State, "Annual Report on the Implementation of the Sergei Magnitsky Rule of Law Accountability Act," Press statement (December 29, 2014); U.S. Department of State, "Annual Report on the Implementation of the Sergei Magnitsky Rule of Law Accountability Act," Press statement (February 2, 2016); and Mark Landler, "U.S. Blacklists 5 Russians, a Close Putin Aide Among Them," *New York Times* (January 9, 2017).

44. Author's interview of Daniel Fried (February 6, 2016).

45. Anne Gearan, "No Names Added to Blacklist of Russian Officials," *Washington Post* (December 20, 2013).

46. Josh Rogin, "Congress Presses Obama on Russia Sanctions," *Daily Beast* (January 17, 2014).

47. Global Magnitsky Human Rights Accountability Act, enacted as part of the National Defense Authorization Act for Fiscal Year 2017 (Public Law 114-328).

48. U.S. Department of State, "Global Magnitsky Human Rights Act Accountability Act Annual Report," U.S. Federal Register 84, 250 (December 31, 2019), 72424–72430. See also Tama 2018a.

49. Hearing Before the U.S. Commission on Security and Cooperation in Europe, "The Magnitsky Act at Five: Assessing Accomplishments and Challenges," CSCE 115-1-7 (December 14, 2017); Human Rights Watch, "Submission to the Australian Parliamentary Joint Standing Committee on Foreign Affairs, Defence, and Trade" (February 13, 2020); Human Rights First, "Human Rights First Welcomes Australia's Adoption of Magnitsky-Style Sanctions," Press release (December 2, 2021).

50. Remarks by Irwin Cotler, Hrg., U.S. Commission on Security and Cooperation in Europe, "The Magnitsky Act at Five."

51. Author's interview of Matthew Rojansky (February 7, 2014).

52. Elias Groll, "Here's the Memo the Kremlin-Linked Lawyer Took to the Meeting with Donald Trump Jr.," *Foreign Policy* (October 16, 2017).

53. U.S. Department of the Treasury, "Treasury Targets Individuals Involved in the Sergei Magnitsky Case and Other Gross Violations of Human Rights in Russia," Press release (December 20, 2017); U.S. Department of the Treasury, "Magnitsky Act-Related Designations," Resource Center (May 16, 2019).

54. Margon 2018.

55. In 2006, the Chicago Council on Foreign Relations changed its name to the Chicago Council on Global Affairs.

56. Chicago Council on Foreign Relations and Program on International Policy Attitudes, "Americans on Promoting Democracy" (September 29, 2005), 11.

57. Smeltz 2012.

58. Price 2014.

59. Smeltz, Busby, et al. 2015.

60. Foreign Policy Initiative Russia Working Group, "Statement on Russia's December 4 Duma Elections," Press release (December 7, 2011); Ariel Cohen and Bryan Riley, "After WTO Membership: Promoting Human Rights in Russia with the Magnitsky Act," Heritage Foundation Backgrounder (May 14, 2012); Rachel Kleinfeld, "Pass the Magnitsky Bill," *Huffington Post* (June 7, 2012); Bipartisan Policy Center 2012.

61. Kleinfeld, "Pass the Magnitsky Bill."

62. *Washington Post*, "Punish the Russian Abusers" (June 17, 2012).

63. *Wall Street Journal*, "Sergei's Law" (November 19, 2012).

64. See the Center for Responsive Politics data on campaign contributions by Human Rights Watch and Human Rights First, https://www.opensecrets.org.

65. Freedom House does not provide campaign contributions to politicians, but Republicans have been heavily represented among its board and executive staff. During the Magnitsky Act debate, Freedom House was led by David Kramer, a former George W. Bush administration official with close ties to Senator John McCain, among other Republicans. Kramer's predecessor as Freedom House president was Mark Lagon, who had served both in the Bush administration and as a senior Republican aide on Capitol Hill. For a discussion of liberal and conservative support for the protection of human rights more generally, see Lagon and Schulz 2012.

66. See Hearing Before the U.S. Senate Subcommittee on European Affairs of the Committee on Foreign Relations, "The State of Human Rights and the Rule of Law in Russia: U.S. Policy Options," S. Hrg. 112-367 (December 14, 2011), 29–38.

67. Joint Baltic American National Committee, Inc., "JBANC Annual Report 2011–2012," http://altcenter.org/wp-content/uploads/2013/09/JBANC-Annual-Report-2012-4-20-1.pdf.

68. MapLight, "Bill Positions" data set, www.maplight.org.

69. Ibid.

70. Author's interview of labor union official (February 2013); author's interview of John Murphy (April 24, 2020).

71. Philip Aldrich, "Bill Browder: The Man Making Moscow Squirm over the Death of Sergei Magnitsky," *The Telegraph* (August 20, 2011).

72. Browder 2015.

73. Author's interview of Margaret Taylor (April 30, 2020).

74. Author's interview of Charles Kupchan (May 8, 2020).

75. Ibid.

76. Letter from Senators Ben Cardin, Robert Menendez, Bob Corker, John Barrasso, Richard Durbin, Ron Johnson, Edward Markey, John McCain, Chris Murphy, Jim Risch, Marco Rubio, and Jeanne Shaheen to President Barack Obama (February 28, 2014), https://www.foreign.senate.gov/imo/media/doc/02-28-14_SFRC_Letter_to_POTUS_on_Ukraine.pdf.

77. Burgess Everett and Seung Min Kim, "Hill Moving on Aid, Sanctions," *Politico* (March 5, 2014).

78. H.R. 4152, Support for the Sovereignty, Integrity, Democracy, with and Economic Stability of Ukraine Act of 2014 (113th Cong.).

79. Author's interview of Daniel Fried (February 4, 2016).

80. Public Law 113-95; House Vote 114 on H.R. 4152, Support for the Sovereignty, Integrity, Democracy, and Economic Stability of Ukraine Act of 2014 (March 6, 2014); Senate Voice Vote on H.R. 4152 (March 27, 2014).

81. Author's interview of Daniel Fried (February 4, 2016); Paul Lewis, "Obama Wary of Fight with Republicans over Russia Sanctions," *The Guardian* (March 4, 2014).

82. Executive Order 13660, "Blocking Property of Certain Persons Contributing to the Situation in Ukraine," *Federal Register* 79, 46 (2014), 13493–13495; Executive Order 13661, "Blocking Property of Additional Persons Contributing to the Situation in Ukraine," *Federal Register* 79, 53 (2014), 15535–15537; Executive Order 13662, "Blocking Property of Additional Persons Contributing to the Situation in Ukraine," *Federal Register* 79, 56 (2014), 16169–16171; Department of the Treasury, "Ukraine-Related Sanctions Regulations," *Federal Register* 79, 89 (2014), 26365–26373; Department of the Treasury, "Designation of Individuals and Entities Pursuant to Executive Order 13660 or 13661," *Federal Register* 79, 152 (2014), 46302–46305; Department of the Treasury, "Sanctions Actions Pursuant to Executive Orders 13660, 13661, and 13662," *Federal Register* 79, 203 (2014), 63021–63209; Executive Order 13685, "Blocking Property of Certain Persons and Prohibiting Certain Transactions with Respect to the Crimea Region of Ukraine," *Federal Register* 79, 247 (2014), 77357–77359. See also Congressional Research Service 2020, 9–15.

83. Author's interview of David Kramer (August 3, 2017).

84. S. 2277, Russian Aggression Prevention Act of 2014 (113th Cong.).

85. Author's interview of Daniel Fried (February 4, 2016).

86. Author's interview of Jamil Jaffer (April 22, 2020).

87. S. 2828, Ukraine Freedom Support Act of 2014 (113th Cong.).

88. Author's interview of Kyle Parker (September 22, 2017).

89. Remarks by Barack Obama at a meeting of the President's Export Council (December 11, 2014).

90. Public Law 113-272, Ukraine Freedom Support Act of 2014.

91. Peter Baker, "Obama Signals Support for New U.S. Sanctions to Pressure Russian Economy," *New York Times* (December 17, 2014).

92. Author's interview of Kyle Parker (September 22, 2017).

93. Author's interview of Daniel Fried (February 4, 2016).

94. Steven Mufson, "Russian Energy Sector Struggles as U.S. and Europe Tighten Sanctions," *Washington Post* (December 22, 2015).

95. Smeltz, Daalder, and Kafura 2014.

96. Smeltz, Daalder, and Kafura 2014; Smeltz, Busby, et al. 2015; Pew Research Center, "Far More Continue to View Russia as a 'Serious Problem' Than as an 'Adversary'" (July 28, 2014).

97. Pew Research Center, "Increased Public Support for the U.S. Arming Ukraine" (February 23, 2015).

98. Peyton M. Craighill and Scott Clement, "Americans Split on Obama's Handling of Russia, Post-ABC Poll Finds," *Washington Post* (March 11, 2014); CNN.com, "CNN Poll: Most See Russia as a Threat to U.S." (March 14, 2014); Quinnipiac University Poll, "Obama Approval Inches Up, Tied with Putin as Leader, Quinnipiac University National Poll Finds" (April 2, 2014); Pew Research Center, "Bipartisan Support for Increased U.S. Sanctions Against Russia" (April 28, 2014); Smeltz, Daalder, et al. 2015.

99. Craighill and Clement, "Americans Split on Obama's Handling of Russia, Post-ABC Poll Finds;" CNN.com, "CNN Poll: Most See Russia as a Threat to U.S."

100. Oleh Wolowyna, "Ukrainians in the United States Have Reached 1 Million," *The Ukrainian Weekly* (May 11, 2018).

101. Ukrainian Federation of America, "Programs—Advocacy & Information," n.d., http://www.ukrainianfederationofamerica.org/AdvocacyInformation.html.

102. Orest Deychakiwsky, "Ukraine in Congress: Century of US Congressional Support for Ukraine," U.S. Ukraine Foundation (August 29, 2018).

103. Author's interview of Charles Kupchan (May 8, 2020).

104. Central and East European Coalition, "Statement on Ukraine and Call for Further Action," Press release (April 17, 2014).

105. Center for Responsive Politics lobbying records, https://www.opensecrets.org.

106. Author's interview of Kyle Parker (September 22, 2017).

107. Center for Responsive Politics lobbying records; Author's interview of Kyle Parker (September 22, 2017); Matt Egan and Tal Kopan, "Despite Paper Trail, Tillerson Denies Exxon Lobbied Against Sanctions, CNN.com (January 11, 2017).

108. Author's interview of Kyle Parker (September 22, 2017).

109. U.S. Office of the Director of National Intelligence, "Assessing Russian Activities and Intentions in Recent US Elections," Intelligence Community Assessment 2017-01D (January 6, 2017).

110. Kriner and Schickler 2018.

111. Mueller 2019.

112. Helderman and Zapotosky 2019.

113. See, e.g., Maggie Miller, "Bipartisan Senate Report Reaffirms Intelligence Findings That Russia Meddled in 2016 Elections," *The Hill* (April 21, 2020); Nicholas Fandos and Sharon LaFraniere, "Republicans on House Intelligence Panel Absolve Trump Campaign in Russian Meddling," *New York Times* (April 27, 2018).

114. Rice 2019, 447–449.

115. Office of Senator Ben Cardin, "Cardin Statement on White House Announcement of Russia Sanctions Following U.S. Cyber Attacks" (December 29, 2016).

116. Jacob Pramuk, "McCain, Graham Say They Will Seek 'Stronger Sanctions' on Russia," CNBC.com (December 29, 2016).

117. Theodore Schleifer, "Lindsay Graham: Donald Trump Disagrees with Senate Consensus on Russia," CNN.com (December 29, 2016).

118. Seung Min Kim, Burgess Everett, and Austin Wright, "McConnell to Trump: Do Not Lift Sanctions on Russia," *Politico* (January 27, 2017).

119. S. 341, Russia Sanctions Review Act of 2017 (115th Cong.).

120. H.R. 1059, Russia Sanctions Review Act of 2017 (115th Cong.).

121. S. 94, Countering Russian Hostilities Act of 2017 (115th Cong.).

122. Author's interview of Margaret Taylor (April 30, 2020).

123. Senate Vote 144 on Senate Amendment 232 to S. 722, Countering Iran's Destabilizing Activities Act of 2017 (June 14, 2017).

124. Remarks by Chuck Schumer, 163 Cong. Rec. S3428 (June 13, 2017).

125. Remarks by Mitch McConnell, 163 Cong. Rec. S3440 (June 13, 2017).

126. U.S. Senate Committee on Foreign Relations, "Review of the Fiscal Year 2018 State Department Budget Request," S. Hrg. 115-726 (June 13, 2017), 18.

127. Hearing Before the U.S. House of Representatives Committee on Foreign Affairs, "The FY 2018 Foreign Affairs Budget," Serial No. 115-61 (June 14, 2017), 4.

128. Hirschfeld Davis and Flegenheimer, "White House Tries to Get G.O.P. to Water Down Russia Sanctions Bill"; DeBonis and Wagner, "White House Will Step Up Lobbying Against Stalled Russia Sanctions Bill."

129. Julia Manchester, "Scaramucci Floats Trump Veto on Sanctions Bill," *The Hill* (July 27, 2017).

130. Natalie Andrews, "Trump to Sign Russia Sanctions Bill," *Wall Street Journal* (July 28, 2017).

131. Julia Manchester, "Trump Slams 'Sad' Republicans Who Won't 'Protect' Him," *The Hill* (July 23, 2017).

132. Andrew Osborn, "Russia Orders out U.S. Diplomats in Sanctions· Retaliation," Reuters (July 28, 2017).

133. Felicia Schwartz, "Administration Begins to Implement Russia Sanctions under New U.S. Law," *Wall Street Journal* (October 26, 2017); Hearing Before U.S. House of Representatives Committee on Foreign Affairs, "Sanctions and Financial Pressure: Major National Security Tools," Serial No. 115-107 (January 10, 2018).

134. Congressional Research Service, "U.S. Sanctions on Russia" (January 17, 2020), 17–19.

135. Laura Smith-Spark and Radina Gigova, "Russia to Expand American 'Blacklist' After New US Sanctions," CNN.com (March 16, 2018).

136. Congressional Research Service 2020, 23.

137. Testimony Before U.S. Senate Committee on Foreign Relations, remarks by Christopher A. Ford, "Countering Russian Intimidation and Aggression and Building a Better Security Environment" S. Hrg. 116-184 (December 3, 2019).

138. Bolton 2020.

139. Author's interview of David Kramer (August 3, 2017).

140. Quinnipiac University Poll, "American Voters Say Russia Interfered in Election, Quinnipiac University National Poll Finds" (January 30, 2017).

141. Quinnipiac University Poll, "Trump Ties to Russia Are Illegal or Unethical, U.S. Voters Tell Quinnipiac University National Poll" (June 7, 2017).

142. Smeltz and Wojtowicz 2017.
143. Art Smith, "Putin's Already Negative U.S. Image Worsens," Gallup (June 23, 2017).
144. Busby, Kafura, Smeltz, et al. 2020.
145. Quinnipiac University Poll, "American Voters Say Russia Interfered in Election."
146. Smeltz and Wojtowicz 2017.
147. Scott Clement, "Large Majority Supports Tougher Russia Sanctions, Post-ABC Poll Finds," *Washington Post* (April 17, 2018).
148. Böller and Herr 2020.
149. Author's interview of Andrew King (April 21, 2020).
150. Susan B. Glasser, "The Russian Bots Are Coming. This Bipartisan Duo Is on It," *Politico* (February 26, 2018).
151. Author's interview of Kyle Parker (September 22, 2017).
152. Human Rights First, "Comprehensive Sanctions Package Is Decisive Action Against Russian Abuses" (June 13, 2017); Central and East European Coalition, "115th Congress Policy Brief" (Summer 2017); Joint Baltic American National Committee, "Summer of Advocating for the Baltics: The Campaign to Support the Russia Sanctions Bill" (August 24, 2017).
153. Author's interview of senior House Democratic aide (August 2017).
154. Anthony Adragna, "Energy Companies Get Something in Russian Sanctions Deal," *Politico* (July 24, 2017); Peter Behr, "Congress Ties Trump's Hands on Russian Energy Sanctions," *E&E News* (July 26, 2017).

Chapter 7

1. Author's interview of Colin Kahl (April 22, 2014); author's interview of Dennis Ross (August 26, 2014); Testimony of Robert Cohen, U.S. Senate Committee on Foreign Relations, "U.S. Strategic Objectives Toward Iran," S. Hrg. 112-366 (December 1, 2011).
2. Senate Roll Call Vote 216 on Senate Amendment 1414 to S. 1867, The National Defense Authorization Act for Fiscal Year 2012 (December 2, 2011).
3. The White House, "Statement by the President on H.R. 1540" (December 31, 2011).
4. Senate Roll Call Vote 264 on Senate Amendment 2640 to H.J. Res. 61, The Hire More Heroes Act of 2015 (September 10, 2015).
5. Parts of this chapter draw on Tama 2020.
6. Alvandi 2014, 126–171.
7. Iran and Libya Sanctions Act of 1996 (Public Law 104-172).
8. Iran Nonproliferation Act of 2000 (Public Law 106-178).
9. The Iran and Libya Sanctions Act of 1996 was approved by a vote of 415-0 in the House on June 19, 1996 (House Roll Call Vote 250) and approved by unanimous consent in the Senate on July 16, 1996. The Iran Nonproliferation Act of 2000 was approved by a vote of 98-0 in the Senate on February 24, 2000 (Senate Roll Call Vote 12) and approved by a vote of 420-0 in the House on March 1, 2000 (House Roll Call Vote 28).

10. Congressional Quarterly 1996.

11. Walt Barron, "House Clears Sanctions on Iran Arms Aid," *CQ Weekly* (March 4, 2000), 487.

12. The White House, "Message from the President of the United States Transmitting His Veto of H.R. 2709, The Iran Missile Proliferation Sanctions Act of 1998," House Document 105-276 (June 24, 1998); Congressional Quarterly 1998.

13. Congressional Quarterly 1996, 2000.

14. Congressional Quarterly 2001.

15. Public Law 107-24, ILSA Extension Act of 2001. The legislation was approved by a vote of 409-6 in the House on July 26, 2001 (House Roll Call Vote 276) and approved by unanimous consent in the Senate on July 27, 2001.

16. Arms Control Today, "Timeline of Nuclear Diplomacy with Iran" (n.d.), https://www.armscontrol.org/factsheet/Timeline-of-Nuclear-Diplomacy-With-Iran.

17. H.R. 1400, The Iran Counter-Proliferation Act of 2007 (110th Cong.).

18. Author's interview of Richard Nephew (February 19, 2016); Jacobson 2008, 83; Eli Lake, "An Effort to Take a Harder Stance on Iran Is Derailed," *New York Sun* (June 16, 2006).

19. House Roll Call Vote 895 on H.R. 1400, Iran Counter-Proliferation Act of 2007 (September 25, 2007).

20. Nathan Guttman, "White House Blocks Congress on Iran," *Forward* (September 26, 2008).

21. Hearing Before the U.S. Senate Committee on Banking, Housing, and Urban Affairs, "Minimizing Potential Threats from Iran: Administration Perspectives on Economic Sanctions and Other U.S. Policy Options," S. Hrg. 111-410 (October 9, 2009).

22. H.R. 2914 and S. 2799, The Comprehensive Iran Sanctions, Accountability, and Divestment Act of 2009.

23. Josh Rogin, "Exclusive: State Department Letter to Kerry Outlines 'Serious Substantive Concerns' with Iran Sanctions Bill," *Foreign Policy* (December 11, 2009).

24. House Roll Call Vote 975 on H.R. 2194, Iran Refined Petroleum Act of 2009 (December 15, 2009); Senate approval by unanimous consent of H.R. 2194 (March 11, 2010); McArthur 2010.

25. Parsi 2017, 115.

26. Author's interview of Dennis Ross (August 26, 2014).

27. Author's interview of Howard Berman (July 19, 2022).

28. Senate Roll Call Vote 199 on H.R. 2194, Comprehensive Iran Sanctions, Accountability, and Divestment Act of 2010 (June 24, 2010); House Roll Call Vote 394 on H.R. 2194 (June 24, 2010).

29. Comprehensive Iran Sanctions, Accountability, and Divestment Act of 2010 (Public Law 111-195); Colum Lynch and Thomas Erdbrink, "Congress Strikes Deal on Tougher Sanctions for Iran's Suppliers," *Washington Post* (June 22, 2010).

30. Testimony of Cohen, "U.S. Strategic Objectives Toward Iran."

31. H.R. 1905, The Iran Threat Reduction and Syria Human Rights Act of 2012 (112th Cong.).

32. Author's interview of Richard Nephew (February 19, 2016); author's interview of former administration official (June 2014).

33. House Roll Call Vote 546 on H.R. 1905, Iran Threat Reduction and Syria Human Rights Act of 2012 (August 1, 2012); Senate approval by unanimous consent of H.R. 1905 (August 1, 2012); Public Law 112-158, Iran Threat Reduction and Syria Human Rights Act of 2012; Mark Landler and Steven Lee Myers, "White House and Congress Are in Step over Iran Sanctions," *New York Times* (July 31, 2012).

34. Josh Rogin, "White House Opposed New Iran Sanctions," *The Cable* (November 30, 2012).

35. Senate Roll Call Vote 215 on Senate Amendment 3232 to S. 3254, The National Defense Authorization Act for Fiscal Year 2013 (November 30, 2012); Public Law 112-239; Emily Cadei, "2012 Legislative Summary: Iran Sanctions," *CQ Weekly* (January 14, 2013), 87.

36. For more detail on the impact of Iran sanctions legislation, see Tama 2020.

37. Author's interview of Richard Nephew (February 19, 2016).

38. Author's interview of Mark Dubowitz (November 12, 2014).

39. Author's interview of Colin Kahl (April 22, 2014).

40. Gallup, "Iran" (n.d.), http://www.gallup.com/poll/116236/iran.aspx.

41. Fox News, "Fox News/Opinion Dynamics Poll" (January 26, 2006).

42. Gallup, "Iran."

43. Smeltz 2012.

44. Washington Post, "Washington Post-ABC News Poll" (January 27, 2006).

45. Pew Research Center for the People and the Press, "Support for Talks and Sanctions, Skepticism They Will Work" (October 6, 2009).

46. PollingReport.com, "Iran" (n.d.), https://www.pollingreport.com/iran.htm.

47. Author's interview (October 2014).

48. Smeltz, Friedhoff, et al. 2017; Busby, Kafura, Smeltz, et al. 2020.

49. Zack Beauchamp, "Why the US Has the Most Pro-Israel Foreign Policy in the World," *Vox* (July 24, 2014).

50. Congressional Quarterly 1996, 1998; Hurst 2016. Tim Starks, "Preparing for the Worst on Iran," *CQ Weekly* (March 5, 2007); Jonathan Broder, "Israel's Voice Rings on Hill as Change Roils Mideast," *CQ Weekly* (May 16, 2011).

51. Parsi 2012; Bruck 2014; author's interviews of congressional aides (2014–2020); author's interview of Howard Berman (July 19, 2022).

52. Kathy Gilsinan, "Iran's Enemy du Jour: A Guy Who Runs a Think Tank," *The Atlantic* (August 29, 2019); author's interviews of congressional aides (2014–2020).

53. Author's interviews of congressional aides (2014–2020).

54. Author's interview of congressional aide (October 2014).

55. Leech 2011.

56. Parsi 2012; Bruck 2014.

57. H.R. 850, The Nuclear Iran Prevention Act of 2013 (113th Cong.); S. 1881, The Nuclear Weapon Free Iran Act of 2013 (113th Cong.).

58. House Roll Call Vote 427 on H.R. 850, The Nuclear Iran Prevention Act of 2013 (July 31, 2013).

59. Burns 2019, 337–387.

60. "Joint Plan of Action" (November 2013), available at eeas.europa.eu/statements/docs/2013/131124_03_en.pdf.

61. Karen DeYoung and Joby Warrick, "Obama Twisting Arms over Iran Bill," *Washington Post* (December 2, 2013); Bruck 2014, 60–61.

62. President Barack Obama, State of the Union Address (January 28, 2014).

63. Letter from Senators Tim Johnson, Dianne Feinstein, Carl Levin, Barbara Mikulski, Barbara Boxer, John Rockefeller, Thomas Carper, Patrick Leahy, Ron Wyden, and Tom Harkin to Senator Harry Reid (December 18, 2013), available at https://www.scribd.com/doc/192583694/Chairmen-s-Letter-Final.

64. Mark Landler, "Potent Pro-Israel Group Finds Its Momentum Blunted," *New York Times* (February 4, 2014).

65. Jeremy Herb, "Reid, Dems Back Away from Iran Sanctions Legislation," *The Hill* (January 15, 2014).

66. Author's interview of congressional aide (October 2014).

67. Friedrichs 2021, 82–126.

68. Stephanie Condon, "Eric Cantor Blasts Obama's Foreign Policy: 'Hope is Not a Strategy,'" CBSNews.com (February 17, 2014).

69. S. 269, the Nuclear Weapon Free Iran Act of 2015 (114th Cong.).

70. President Barack Obama, State of the Union Address (January 20, 2015).

71. "An Open Letter to the Leaders of the Islamic Republic of Iran" (March 9, 2015), available at http://www.nytimes.com/interactive/2015/03/09/world/middleeast/document-the-letter-senate-republicans-addressed-to-the-leaders-of-iran.html?_r=1.

72. Jennifer Steinhauer and Julie Hirschfeld Davis, "Irate Democrats Denounce G.O.P. on Iran Letter," *New York Times* (March 10, 2015).

73. "Joint Comprehensive Plan of Action" (July 14, 2015), available at eeas.europa.eu/statements-eeas/docs/iran_agreement/iran_joint-comprehensive-plan-of-action_en.pdf.

74. Wolfensberger 2018, 104–121; Yishai Schwartz, "Why the Administration Is Perfectly Pleased with the Iran Nuclear Agreement Review Act," *Lawfare* (April 14, 2015).

75. William Jordan, "Americans Tend to Favor Iran Deal, Despite Serious Doubts," YouGov (July 17, 2015); Scott Clement, "56% of People Support Obama's Iran Deal. But They Don't Think It Will Work," *Washington Post* (July 20, 2015); Pew Research Center, "Iran Nuclear Agreement Meets with Public Skepticism" (July 21, 2015); Mark Murray, "Poll: American Public Divided on Iran Nuclear Deal," NBC News (August 3, 2015); Sarah Dutton, Jennifer De Pinto, Anthony Salvanto, and Fred Backus, "CBS News Poll: More Americans Disapprove Than Approve of the Iran Deal," CBS News (August 4, 2015); Monmouth University, "National: Iran Got Better End of Deal" (August 10, 2015); CNN.com, "CNN/ORC Poll: Iran Full Results" (August 20, 2015); Pew Research Center, "Support for Iran Nuclear Agreement Falls" (September 8, 2015); CNN.com, "CNN/ORC Poll" (September 13, 2015); PollingReport.com, "Iran."

76. Smeltz, Busby, et al. 2015.

77. Author's interview of Ilan Goldenberg (January 16, 2018).

78. Author's interview of Lester Munson (June 22, 2022).

79. Dueck 2010; Gries 2014.

80. Author's interview of House Republican aide (April 2020).

81. Author's interviews of former congressional aides and Obama administration legislative affairs officials (August 2017); Ailsa Chang, "Lobbyists Spending Millions to Sway the Undecided on Iran Deal," NPR (August 6, 2015); Karoun Demirjian and Carol Morello, "How AIPAC Lost the Iran Deal Fight," Washington Post (September 3, 2015).

82. Hurst 2016; Parsi 2017; Lantis 2019b; Karen DeYoung, "As an Iran Deal Nears, the Lobbying, Pro and Con, Intensifies," Washington Post (June 11, 2015); Anna Palmer and Tarini Parti, "Iran Deal Launches Lobbying War," Politico (July 14, 2015); Julie Hirschfeld Davis, "Lobbying Fight over Iran Nuclear Deal Centers on Democrats," New York Times (August 17, 2015).

83. Parsi 2017, 328.

84. Author's interview of former House Democratic aide (August 2017).

85. Hurst 2016; CQ Magazine, "Divide over Israel Widens in Democratic Party" (July 23, 2018); Sheryl Gay Stolberg, "Israel Lobby Convenes in Washington amid Fraying Bipartisanship and Rising Tension," New York Times (March 23, 2019).

86. Krishnadev Calamur, "In a Speech to Congress, Netanyahu Blasts 'A Very Bad Deal' with Iran," NPR (March 3, 2015).

87. Author's interview of Ryan Costello (June 29, 2022).

88. Rhodes 2018, 323–333; author's interviews of Obama administration officials (August 2017).

89. Author's interview of Obama administration official (August 2017).

90. Kerry 2018; Sherman 2018.

91. Author's interview of Margaret Taylor (April 30, 2020).

92. Author's interview of senior Democratic congressional aide (August 2017).

93. Yeganeh Torbati, "Trump Election Puts Iran Nuclear Deal on Shaky Ground," Reuters (November 9, 2016).

94. McMaster 2020, 295.

95. Michael R. Pompeo, "After the Deal: A New Iran Strategy," Remarks at the Heritage Foundation (May 21, 2018).

96. Bolton 2020, 362–370; Dina Esfandiary, "The Trump Administration's Maximum Pressure Campaign: A Prelude to War with Iran?," Bulletin of the Atomic Scientists (May 6, 2019); Andrew Hanna, "Sanctions 5: Trump's 'Maximum Pressure' Targets," The Iran Primer, United States Institute of Peace (March 3, 2021).

97. The Iran Primer, "Exiting the Deal Part 5: Congressional Remarks," United States Institute of Peace (May 9, 2018).

98. Lindsey McPherson, "7 Lawmakers Who Opposed Iran Deal and Trump's Decision to Withdraw from It," Roll Call (May 8, 2018).

99. Ben Cardin, "I Voted Against Iran Deal. Withdrawing from It Is a Mistake," Jewish Telegraphic Agency (May 8, 2018).

100. The Iran Primer, "Exiting the Deal Part 5."

101. The New York Times, "Trump Withdrew from the Iran Deal. Here's How Republicans, Democrats and the World Reacted" (May 8, 2018); The Iran Primer, "Exiting the Deal Part 5."

102. The Iran Primer, "Exiting the Deal Part 5."
103. Dan Sullivan, "Don't 'Tear Up' the Iran Deal. Let It Fall on Its Own," *Washington Post* (February 1, 2017); The Iran Primer, "Exiting the Deal Part 5"; McPherson, "7 Lawmakers Who Opposed Iran Deal and Trump's Decision to Withdraw from It."
104. Author's interview of House Republican aide (April 2020).
105. Autor's interview of Ilan Goldenberg (January 16, 2018); author's interview of Margaret Taylor (April 30, 2020).
106. Senate Roll Call Vote 147 on S. 722, The Countering Iran's Destabilizing Activities Act of 2017 (June 15, 2017).
107. Public Law 115-44, Countering America's Adversaries Through Sanctions Act.
108. Author's interview of Senate Democratic foreign policy aide (August 2017).
109. Author's interview of House Republican foreign policy aide (April 2020).
110. Ryan Struyk, "CNN Poll: Two-Thirds Want to Stay in Iran Nuclear Deal," CNN.com (October 20, 2017).
111. Grace Sparks, "Majority Say US Should Not Withdraw from Iran Nuclear Agreement," CNN.com (May 9, 2018).
112. Jennifer De Pinto, Fred Backus, Kabir Khanna, and Anthony Salvanto, "Most Americans Don't Know What U.S. Should Do on Iran Deal—CBS News Poll," CBS News (May 7, 2018).
113. Smeltz et al. 2018.
114. Busby, Kafura, Smeltz, et al. 2020.
115. Lantis 2019b.
116. Michael Wilner, "AIPAC Partners to Redefine Debate on Iran Agreement," *Jerusalem Post* (October 9, 2017).
117. Ibid.
118. Author's interview of Ilan Goldenberg (January 16, 2018).
119. Testimony of Michael Singh, U.S. Senate Armed Services Committee, "The Joint Comprehensive Plan of Action (JCPOA) and the Military Balance in the Middle East" (August 5, 2015); Testimony of Michael Singh, U.S. Senate Foreign Relations Committee, "The View from Congress: U.S. Policy on Iran" (March 28, 2017).
120. John Haltiwanger, "Even Some of the Iran Deal's Most Vocal Critics Aren't Sure Trump Made the Right Choice in Withdrawing from It," *Business Insider* (May 8, 2018); Gardiner Harris, "He Was a Tireless Critic of the Iran Deal. Now He Insists He Wanted to Save It," *New York Times* (May 13, 2018).

Chapter 8

1. Fergusson and Williams 2016, 1.
2. President Barack Obama, "Statement by the President on the Trans-Pacific Partnership" (October 5, 2015).
3. House Vote 374 on Motion to Concur in Senate Amendment with Amendment to H.R. 2146, Defending Public Safety Employees' Retirement Act (June 18, 2015); Senate Vote 219 on Motion to Concur in the House Amendment to the Senate Amendment to H.R. 2146 (June 24, 2015).

4. Hermann, Tetlock, and Diascro 2001; Rathbun 2016; Guisinger 2017. For a detailed analysis of factors that influence people's attitudes on trade, see Fordham and Kleinberg 2012.

5. Baldwin and Magee 2000; Hiscox 2002; Destler 2005.

6. Drezner 2015.

7. Office of Senator Thom Tillis, "Tobacco Draws a Fight in Trade Deal," Press release (October 11, 2015).

8. WXYZ-TV, "Senator Stabenow Says TPP Isn't Right for Mich." (June 2, 2016).

9. John T. Bennett, "Trump Castigates Global Trade Pacts, Lawmakers Caught in a Vice," *Roll Call* (September 26, 2016); Jim Tankersley, "How the Politics of Trade Swung So Fast," *Washington Post* (October 9, 2016).

10. Jackie Calmes, "Obama Readies One Last Push for Trans-Pacific Partnership," *New York Times* (August 21, 2016); William Mauldin, "Obama Administration Gives Up on Pacific Trade Deal," *Wall Street Journal* (November 11, 2016).

11. Siobhan Hughes, "GOP Backers of Trade Deal Ponder Next Steps," *Wall Street Journal* (January 23, 2017).

12. Testimony of Susan C. Schwab, Joint Hearing Before the U.S. House of Representatives Subcommittee on Terrorism, Nonproliferation, and Trade and the Subcommittee on Asia and the Pacific of the Committee on Foreign Affairs, "The Trans-Pacific Partnership Agreement: Challenges and Potential," Serial No. 112-144 (May 17, 2012), 10–13.

13. Elms 2016.

14. Remarks by President Obama at Suntory Hall, Tokyo (November 14, 2009).

15. Clinton 2011; Campbell and Andrews 2013; Bader and Dollar 2015.

16. Federal News Service, "Reps. Camp, Brady Welcome US Participation in Trans-Pacific Partnership Talks" (November 14, 2009).

17. Ibid.

18. Tom Wright, Jonathan Weisman, and Peter Fritsch, "Obama in Asia: Pacific-Trade Plan Shows Constraints on U.S.," *Wall Street Journal* (November 16, 2009); Office of Senator John Kerry, "Kerry, Webb Support Second Round of Trans-Pacific Partnership Trade Deal Negotiations," Press release (June 14, 2010).

19. Ways and Means Committee Democrats, "Lawmakers on Announcement of U.S. Engagement on Trans Pacific Partnership Free Trade Agreement," Press release (November 16, 2009).

20. Office of Senator Sherrod Brown, "Senators Write to U.S. Trade Rep. in Advance of Trans-Pacific Partnership Negotiations," Press release (March 13, 2010); Ways and Means Committee Democrats, "Ways and Means Democrats Call for Robust, Enforceable Disciplines on State-Owned and State-Supported Enterprises in Trans-Pacific Partnership Agreement," Press release (June 28, 2011); Office of Senator Sherrod Brown, "As Japan Announces Intent to Join the Trans-Pacific Partnership, Brown Tells Obama—Don't Leave American Automakers and Manufacturers behind," Press release (November 9, 2011).

21. Testimony of Senator Debbie Stabenow, Hearing Before U.S. Senate Committee on Finance, "The Trans-Pacific Partnership: Opportunities and Challenges," S. Hrg. 113-160 (April 24, 2013), 16.

22. For a detailed analysis of the debate over the TPP, see Friedrichs 2021, 151–193.

23. Congressional Research Service 2019a.

24. Among Republicans, 84% of representatives and 88% of senators voted for the legislation. Among Democrats, 12% of representatives and 43% of senators voted for it. House Vote 370 on H.R. 3009, Trade Act of 2002, On Agreeing to the Conference Report (July 27, 2002); Senate Vote 207 on H.R. 3009, Trade Act of 2002, On Agreeing to the Conference Report (August 1, 2002).

25. Author's interview of Michael Froman (July 18, 2022).

26. Lantis 2019a, 88–93; Lantis and Homan 2019, 167–170.

27. Office of Representative Rosa DeLauro, "DeLauro, Miller Lead 151 House Dems Telling President They Will Not Support Outdated Fast Track for Trans-Pacific Partnership," Press release (November 13, 2013).

28. Remarks of Representative Barbara Lee, "Progressive Caucus: Opposition to the Trans-Pacific Partnership," 160 Cong. Rec. H460 (January 15, 2014).

29. Citizens Trade Campaign, "Congress Voices Bipartisan Opposition to Fast Track" (November 13, 2013).

30. Lantis 2019a, 88–93; Lantis and Homan 2019, 167–170.

31. H.R. 1890 and S. 995, Bipartisan Congressional Trade Priorities and Accountability Act of 2015 (114th Cong.).

32. Congressional Research Service 2019a.

33. Jonathan Weisman, "Deal Reached on Fast-Track Authority for Obama on Trade Accord," *New York Times* (April 16, 2015).

34. Hearing Before the U.S. Senate Committee on Finance, "Congress and U.S. Tariff Policy," S. Hrg. 114-221 (April 16 and April 21, 2015).

35. Hearing Before the U.S. House of Representatives Committee on Ways and Means, "Expanding American Trade with Accountability and Transparency," Serial No. 114-FC04 (April 22, 2015), 5.

36. Hearing Before the U.S. House of Representatives Committee on Foreign Affairs, "Advancing U.S. Economic Interests in Asia," Serial No. 114-50 (May 14, 2015), 33.

37. Hrg., Senate Committee on Finance, "Congress and U.S. Tariff Policy," 16.

38. Ibid., 19–20, 28–29, 31–35.

39. Ibid., 25–26; Hrg., House of Representatives Committee on Foreign Affairs, "Advancing U.S. Economic Interests in Asia," 26.

40. Report (to accompany S. 995), "Bipartisan Congressional Trade Priorities and Accountability Act of 2015," U.S. Senate Rept. 114-42 (May 12, 2015); Philip Brasher, "Senate Committee OKs Fast-Track Trade Bill," Agri Pulse (April 22, 2015).

41. Report together with dissenting views (to accompany H.R. 1890), "Bipartisan Congressional Trade Priorities and Accountability Act of 2015," U.S. House Rept. 114-100, Part 1 (May 1, 2015), 77.

42. Ibid., 30.

43. Ibid., 134–143.
44. House Vote 374.
45. Senate Vote 219.
46. Senate Vote 220 on Motion to Invoke Cloture on the Motion to Concur in the House Amendment to the Senate Amendment to H.R. 1295 with Amendment No. 2065(June 24, 2015); House Vote 388 on H.R. 1295, Trade Preferences Extension Act of 2015 (June 25, 2015).
47. Public Law 114-26; Public Law 114-27.
48. Office of Senate Majority Leader, "McConnell Statement on Senate Passage of Trade Promotion Authority," Press release (June 24, 2015).
49. The White House, "Statement by the President," Press release (June 25, 2015).
50. Fergusson and Williams 2016.
51. William Mauldin, "U.S. Reaches Trans-Pacific Partnership Trade Deal with 11 Pacific Nations," *Wall Street Journal* (October 5, 2015); Fergusson and Williams 2016, 49–50.
52. Yoshimatsu 2016, 1164.
53. Alana Semuels, "The TPP's Uneven Attempt at Labor Protection," *The Atlantic* (January 22, 2016).
54. U.S. Department of the Treasury, "Fact Sheet: Joint Declaration of the Macroeconomic Policy Authorities of the TPP Countries" (November 5, 2015).
55. Fergusson and Williams 2016, 7–8.
56. Nick Timiraos and William Mauldin, "Odds Worsen for TPP Trade Deal," *Wall Street Journal* (July 29, 2016).
57. Drezner 2015.
58. Calmes, "Obama Readies One Last Push for Trans-Pacific Partnership"; Bennett, "Trump Castigates Global Trade Pacts."
59. Author's interview of Nasim Fussell (June 17, 2022).
60. U.S. Senate Committee on Finance, "Hatch Statement on Trans-Pacific Partnership Negotiations," Press release (October 5, 2015).
61. Jackie Calmes, "Utah Senator, Crucial Ally for the Pacific Rim Trade Deal, Is Now Its Main Hurdle," *New York Times* (November 13, 2015).
62. Thomas J. Bollyky, "TPP Tobacco Exception Proves the New Rule in Trade," Council on Foreign Relations (February 4, 2016); Calmes, "Obama Readies One Last Push for Trans-Pacific Partnership"; Fergusson and Williams 2016.
63. Andrew Kahn, Chris Kirk, and Will Oremus, "The GOP Horse Race," *Slate* (February 3, 2016).
64. Adam Taylor, "A Timeline of Trump's Complicated Relationship with the TPP," *Washington Post* (April 13, 2018).
65. Bennett, "Trump Castigates Global Trade Pacts"; Tankersley, "How the Politics of Trade Swung So Fast."
66. Daniel Strauss, "Bernie Sanders Bashes Trade Agreement as 'Disastrous,'" *Politico* (October 5, 2015).
67. Ben Jacobs, Lauren Gambino, and Sabrina Siddiqui, "Hillary Clinton Breaks with Obama to Oppose Trans Pacific Partnership," *The Guardian* (October 7, 2015).

68. President Barack Obama, "Statement by the President on the Signing of the Trans-Pacific Partnership" (February 3, 2016).

69. Author's interview of Michael Froman (July 18, 2022).

70. Hearing Before the U.S. Senate Committee on Finance, "Free Trade Agreement Implementation: Lessons from the Past," S. Hrg. 114-549 (March 3, 2016).

71. Remarks by Senator Jeff Sessions, 162 Cong. Rec. S2403 (April 25, 2016); Remarks by Representatives Mark Pocan, Paul Tonko, and Michael M. Honda, 162 Cong. Rec. H5491 (September 14, 2016); Remarks by Representative Nydia Velazquez, 162 Cong. Rec. H5720 (September 21, 2016); Remarks by Representative Barbara Lee, 162 Cong. Rec. E1341 (September 22, 2016).

72. Remarks by Senator Sherrod Brown, 162 Cong. Rec. S6261 (September 29, 2016).

73. Author's interview of Susan Rice (June 13, 2019).

74. Author's interview of John Murphy (April 24, 2020).

75. Calmes, "Obama Readies One Last Push for Trans-Pacific Partnership."

76. William Mauldin, "Obama Administration Gives Up on Pacific Trade Deal," *Wall Street Journal* (November 11, 2016).

77. Author's interview of former Obama administration legislative affairs official (August 2017).

78. Author's interview of former senior House Democratic aide (April 2020).

79. President Donald Trump, "Withdrawal of the United States from the Trans-Pacific Partnership Negotiations and Agreement," Memo (January 23, 2017).

80. Philip Rucker and Robert Costa, "Bannon Vows a Daily Fight for 'Deconstruction of the Administrative State,'" *Washington Post* (January 23, 2017).

81. Peter Baker, "Trump Abandons Trans-Pacific Partnership, Obama's Signature Trade Deal," *New York Times* (January 23, 2017).

82. Remarks of Senator Charles Schumer, 163 Cong. Rec. S369 (January 23, 2017).

83. Ibid.

84. Office of Representative Chellie Pingree, "Statement on Withdrawal from Trans Pacific Partnership," Press release (January 23, 2017).

85. Hearing Before the U.S. House of Representatives Committee on Ways and Means, "U.S. Trade Policy Agenda," Serial No. 115-FC05 (June 22, 2017).

86. Siobhan Hughes, "GOP Backers of Trade Deal Ponder Next Steps," *Wall Street Journal* (January 23, 2017).

87. Ibid.

88. Jeff Stein, "Paul Ryan Used to Love TPP. Then Came Donald Trump," *Vox* (January 23, 2017).

89. Ibid.

90. Author's interview of Jeff Flake (December 11, 2018).

91. Ana Swanson, "Trump Proposes Rejoining Trans-Pacific Partnership," *New York Times* (April 12, 2018).

92. Tweet by Donald Trump (April 12, 2018), https://twitter.com/realdonaldtrump/status/984631073865953280?lang=en.

93. Tweet by Donald Trump (April 17, 2018), https://twitter.com/realdonaldtrump/status/986436520444866560?lang=en.

94. Center for Strategic and International Studies, "The CPTPP at Three" (October 28, 2021).

95. Hermann, Tetlock, and Diascro 2001; Rathbun 2016; Guisinger 2017.

96. Lydia Saad, "Americans' Vanishing Fear of Foreign Trade," Gallup (February 26, 2020).

97. Author's interview of John Murphy (April 24, 2020).

98. Smeltz et al. 2016.

99. Smeltz and Kafura 2018.

100. Pew Research Center, "Free-Trade Agreements Seen as Good for U.S., but Concerns Persist" (May 2015).

101. Bruce Stokes, "Republicans, Especially Trump Supporters, See Free Trade Deals as Bad for US" Pew Research Center (March 31, 2016); Pew Research Center, "Clinton, Trump Supporters Have Starkly Different Views of a Changing Nation" (August 2016), 29; Jacob Poushter, "American Public, Foreign Policy Experts Sharply Disagree over Involvement in Global Economy," Pew Research Center (October 28, 2016); Bradley Jones, "Support for Free Trade Agreement Rebounds Modestly, but Wide Partisan Differences Remain," Pew Research Center (April 25, 2017); Bradley Jones, "Americans Are Generally Positive about Free Trade Agreements, More Critical of Tariff Increases," Pew Research Center (May 10, 2018).

102. Jacob Poushter, "Americans Favor TPP, but Less Than Those in Other Countries Do," Pew Research Center (June 23, 2015).

103. Pew Research Center, "Clinton, Trump Supporters Have Starkly Different Views of a Changing Nation" (August 2016), 27.

104. Ibid.

105. Ryan Rainey, "As Trade Plays in Campaigns, Most Americans Don't Know What TPP Is," Morning Consult (April 21, 2016); Ryan Rainey, "Support for TPP Grows as Americans Become More Familiar with Trade Deal," Morning Consult (August 11, 2016).

106. Smeltz, Friedhoff, et al. 2017.

107. Busby, Kafura, Smeltz, et al. 2020, 4.

108. Guisinger 2009.

109. Jackie Calmes, "Who Hates Free Trade Treaties? Surprisingly, Not Voters," New York Times (September 21, 2016).

110. On interest group activity on trade generally, see Milner 1988; Baldwin 1989; Hiscox 2002.

111. Baldwin and Magee 2000; Destler 2005.

112. Baldwin and Magee 2000; Hiscox 2002, 62–70; Guisinger 2017, 31–33.

113. Author's interview of Everett Eissenstat (August 4, 2022).

114. Calmes, "Obama Readies One Last Push for Trans-Pacific Partnership"; Bob Davis and William Mauldin, "New Push to Salvage Trade Pact—Business Groups Press Trump Officials to Revamp Trans-Pacific Partnership Deal," Wall Street Journal (January 18, 2017).

115. Testimony of Thomas J. Donahue, Hearings before the Committee on Finance, U.S. Senate, "Congress and U.S. Tariff Policy," S. Hrg. 114-221 (April 16 and April 21, 2015), 58.

116. Robert Holly, "U.S. Agribusinesses Lobby Heavily for Trans-Pacific Deal," *Des Moines Register* (November 22, 2015).

117. Fergusson and Williams 2016, 35–36; Adam Behsudi, "Tech Industry Pushes for TPP," *Politico* (September 13, 2016).

118. Fergusson and Williams 2016, 43, 49–50.

119. Fergusson and Williams 2016, 33–34; author's interview of John Murphy (April 24, 2020).

120. Author's interview of Nilmini Rubin (August 21, 2017).

121. Author's interview of former Obama administration legislative affairs official (August 2017).

122. BlueGreen Alliance, "Labor, Environmental Leaders Call on Congress to Reject Trans-Pacific Partnership Agreement," Press release (November 10, 2015).

123. Leo Gerard, "Unless You're a Corporation, Nothing Good Will Come of the Trans-Pacific Partnership," *In These Times* (October 15, 2015).

124. BlueGreen Alliance, "Labor, Environmental Leaders Call on Congress to Reject Trans-Pacific Partnership Agreement," Press release (November 10, 2015).

125. Young 2016.

126. Lantis 2019a, 93–96; Jonathan Weisman, "Deal Reached on Fast-Track Authority for Obama on Trade Accord," *New York Times* (April 16, 2015); Calmes, "Obama Readies One Last Push for Trans-Pacific Partnership."

127. Author's interview of Edward Alden (April 24, 2020).

128. Author's interview of Nilmini Rubin (August 21, 2017).

129. Boucher and Thies 2019; Ken Thomas and Paul Wiseman, "Trade War? Trump Orders Aluminum, Steel Tariffs," Associated Press (March 2, 2018).

130. Jacqueline Varas, "The Total Cost of Trump's Tariffs," American Action Forum (February 5, 2020).

131. David J. Lynch, Philip Rucker, and Erica Werner, "Pushback Begins as Tariffs Are Enacted," *Washington Post* (March 9, 2018); Nolan D. McCaskill, "McConnell Hits at Trump's Tariffs," *Politico* (March 6, 2018).

132. Senate Democrats, "Schumer Floor Remarks on Trade Tariffs and the GOP Tax Bill Leading to Huge Stock Buybacks," Press release (March 8, 2018).

133. David J. Lynch, Philip Rucker, and Erica Werner, "Pushback Begins as Tariffs Are Enacted," *Washington Post* (March 9, 2018).

134. Jim Tankersley, "Rebuffed by Trump on Tariffs, Businesses Mount Coordinated Pushback," *New York Times* (September 12, 2018).

135. U.S. Chamber of Commerce, "Trade Works. Tariffs Don't" (n.d.), https://action. uschamber.com/MYWsiem.

136. Author's interview of John Murphy (April 24, 2020).

137. AFL-CIO, "Steel and Aluminum Tariffs Good for Working People," Press release (March 1, 2018); AFL-CIO, "Strategic Tariffs Against China Are Critical Part of Trade Reform to Create More Jobs and Better Pay," Press release (March 22, 2018).

138. S.3013, A bill to amend the Trade Expansion Act of 1962 to require Congressional approval before the President adjusts imports that are determined to threaten to impair national security (115th Cong.).

139. Senate Foreign Relations Committee, "Senators Introduce Legislation to Require Congressional Approval of National Security-Designated Tariffs," Press release (June 6, 2018).

140. Ibid.

141. Senate Foreign Relations Committee, "Support Continues to Grow for Legislation Requiring Congressional Approval of National Security-Designated Tariffs," Press release (June 7, 2018).

142. Haley Bird, "Deferring to Trump on Trade," *Washington Examiner* (June 15, 2018).

143. Author's interview of Bob Corker (June 29, 2022).

144. Author's interview of Jeff Flake (December 11, 2018).

145. For more information on tariff actions and debates under Trump, see Packard and Wallach 2018; Congressional Research Service 2019b; Harrell 2019.

146. Author's interview of former senior House Democratic aide (April 2020).

147. Hrg., House of Representatives Committee on Ways and Means, "U.S. Trade Policy Agenda," 3; Hearing Before the U.S. Senate Committee on Finance, "President's Trade Policy Agenda and Fiscal Year 2018 Budget," S. Hrg. 115-247 (June 21, 2017), 6.

148. Author's interview of Nasim Fussell (June 17, 2022).

149. Author's interview of Edward Alden (April 24, 2020).

150. Author's interview of former senior House Democratic aide (April 2020).

151. Lighthizer 2020.

152. Edward Alden, "In the NAFTA Deal, Trump Got What Democrats Couldn't," *Politico* (October 2, 2018). See also Friedrichs 2022.

153. AFL-CIO, "AFL-CIO Endorses USMCA After Successfully Negotiating Improvements," Press release (December 10, 2019).

154. Alexia Fernández Campbell, "Workers in Mexico Just Won the Right to Organize Real Labor Unions. Trump Helped," *Vox* (May 1, 2019); Rachel Cohrs, "Biologic Exclusivity Provision Stripped from Revised USMCA Deal," Modern Healthcare (December 10, 2019).

155. U.S. Chamber of Commerce, "Coalition Letter on the USMCA," Press release (December 17, 2019).

156. Author's interview of John Murphy (April 24, 2020).

157. Author's interview of Everett Eissenstat (August 4, 2022).

158. Jeff Stein, "Trump Signs Trade Agreement with Canada and Mexico," *Washington Post* (January 30, 2020).

159. The White House, "Remarks by President Trump at a Signing Ceremony for the United States-Canada-Mexico Trade Agreement" (January 29, 2020).

Chapter 9

1. Congressional Research Service 2021.
2. Krasner 1978, 63–64; Canes-Wrone, Howell, and Lewis 2008, 5; Meernik and Oldmixon 2008, 187; Howell, Jackman, and Rogowski 2013, 37–39; Milner and Tingley 2015, 32.
3. But see Hicks, Lauter, and McElhinny 2018 for an analysis highlighting the internationalism of many members of Congress.
4. Milner and Tingley 2013; Gries 2014; Wenzelburger and Böller 2019; Raunio and Wagner 2020.
5. Lindsay 1994; Milner and Tingley 2015.
6. Congressional Research Service 2013. Congress later increased the spending caps for subsequent years. Alicia Parlapiano, "How Congress Has Worked to Avoid the 'Sequester' Spending Caps," *New York Times* (October 29, 2015).
7. US Global Leadership Coalition, "Military Leaders Letter to Congress" (March 30, 2011), http://www.usglc.org/wp-content/uploads/2011/03/NSAC-letter-2011.pdf.
8. Ibid.
9. US Global Leadership Coalition, "Business Leaders to Congress: Support a Strong & Effective International Affairs Budget" (June 29, 2011), https://www.usglc.org/wp-content/uploads/2011/06/FY12_Business-Leaders-Letter-to-Congress.pdf.
10. US Global Leadership Coalition, "Senator Graham and Top Military, Business Leaders Discuss U.S. Global Leadership," Press release (November 21, 2011).
11. Sara Sorcher, "Granger Stands at Center of Foreign-Aid Debates," *National Journal* (April 27, 2012).
12. Author's interview of executive branch official involved in foreign aid policy (March 2013).
13. For instance, see Joanna Anderson, "Family-Planning Funding Rolled Back in House State-Foreign Draft Bill," *CQ Weekly* (May 21, 2012).
14. Author's interview of Andrew King (April 21, 2020).
15. Author's interview of Jamie Curtis (April 17, 2020).
16. Appropriations Committee Republicans, "Chairwoman Granger Opening Statement on FY 2013 State and Foreign Operations Appropriations Bill for Subcommittee Markup" (May 9, 2012).
17. Author's interview of Andrew King (April 21, 2020).
18. Kaiser Family Foundation, "Congressional Delegation Visits Africa to Assess Impact of U.S.-Sponsored Projects" (January 9, 2012).
19. Mary Troyan, "How Lindsey Graham Promotes Foreign Aid," *Greenville News* (June 2, 2015).
20. Michael Wines, "Man in the News; Kentucky Blend of Understatement and Ambition—Addison Mitchell McConnell," *New York Times* (September 7, 1995); Isaac Chotiner, "Regrets, Mitch McConnell Has A Few," *New Republic* (May 20, 2013).
21. Hicks, Lauter, and McElhinny 2018, 154–183; Public Law 114-121, Electrify Africa Act; Public Law 114-191, Foreign Aid Transparency and Accountability Act; Public Law 114-195, Global Food Security Act.

22. Mark Hensch, "Trump Pitches 37% Cut to State Department Budget," *The Hill* (February 28, 2017).

23. Letter from 121 retired generals and admirals to Speaker of the House Paul Ryan, Senate Majority Leader Mitch McConnell, House Minority Leader Nancy Pelosi, and Senate Minority Leader Chuck Schumer (February 27, 2017), available at https://www.usglc.org/downloads/2017/02/FY18_International_Affairs_Budget_House_Senate.pdf.

24. Letter from 106 Christian leaders to Speaker of the House Paul Ryan, Senate Majority Leader Mitch McConnell, House Minority Leader Nancy Pelosi, and Senate Minority Leader Chuck Schumer (March 16, 2017), available at https://www.worldvision.org/wp-content/uploads/2017/03/Faith-Letter-to-House_Senate-Leadership-on-International-Affairs-Budget-03162017.pdf.

25. Letter from 225 business leaders to Secretary of State Rex Tillerson (May 22, 2017), available at https://www.usglc.org/downloads/2017/05/Business-Letter-Tillerson-May-22.pdf.

26. Hilary Clark, Kara Fox, and Richard Allen Greene, "Alarm Bells Ring for Charities as Trump Pledges to Slash Foreign Aid Budget," CNN.com (March 1, 2017); Rich Edson, "Faith Leaders Lobby Congress Against Foreign Aid Cuts," FoxNews.com (March 16, 2017); Carol Morello, "Foreign Aid Under the Ax in State Department Budget Proposal," *Washington Post* (May 23, 2017).

27. Ali Breland, "Gates Advocates for Foreign Aid During Capitol Hill Meetings," *The Hill* (March 22, 2017); Morello, "Foreign Aid Under the Ax."

28. Author's interview of John Glenn (October 5, 2017).

29. Patricia Zengerle, "Trump Plan to Slash State, Foreign Aid Spending Has Foes in Congress," Reuters (February 28, 2017).

30. Josh Rogin, "Trump Slashing of State Dept. and Foreign Aid Budget Would Be 'Dead on Arrival,'" *Washington Post* (February 28, 2017).

31. U.S. Senate Committee on Appropriations Subcommittee on State, Foreign Operations, and Related Programs, "Hearing to Review the FY2018 Budget for the U.S. Department of State," S. Hrg. 115-726 (June 14, 2017).

32. Erica Werner, "McConnell Rejects Trump's Proposed Cuts to Foreign Aid, Medical Research," Associated Press (March 21, 2017).

33. Kelsey Snell and Karoun Demirjian, "Capitol Hill Republicans Not on Board with Trump Budget," *Washington Post* (March 16, 2017).

34. Tweets by Senator Marco Rubio and Senator Chris Murphy (February 28, 2017), https://twitter.com/chrismurphyct/status/836596946731163648?lang=en.

35. Office of Management and Budget 2017.

36. U.S. Senate Committee on Appropriations Subcommittee on State, Foreign Operations, and Related Programs, "Hearing to Review the FY2018 Budget for the U.S. Department of State."

37. U.S. Senate, "Department of State, Foreign Operations, and Related Programs Appropriations Bill, 2018," Senate Rept. 115-152 (2017), 6.

38. Ibid., 6–7.

39. Public Law 115-141, Consolidated Omnibus Appropriations Act, 2018; US Global Leadership Coalition, "Congress Finalizes FY18 Spending: Rejects 'Doctrine of Retreat,' Restores Funding for International Affairs Budget" (May 23, 2018).

40. Office of Management and Budget 2018.

41. Samantha Urban, "Congress Should Ignore President Trump's 2019 Budget Request," ONE Campaign (February 12, 2018).

42. Letter from 1,215 veterans to Speaker of the House Paul Ryan, Senate Majority Leader Mitch McConnell, House Minority Leader Nancy Pelosi, and Senate Minority Leader Chuck Schumer (February 12, 2018), available at https://www.usglc.org/media/2018/02/1215-Veterans-Congressional-Leadership-Feb-2018.pdf.

43. Nahal Toosi, "Lawmakers Promise Bipartisan 'No' to Trump Plan for Cutting Diplomacy and Aid Money," *Politico* (February 12, 2018).

44. Office of Representative Eliot Engel, "Engel Statement on Proposed FY 19 International Affairs Budget," Press release (February 12, 2018).

45. US Global Leadership Coalition, "Congress Finalizes FY 19 Spending" (February 15, 2019).

46. Public Law 116-6, Consolidated Appropriations Act 2019.

47. Office of Management and Budget 2019. The funding level was initially described as $42.7 billion, but the congressional budget office later determined that the actual proposed amount was $43.3 billion. See US Global Leadership Coalition, "Congress Finalizes FY 20 Spending: International Affairs Budget Sees Small Increase as Global Challenges Grow" (December 20, 2019).

48. "Statement by Former U.S. Combatant Commanders" (March 10, 2019), available at https://www.usglc.org/media/2019/03/Statement-by-Former-US-Combatant-Commanders.pdf.

49. Oxfam, "Leading Humanitarian, Development, and Global Health Organizations Urge Congress to Reject Cuts to Foreign Assistance," Press release (March 11, 2019).

50. U.S. House of Representatives Committee on Appropriations, "Chairwoman Lowey Statement at State-Foreign Operations Public Witness Day," Press release (March 12, 2019).

51. Edward Wong and Catie Edmondson, "Lawmakers Rough Up Pompeo over Proposed State Department Cuts," *New York Times* (March 27, 2019).

52. US Global Leadership Coalition, "House Passes FY20 State-Foreign Operations Bill; Bipartisan Majority Defeats Cutting Amendments" (June 20, 2019).

53. US Global Leadership Coalition, "Congress Finalizes FY 20 Spending."

54. Office of Management and Budget 2020. Trump's repeated proposals of large cuts to the budget despite the bipartisan congressional rejection of them each year raises the question of why Trump kept making requests that Congress was almost certain to reject. It is likely that the repeated proposals for cuts were driven by the ideological antipathy of Trump and some of his key budget advisors, such as Office of Management and Budget Director Mick Mulvaney, to foreign aid spending.

55. US Global Leadership Coalition, "Out of Touch with America's Interests: International Affairs Programs Slashed for Fourth Straight Year Despite Growing Global Crises" (February 10, 2020), 3.

56. U.S. House of Representatives Committee on Foreign Affairs, "Engel Blasts Trump Proposal to Slash Diplomacy and Development Budget," Press release (February 10, 2020).
57. Foreign Affairs Committee Republicans, "McCaul Statement on the Administration's FY 2021 Budget Request," Press release (February 10, 2020).
58. Congressional Research Service 2021.
59. Carol Morello and Karoun Demirjian, "Trump Administration Is Considering Pulling Back $3 Billion in Foreign Aid," *Washington Post* (August 16, 2018).
60. Michael Igoe, "White House Abandons Plan to Rescind Billions in US Foreign Aid," Devex (August 29, 2018).
61. Rachel Oswald, "Lawmakers Wary of Potential Trump Cuts to Foreign Aid," *Roll Call* (August 17, 2018).
62. Morello and Demirjian, "Trump Administration Is Considering Pulling Back $3 Billion in Foreign Aid."
63. Patricia Zengerle and Lesley Wroughton, "Trump Backs Off Plan to Roll Back Foreign Aid Funding: Officials," *Reuters* (August 28, 2018).
64. Edward Wong, "U.S. Orders Freeze of Foreign Aid, Bypassing Congress," *New York Times* (August 7, 2019).
65. Ibid.
66. Interaction, "90+ NGOs: Letter to Congressional Leadership Regarding Possible Rescissions," Press release (August 19, 2019).
67. U.S. House of Representatives Committee on Foreign Affairs, "Engel Statement on Administration's Plan to Withhold Funding for Foreign Affairs Efforts," Press release (August 7, 2019).
68. Office of Senator Lindsey Graham, "Graham, Rogers Express Concerns About Proposed USAID Rescission," Press release (August 16, 2019).
69. Bolton 2020, 470–471; Steve Holland and Patricia Zengerle, "Trump Drops Bid to Slash Foreign Aid After Congress Objects," Reuters (August 22, 2019).
70. US Global Leadership Coalition, "Congress Finalizes FY20 Spending."
71. Kull 2017.
72. Wojtowicz and Hanania 2017.
73. Kull and Destler 1999; Kull 2017.
74. Kull 2017, 3–5.
75. Milner and Tingley 2013, 393.
76. Wojtowicz and Hanania 2017.
77. Smeltz, Daalder, et al. 2017.
78. Kafura 2018.
79. Ibid.
80. Program for Public Consultation, "Trump's Budget at Odds with Public's Priorities" (March 23, 2017).
81. Busby, Kafura, Smeltz, et al. 2020.
82. Ibid.
83. Otter 2003.

84. US Global Leadership Coalition, "After Tumultuous Election, Foreign Policy Direction Less Clear" (November 9, 2016), 3.

85. US Global Leadership Coalition, "After Tumultuous Midterm Cycle, Strong Signals for Internationalist Congress" (November 7, 2018), 3.

86. Author's interview of Diana Ohlbaum (July 18, 2017).

87. For another example of a diverse advocacy coalition exercising influence on foreign aid policy, see Milner and Tingley 2015, 238–239.

88. Carter and Scott 2009, 188.

89. Taroff and Lawson 2016, 31.

90. Judy Sarasohn, "Strange Bedfellows for International Affairs," *Washington Post* (March 3, 2005).

91. Author's interview of John Glenn (October 5, 2017).

92. US Global Leadership Coalition, https://www.usglc.org/.

93. Author's interview of John Glenn (October 5, 2017).

94. Ibid.

95. Author's interview of Diana Ohlbaum (July 18, 2017).

96. Author's interview of Dafna Rand (June 6, 2018).

97. Author's interview of Nilmini Rubin (August 2, 2017).

98. Author's interview of Mark Lagon (August 9, 2017).

99. Busby 2007.

100. ONE Leadership, https://www.one.org/us/about/leadership/.

101. Author's interview of Senate Democratic foreign policy aide (August 2017).

102. Amstutz 2014, 143–144.

103. Ibid., 159–165; see also Goldstein and Moss 2005.

104. Center for Responsive Politics, "PAC Profile: 150 PAC.org" (n.d.), https://www.open secrets.org/political-action-committees-pacs/C00614552/summary/2020.

105. Easterly 2006; Brett D. Schaefer, "Trump's Budget Grasps What Congress Doesn't: America's Global Leadership Doesn't Come Free," Heritage Foundation (May 29, 2017).

106. Author's interview of Diana Ohlbaum (July 18, 2017).

107. Ibid.

108. Alex Leary, "Long Time Florida Rep. Cliff Stearns Undone by His Own Party, Horse Doctor Ted Yoho," *Tampa Bay Times* (August 15, 2012).

109. See Project Vote Smart, "Ted Yoho's Ratings and Endorsements" (n.d.), https://votesmart.org/candidate/evaluations/137622/ted-yoho#.XI6MxyhKgdU.

110. Adva Saldinger, "Q&A: Representative Ted Yoho on His Foreign Aid Philosophy," Devex (February 24, 2017).

111. Alison Sherry, "Sixth District Rep. Tom Emmer's Eyes Opened on Congressional African Trip," *Star Tribune* (April 18, 2015).

112. Ibid.

113. Author's interview of Nilmini Rubin (August 2, 2017).

114. Author's interview of Steven Feldstein (August 4, 2017).

115. Author's interview of Nilmini Rubin (August 2, 2017); Consensus for Development Reform, "Mission Statement" (n.d.), http://www.developmentreform.org/.

116. For more information on MFAN, see http://modernizeaid.net/.

117. Author's interview of Lester Munson (June 22, 2022).

118. Norris and Veillette 2012.

119. Modernizing Foreign Assistance Network, "Reps. Crenshaw and Smith Announce Caucus for Effective Foreign Assistance," Press release (May 5, 2011).

120. Modernizing Foreign Assistance Network 2014, 2015.

121. David Beckmann, George Ingram, and Jim Kolbe, "Transforming Foreign Assistance," Brookings Institution (April 15, 2013).

122. Author's interview of executive branch official involved in foreign aid policy (March 2013).

123. Emily Cadei, "USAID's Shah Forges Unlikely Relationships with Conservative Members of Congress," *The Hill* (January 21, 2013); John Hudson, "USAID Administrator Rajiv Shah to Step Down," *Foreign Policy* (December 16, 2014).

124. Levine, Reinelt, and Kane 2017, 7–10.

125. Public Law 114-191, Foreign Aid Transparency and Accountability Act of 2016.

126. Public Law 115-254, Better Utilization of Investments Leading to Development (BUILD) Act of 2018.

Chapter 10

1. *The Economist*, "More Than Any President, Joe Biden Emphasized Unity at His Inauguration" (January 21, 2021).

2. On the informal influence of Congress in foreign policy, see Auerswald 2000; Howell and Pevehouse 2007; Kriner 2010.

3. Putnam 1988; Bennett 2002.

4. Jeffrey M. Jones, "Biden One Year Approval Ratings Subpar, Extremely Polarized," Gallup (January 18, 2022).

5. Senate Vote 110 and House Vote 72 on H.R. 1319, American Rescue Plan Act of 2021 (March 6 and March 10, 2021).

6. House Vote 260 and Senate Vote 459 on H.R. 4 and S. 4, John R. Lewis Voting Rights Advancement Act of 2021 (August 24, 2021, and November 3, 2021).

7. Senate Vote 134 on the Confirmation of Ketanji Brown Jackson as an Associate Justice of the Supreme Court of the United States (April 7, 2022).

8. Senate Vote 325 and House Vote 420 on H.R. 5376, Inflation Reduction Act of 2022 (August 7 and August 12, 2022).

9. Senate Vote 314 on H.R. 3684, Infrastructure Investment and Jobs Act (August 10, 2021).

10. House Vote 369 on H.R. 3684, Infrastructure Investment and Jobs Act (November 5, 2021).

11. Alexa Lardieri, "Majority of Americans Favor Increasing Infrastructure Spending, Poll Finds," U.S. News & World Report (July 22, 2021); Alana Abramson, "How a Coalition of Business and Labor Groups Helped Save the Infrastructure Bill," *Time* (July 30, 2021).

12. Curry and Lee 2020.
13. Domenico Montanaro, "5 Takeaways from Biden's State of the Union Address," NPR (March 2, 2022).
14. Jonathan Masters and Will Merrow, "How Much Aid Has the US Sent Ukraine? Here Are Six Charts," Council on Foreign Relations (last updated February 22, 2023).
15. Patricia Zengerle, "U.S. Congress Votes to Strip Russia of 'Most Favored' Trade Status, Ban Its Oil," Reuters (April 7, 2022).
16. Josh Rogin, "Biden Doesn't Want to Change China. He Wants to Beat It," *Washington Post* (February 13, 2022).
17. Senate Voice Vote and House Vote 412 on S. 65 and H.R. 1155, Uyghur Forced Labor Prevention Act (July 14, 2021, and December 8, 2021).
18. Amy B. Wang and Marianna Sotomayor, "House Passes Bill to Subsidize U.S-Made Semiconductor Chips in Win for Biden," *Washington Post* (July 28, 2022).
19. Luke Broadwater, "Lawmakers Rush to Help Afghans Seeking Visas for Helping the U.S.," *New York Times* (June 18, 2021); Senate Vote 287 and House Vote 250 on H.R. 3237, Emergency Security Supplemental Appropriations Act, 2021 (July 29, 2021).
20. Karoun Demirjian, "Senate Votes to Approve NATO Membership for Sweden and Finland," *New York Times* (August 3, 2022).
21. Benjamin J. Hulac, "Senate Approves Treaty That Would Limit Potent Greenhouse Gases," *Roll Call* (September 21, 2022).
22. Ibid.
23. Office of Senator Bob Menendez, "Chairman Menendez Celebrates Passage of State Department Authorization Bill," Press release (December 15, 2021); Rachel Oswald, "Vehicle for State Reauthorization Leaves Some Policy Goals Behind," *Roll Call* (December 20, 2021).
24. Andrew Desiderio and Connor O'Brien, "Partisan Lines Blur as Congress Tries to Curb Biden's War Powers," *Politico* (March 25, 2021); House Vote 172 on H.R. 256, To Repeal the Authorization for Use of Military Force against Iraq Resolution of 2002 (June 17, 2021); Andrew Desiderio and Connor O'Brien, "Push to Repeal Iraq War Powers Snags in Overloaded Senate," *Politico* (December 7, 2021); author's interview of Reid Smith (July 5, 2022); author's interview of congressional foreign policy aide (July 2022).
25. Maria Carrasco, "House Votes to Limit Arms Sales to Saudi Arabia over Khashoggi Killing," *Politico* (April 21, 2021).
26. Eduardo Medina, "The U.S. Senate Passes a Resolution Seeking to Label Russia as a State Sponsor of Terrorism," *New York Times* (July 28, 2022).
27. Patricia Zengerle, "U.S. Senators Introduce Bill to Designate Russian State Sponsor of Terrorism," Reuters (September 14, 2022).
28. John T. Bennett, "Pelosi Defies Biden, Pokes China with Taiwan Visit," *Roll Call* (August 2, 2022).
29. Jacob Knutson, "McConnell, 25 Senate Republicans Say They Support Pelosi's Taiwan Trip," *Axios* (August 2, 2022).
30. Andrew Desiderio, "U.S.-Taiwan Bill Sails Through Senate Panel Despite White House Misgivings," *Politico* (September 14, 2022).

31. Phil Stewart and Patricia Zengerle, "'Unmitigated Disaster': Republicans Attack Biden's Defense of Afghan Pullout," *Reuters* (September 29, 2021).

32. Ibid.

33. Haris Alic, "49 Senate Republicans Pledge to Reject Any New Iran Deal Negotiated by Biden," *Washington Times* (March 14, 2022).

34. Crabb 1957.

35. Tuttle 2022.

36. Martin 2000; Schultz 2001; Howell and Pevehouse 2007; Kupchan and Trubowitz 2007; Schultz 2017; Jervis et al. 2018; Kupchan and Trubowitz 2021; Myrick 2022.

37. Persily 2015; Drutman 2020; Page and Gilens 2020.

38. Theriault 2013; Wolfensberger 2018.

39. Persily 2015; Chergosky and Roberts 2018; Guenov and Ross 2018; Ross 2018; American Political Science Association 2019; Burgat 2019; Harbridge-Yong 2020b; Thomsen 2020; Bolton and Thrower 2022.

40. Alduncin, Parker, and Theriault 2017; Bordewich 2020; Curry and Roberts 2022.

41. Paul Kane, "Bipartisan Senate Lunch Crew Hopes to Do More Than Just Break Bread Together," *New York Times* (March 25, 2021).

42. Menachem Wecker, "Continuing Education for Congress: Building Trust and Expertise—To Get Things Done," *Carnegie Reporter* (Spring 2021); Bipartisan Policy Center, "American Congressional Exchange" (n.d.), https://bipartisanpolicy.org/proj ect/american-congressional-exchange/; Scott R. Anderson, "Congressional Study Group on Foreign Relations and National Security," Brookings Institution (December 30, 2020); Council on Foreign Relations, "Congress" (n.d.), https://www.cfr.org/ congress; Jean Parvin Bordewich, "Building Bipartisan Relationships in Congress," William-Flora Hewlett Foundation (April 17, 2020); Lugar Center, "University Project for Bipartisan Collaboration" (n.d.), https://www.thelugarcenter.org/ourw ork-Effective-Bipartisan-Governance.html; LegBranch.org, "About LegBranch" (n.d.), https://www.legbranch.org/about-legbranch/; Partnership for a Secure America, "Congressional Partnership Program" (n.d.), https://psaonline.org/congre ssional-partnership-program/; Woodrow Wilson Center, "Foreign Policy Fellowship Program" (n.d.), https://www.wilsoncenter.org/foreignpolicyfellowship.

43. Tama 2011; Binder and Lee 2015; Mansbridge and Martin 2016; Anderson, Butler, and Harbridge-Yong 2020.

44. Fowler 2015; Curry and Lee 2020.

45. Yglesias and Teles 2021.

46. Marianne Levine and Burgess Everett, "Latest Bipartisan Gang Tries to Save Senate from Itself," *Politico* (March 18, 2021).

47. Hurlburt and Polimédio 2016, 10.

48. Hurlburt and Polimédio 2016; Heaney 2017; Page and Gilens 2020.

49. Lugar Center, "Bipartisan Index" (n.d.), https://www.thelugarcenter.org/ourwork-Bipartisan-Index.html.

50. Paris 2017; Wolak 2020.

51. Harbridge, Malhotra, and Harrison 2014.

References

Aberbach, Joel D., and Bert A. Rockman. 2002. "Conducting and Coding Elite Interviews." *PS: Political Science & Politics* 35 (4): 673–676.

Abramowitz, Alan I. 2010. *The Disappearing Center: Engaged Citizens, Polarization, and American Democracy.* New Haven, CT: Yale University Press.

Abramowitz, Alan I. 2018. *The Great Alignment: Race, Party Transformation, and the Rise of Donald Trump.* New Haven, CT: Yale University Press.

Abramowitz, Alan I., and Steven Webster. 2016. "The Rise of Negative Partisanship and the Nationalization of US Elections in the 21st Century." *Electoral Studies* 41: 12–22.

Adams, Gordon. 1981. *The Politics of Defense Contracting: The Iron Triangle.* New Brunswick, NJ: Transaction.

Adams, Gordon, and Shoon Murray. 2014. *Mission Creep: The Militarization of US Foreign Policy?* Washington, DC: Georgetown University Press.

Adler, E. Scott, and John D. Wilkerson. 2012. *Congress and the Politics of Problem Solving.* New York: Cambridge University Press.

Aldrich, John H., Adam P. Brinegar, Claire V. Kramer, and Jennifer L. Merolla. 2006. *Tough Choices: Determinants of Senator's Trade Votes.* Institute of Governmental Studies, UC Berkeley.

Aldrich, John H., Christopher Gelpi, Peter Feaver, Jason Reifler, and Kristin Thompson Sharp. 2006. "Foreign Policy and the Electoral Connection." *Annual Review of Political Science* 9: 477–502.

Alduncin, Alex, David C. W. Parker, and Sean M. Theriault. 2017. "Leaving on a Jet Plane: Polarization, Foreign Travel, and Comity in Congress." *Congress and the Presidency* 44 (2): 179–200.

Alliance for Securing Democracy. 2020. *Linking Values and Strategy: How Democracies Can Offset Autocratic Advances.* Task Force Report, October.

Alvandi, Roham. 2014. *Nixon, Kissinger, and the Shah.* New York: Oxford University Press.

Ambrosio, Thomas, ed. 2002. *Ethnic Identity Groups and U.S. Foreign Policy.* Westport, CT: Praeger.

American Political Science Association. 2019. *Report of the Task Force Project on Congressional Reform,* October.

Amstutz, Mark R. 2014. *Evangelicals and American Foreign Policy.* Oxford: Oxford University Press.

Anderson, Sarah E., Daniel M. Butler, and Laurel Harbridge-Yong. 2020. *Rejecting Compromise: Legislators' Fear of Primary Voters.* New York: Cambridge University Press.

Arnold, Douglas R. 1990. *The Logic of Congressional Action.* New Haven, CT: Yale University Press.

Auerswald, David P. 2000. *Disarmed Democracies: Domestic Institutions and the Use of Force.* Ann Arbor: University of Michigan Press.

Auerswald, David P. 2012. "Arms Control." In *Congress and the Politics of National Security*, edited by David P. Auerswald and Colton C. Campbell, 189–212. New York: Cambridge University Press.

Auerswald, David P., and Colton C. Campbell, eds. 2012. *Congress and the Politics of National Security*. New York: Cambridge University Press.

Auerswald, David P., and Colton C. Campbell, eds. 2015. *Congress and Civil-Military Relations*. Washington, DC: Georgetown University Press.

Auerswald, David, and Forrest Maltzman. 2003. "Policymaking Through Advice and Consent: Treaty Consideration by the United States Senate." *Journal of Politics* 65 (4): 1097–1110.

Bader, Jeffrey A., and David Dollar. 2015. "Why the TPP Is the Linchpin of the Asia Rebalance." Brookings Institution, July 28.

Baker, Ross K. 2015. *Is Bipartisanship Dead? A Report from the Senate*. Boulder: Paradigm.

Baker, William D., and John R. Oneal. 2001. "Patriotism or Opinion Leadership? The Nature and Origins of the 'Rally 'Round the Flag' Effect." *Journal of Conflict Resolution* 45 (5): 661–687.

Baldassarri, Delia, and Andrew Gelman. 2008. "Partisans Without Constraint: Political Polarization and Trends in American Public Opinion." *American Journal of Sociology* 114 (2): 408–446.

Baldwin, Robert E. 1989. "The Political Economy of Trade Policy." *Journal of Economic Perspectives* 3 (4): 119–135.

Baldwin, Robert E., and Christopher S. Magee. 2000. "Is Trade Policy for Sale? Congressional Voting on Recent Trade Bills." *Policy Choice* 105 (1–2): 79–101.

Barber, Michael, and Nolan McCarty. 2016. "Causes and Consequences of Polarization." In *Political Negotiation: A Handbook*, edited by Jane Mansbridge and Cathie Jo Martin, 37–90. Washington, DC: Brookings Institution Press.

Bardes, Barbara A., and Robert W. Oldendick. 2017. *Public Opinion: Measuring the American Mind*. 5th ed. Lanham, MD: Rowman & Littlefield.

Barker, David C., and Elizabeth Suhay, eds. 2021. *The Politics of Truth in Polarized America*. New York: Oxford University Press.

Bartels, Larry M. 1991. "Constituency Opinion and Congressional Policy Making: The Reagan Defense Build Up." *American Political Science Review* 85 (2): 457–474.

Baum, Matthew A. 2002. "The Constituent Foundations of the Rally-Round-the-Flag Phenomenon." *International Studies Quarterly* 46 (2): 263–298.

Baum, Matthew A. 2004. "How Public Opinion Constrains the Use of Force: The Case of Operation Restore Hope." *Presidential Studies Quarterly* 34 (2): 187–226.

Baumgartner, Frank R., Jeffrey M. Berry, Marie Hojnacki, David C. Kimball, and Beth L. Leech. 2009. *Lobbying and Policy Change: Who Wins, Who Loses, and Why*. Chicago: University of Chicago Press.

Baumgartner, Frank R., and Beth L. Leech. 2001. "Interest Niches and Policy Bandwagons: Patterns of Interest Group Involvement in National Politics." *Journal of Politics* 63 (4): 1191–1213.

Bawm, Kathleen, Martin Cohen, David Karol, Seth Masket, Hans Noel, and John Zaller. 2012. "A Theory of Political Parties: Groups, Policy Demands and Nominations in American Politics." *Perspectives on Politics* 10 (3): 571–597.

Baylor, Christopher. 2017. *First to the Party: The Group Origins of Political Transformation*. Philadelphia: University of Pennsylvania Press.

Bendix, William, and Gyung-Ho Jeong. 2021. "The Polarization of the Defense and Foreign Policy Committees." In *Congress and U.S. Foreign Policy: Activism, Assertiveness, and Acquiescence in a Polarized Era*, edited by Ralph G. Carter and James M. Scott, 37–58. Lanham, MD: Rowman & Littlefield.

Bendix, William, and Gyung-Ho Jeong. 2022. "Beyond Party: Ideological Convictions and Foreign Policy Conflicts in the US Congress." *International Politics* 59 (5): 827–850.

Bennett, Andrew. 2002. "Who Rules the Roost? Congressional-Executive Relations on Foreign Policy After the Cold War." In *Eagle Rules? Foreign Policy and American Primacy in the 21st Century*, edited by Robert J. Lieber, 47–69. Upper Saddle River, NJ: Prentice Hall.

Bergen, Peter. 2019. *Trump and His Generals: The Cost of Chaos*. New York: Penguin Press.

Berinsky, Adam J. 2009. *In Time of War: Understanding American Public Opinion from World War II to Iraq*. Chicago: University of Chicago Press.

Berry, Jeffrey M., and Clyde Wilcox. 2009. *The Interest Group Society*. 5th ed. New York: Pearson.

Binder, Sarah. 2017. "Polarized We Govern?" In *Governing in a Polarized Age: Elections, Parties, and Political Representation in America*, edited by Alan S. Gerber and Eric Schickler, 223–242. New York: Cambridge University Press.

Binder, Sarah. 2020. "The Republican Senate Just Rebuked Trump Using the War Powers Act—For the Third Time. That's Remarkable." *Washington Post*, February 14.

Binder, Sarah A. 2003. *Stalemate: Causes and Consequences of Legislative Gridlock*. Washington, DC: Brookings Institution Press.

Binder, Sarah, James Goldgeier, and Elizabeth N. Saunders. 2020. "The Imperial Presidency Is Alive and Well." *Foreign Affairs*, January 21.

Binder, Sarah A., and Frances E. Lee. 2015. "Making Deals in Congress." In *Solutions to Political Polarization in America*, edited by Nathaniel Persily, 240–261. New York: Cambridge University Press.

Bipartisan Policy Center. 2012. *A Bull in Bear's Clothing: Russia, WTO and Jackson-Vanik*, January.

Bishin, Benjamin G. 2010. *Tyranny of the Minority: The Subconstituency Politics Theory of Representation*. Philadelphia: Temple University Press.

Böller, Florian. 2022. "Brakeman or Booster? Presidents, Ideological Polarization, Reciprocity, and the Politics of US Arms Control." *International Politics* 59 (4): 725–748.

Böller, Florian, and Lukas D. Herr. 2020. "From Washington Without Love: Congressional Foreign Policy Making and US-Russian Relations Under President Trump." *Contemporary Politics* 26 (1): 17–37.

Böller, Florian, and Marcus Müller. 2018. "Unleashing the Watchdogs: Explaining Congressional Assertiveness in the Politics of US Military Interventions." *European Political Science Review* 10 (4): 637–662.

Bolton, Alexander, and Sharece Thrower. 2022. *Checks in the Balance: Legislative Capacity and the Dynamics of Executive Power*. Princeton: Princeton University Press.

Bolton, John. 2020. *The Room Where It Happened: A White House Memoir*. New York: Simon & Schuster.

Bonica, Adam. 2013. "Ideology and Interests in the Political Marketplace." *American Journal of Political Science* 57 (2): 294–311.

Bonica, Adam. 2014. "Mapping the Ideological Marketplace." *American Journal of Political Science* 58 (2): 367–386.

Bordewich, Jean Parvin. 2020. "Building Bipartisan Relationships in Congress." William-Flora Hewlett Foundation, April 17.

Boucher, Jean-Christophe, and Cameron G. Thies. 2019. "'I Am a Tariff Man:' The Power of Populist Foreign Policy Rhetoric Under President Trump." *Journal of Politics* 81 (2): 712–722.

Brady, David W. 2011. "Public Opinion and Congressional Policy." In *The Oxford Handbook of the American Congress*, edited by Eric Schickler and Frances E. Lee, 340–354. Oxford: Oxford University Press.

Bresolin, Justin. 2014. *The Nunn-Lugar Cooperative Threat Reduction Program.* Center for Arms Control and Nonproliferation, June.

Broockman, David E., and Christopher Skovron. 2018. "Bias in Perceptions of Public Opinion Among Political Elites." *American Political Science Review* 112 (3): 542–563.

Browder, Bill. 2015. *Red Notice: A True Story of High Finance, Murder, and One Man's Fight for Justice.* New York: Simon & Schuster.

Broz, J. Lawrence. 2011. "The United States Congress and IMF Financing, 1944–2009." *Review of International Organizations* 6: 341–368.

Broz, J. Lawrence, and Michael Brewster Hawes. 2006. "Congressional Politics of Financing the International Monetary Fund." *International Organization* 60 (2): 367–399.

Bruck, Connie. 2014. "Friends of Israel." *The New Yorker*, September 1, 50–63.

Bryan, James, and Jordan Tama. 2022. "The Prevalence of Bipartisanship in U.S. Foreign Policy: An Analysis of Important Congressional Votes." *International Politics* 59 (5): 874–898.

Burgat, Casey. 2019. *Congressional Undersight.* R Street Policy Study No. 188.

Burns, Sarah. 2020. *The Politics of War Powers: The Theory and History of Presidential Unilateralism.* Lawrence: University Press of Kansas.

Burns, Sarah, and Andrew Stravers. 2020. "Obama, Congress, and Audience Costs: Shifting the Blame on the Red Line." *Political Science Quarterly* 135 (1): 67–101.

Burns, William J. 2019. *The Back Channel: A Memoir of American Diplomacy and the Case for Its Renewal.* New York: Random House.

Busby, Joshua, Craig Kafura, Jonathan Monten, and Jordan Tama. 2020. "Multilateralism and the Use of Force: Experimental Evidence on the Views of Foreign Policy Elites." *Foreign Policy Analysis* 16 (1): 118–129.

Busby, Joshua, Craig Kafura, Dina Smeltz, Jordan Tama, Jonathan Monten, Joshua D. Kertzer, and Brendan Helm. 2020. *Coming Together or Coming Apart? Attitudes of Foreign Policy Opinion Leaders and the Public in the Trump Era.* Chicago Council on Global Affairs.

Busby, Joshua William. 2007. "Bono Made Jesse Helms Cry: Jubilee 2000, Debt Relief, and Moral Action in International Politics." *International Studies Quarterly* 51 (2): 247–275.

Cameron, Charles M. 2000. *Veto Bargaining: Presidents and the Politics of Negative Power.* New York: Cambridge University Press.

Campbell, Kurt, and Brian Andrews. 2013. *Explaining the US "Pivot" to Asia.* Chatham House.

Canes-Wrone, Brandice. 2006. *Who Leads Whom? Presidents, Policy, and the Public.* Chicago: University of Chicago Press.

Canes-Wrone, Brandice, William G. Howell, and David E. Lewis. 2008. "Toward a Broader Understanding of Presidential Power: A Reevaluation of the Two Presidencies Thesis." *Journal of Politics* 70 (1): 1–16.

Carcelli, Shannon. 2022. "Congressional Polarization and Limitation Riders in Foreign Aid Appropriations." *International Politics* 59 (5): 898–924.

Carmines, Edward G., and Nicholas J. D'Amico. 2015. "The New Look in Political Ideology Research." *Annual Review of Political Science* 18: 205–216.

Carrubba, Clifford J., Matthew Gabel, Lacey Murrah, Ryan Clough, Elizabeth Montgomery, and Rebecca Schambach. 2006. "Off the Record: Unrecorded Legislative Votes, Selection Bias and Roll-Call Vote Analysis." *British Journal of Political Science* 36 (4): 691–704.

Carter, Ralph G., and James M. Scott. 2009. *Choosing to Lead: Understanding Congressional Foreign Policy Entrepreneurs.* Durham, NC: Duke University Press.

Carter, Ralph G., and James M. Scott. 2021a. "Conclusion: Patterns and Prospects." In *Congress and U.S. Foreign Policy: Activism, Assertiveness, and Acquiescence in a Polarized Era*, edited by Ralph G. Carter and James M. Scott, 195–203. Lanham, MD: Rowman & Littlefield.

Carter, Ralph G., and James M. Scott, eds. 2021b. *Congress and U.S. Foreign Policy: Activism, Assertiveness, and Acquiescence in a Polarized Era.* Lanham, MD: Rowman & Littlefield.

Carter, Ralph G., and James M. Scott. 2021c. "Opening Windows in Shrinking Spaces: Polarization and Congressional Foreign Policy Entrepreneurship." In *Congress and U.S. Foreign Policy: Activism, Assertiveness, and Acquiescence in a Polarized Era*, edited by Ralph G. Carter and James M. Scott, 123–139. Lanham, MD: Rowman & Littlefield.

Caruson, Kiki, and Victoria A. Farrar-Myers. 2007. "Promoting the President's Foreign Policy Agenda: Presidential Use of Executive Agreements as Policy Vehicles." *Political Research Quarterly* 60 (4): 631–644.

Cato Institute. 2017. *Cato Handbook for Policymakers.* 8th ed. Washington, DC: Cato Institute.

Chaudoin, Stephen, Helen V. Milner, and Dustin Tingley. 2021. "'America First' Meets Liberal Internationalism." H-Diplo/ISSF Policy Series, America and the World: The Effects of the Trump Presidency.

Chaudoin, Stephen, Helen V. Milner, and Dustin H. Tingley. 2010. "The Center Still Holds: Liberal Internationalism Survives." *International Security* 35 (1): 75–94.

Chergosky, Antony J., and Jason M. Roberts. 2018. "The De-Institutionalization of Congress." *Political Science Quarterly* 133 (3): 475–495.

Chollet, Derek. 2016. *The Long Game: How Obama Defied Washington and Redefined America's Role in the World.* New York: Public Affairs.

Chollet, Derek, and Tod Lindberg. 2008. "Bridging the Foreign Policy Divide." In *Bridging the Foreign Policy Divide: Liberals and Conservatives Find Common Ground on 10 Key Global Challenges*, edited by Derek Chollet, Tod Lindberg and David Shorr, 1–7. New York: Routledge.

Christenson, Dino P., and Douglas L. Kriner. 2020. *The Myth of the Imperial Presidency: How Public Opinion Checks the Unilateral Executive.* Chicago: University of Chicago Press.

Citrin, Jack, and John Sides. 2008. "Immigration and the Imagined Community in Europe and the United States." *Political Studies* 56 (1): 33–56.

Clinton, Hillary. 2011. "America's Pacific Century." *Foreign Policy* 189: 56–63.

Clinton, Hillary. 2014. *Hard Choices.* New York: Simon and Schuster.

Cohen, Jeffrey E. 2019. *The President on Capitol Hill: A Theory of Institutional Influence.* New York: Columbia University Press.

Collier, Ellen C. 2011. *Bipartisanship and the Making of Foreign Policy: A Historical Survey*. Second ed. United States: Xlibris.

Congressional Quarterly. 1935. "American Policy on the League of Nations and the World Court." Editorial Research Reports. Washington, DC: CQ Press.

Congressional Quarterly. 1996. "Law Hits Trade with Iran, Libya." In *CQ Almanac 1996*. 52nd ed., Chapter 9, 5–6. Washington, DC: Congressional Quarterly Inc.

Congressional Quarterly. 1998. "Clinton Vetoes Iran Sanctions but Vows to Punish Russians for Aiding Iranian Military." In *CQ Almanac 1998*. 54th ed., Chapter 16, 16–23. Washington, DC: Congressional Quarterly Inc.

Congressional Quarterly. 2000. "Lawmakers Seek to Curb Russian Involvement in Iran's Weapons Program." In *CQ Almanac 2000*. 56th ed., Chapter 11, 10–14. Washington, DC: Congressional Quarterly Inc.

Congressional Quarterly. 2001. "Iran-Libya Sanctions Extended." In *CQ Almanac 2001*. 57th ed., Chapter 11, 6–7. Washington, DC: Congressional Quarterly Inc.

Congressional Research Service. 2013. *The Budget Control Act, Sequestration, and the Foreign Affairs Budget: Background and Possible Impacts*, December 20.

Congressional Research Service. 2019a. *Trade Promotion Authority (TPA): Frequently Asked Questions*, June 21.

Congressional Research Service. 2019b. *Trump Administration Tariff Actions (Sections 201, 232, and 301): Frequently Asked Questions*, February 22.

Congressional Research Service. 2020. *U.S. Sanctions on Russia*, January 17.

Congressional Research Service. 2021. *Department of State, Foreign Operations, and Related Programs: FY2021 Budget and Appropriations*, September 24.

Coons, Chris. 2020. "A Bipartisan Foreign Policy Is Still Possible." *Foreign Affairs*, October 7.

Cooper, Joseph, and Garry Young. 1997. "Partisanship, Bipartisanship, and Crosspartisanship in Congress and the New Deal." In *Congress Reconsidered*, edited by Lawrence C. Dodd and Bruce I. Oppenheimer, 246–273. Washington, DC: CQ Press.

Crabb, Cecil V., Jr. 1957. *Bipartisan Foreign Policy: Myth or Reality?* Evanston, IL: Row, Peterson.

Cronin, Patrick, and Benjamin O. Fordham. 1999. "Timeless Principles or Today's Fashion? Testing the Stability of the Linkage Between Ideology and Foreign Policy in the Senate." *Journal of Politics* 61 (4): 967–998.

Crouch, Jeffrey, Mark J. Rozell, and Mitchel A. Sollenberger. 2020. *The Unitary Executive Theory: A Danger to Constitutional Government*. Lawrence: University Press of Kansas.

Curry, James M., and Frances E. Lee. 2020. *The Limits of Party: Congress and Lawmaking in a Polarized Era*. Chicago: University of Chicago Press.

Curry, James M., and Jason M. Roberts. 2022. "Interpersonal Relationships and Legislative Collaboration in Congress." *Legislative Studies Quarterly*. DOI: https://doi.org/10.1111/lsq.12381.

Cutrone, Ellen A., and Benjamin O. Fordham. 2010. "Commerce and Imagination: The Sources of Concern About International Human Rights in the U.S. Congress." *International Studies Quarterly* 54 (3): 633–655.

Daugirdas, Kristina, and Julian Davis Mortensen. 2017. "Congress Overrides Obama's Veto to Pass Justice Against Sponsors of Terrorism Act." *American Journal of International Law* 111 (1): 156–162.

David, Charles-Philippe. 2020. *L'Effet Trump: Quel Impact sur la Politique Etrangère des Etats-Unis?* Montréal: Les Presses de l'Université de Montréal.

Davidson, Roger H., Walter J. Oleszek, Frances E. Lee, and Eric Schickler. 2018. *Congress and Its Members*. 16th ed. Thousand Oaks, CA: CQ Press.

Dearborn, John A. 2021. *Power Shifts: Congress and Presidential Representation*. Chicago: University of Chicago Press.

Deering, Christopher J., and Steven S. Smith. 1997. *Committees in Congress*. 3rd ed. Washington, DC: Congressional Quarterly Inc.

Deibel, Terry. 2002. "The Death of a Treaty." *Foreign Affairs* 81 (5): 142–161.

DeLaet, C. James, and James M. Scott. 2006. "Treaty-Making and Partisan Politics: Arms Control and the U.S. Senate, 1960–2001." *Foreign Policy Analysis* 2 (2): 177–200.

Destler, I. M. 2005. *American Trade Politics*. 4th ed. Washington, DC: Institute for International Economics.

Destler, I. M., Leslie H. Gelb, and Anthony Lake. 1984. *Our Own Worst Enemy: The Unmaking of American Foreign Policy*. New York: Simon & Schuster.

Destler, I. M., and C. Randall Henning. 1989. *Dollar Politics: Exchange Rate Policymaking in the United States*. Washington, DC: Institute for International Economics.

DeWind, Josh, and Renata Segura, eds. 2014. *Diaspora Lobbies and the US Government: Convergence and Divergence in Making Foreign Policy*. New York: New York University Press.

Dieck, Hélène. 2014. "The United States and the Syrian Crisis: The Influence of Public Opinion on the Non-Intervention Policy." *Sciences-Po Centre de Recherches Internationales*, January 1.

Drezner, Daniel W. 2008. "The Realist Tradition in American Public Opinion." *Perspectives on Politics* 6 (1): 51–70.

Drezner, Daniel W. 2015. "Will Congress Approve the Trans-Pacific Partnership?" *Washington Post*, October 6.

Drezner, Daniel W. 2019a. "Charles Koch and George Soros Teamed up on a New Foreign-Policy Think Tank. I Have Questions." *Washington Post*, July 11.

Drezner, Daniel W. 2019b. "This Time Is Different: Why U.S. Foreign Policy Will Never Recover." *Foreign Affairs* 98 (3): 10–17.

Drutman, Lee. 2020. *Breaking the Two-Party Doom Loop: The Case for Multiparty Democracy in America*. New York: Oxford University Press.

Dueck, Colin. 2010. *Hard Line: The Republican Party and U.S. Foreign Policy Since World War II*. Princeton: Princeton University Press.

Dueck, Colin. 2020. *Age of Iron: On Conservative Nationalism*. Oxford: Oxford University Press.

Easterly, William. 2006. *The White Man's Burden: Why the West's Efforts to Aid the Rest Have Done So Much Ill and So Little Good*. New York: Penguin Press.

Edelson, Chris. 2016. *Power Without Constraint: The Post-9/11 Presidency and National Security*. Madison: University of Wisconsin Press.

Ellis, Christopher, and James A. Stimson. 2012. *Ideology in America*. New York: Cambridge University Press.

Elms, Deborah. 2016. "The Origins and Evolution of the Trans-Pacific Partnership Trade Negotiations." *Asian Survey* 56 (6): 1017–1039.

Erikson, Robert S., Michael B. MacKuen, and James A. Stimson. 2002. *The Macro Polity*. Cambridge: Cambridge University Press.

Esterberg, Kristin G. 2002. *Qualitative Methods in Social Research*. Boston: McGraw-Hill.

Facchini, Giovanni, Anna Maria Mayda, and Prachi Mishra. 2011. "Do Interest Groups Affect US Immigration Policy?" *Journal of International Economics* 85 (1): 114–128.

Fenno, Richard F., Jr. 1973. *Congressmen in Committees*. Boston: Little, Brown.

Fergusson, Ian F., and Brock R. Williams. 2016. *The Trans-Pacific Partnership (TPP): Key Provisions and Issues for Congress*. Congressional Research Service, June 14.

Fiorina, Morris P., and Samuel J. Abrams. 2008. "Political Polarization in the American Public." *Annual Review of Political Science* 11: 563–588.

Fisher, Louis. 2000. *Congressional Abdication on War and Spending*. College Station: Texas A&M University Press.

Fisher, Louis. 2015. "Closing Guantánamo: A Presidential Commitment Unfulfilled." In *Congress and Civil-Military Relations*, edited by Colton C. Campbell and David P. Auerswald, 148–165. Washington, DC: Georgetown University Press.

Fleisher, Richard, Jon Bond, Glen Krutz, and Stephen Hanna. 2000. "The Demise of the Two Presidencies." *American Politics Quarterly* 28 (1): 3–25.

Flores-Macías, Gustavo A., and Sarah E. Kreps. 2013. "Political Parties at War: A Study of American War Finance, 1789–2010." *American Political Science Review* 107 (4): 833–848.

Flynn, Michael E. 2014. "The International and Domestic Sources of Bipartisanship in U.S. Foreign Policy." *Political Research Quarterly* 67 (2): 398–412.

Foran, Clare. 2017. "Trump's Support from Democrats on Syria." *The Atlantic*, April 7.

Fordham, Benjamin O. 1998. "Economic Interests, Party and Ideology in Early Cold War Era U.S. Foreign Policy." *International Organization* 52 (2): 359–396.

Fordham, Benjamin O., and Katja B. Kleinberg. 2012. "How Can Economic Interests Influence Support for Free Trade?" *International Organization* 66 (2): 311–328.

Fordham, Benjamin O., and Michael Flynn. 2022. "Everything Old Is New Again: The Persistence of Republican Opposition to Multilateralism in American Foreign Policy." *Studies in American Political Development*. DOI: https://doi.org/10.1017/S0898588x2 2000165.

Fordham, Benjamin O., and Timothy J. McKeown. 2003. "Selection and Influence: Interest Groups and Congressional Voting on Trade Policy." *International Organization* 57 (3): 519–549.

Forsythe, David P. 1987. "Congress and Human Rights in US Foreign Policy: The Fate of General Legislation." *Human Rights Quarterly* 9: 382–404.

Fowler, Linda L. 2015. *Watchdogs on the Hill: The Decline of Congressional Oversight of U.S. Foreign Relations*. Princeton: Princeton University Press.

Fowler, Linda L. 2021. "The Continued Decline of Congressional Oversight of U.S. Foreign Policy." In *Congress and U.S. Foreign Policy: Activism, Assertiveness, and Acquiescence in a Polarized Era*, edited by Ralph G. Carter and James M. Scott, 59–79. Lanham, MD: Rowman & Littlefield.

Foyle, Douglas C. 2012. "Vox Populi as a Foundation for Foreign Policy Renewal? Unity and Division in Post-Bush Administration Public Opinion." In *U.S. Foreign Policy Today: American Renewal?*, edited by Steven W. Hook and James M. Scott, 54–76. Washington, DC: CQ Press.

Franck, Thomas M., and Edward Weisband. 1979. *Foreign Policy by Congress*. New York: Oxford University Press.

Freeman, Gary P., and Stuart M. Tendler. 2012. "Interest Group Politics and Immigration Policy." In *Oxford Handbook of the Politics of International Migration*, edited by Mark R. Rosenblum and Daniel J. Tichenor, 324–344. New York: Oxford University Press.

Friedrichs, Gordon M. 2021. *U.S. Global Leadership Role and Domestic Polarization: A Role Theory Approach*. New York: Routledge.

Friedrichs, Gordon M. 2022. "Polarized We Trade? Intraparty Polarization and US Trade Policy." *International Politics* 59 (5): 956–980.

Friedrichs, Gordon M., and Jordan Tama. 2022. "Polarization and US Foreign Policy: Key Debates and New Findings." *International Politics* 59 (5): 767–785.

Friedman, Jeffrey A. 2022. "Are the Political Foundations of Deep Engagement Eroding? Party Polarization and U.S. Grand Strategy, 1948–2020." Working paper.

Gagnon, Frédéric. 2018. "The Most Dynamic Club: Vandenberg, Fulbright, Helms, and the Activism of the Chairman of the US Senate Foreign Relations Committee." *Foreign Policy Analysis* 14 (2): 191–211.

Garcia, Michael John. 2009. *NATO Enlargement: Senate Advice and Consent.* Congressional Research Service.

Garrett, Stephen A. 1978. "Eastern European Ethnic Groups and American Foreign Policy." *Political Science Quarterly* 93 (2): 301–323.

Gibson, Martha L. 2000. *Conflict Amid Consensus in American Trade Policy.* Washington, DC: Georgetown University Press.

Gilens, Martin, and Benjamin I. Page. 2014. "Testing Theories of American Politics: Elites, Interest Groups, and Average Citizens." *Perspectives on Politics* 12 (3): 564–581.

Gimpel, James G., Frances E. Lee, and Michael Parrott. 2014. "Business Interests and the Party Coalitions: Industry Sector Contributions to U.S. Congressional Campaigns." *American Politics Research* 42 (6): 1034–1076.

Glennon, Michael J. 2015. *National Security and Double Government.* Oxford: Oxford University Press.

Goldberg, Jeffrey. 2016. "The Obama Doctrine." *The Atlantic,* April.

Goldgeier, James. 2019. "NATO at 70: Is the USA Still in It for the Long Haul?" *Journal of Transatlantic Studies* 17: 255–267.

Goldgeier, James, and Elizabeth N. Saunders. 2018. "The Unconstrained Presidency: Checks and Balances Eroded Long Before Trump." *Foreign Affairs* 97 (5): 144–156.

Goldstein, Markus P., and Todd J. Moss. 2005. "Compassionate Conservatives or Conservative Compassionates? US Political Parties and Bilateral Foreign Assistance to Africa." *Journal of Development Studies* 41 (7): 1288–1302.

Gries, Peter Hays. 2014. *The Politics of American Foreign Policy: How Ideology Divides Liberals and Conservatives over Foreign Affairs.* Stanford: Stanford University Press.

Groeling, Tim, and Matthew A. Baum. 2008. "Crossing the Water's Edge: Elite Rhetoric, Media Coverage, and the Rally-Round-the-Flag Phenomenon." *Journal of Politics* 70 (4): 1065–1085.

Grossman, Matt. 2009. "Who Gets What Now? Interest Groups under Obama." *The Forum* 7 (1).

Grossman, Matt. 2012. "Interest Group Influence on US Policy Change: An Assessment Based on Policy History." *Interest Groups & Advocacy* 1: 171–192.

Grossman, Matt, and David A. Hopkins. 2016. *Asymmetric Politics: Ideological Republicans and Group Interest Democrats.* New York: Oxford University Press.

Guenov, Tressa, and Tommy Ross. 2018. "At a Crossroads, Part I: How Congress Can Find Its Way Back to Effective Defense Oversight." *War on the Rocks,* March 9.

Guisinger, Alexandra. 2009. "Determining Trade Policy: Do Voters Hold Politicians Accountable?" *International Organization* 63 (3): 533–557.

Guisinger, Alexandra. 2017. *American Opinion on Trade: Preferences Without Politics.* New York: Oxford University Press.

Guisinger, Alexandra, and Elizabeth N. Saunders. 2017. "Mapping the Boundaries of Elite Cues: How Elites Shape Mass Opinion Across International Issues." *International Studies Quarterly* 61 (2): 425–441.

Haesebrouck, Tim, and Patrick Mello. 2020. "Patterns of Political Ideology and Security Policy." *Foreign Policy Analysis* 16 (4): 565–586.

Hafner-Burton, Emilie M., Thad Kousser, and David G. Victor. 2015. *Lobbying at the Water's Edge: Corporations and Congressional Foreign Policy Lobbying.* Working Paper No. 22, Laboratory on International Law and Regulation.

Hammer, Bettina, and Craig Kafura. 2019. *Republicans and Democrats in Different Worlds on Immigration.* Chicago Council on Global Affairs.

Harbridge, Laurel. 2015. *Is Bipartisanship Dead? Policy Agreement and Agenda-Setting in the House of Representatives.* New York: Cambridge University Press.

Harbridge, Laurel, Neil Malhotra, and Brian F. Harrison. 2014. "Public Preferences for Bipartisanship in the Policymaking Process." *Legislative Studies Quarterly* 39 (3): 327–355.

Harbridge-Yong, Laurel. 2020a. "The Challenges of Partisan Conflict for Lawmaking in Congress." In *New Directions in Congressional Politics*, edited by Jamie L. Carson and Michael S. Lynch, 187–205. New York: Routledge.

Harbridge-Yong, Laurel. 2020b. "Congressional Capacity and Bipartisanship in Congress." In *Congress Overwhelmed: The Decline in Congressional Capacity and Prospects for Reform*, edited by Timothy M. LaPira, Lee Drutman and Kevin R. Kosar, 239–252. Chicago: University of Chicago Press.

Harrell, Peter. 2019. *Reforming National Security Tariff Tools: Issues and Recommendations for Policymakers.* Center for a New American Security, June 27.

Hartley, Thomas, and Bruce Russett. 1992. "Public Opinion and the Common Defense: Who Governs Military Spending in the United States?" *American Political Science Review* 86 (4): 905–915.

Hatipoglu, Emre. 2014. "A Story of Institutional Misfit: Congress and US Economic Sanctions." *Foreign Policy Analysis* 10 (4): 431–445.

Heaney, Michael T. 2012. "Bridging the Gap Between Political Parties and Interest Groups." In *Interest Group Politics*, edited by Allan J. Cigler and Burdett A. Loomis, 194–218. Washington, DC: CQ Press.

Heaney, Michael T. 2017. "Activism in an Era of Partisan Polarization." *PS: Political Science & Politics* 50 (4): 1000–1003.

Helderman, Rosalind S., and Matt Zapotosky. 2019. "Introduction: A President, a Prosecutor, and the Protection of American Democracy." In *The Mueller Report*, edited by Washington Post, 9–27. New York: Scribner.

Hendrickson, Ryan C. 2015. *Obama at War: Congress and the Imperial Presidency.* Lexington: University Press of Kentucky.

Hermann, Richard K., Philip E. Tetlock, and Matthew N. Diascro. 2001. "How Americans Think About Trade: Reconciling Conflicts Among Money, Power, and Principles." *International Studies Quarterly* 45 (2): 191–218.

Hertzke, Allen D. 2004. *Freeing God's Children: The Unlikely Alliance for Global Human Rights.* Lanham, MD: Rowman & Littlefield.

Hicks, Kathleen. 2017. "Now What? The American Citizen, World Order, and Building a New Foreign Policy Consensus." *Texas National Security Review* 1 (1): 108–119.

Hicks, Kathleen H., Louis Lauter, and Colin McElhinny. 2018. *Beyond the Water's Edge: Measuring the Internationalism of Congress*. Center for Strategic and International Studies.

Hildebrandt, Timothy, Courtney Hillebrecht, Peter M. Holm, and Jon Pevehouse. 2013. "The Domestic Politics of Humanitarian Intervention: Public Opinion, Partisanship, and Ideology." *Foreign Policy Analysis* 9 (3): 243–266.

Hinckley, Barbara. 1994. *Less Than Meets the Eye: Foreign Policy Making and the Myth of the Assertive Congress*. Chicago: University of Chicago Press.

Hiscox, Michael J. 2002. *International Trade and Political Conflict: Commerce, Coalitions, and Mobility*. Princeton: Princeton University Press.

Holsti, Ole R. 2004. *Public Opinion and American Foreign Policy*. Ann Arbor: University of Michigan Press.

Homan, Patrick, and Jeffrey S. Lantis. 2020. *The Battle for U.S. Foreign Policy: Congress, Parties, and Factions in the 21st Century*. Cham, Switzerland: Palgrave Macmillan.

Howell, William G. 2003. *Power Without Persuasion: The Politics of Direct Presidential Action*. Princeton: Princeton University Press.

Howell, William G. 2013. "Count on Congress: The Logic of Handing Syria over to the Lawmakers." *Foreign Affairs*, September 3.

Howell, William G., Saul P. Jackman, and Jon C. Rogowski. 2013. *The Wartime President*. Chicago: University of Chicago Press.

Howell, William G., and Terry M. Moe. 2021. "America's Crisis of Democracy." *Political Science Quarterly* 136 (1): 105–127.

Howell, William G., and Jon C. Pevehouse. 2007. *While Dangers Gather: Congressional Checks on Presidential War Powers*. Princeton: Princeton University Press.

Hufbauer, Gary Clyde, Jeffrey J. Schott, Kimberly Ann Elliott, and Barbara Oegg. 2009. *Economic Sanctions Reconsidered*. 3rd ed. Washington, DC: Peterson Institute for International Economics.

Human Rights Watch. 2015. *If the Dead Could Speak: Mass Deaths and Torture in Syria's Detention Facilities*. December 16.

Hurlburt, Heather, and Chayenne Polimédio. 2016. *Can Transpartisan Coalitions Overcome Polarization: Lessons from Four Case Studies*. New America.

Hurst, Steven. 2016. "The Iranian Nuclear Negotiations as a Two-Level Game: The Importance of Domestic Politics." *Diplomacy & Statecraft* 27 (3): 545–567.

Hurst, Steven, and Andrew Wroe. 2016. "Partisan Polarization and US Foreign Policy: Is the Centre Dead or Holding?" *International Politics* 53 (5): 666–682.

Hurwitz, Jon, and Mark Peffley. 1987. "How Are Foreign Attitudes Structured? A Hierarchical Model." *American Political Science Review* 81 (4): 1099–1120.

Ingber, Rebecca. 2020. "Congressional Administration of Foreign Affairs." *Virginia Law Review* 106 (2): 395–465.

Iyengar, Shanto, Yphtach Lelkes, Matthew Levendusky, Neil Malhotra, and Sean J. Westwood. 2019. "The Origins and Consequences of Affective Polarization in the United States." *Annual Review of Political Science* 22: 129–146.

Iyengar, Shanto, and Sean J. Westwood. 2015. "Fear and Loathing Across Party Lines: New Evidence on Group Polarization." *American Journal of Political Science* 59 (3): 690–707.

Jacobs, Lawrence R., and Benjamin I. Page. 2005. "Who Influences U.S. Foreign Policy?" *American Political Science Review* 99 (1): 107–123.

Jacobson, Gary C. 2013. "Partisan Polarization in American Politics: A Background Paper." *Presidential Studies Quarterly* 43 (4): 688–708.

Jacobson, Michael. 2008. "Sanctions Against Iran: A Promising Struggle." *Washington Quarterly* 31 (3): 69–88.

Jentleson, Adam. 2021. *Kill Switch: The Rise of the Modern Senate and the Crippling of American Democracy*. New York: Liveright.

Jentleson, Bruce W. 1992. "The Pretty Prudent Public: Post Post-Vietnam American Opinion on the Use of Military Force." *International Studies Quarterly* 36 (1): 49–73.

Jeong, Gyung-Ho, and Paul J. Quirk. 2019. "Division at the Water's Edge: The Polarization of Foreign Policy." *American Politics Research* 47 (1): 58–87.

Jervis, Robert, Francis J. Gavin, Joshua Rovner, and Diane N. Labrosse. 2018. *Chaos in the Liberal Order: The Trump Presidency and International Politics in the Twenty-First Century*. New York: Columbia University Press.

Jochim, Ashley E., and Bryan D. Jones. 2013. "Issue Politics in a Polarized Congress." *Political Research Quarterly* 66 (2): 352–369.

Johnson, Robert David. 2006. *Congress and the Cold War*. Cambridge: Cambridge University Press.

Kaempfer, William H., and Anton D. Lowenberg. 2000. "A Public Choice Analysis of the Political Economy of International Sanctions." In *Sanctions as Economic Statecraft: Theory and Practice*, edited by Steve Chan and A. Cooper Drury, 158–186. New York: Palgrave.

Kafura, Craig. 2018. *Public Support for Foreign Aid Programs*. Chicago Council on Global Affairs.

Kagan, Kimberly. 2013. "The Smart and Right Thing in Syria." *Strategika* 1: 11–13.

Kandel, Maya. 2010. "Une Diplomatie des Diasporas? La Mobilisation des Diasporas 'Yougoslaves' aux États-Unis et Leur Influence sur la Politique Étrangère Américaine Pendant les Guerres Balkaniques des Années 1990." *Relations Internationales* 1: 83–97.

Karol, David. 2000. "Divided Government and US Trade Policy: Much Ado About Nothing?" *International Organization* 54 (4): 825–844.

Karol, David. 2009. *Party Position Change in American Politics: Coalition Management*. New York: Cambridge University Press.

Karol, David. 2015. "Party Activists, Interest Groups, and Polarization in American Politics." In *American Gridlock: The Sources, Character, and Impact of Political Polarization*, edited by James A. Thurber and Antoine Yoshinaka, 68–85. New York: Cambridge University Press.

Karol, David. 2019. *Red, Green, and Blue: The Partisan Divide on Environmental Issues*. Cambridge, UK: Cambridge University Press.

Kaufman, Zachary D. 2019. "Legislating Atrocity Prevention." *Harvard Journal on Legislation* 57: 163–218.

Kelley, Judith G., and Jon C. W. Pevehouse. 2015. "An Opportunity Cost Theory of US Treaty Behavior." *International Studies Quarterly* 59: 531–543.

Kerry, John. 2018. *Every Day Is Extra*. New York: Simon & Schuster.

Kertzer, Joshua D. 2022. "Reassessing Elite-Public Gaps in Political Behavior." *American Journal of Political Science* 66 (3): 539–553.

Kertzer, Joshua D., Deborah Jordan Brooks, and Stephen G. Brooks. 2021. "Do Partisan Types Stop at the Water's Edge?" *Journal of Politics* 83 (4): 1764–1782.

Kertzer, Joshua D., Kathleen E. Powers, Brian Rathbun, and Ravi Iyer. 2014. "Moral Support: How Moral Values Shape Foreign Policy Attitudes." *Journal of Politics* 76 (3): 825–840.

Kertzer, Joshua D., and Thomas Zeitzoff. 2017. "A Bottom-Up Theory of Public Opinion About Foreign Policy." *American Journal of Political Science* 61 (3): 543–558.

Klein, Ezra. 2020. *Why We're Polarized*. New York: Simon & Schuster.

Kosar, Kevin, ed. 2020. *Congress and Foreign Affairs: Reasserting the Power of the First Branch*. R Street.

Krasner, Stephen D. 1978. *Defending the National Interest: Raw Materials Investments and U.S. Foreign Policy*. Princeton: Princeton University Press.

Krebs, Ronald R. 2015. "How Dominant Narratives Rise and Fall: Military Conflict, Politics, and the Cold War Consensus." *International Organization* 69 (4): 809–845.

Kreps, Sarah E. 2018. *Taxing Wars: The American Way of War Finance and the Decline of Democracy*. New York: Oxford University Press.

Kreps, Sarah E., Elizabeth N. Saunders, and Kenneth A. Schultz. 2018. "The Ratification Premium: Hawks, Doves, and Arms Control." *World Politics* 70 (4): 479–514.

Kriner, Douglas L. 2010. *After the Rubicon: Congress, Presidents, and the Politics of Waging War*. Chicago: University of Chicago Press.

Kriner, Douglas L. 2014. "Obama's Authorization Paradox: Syria and Congress's Continued Relevance in Military Affairs." *Presidential Studies Quarterly* 44 (2): 309–327.

Kriner, Douglas L. 2018. "Congress, Public Opinion, and an Informal Constraint on the Commander-in-Chief." *British Journal of Politics and International Relations* 20 (1): 52–68.

Kriner, Douglas L., and Andrew Reeves. 2015. "Presidential Particularism and Divide-the-Dollar Politics." *American Political Science Review* 109 (1): 155–171.

Kriner, Douglas L., and Eric Schickler. 2016. *Investigating the President: Congressional Checks on Presidential Power*. Princeton: Princeton University Press.

Kriner, Douglas, and Eric Schickler. 2018. "The Resilience of Separation of Powers? Congress and the Russia Investigation." *Presidential Studies Quarterly* 48 (3): 436–455.

Kriner, Douglas, and Francis Shen. 2014. "Responding to War on Capitol Hill: Battlefield Casualties, Congressional Response, and Public Support for the War in Iraq." *American Journal of Political Science* 58 (1): 157–174.

Kronlund, Anna, and Teemu Mäkinen. 2015. *Topicality of the Separation of Powers: The US Congress and Foreign Policy Processes*. Finnish Institute of International Affairs.

Krutz, Glen S., and Jeffrey S. Peake. 2011. *Treaty Politics and the Rise of Executive Agreements: International Commitments in a System of Shared Powers*. Ann Arbor: University of Michigan Press.

Kull, Steven. 2017. *American Public Support for Foreign Aid in the Age of Trump*. Brookings Institution.

Kull, Steven, and I. M. Destler. 1999. *Misreading the Public: The Myth of a New Isolationism*. Washington, DC: Brookings Institution Press.

Kupchan, Charles A., and Peter L. Trubowitz. 2007. "Dead Center: The Demise of Liberal Internationalism in the United States." *International Security* 32 (2): 7–44.

Kupchan, Charles A., and Peter L. Trubowitz. 2021. "The Home Front: Why an Internationalist Foreign Policy Needs a Stronger Domestic Foundation." *Foreign Affairs* 100 (3): 92–101.

Lagon, Mark P., and William F. Schulz. 2012. "Conservatives, Liberals, and Human Rights." *Policy Review* 171: 23–32.

Lake, David A. 1988. "The State and American Trade Strategy in the Pre-Hegemonic Era." *International Organization* 42 (1): 33–58.

Lantis, Jeffrey S. 2019a. *Foreign Policy Advocacy and Entrepreneurship: How a New Generation in Congress Is Shaping US Engagement with the World*. Ann Arbor: University of Michigan Press.

Lantis, Jeffrey S. 2019b. "'Winning' and 'Losing' the Iran Nuclear Deal: How Advocacy Coalitions and Competition Shape U.S. Foreign Policy." *Politics & Policy* 47 (3): 464–505.

Lantis, Jeffrey S. 2021. "Advocacy Coalitions and Foreign Policy Change: Understanding US Responses to the Syrian Civil War." *Journal of Global Security Studies* 6 (1): ogaa016.

Lantis, Jeffrey S., and Patrick Homan. 2019. "Factionalism and US Foreign Policy: A Social Psychological Model of Minority Influence." *Foreign Policy Analysis* 15 (2): 157–175.

Lapinski, John. 2013. *The Substance of Representation: Congress, American Political Development, and Lawmaking*. Princeton: Princeton University Press.

LaPira, Timothy M., Lee Drutman, and Kevin R. Kosar, eds. 2020. *Congress Overwhelmed: The Decline in Congressional Capacity and Prospects for Reform*. Chicago: University of Chicago Press.

Lavelle, Kathryn C. 2011a. *Legislating International Organization: The US Congress, the IMF, and the World Bank*. Oxford: Oxford University Press.

Lavelle, Kathryn C. 2011b. "Multilateral Cooperation and Congress: The Legislative Process of Securing Funding for the World Bank." *International Studies Quarterly* 55 (1): 199–222.

Layman, Geoffrey C., Thomas M. Carsey, John C. Green, Richard Herrera, and Rosalyn Cooperman. 2010. "Activists and Conflict Extension in American Party Politics." *American Political Science Review* 104 (2): 324–346.

Lee, Carrie A. 2019. "Electoral Politics, Party Polarization, and Arms Control: New START in Historical Perspective." *Orbis* 63 (4): 545–564.

Lee, Frances E. 2005. "Interests, Constituencies, and Policy Making." In *The Legislative Branch*, edited by Paul J. Quirk and Sarah A. Binder, 281–313. Oxford: Oxford University Press.

Lee, Frances E. 2009. *Beyond Ideology: Politics, Principles, and Partisanship in the U.S. Senate*. Chicago: University of Chicago Press.

Lee, Frances E. 2016. *Insecure Majorities: Congress and the Perpetual Campaign*. Chicago: University of Chicago Press.

Leech, Beth L. 2011. "Lobbying and Interest Group Advocacy." In *The Oxford Handbook of the American Congress*, edited by Eric Schickler and Frances E. Lee, 598–617. Oxford: Oxford University Press.

Lelkes, Yphtach. 2016. "Mass Polarization: Manifestations and Measurements." *Public Opinion Quarterly* 80 (1): 392–410.

Levendusky, Matthew S. 2009. *The Partisan Sort: How Liberals Became Democrats and Conservatives Became Republicans*. Chicago: University of Chicago Press.

Levine, Carlisle, Claire Reinelt, and Robin Kane. 2017. *The Modernizing Foreign Assistance Network (MFAN), Evaluation Report: 2008–2016*. BLE Solutions.

Lewis, David E. 2003. *Presidents and the Politics of Agency Design: Political Insulation in the United States Government Bureaucracy, 1946–1997*. Stanford: Stanford University Press.

Lewis, Verlan. 2019. *Ideas of Power: The Politics of American Party Ideology Development*. Cambridge, UK: Cambridge University Press.

Lighthizer, Robert E. 2020. "How to Make Trade Work for Workers: Charting a Path Between Protectionism and Globalism." *Foreign Affairs* 99 (4): 78–92.

Lindsay, James M. 1986. "Trade Sanctions as Policy Instruments: A Re-Examination." *International Studies Quarterly* 30 (2): 153–173.

Lindsay, James M. 1994. *Congress and the Politics of U.S. Foreign Policy*. Baltimore: Johns Hopkins University Press.

Lipset, Seymour Martin. 1966. "The President, the Polls, and Vietnam." *Trans-action* 3 (6): 19–24.

Lupton, Danielle. 2021. "Veterans in the Post-2001 House: The Impact of Military Service on War Oversight." In *Congress and U.S. Foreign Policy: Activism, Assertiveness, and Acquiescence in a Polarized Era*, edited by Ralph G. Carter and James M. Scott, 161–176. Lanham, MD: Rowman & Littlefield.

Mahoney, Christine. 2007. "Lobbying Success in the United States and the European Union." *Journal of Public Policy* 27 (1): 35–56.

Malley, Robert, and Stephen Pomper. 2021. "Accomplice to Carnage: How America Enables War in Yemen." *Foreign Affairs* 100 (2): 73–88.

Mann, Thomas E., and Norman J. Ornstein. 2006. *The Broken Branch: How Congress Is Failing America and How to Get It Back on Track*. Oxford: Oxford University Press.

Mann, Thomas E., and Norman J. Ornstein. 2012. *It's Even Worse Than It Looks: How the American Constitutional System Collided with the New Politics of Extremism*. New York: Basic Books.

Mansbridge, Jane, and Cathie Jo Martin, eds. 2016. *Political Negotiation: A Handbook*. Washington, DC: Brookings Institution.

Margon, Sarah. 2018. "Giving up the High Ground: America's Retreat on Human Rights." *Foreign Affairs* 97 (2): 39–45.

Marshall, Bryan W., and Patrick J. Haney. 2022. "The Impact of Party Conflict on Executive Ascendancy and Congressional Abdication in US Foreign Policy." *International Politics* 59 (4): 661–686.

Martin, Lisa L. 1992. *Coercive Cooperation: Explaining Multilateral Economic Sanctions*. Princeton: Princeton University Press.

Martin, Lisa L. 2000. *Democratic Commitments: Legislatures and International Cooperation*. Princeton: Princeton University Press.

Mason, Lilliana. 2018. *Uncivil Agreement: How Politics Became Our Identity*. Chicago: University of Chicago Press.

Maxey, Sarah. 2020. "The Power of Humanitarian Narratives: A Domestic Coalition Theory of Justifications for Military Action." *Political Research Quarterly* 73 (3): 680–695.

Mayda, Anna Maria, and Dani Rodrik. 2005. "Why Are Some People (and Countries) More Protectionist Than Others?" *European Economic Review* 49 (6): 1393–1430.

Mayhew, David R. 2000. *America's Congress: Actions in the Public Sphere, James Madison Through Newt Gingrich*. New Haven, CT: Yale University Press.

Mayhew, David R. 2004. *Congress: The Electoral Connection*. 2nd ed. New Haven, CT: Yale University Press.

Mayhew, David R. 2005. *Divided We Govern: Party Control, Lawmaking, and Investigations, 1946–2002*. 2nd ed. New Haven, CT: Yale University Press.

McArthur, Shirl. 2010. "Senate Passes Omnibus Iran Sanctions Bill." *Washington Report on Middle East Affairs* 29 (3): 22–23.

McCain, John, and Mark Salter. 2018. *The Restless Wave: Good Times, Just Causes, Great Fights, and Other Appreciations*. New York: Simon & Schuster.

McCarty, Nolan. 2019. *Polarization: What Everyone Needs to Know*. New York: Oxford University Press.

McCarty, Nolan, Keith T. Poole, and Howard Rosenthal. 2006. *Polarized America: The Dance of Ideology and Unequal Riches*. Cambridge: MIT Press.

McCormick, James M. 2012. "Ethnic Interest Groups and American Foreign Policy: A Growing Influence?" In *Interest Group Politics*, edited by Allan J. Cigler and Burdett A. Loomis, 317–344. Washington, DC: CQ Press.

McCormick, James M. 2014. "American Foreign Policy and the Partisan Divide: How Deep and Widespread?" International Studies Association Annual Meeting, Toronto, Canada.

McCormick, James M., and Michael Black. 1983. "Ideology and Senate Voting on the Panama Canal Treaties." *Legislative Studies Quarterly* 8 (1): 45–63.

McCormick, James M., and Neil J. Mitchell. 2007. "Commitments, Transnational Interests, and Congress: Who Joins the Congressional Human Rights Caucus?" *Political Research Quarterly* 60 (4): 579–592.

McCormick, James M., and Eugene R. Wittkopf. 1990. "Bipartisanship, Partisanship, and Ideology in Congressional-Executive Foreign Policy Relations, 1947–1988." *Journal of Politics* 52 (4): 1077–1100.

McCormick, James M., and Eugene R. Wittkopf. 1992. "At the Water's Edge: The Effects of Party, Ideology, and Issues on Congressional Foreign Policy Voting, 1947–1988." *American Politics Quarterly* 20 (1): 26–53.

McFaul, Michael. 2018. *From Cold War to Hot Peace: An American Ambassador in Putin's Russia*. Boston: Mariner Books.

McMaster, H. R. 2020. *Battlegrounds: The Fight to Defend the Free World*. New York: Harper.

Meernik, James. 1993. "Presidential Support in Congress: Conflict and Consensus on Foreign and Defense Policy." *Journal of Politics* 55 (3): 569–587.

Meernik, James, and Elizabeth Oldmixon. 2008. "The President, the Senate, and the Costs of Internationalism." *Foreign Policy Analysis* 4 (2): 187–206.

Melanson, Richard A. 2005. *American Foreign Policy Since the Vietnam War: The Search for Consensus from Richard Nixon to George W. Bush*. 4th ed. Armonk, NY: M. E. Sharpe.

Miler, Kristina C. 2014. *Constituency Representation in Congress: The View from Capitol Hill*. New York: Cambridge University Press.

Miller, Warren E., and Donald E. Stokes. 1963. "Constituency Influence in Congress." *American Political Science Review* 57 (1): 45–56.

Milner, Helen V. 1988. *Resisting Protectionism: Global Industries and the Politics of International Trade*. Princeton: Princeton University Press.

Milner, Helen V. 1997. *Interests, Institutions, and Information: Domestic Politics and International Relations*. Princeton: Princeton University Press.

Milner, Helen V. 1999. "The Political Economy of International Trade." *Annual Review of Political Science* 2: 91–114.

Milner, Helen V., and Dustin Tingley. 2011. *The Economic and Political Influences on Different Dimensions of United States Immigration Policy*. Social Science Research Network.

Milner, Helen V., and Dustin Tingley. 2013. "Public Opinion and Foreign Aid: A Review Essay." *International Interactions* 39 (3): 389–401.

Milner, Helen V., and Dustin Tingley. 2015. *Sailing the Water's Edge: The Domestic Politics of American Foreign Policy*. Princeton: Princeton University Press.

Modernizing Foreign Assistance Network. 2014. *The Way Forward: A Reform Agenda for 2014 and Beyond*.

Modernizing Foreign Assistance Network. 2015. *ACCOUNTdown to 2017: Strengthening a Bipartisan Legacy of Modernizing Foreign Assistance*.

Mueller, John E. 1970. "Presidential Popularity from Truman to Johnson." *American Political Science Review* 64 (1): 18–34.

Mueller, Robert S., III. 2019. *Report on the Investigation into Russian Interference in the 2016 Presidential Election*. Washington, DC: U.S. Department of Justice.

Murray, Shoon Kathleen. 2002. *Anchors Against Change: American Opinion Leaders' Beliefs After the Cold War*. Ann Arbor: University of Michigan Press.

Murray, Shoon Kathleen. 2015. "Stretching the 2001 AUMF: A History of Two Presidencies." *Presidential Studies Quarterly* 45 (1): 175–198.

Murray, Shoon Kathleen, Jonathan A. Cowden, and Bruce M. Russett. 1999. "The Convergence of American Elites' Domestic Beliefs with Their Foreign Policy Beliefs." *International Interactions* 25 (2): 153–180.

Myrick, Rachel. 2022. "The Reputational Consequences of Polarization for American Foreign Policy: Evidence from the U.S.-U.K. Bilateral Relationship." *International Politics* 59 (5): 1004–1027.

Nau, Henry. 2015. *Conservative Internationalism: Armed Diplomacy Under Jefferson, Polk, Truman, and Reagan*. Princeton: Princeton University Press.

Newhouse, John. 2009. "Diplomacy, Inc.: The Influence of Lobbies on U.S. Foreign Policy." *Foreign Affairs* 88 (3): 73–92.

Nincic, Miroslav, and Jennifer M. Ramos. 2010. "Ideological Structure and Foreign Policy Preferences." *Journal of Political Ideologies* 15 (2): 119–141.

Noel, Hans. 2013. *Political Ideologies and Political Parties in America*. New York: Cambridge University Press.

Noel, Hans. 2016. "Ideological Factions in the Republican and Democratic Parties." *Annals of the American Academy of Political and Social Science* 667 (1): 166–188.

Norris, John, and Connie Veillette. 2012. *Engagement Amid Austerity: Reorienting the International Affairs Budget*. Center for American Progress and Center for Global Development.

Office of Management and Budget. 2017. *Budget for the U.S. Government: A New Foundation for American Greatness*. Washington, DC: Executive Office of the President.

Office of Management and Budget. 2018. *An American Budget: Efficient, Effective, Accountable*. Washington, DC: Executive Office of the President.

Office of Management and Budget. 2019. *A Budget for a Better America*. Washington, DC: Executive Office of the President.

Office of Management and Budget. 2020. *A Budget for America's Future: Budget of the U.S. Government*. Washington, DC: Executive Office of the President.

Otter, Mark. 2003. "Domestic Public Support For Foreign Aid: Does It Matter?" *Third World Quarterly* 24 (1): 115–125.

Overby, Marvin L. 1991. "Assessing Constituency Influence: Congressional Voting on the Nuclear Freeze, 1982–83." *Legislative Studies Quarterly* 16 (2): 297–312.

Packard, Clark, and Philip Wallach. 2018. *Restraining the President: Congress and Trade Policy*. R Street Policy Study No. 158.

Page, Benjamin I., and Jason Barabas. 2000. "Foreign Policy Gaps Between Citizens and Leaders." *International Studies Quarterly* 44 (3): 339–364.

Page, Benjamin I., and Marshall M. Bouton. 2006. *The Foreign Policy Disconnect: What Americans Want from Our Leaders but Don't Get*. Chicago: University of Chicago Press.

Page, Benjamin I., and Martin Gilens. 2020. *Democracy in America? What Has Gone Wrong and What We Can Do About It*. Chicago: University of Chicago Press.

Panetta, Leon. 2014. *Worthy Fights*. New York: Penguin Press.

Paris, Celia. 2017. "Breaking Down Bipartisanship: When and Why Citizens React to Cooperation Across Party Lines." *Public Opinion Quarterly* 81 (2): 473–494.

Parsi, Trita. 2012. *A Single Roll of the Dice: Obama's Diplomacy with Iran*. New Haven, CT: Yale University Press.

Parsi, Trita. 2017. *Losing an Enemy: Obama, Iran, and the Triumph of Diplomacy*. New Haven, CT: Yale University Press.

Peake, Jeffrey S. 2002. "Coalition Building and Overcoming Legislative Gridlock in Foreign Policy, 1947–98." *Presidential Studies Quarterly* 32 (1): 67–83.

Peake, Jeffrey S., Glen S. Krutz, and Tyler Hughes. 2012. "President Obama, the Senate and the Polarized Politics of Treaty-Making." *Social Science Quarterly* 93 (5): 1295–1315.

Peck, Justin C., and Jeffrey A. Jenkins. 2020. "The 'Flip-Side' of Delegation: Examining Congressional Reassertion Efforts." In *New Directions in Congressional Politics*, edited by Jamie L. Carson and Michael S. Lynch, 251–273. New York: Routledge.

Persily, Nathaniel, ed. 2015. *Solutions to Political Polarization in America*. New York: Cambridge University Press.

Peters, Margaret. 2015. "Open Trade, Closed Borders: Immigration in the Era of Globalization." *World Politics* 67 (1): 114–154.

Price, Kathryn M. 2014. "American Public Opinion on Human Rights and the Challenge of Humanitarian Intervention." Master's thesis, University of Oregon.

Prins, Brandon C., and Bryan W. Marshall. 2001. "Congressional Support of the President: A Comparison of Foreign, Defense, and Domestic Policy Decision Making During and After the Cold War." *Presidential Studies Quarterly* 31 (4): 660–678.

Putnam, Robert D. 1988. "Diplomacy and Domestic Politics: The Logic of Two-Level Games." *International Organization* 42 (3): 427–460.

Rathbun, Brian. 2016. "Wedges and Widgets: Liberalism, Libertarianism, and the Trade Attitudes of the American Mass Public and Elites." *Foreign Policy Analysis* 12 (1): 85–108.

Rathbun, Brian C. 2004. *Partisan Interventions: European Party Politics and Peace Enforcement in the Balkans*. Ithaca: Cornell University Press.

Rathbun, Brian C. 2007. "Hierarchy and Community at Home and Abroad: Evidence of a Common Structure of Domestic and Foreign Policy Beliefs in American Elites." *Journal of Conflict Resolution* 51 (3): 379–407.

Rathbun, Brian C. 2012. *Trust in International Cooperation: International Security Institutions, Domestic Politics and American Multilateralism*. Cambridge: Cambridge University Press.

Rathbun, Brian C., Joshua D. Kertzer, Jason Reifler, Paul Goren, and Thomas J. Scotto. 2016. "Taking Foreign Policy Personally: Personal Values and Foreign Policy Attitudes." *International Studies Quarterly* 60 (1): 124–137.

Raunio, Tapio, and Wolfgang Wagner. 2020. "The Party Politics of Foreign and Security Policy." *Foreign Policy Analysis* 16 (4): 515–531.

Recchia, Stefano. 2016. "Why Seek International Organization Approval under Unipolarity? Averting Issue Linkage vs. Appeasing Congress." *International Relations* 30 (1): 78–101.

Reeves, Andrew, and Jon C. Rogowski. 2022. "Unilateral Inaction: Congressional Gridlock, Interbranch Conflict, and Public Evaluations of Executive Power." *Legislative Studies Quarterly* 47 (2): 427–457.

Rhodes, Ben. 2018. *The World As It Is: A Memoir of the Obama White House.* New York: Random House.

Rice, Susan. 2019. *Tough Love: My Story of the Things Worth Fighting For.* New York: Simon & Schuster.

Ripley, Randall B., and James M. Lindsay, eds. 1993. *Congress Resurgent: Foreign and Defense Policy on Capitol Hill.* Ann Arbor: University of Michigan Press.

Rosenfeld, Sam. 2018. *The Polarizers: Postwar Architects of Our Partisan Era.* Chicago: University of Chicago Press.

Ross, Tommy. 2018. "At a Crossroads, Part III: Reasserting Congress' Oversight Role in Foreign Policy." *War on the Rocks*, June 19.

Rozell, Mark J., Clyde Wilcox, and Michael M. Franz. 2012. *Interest Groups in American Campaigns: The New Face of Electioneering.* 3rd ed. New York: Oxford University Press.

Rudalevige, Andrew. 2006. *The New Imperial Presidency: Renewing Presidential Power After Watergate.* Ann Arbor: University of Michigan Press.

Ryan, Joshua. 2019. "Which House Committees Are the Most Partisan?" Legbranch.org, August 27.

Ryan, Joshua M. 2020. "Congress and the Executive in the Age of Trump." In *New Directions in Congressional Politics*, edited by Jamie L. Carson and Michael S. Lynch, 209–225. New York: Routledge.

Safi, Marlo. 2018. "Understanding U.S. Involvement in Yemen's 'Forgotten War.'" *National Review*, November 30.

Saunders, Elizabeth N. 2015. "War and the Inner Circle: Democratic Elites and the Politics of Using Force." *Security Studies* 24 (3): 466–501.

Saunders, Elizabeth N. 2022. "Elites in the Making and Breaking of Foreign Policy." *Annual Review of Political Science* 25: 219–240.

Schultz, Kenneth A. 2001. *Democracy and Coercive Diplomacy.* Cambridge: Cambridge University Press.

Schultz, Kenneth A. 2017. "Perils of Polarization for U.S. Foreign Policy." *Washington Quarterly* 40 (4): 7–28.

Scott, James M., and Ralph G. Carter. 2014. "The Not-So-Silent Partner: Patterns of Legislative-Executive Interaction in the War on Terror, 2001–2009." *International Studies Perspectives* 15 (2): 186–208.

Sherman, Wendy R. 2018. *Not for the Faint of Heart: Lessons in Courage, Power & Persistence.* New York: Public Affairs.

Sigelman, Lee. 1979. "A Reassessment of the Two Presidencies Thesis." *Journal of Politics* 41 (4): 1195–1205.

Sinclair, Barbara. 2006. *Party Wars: Polarization and the Politics of National Policy Making.* Norman: University of Oklahoma Press.

Sinclair, Barbara. 2016. *Unorthodox Lawmaking: New Legislative Processes in the U.S. Congress.* 5th ed. Washington, DC: CQ Press.

Skocpol, Theda, and Alexander Hertel-Fernandez. 2016. "The Koch Network and Republican Party Extremism." *Perspectives on Politics* 14 (3): 681–699.

Smeltz, Dina. 2012. *Foreign Policy in the New Millenium.* Chicago Council on Global Affairs.

Smeltz, Dina, Joshua Busby, Gregory Holyk, Craig Kafura, Jonathan Monten, and Jordan Tama. 2015. *United in Goals, Divided on Means: Opinion Leaders Survey Results and Partisan Breakdowns from the 2014 Chicago Survey of American Opinion on US Foreign Policy.* Chicago Council on Global Affairs.

Smeltz, Dina, Joshua Busby, and Jordan Tama. 2018. "Political Polarization the Critical Threat to US, Foreign Policy Experts Say." *The Hill,* November 9.

Smeltz, Dina, Ivo Daalder, Karl Friedhoff, and Craig Kafura. 2015. *America Divided: Political Partisanship and US Foreign Policy.* Chicago Council on Global Affairs.

Smeltz, Dina, Ivo Daalder, Karl Friedhoff, and Craig Kafura. 2016. *America in the Age of Uncertainty: American Public Opinion and US Foreign Policy.* Chicago Council on Global Affairs.

Smeltz, Dina, Ivo Daalder, Karl Friedhoff, and Craig Kafura. 2017. *What Americans Think About America First.* Chicago Council on Global Affairs.

Smeltz, Dina, Ivo Daalder, Karl Friedhoff, Craig Kafura, and Brendan Helm. 2019. *Rejecting Retreat: Americans Support US Engagement in Global Affairs.* Chicago Council on Global Affairs.

Smeltz, Dina, Ivo H. Daalder, Karl Friedhoff, Craig Kafura, and Lily Wojtowicz. 2018. *America Engaged: American Public Opinion and US Foreign Policy.* Chicago Council on Global Affairs.

Smeltz, Dina, Ivo H. Daalder, and Craig Kafura. 2014. *Foreign Policy in the Age of Retrenchment.* Chicago Council on Global Affairs.

Smeltz, Dina, Karl Friedhoff, Craig Kafura, Joshua W. Busby, Jonathan Monten, and Jordan Tama. 2017. *The Foreign Policy Establishment or Donald Trump: Which Better Reflects American Opinion?* Chicago Council on Global Affairs.

Smeltz, Dina, and Craig Kafura. 2018. *Record Number of Americans Endorse Benefits of Trade.* Chicago Council on Global Affairs.

Smeltz, Dina, and Craig Kafura. 2022. *For First Time, Half of Americans Favor Defending Taiwan If China Invades.* Chicago Council on Global Affairs.

Smeltz, Dina, and Jordan Tama. 2021. "Did Trump Remake the GOP? On Foreign Policy, Not So Much." *Politico,* May 27.

Smeltz, Dina, and Lily Wojtowicz. 2017. *American Opinion on US-Russian Relations: From Bad to Worse.* Chicago Council on Global Affairs, August.

Smith, Tony. 2000. *Foreign Attachments: The Power of Ethnic Groups in the Making of American Foreign Policy.* Cambridge: Harvard University Press.

Snow, Donald M., and Patrick J. Haney. 2018. *U.S. Foreign Policy: Back to the Water's Edge.* 5th ed. Lanham, MD: Rowman & Littlefield.

Snyder, Jack, Robert Y. Shapiro, and Yaeli Bloch-Elkon. 2009. "Free Hand Abroad, Divide and Rule at Home." *World Politics* 61 (1): 155–187.

Snyder, Sarah B. 2013. "'A Call for U.S. Leadership:' Congressional Activism on Human Rights." *Diplomatic History* 37 (2): 372–397.

Snyder, Sarah B. 2018. *From Selma to Moscow: How Human Rights Activists Transformed U.S. Foreign Policy.* New York: Columbia University Press.

Sobel, Richard. 2001. *The Impact of Public Opinion on U.S. Foreign Policy Since Vietnam.* Oxford: Oxford University Press.

Søndergaard, Rasmus Sinding. 2020. *Reagan, Congress, and Human Rights: Contesting Morality in US Foreign Policy.* Cambridge: Cambridge University Press.

Souva, Mark, and David Rohde. 2007. "Elite Opinion Differences and Partisanship in Congressional Foreign Policy, 1975–1996." *Political Research Quarterly* 60 (1): 113–123.

Stark, Alexandra. 2021. "Congress Failed to Block the Sale of Missiles to Saudi Arabia. Why?" *Washington Post*, December 23.

Stern, Paula. 1979. *Water's Edge: Domestic Politics and the Making of American Foreign Policy*. Westport, CT: Greenwood Press.

Tama, Jordan. 2011. "In Defense of the Back-Room Deal." *New York Times*, October 18.

Tama, Jordan. 2018a. "What Is the Global Magnitsky Act, and Why Are U.S. Senators Invoking This on Saudi Arabia?" *Washington Post*, October 12.

Tama, Jordan. 2018b. "Why Is the Senate Challenging Trump on Yemen? Here's What You Need to Know." *Washington Post*, November 30.

Tama, Jordan. 2020. "Forcing the President's Hand: How the US Congress Shapes Foreign Policy Through Sanctions Legislation." *Foreign Policy Analysis* 16 (3): 397–416.

Tama, Jordan. 2021. "Anti-Presidential Bipartisanship in Foreign Policy in the Trump Era." In *Congress and U.S. Foreign Policy: Activism, Assertiveness and Acquiescence in a Polarized Era*, edited by Ralph G. Carter and James M. Scott, 21–36. Lanham, MD: Rowman & Littlefield.

Tansey, Oisin. 2007. "Process Tracing and Elite Interviewing: A Case for Non-Probability Sampling." *PS: Political Science & Politics* 40 (4): 765–772.

Taroff, Curt, and Marian L. Lawson. 2016. *Foreign Aid: An Introduction to U.S. Programs and Policy.* Congressional Research Service, June 17.

Texas National Security Review. 2018. *Policy Roundtable: The Future of Conservative Foreign Policy*, November 30.

Theriault, Sean M. 2008. *Party Polarization in Congress.* Cambridge: Cambridge University Press.

Theriault, Sean M. 2013. *The Gingrich Senators: The Roots of Partisan Warfare in Congress.* Oxford: Oxford University Press.

Thierse, Stefan. 2016. "Going on Record: Revisiting the Logic of Roll-Call Vote Requests in the European Parliament." *European Union Politics* 17 (2): 219–241.

Thomsen, Danielle M. 2020. "Parties and Polarization in Congress." In *New Directions in Congressional Politics*, edited by Jamie L. Carson and Michael S. Lynch, 109–126. New York: Routledge.

Thorpe, Rebecca U. 2014. *The American Warfare State: The Domestic Politics of Military Spending.* Chicago: University of Chicago Press.

Thurber, James A., Colton C. Campbell, and David A. Dulio. 2018. *Congress and Diaspora Politics: The Influence of Ethnic and Foreign Lobbying.* Albany: State University of New York Press.

Thurber, James A., and Antoine Yoshinaka, eds. 2015. *American Gridlock: The Sources, Character, and Impact of Political Polarization.* Cambridge: Cambridge University Press.

Tierney, John T. 1993. "Interest Group Involvement in Congressional Foreign and Defense Policy." In *Congress Resurgent: Foreign and Defense Policy on Capitol Hill*, edited by Randall B. Ripley and James M. Lindsay, 89–111. Ann Arbor: University of Michigan Press.

Trubowitz, Peter. 2011. *Politics and Strategy: Partisan Ambition and American Statecraft.* Princeton: Princeton University Press.

Trubowitz, Peter, and Peter Harris. 2019. "The End of the American Century? Slow Erosion of the Domestic Sources of Usable Power." *International Affairs* 95 (3): 619–639.

Trubowitz, Peter, and Nicole Mellow. 2005. "'Going Bipartisan': Politics by Other Means." *Political Science Quarterly* 120 (3): 433–453.

Trubowitz, Peter, and Nicole Mellow. 2011. "Foreign Policy, Bipartisanship and the Paradox of Post-September 11 America." *International Politics* 48 (2/3): 164–187.

Tuttle, Christopher M. 2022. "Foreign Policy Bipartisanship's Mixed Blessings." Council on Foreign Relations, May 31.

Wagner, Wolfgang. 2020. *The Democratic Politics of Military Interventions: Political Parties, Contestation, and Decisions to Use Force Abroad.* Oxford: Oxford University Press.

Walldorf, C. William, Jr. 2008. *Just Politics: Human Rights and the Foreign Policy of Great Powers.* Ithaca, NY: Cornell University Press.

Warburg, Gerald. 2021. "Restoring the Balance: How Can Congress Reclaim Its Constitutional Authority to Shape Foreign Policy?" *Wilson Quarterly* 45 (1).

Weissman, Stephen R. 1995. *A Culture of Deference: Congress's Failure of Leadership in Foreign Policy.* New York: Basic Books.

Wenzelburger, Georg, and Florian Böller. 2019. "Bomb or Build? How Party Ideologies Affect the Balance of Foreign Aid and Defence Spending." *British Journal of Politics and International Relations* 22 (1): 3–23.

Whang, Taehee. 2011. "Playing to the Home Crowd? Symbolic Use of Economic Sanctions in the United States." *International Studies Quarterly* 55 (3): 787–801.

Wildavsky, Aaron. 1966. "The Two Presidencies." *Trans-action* 4 (2): 7–14.

Wittkopf, Eugene R. 1987. "Elites and Masses: Another Look at Attitudes Toward America's World Role." *International Studies Quarterly* 31 (2): 131–159.

Wittkopf, Eugene R. 1990. *Faces of Internationalism: Public Opinion and American Foreign Policy.* Durham, NC: Duke University Press.

Wlezien, Christopher. 1996. "Dynamics of Representation: The Case of US Spending on Defence." *British Journal of Political Science* 26 (1): 81–103.

Wojtowicz, Lily, and Dina Hanania. 2017. *Americans Support Foreign Aid, but Oppose Paying for It.* Chicago Council on Global Affairs, November 14.

Wolak, Jennifer. 2020. *Compromise in an Age of Party Polarization.* New York: Oxford University Press.

Wolfensberger, Donald R. 2018. *Changing Cultures in Congress: From Fair Play to Power Plays.* New York: Columbia University Press.

Wong, Carolyn. 2006. *Lobbying for Inclusion: Rights Politics and the Making of Immigration Policy.* Stanford: Stanford University Press.

Wood, B. Dan. 2009. *The Myth of Presidential Representation.* New York: Cambridge University Press.

Yglesias, Matthew, and Steven M. Teles. 2021. "A Moderate Proposal." *The Atlantic*, November 4.

Yoshimatsu, Hidetaka. 2016. "US-Japan Negotiations on the Trans-Pacific Partnership." *Asian Survey* 56 (6): 1145–1167.

Young, Alasdair R. 2016. "Not Your Parents' Trade Politics: The Transatlantic Trade and Investment Partnership Negotiations." *Review of International Political Economy* 23 (3): 345–378.

Zaller, John R. 1992. *The Nature and Origins of Mass Opinion.* Cambridge: Cambridge University Press.

Zegart, Amy B. 1999. *Flawed by Design: The Evolution of the CIA, JCS, and NCS.* Stanford: Stanford University Press.

Zegart, Amy B. 2011. *Eyes on Spies: Congress and the United States Intelligence Community*. Stanford: Hoover Institution Press.

Zelizer, Julian E. 2010. *Arsenal of Democracy: The Politics of National Security—From World War II to the War on Terrorism*. New York: Basic Books.

Zingher, Joshua N., and Michael E. Flynn. 2016. "From on High: The Effect of Elite Polarization on Mass Attitudes and Behaviors, 1972–2012." *British Journal of Political Science* 48 (1): 23–45.

Zong, Jie. 2015. "Profile of Syrian Immigrants in the United States." Migration Policy Institute, November.

Index

For the benefit of digital users, indexed terms that span two pages (e.g., 52–53) may, on occasion, appear on only one of those pages.

Tables and figures are indicated by *t* and *f* following the page number